Toshiaki Iwashiro

I've been terribly forgetful lately.

Actually, I've always instantly forgotten things people tell me, but you know it's serious when a serialized manga artist can't remember the story he was working on last week.

I may have already written something somewhere about becoming terribly forgetful...

Or maybe I haven't.

I guess I'll just have to get by on hunches from now on...

Toshiaki Iwashiro was born December 11, 1977, in Tokyo and has the blood type of A. His debut manga was the popular *Mieru Hito*, which ran from 2005 to 2007 in Japan in *Weekly Shonen Jump*, where *Psyren* was also serialized.

PSYREN VOL. 11
SHONEN JUMP Manga Edition

STORY AND ART BY TOSHIAKI IWASHIRO

Translation/Camellia Nieh
Lettering/Annaliese Christman
Design/Matt Hinrichs
Editor/Joel Enos

PSYREN © 2007 by Toshiaki Iwashiro
All rights reserved.
First published in Japan in 2007 by SHUEISHA Inc., Tokyo.
English translation rights arranged by SHUEISHA Inc.

The rights of the author(s) of the work(s) in this publication to be so
identified have been asserted in accordance with the Copyright, Designs
and Patents Act 1988. A CIP catalogue record for this book is available
from the British Library.

Printed in the U.S.A.

Published by VIZ Media, LLC
P.O. Box 77010
San Francisco, CA 94107

10 9 8 7 6 5 4 3 2 1
First printing, July 2013

www.viz.com

THE WORLD'S
MOST POPULAR MANGA
www.shonenjump.com

SHONEN JUMP MANGA EDITION

11

THE TWO TEST SUBJECTS

Story and Art by
Toshiaki Iwashiro

AGEHA YOSHINA

SAKURAKO AMAMIYA

MATSURI YAGUMO

KAGETORA HYODO

ASUKA YOSHINA

Characters

JUNAS

HARUHIKO YUMEJI

MIROKU AMAGI

RAN SHINONOME

Story

HIGH-SCHOOLER AGEHA YOSHINA HAPPENS UPON A RED PHONE CARD EMBLAZONED WITH THE WORD *PSYREN* THAT ULTIMATELY TRANSPORTS HIM TO A FUTURISTIC LIFE-OR-DEATH GAME IN A POSTAPOCALYPTIC WORLD.

AGEHA MANAGES TO RESCUE THE CREATOR OF THE STRANGE NEMESIS Q, WHO THEN REVEALS THE TRUE PURPOSE OF THE PSYREN GAME. AGEHA LEARNS THAT HIS FRIENDS HIRYU AND OBORO ARE ALL RIGHT, BUT UNABLE TO REUNITE WITH HIM. AGEHA, AMAMIYA, AND KABUTO ARE FORCED TO LEAVE PSYREN FOR THEIR OWN TIME AND LEAVE THEIR FRIENDS BEHIND. BACK HOME, THE THREE REUNITE WITH THEIR FRIEND MATSURI AND BEGIN TO FOLLOW THE TRAIL OF MIROKU AMAGI, THE MAN THEY BELIEVE WILL BRING ABOUT THE END OF THE WORLD.

VOL. 11
THE TWO TEST SUBJECTS
CONTENTS

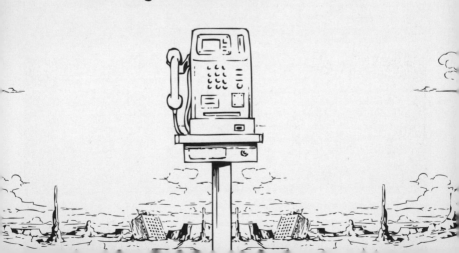

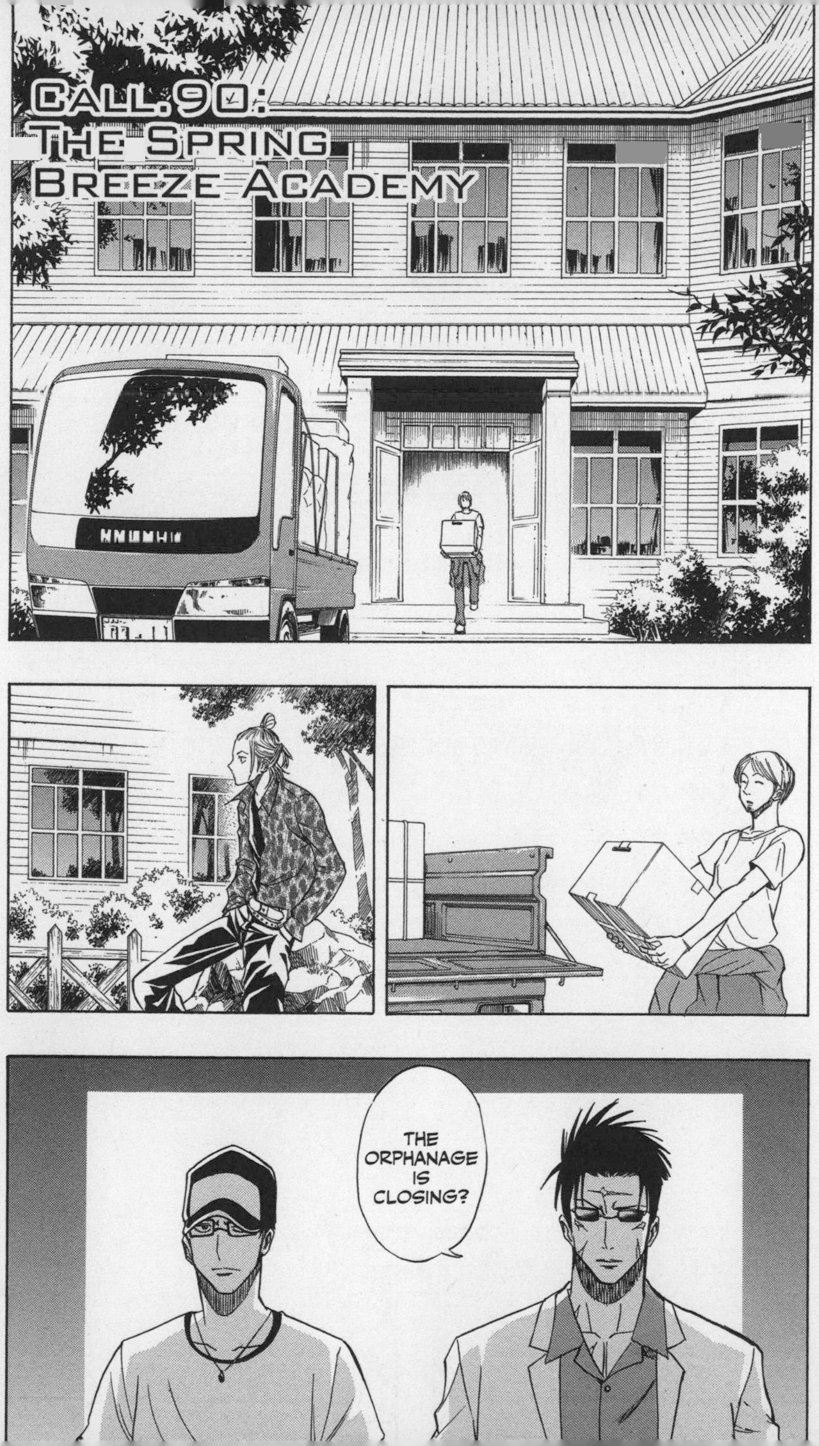
CALL.90:
THE SPRING BREEZE ACADEMY
THE ORPHANAGE IS CLOSING?

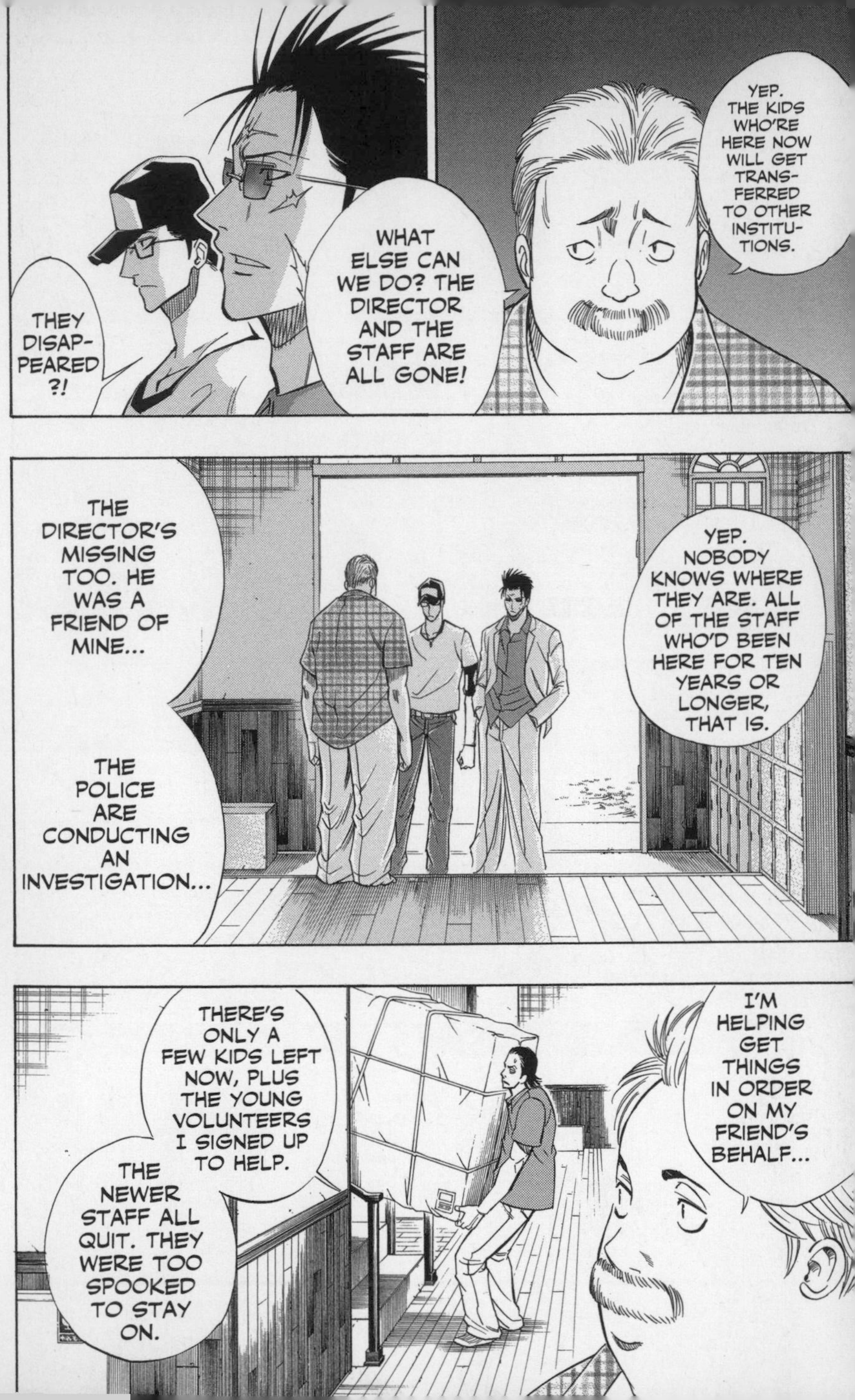
YEP. THE KIDS WHO'RE HERE NOW WILL GET TRANS-FERRED TO OTHER INSTITU-TIONS.
WHAT ELSE CAN WE DO? THE DIRECTOR AND THE STAFF ARE ALL GONE!
THEY DISAP-PEARED ?!
YEP. NOBODY KNOWS WHERE THEY ARE. ALL OF THE STAFF WHO'D BEEN HERE FOR TEN YEARS OR LONGER, THAT IS.
THE DIRECTOR'S MISSING TOO. HE WAS A FRIEND OF MINE...
THE POLICE ARE CONDUCTING AN INVESTIGATION...
I'M HELPING GET THINGS IN ORDER ON MY FRIEND'S BEHALF...
THERE'S ONLY A FEW KIDS LEFT NOW, PLUS THE YOUNG VOLUNTEERS I SIGNED UP TO HELP.
THE NEWER STAFF ALL QUIT. THEY WERE TOO SPOOKED TO STAY ON.

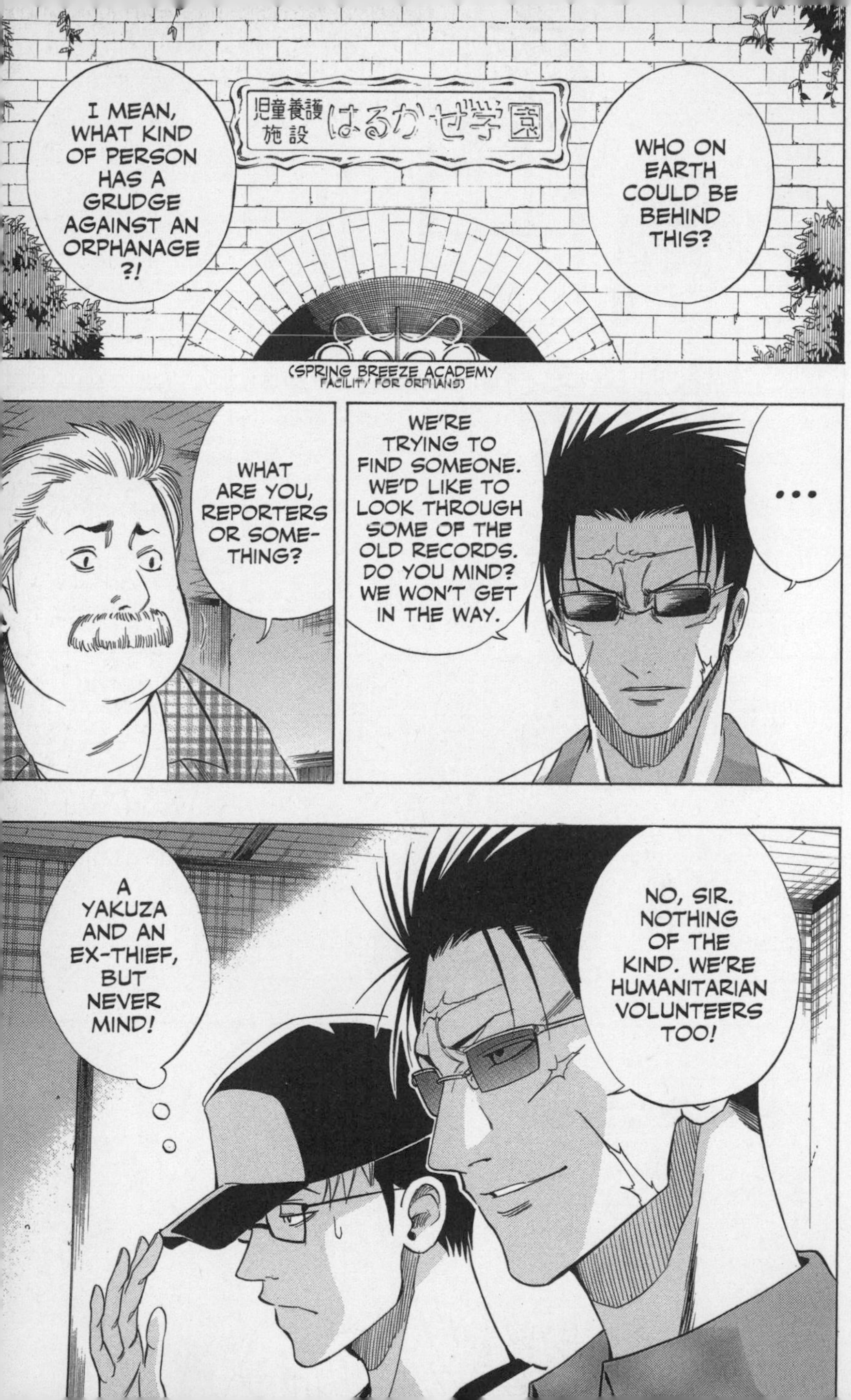
WHO ON EARTH COULD BE BEHIND THIS?
児童養護施設 はるかぜ学園
I MEAN, WHAT KIND OF PERSON HAS A GRUDGE AGAINST AN ORPHANAGE?!
(SPRING BREEZE ACADEMY FACILITY FOR ORPHANS)
...
WE'RE TRYING TO FIND SOMEONE. WE'D LIKE TO LOOK THROUGH SOME OF THE OLD RECORDS. DO YOU MIND? WE WON'T GET IN THE WAY.
WHAT ARE YOU, REPORTERS OR SOME-THING?
NO, SIR. NOTHING OF THE KIND. WE'RE HUMANITARIAN VOLUNTEERS TOO!
A YAKUZA AND AN EX-THIEF, BUT NEVER MIND!

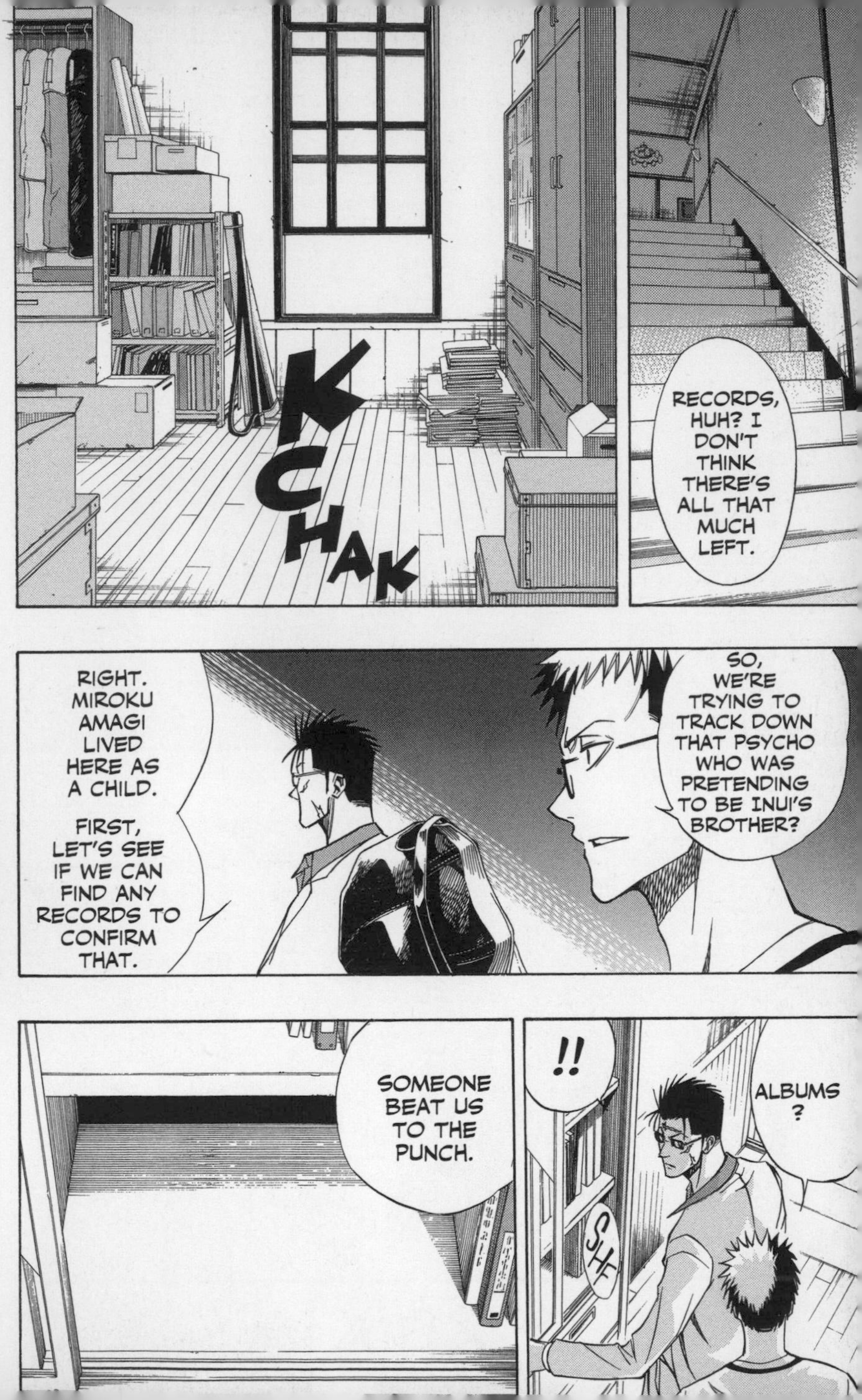
RECORDS, HUH? I DON'T THINK THERE'S ALL THAT MUCH LEFT.
KCHAK
SO, WE'RE TRYING TO TRACK DOWN THAT PSYCHO WHO WAS PRETENDING TO BE INUI'S BROTHER?
RIGHT. MIROKU AMAGI LIVED HERE AS A CHILD.
FIRST, LET'S SEE IF WE CAN FIND ANY RECORDS TO CONFIRM THAT.
ALBUMS ?
!!
SHF
SOMEONE BEAT US TO THE PUNCH.

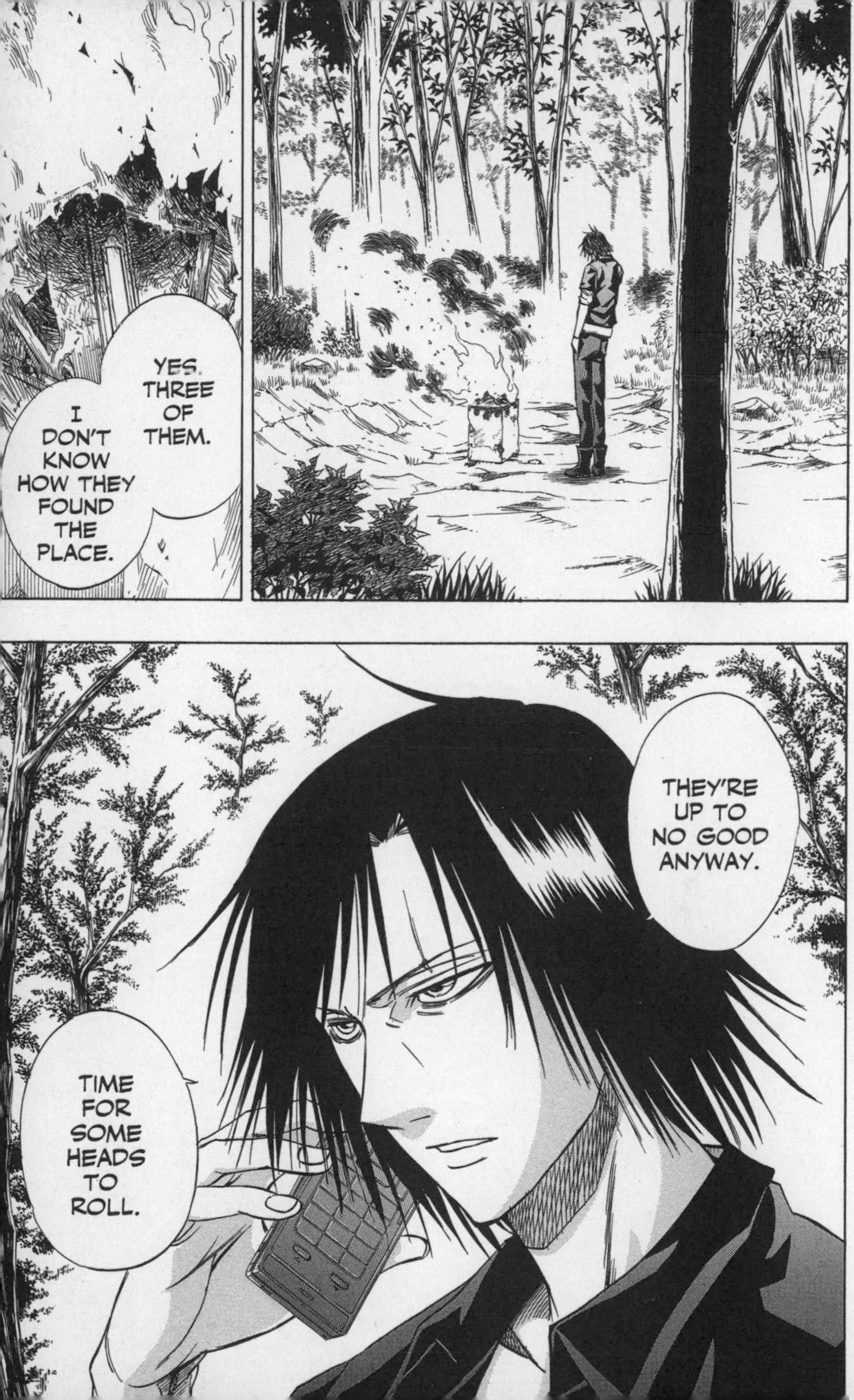
YES. THREE OF THEM.
I DON'T KNOW HOW THEY FOUND THE PLACE.
THEY'RE UP TO NO GOOD ANYWAY.
TIME FOR SOME HEADS TO ROLL.

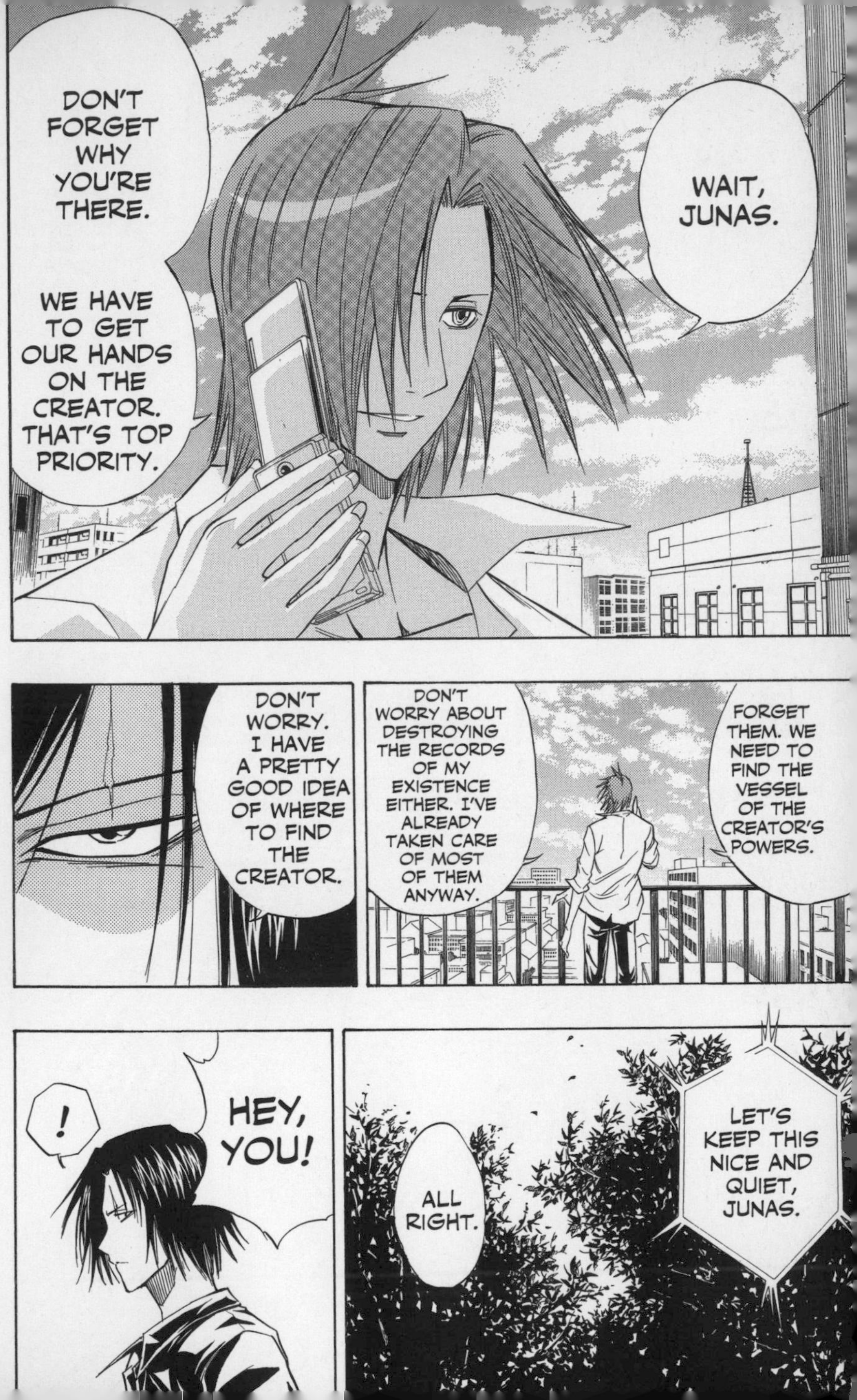
WAIT, JUNAS.
DON'T FORGET WHY YOU'RE THERE.
WE HAVE TO GET OUR HANDS ON THE CREATOR. THAT'S TOP PRIORITY.
FORGET THEM. WE NEED TO FIND THE VESSEL OF THE CREATOR'S POWERS.
DON'T WORRY ABOUT DESTROYING THE RECORDS OF MY EXISTENCE EITHER. I'VE ALREADY TAKEN CARE OF MOST OF THEM ANYWAY.
DON'T WORRY. I HAVE A PRETTY GOOD IDEA OF WHERE TO FIND THE CREATOR.
LET'S KEEP THIS NICE AND QUIET, JUNAS.
ALL RIGHT.
HEY, YOU!
!

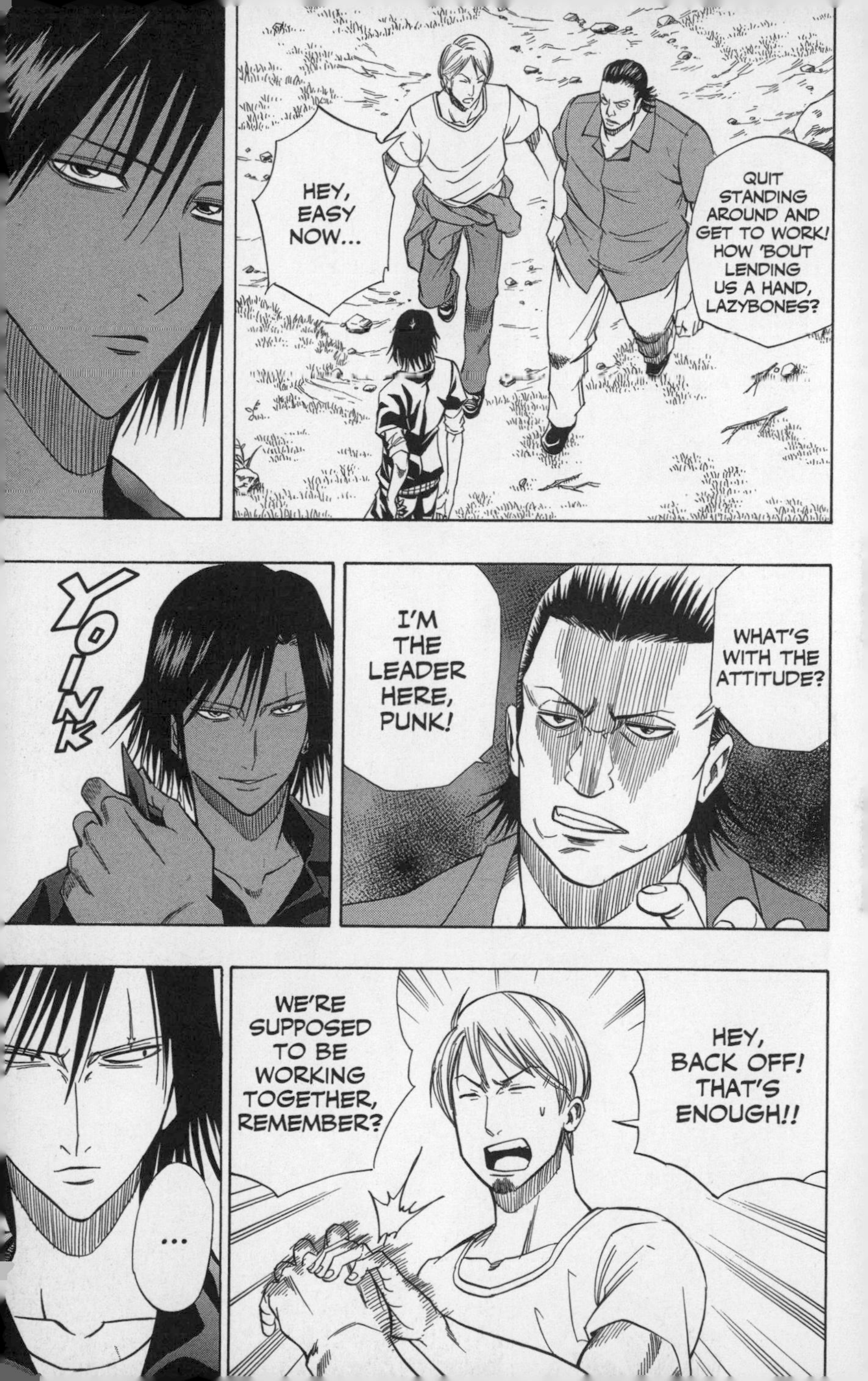
QUIT STANDING AROUND AND GET TO WORK! HOW 'BOUT LENDING US A HAND, LAZYBONES?
HEY, EASY NOW...
WHAT'S WITH THE ATTITUDE?
I'M THE LEADER HERE, PUNK!
YOINK
HEY, BACK OFF! THAT'S ENOUGH!!
WE'RE SUPPOSED TO BE WORKING TOGETHER, REMEMBER?
...

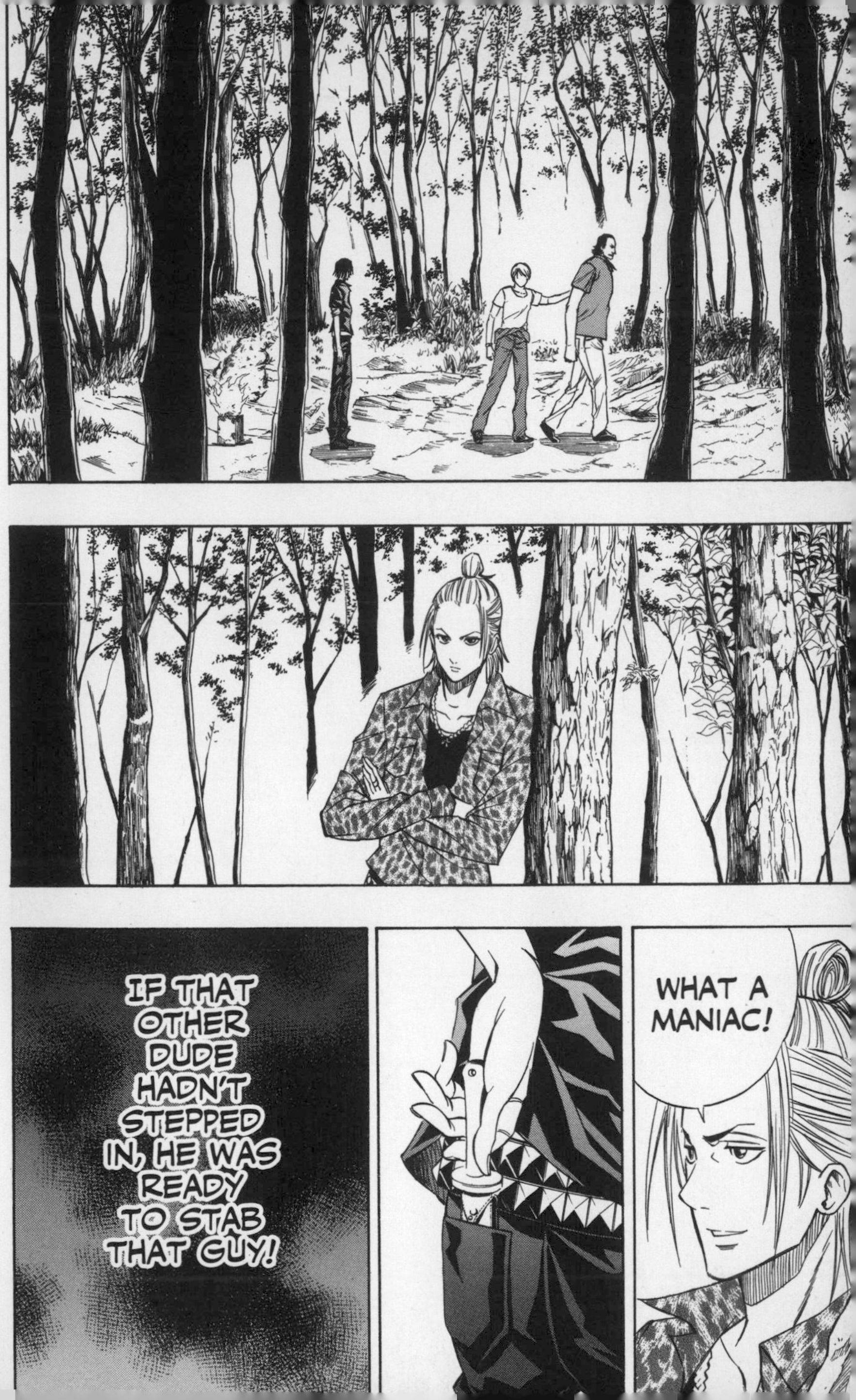
WHAT A MANIAC!
IF THAT OTHER DUDE HADN'T STEPPED IN, HE WAS READY TO STAB THAT GUY!

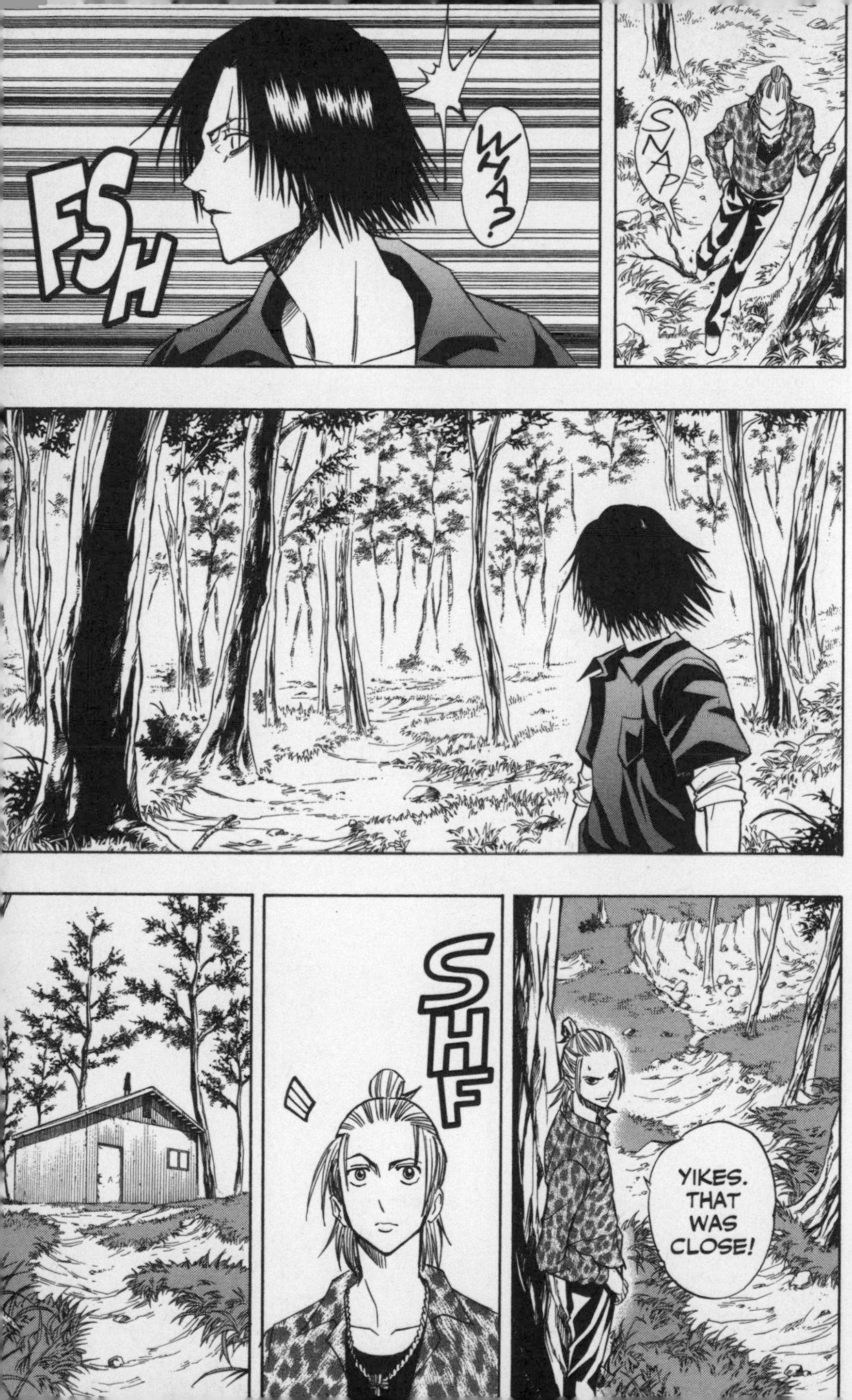
SNAP
WHAP?
FSH
YIKES. THAT WAS CLOSE!
SHF

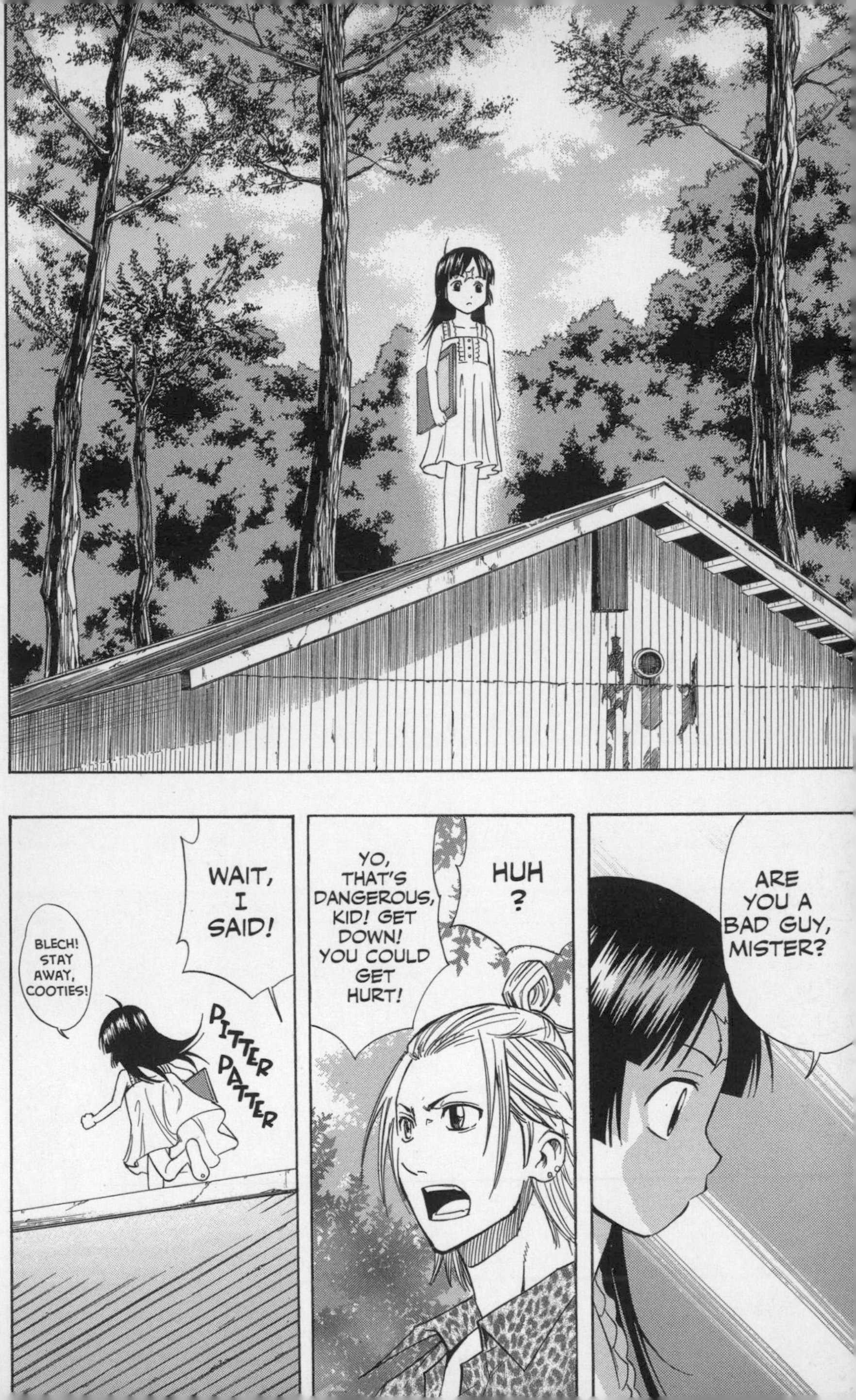
ARE YOU A BAD GUY, MISTER?
HUH?
YO, THAT'S DANGEROUS, KID! GET DOWN! YOU COULD GET HURT!
WAIT, I SAID!
BLECH! STAY AWAY, COOTIES!
PITTER PATTER

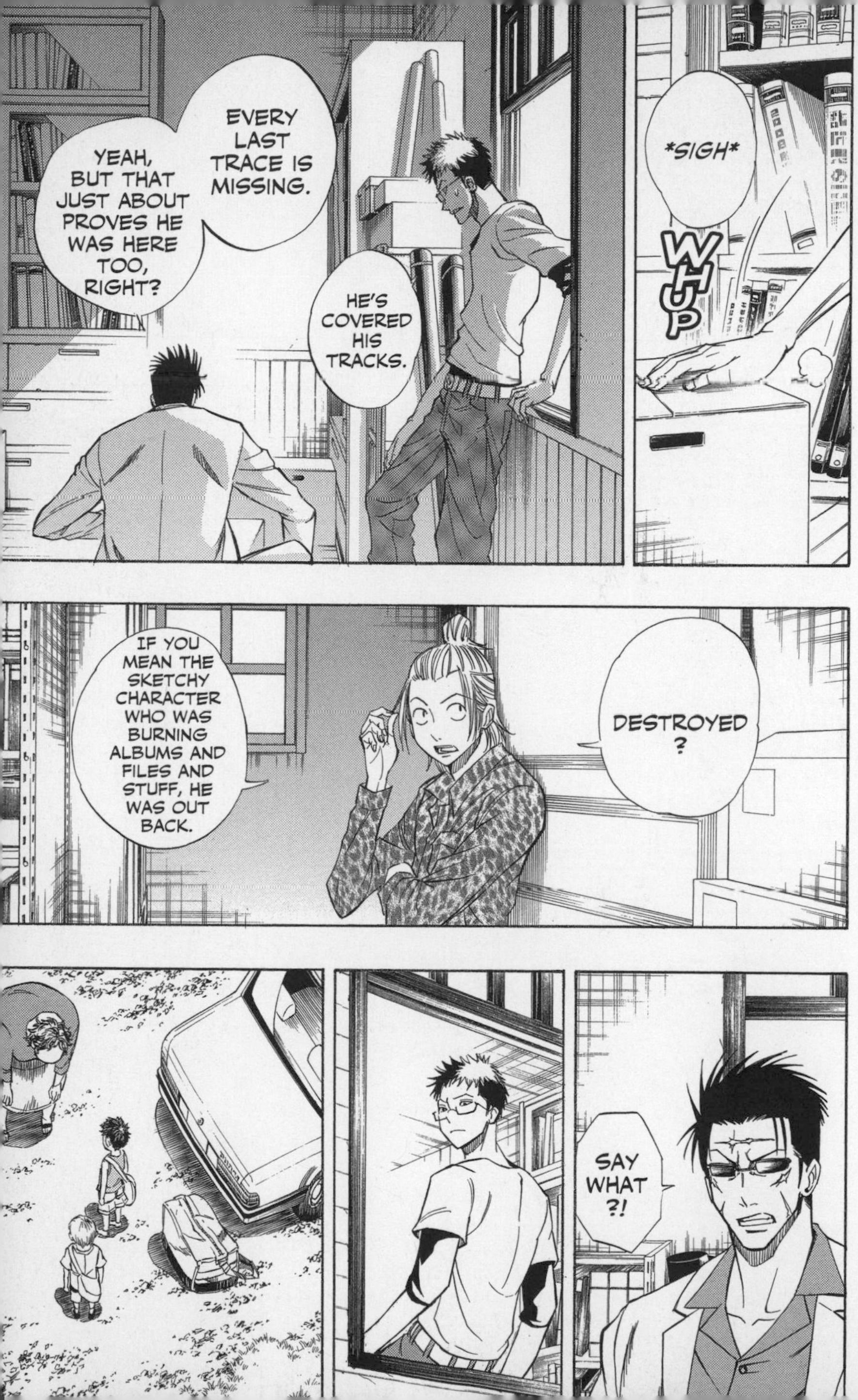
SIGH
WHUP
EVERY LAST TRACE IS MISSING.
HE'S COVERED HIS TRACKS.
YEAH, BUT THAT JUST ABOUT PROVES HE WAS HERE TOO, RIGHT?
DESTROYED?
IF YOU MEAN THE SKETCHY CHARACTER WHO WAS BURNING ALBUMS AND FILES AND STUFF, HE WAS OUT BACK.
SAY WHAT?!

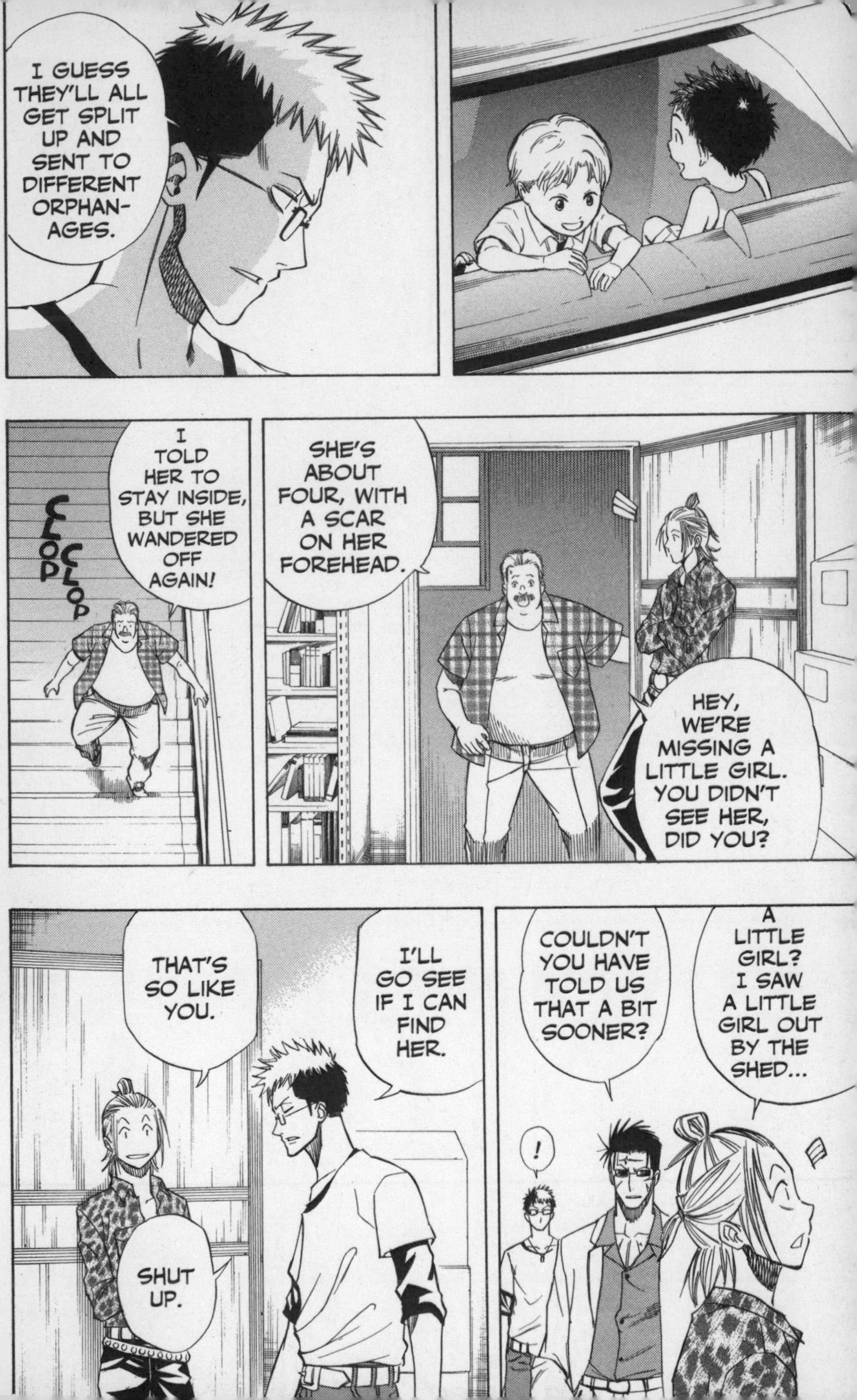
I GUESS THEY'LL ALL GET SPLIT UP AND SENT TO DIFFERENT ORPHAN- AGES.
HEY, WE'RE MISSING A LITTLE GIRL. YOU DIDN'T SEE HER, DID YOU?
SHE'S ABOUT FOUR, WITH A SCAR ON HER FOREHEAD.
I TOLD HER TO STAY INSIDE, BUT SHE WANDERED OFF AGAIN!
CLOP CLOP
A LITTLE GIRL? I SAW A LITTLE GIRL OUT BY THE SHED...
!
COULDN'T YOU HAVE TOLD US THAT A BIT SOONER?
I'LL GO SEE IF I CAN FIND HER.
THAT'S SO LIKE YOU.
SHUT UP.

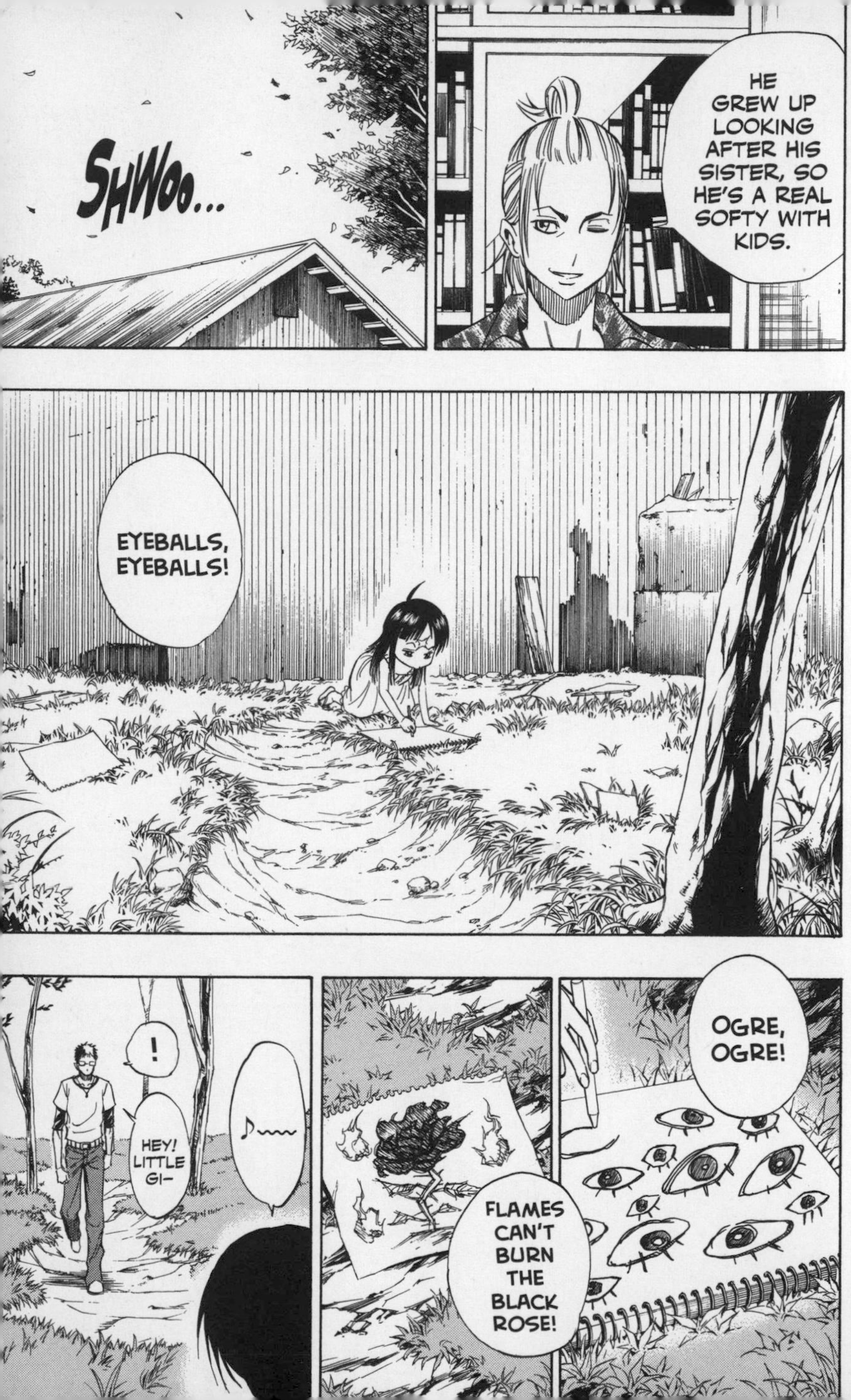
HE GREW UP LOOKING AFTER HIS SISTER, SO HE'S A REAL SOFTY WITH KIDS.
SHWOO...
EYEBALLS, EYEBALLS!
OGRE, OGRE!
FLAMES CAN'T BURN THE BLACK ROSE!
!
HEY! LITTLE GI–
♪~~~

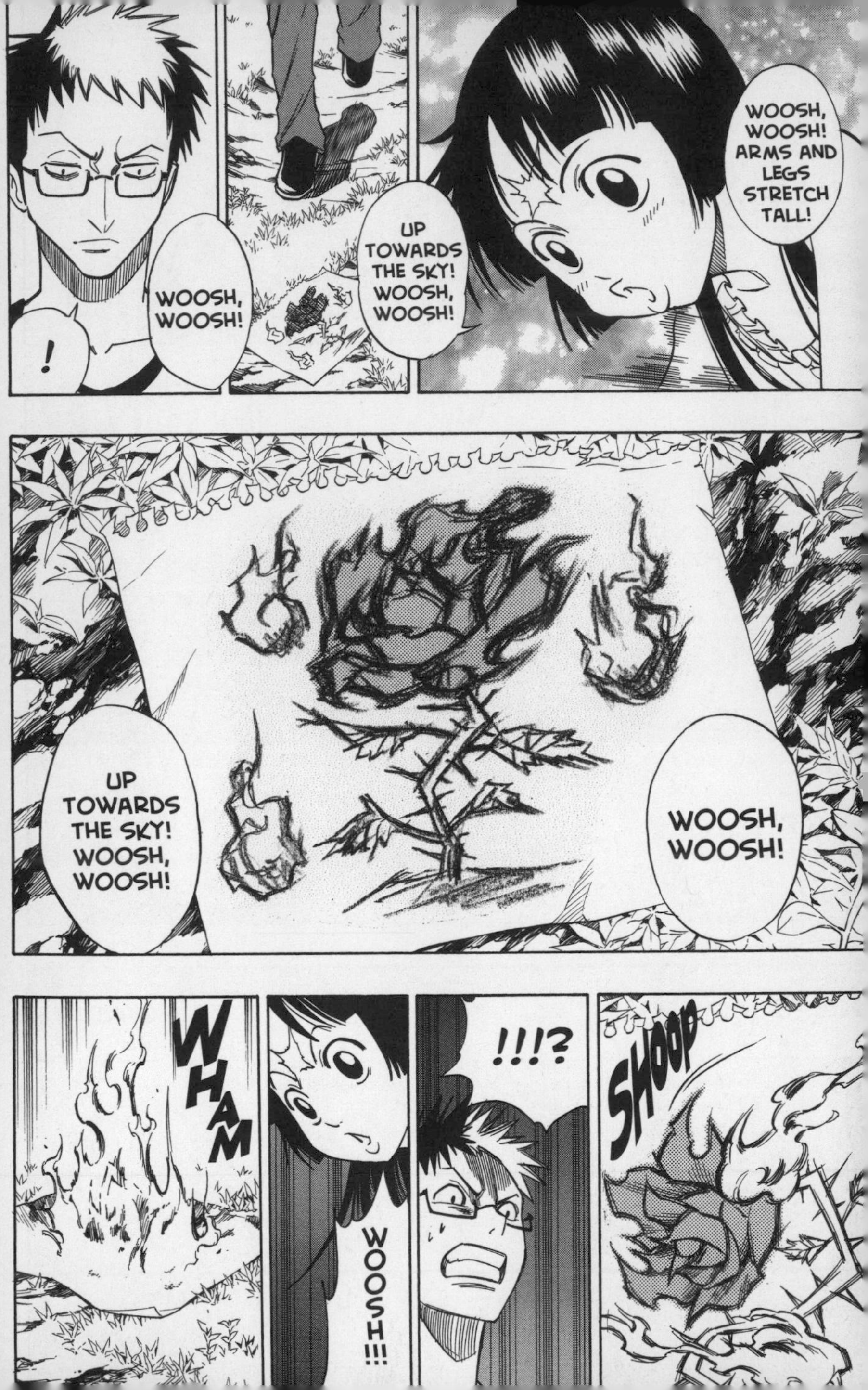
WOOSH, WOOSH! ARMS AND LEGS STRETCH TALL!
UP TOWARDS THE SKY! WOOSH, WOOSH!
WOOSH, WOOSH!
!
WOOSH, WOOSH!
UP TOWARDS THE SKY! WOOSH, WOOSH!
SHOOP
!!!?
WOOSH!!!
WHAM

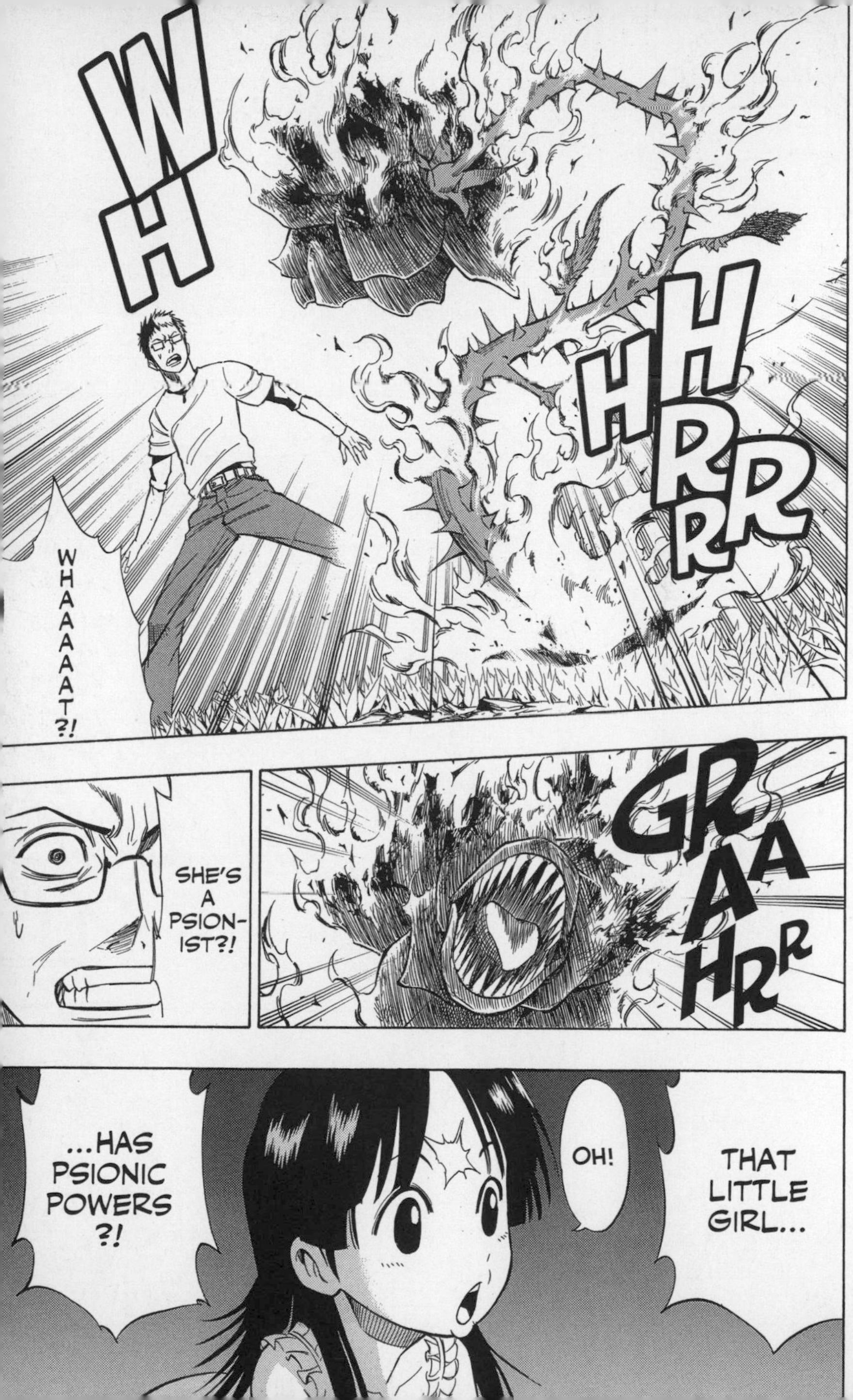

HHRRR
WHH
WHAAAAAT?!
GRAAHRR
SHE'S A PSIONIST?!
THAT LITTLE GIRL...
OH!
...HAS PSIONIC POWERS?!

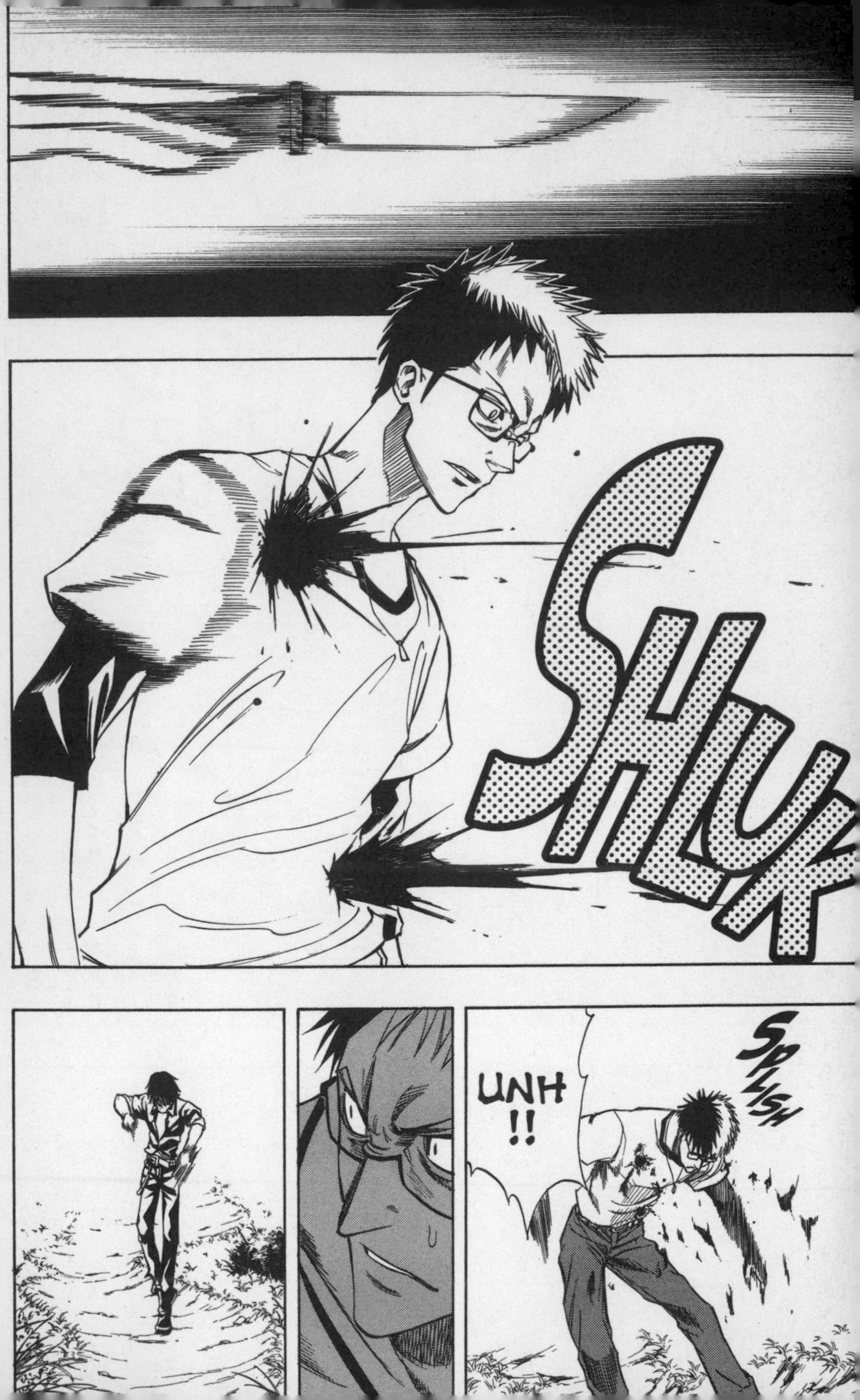
SHLUK
SPLISH
UNH !!

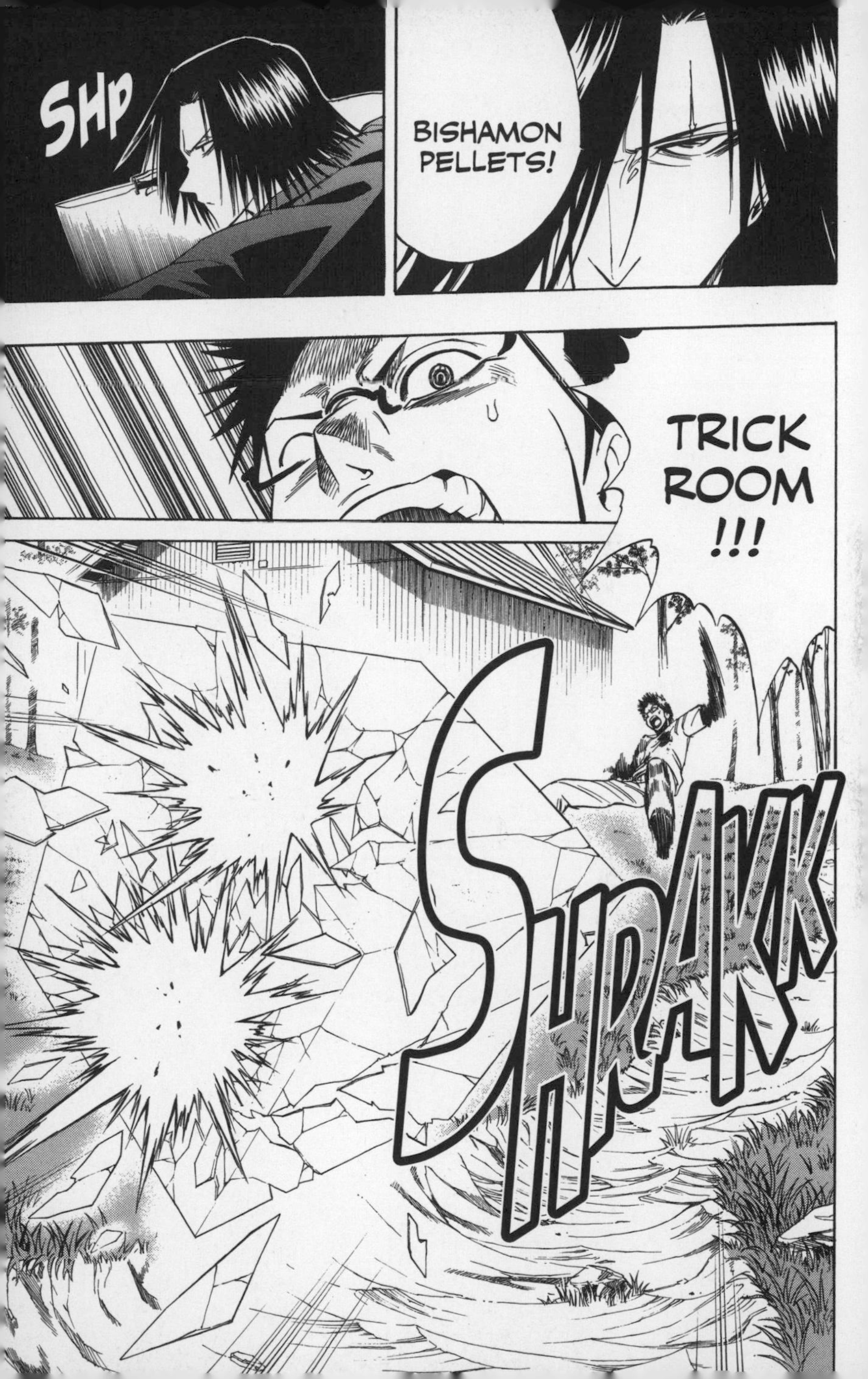
BISHAMON PELLETS!
SHp
TRICK ROOM !!!
SHPAKK

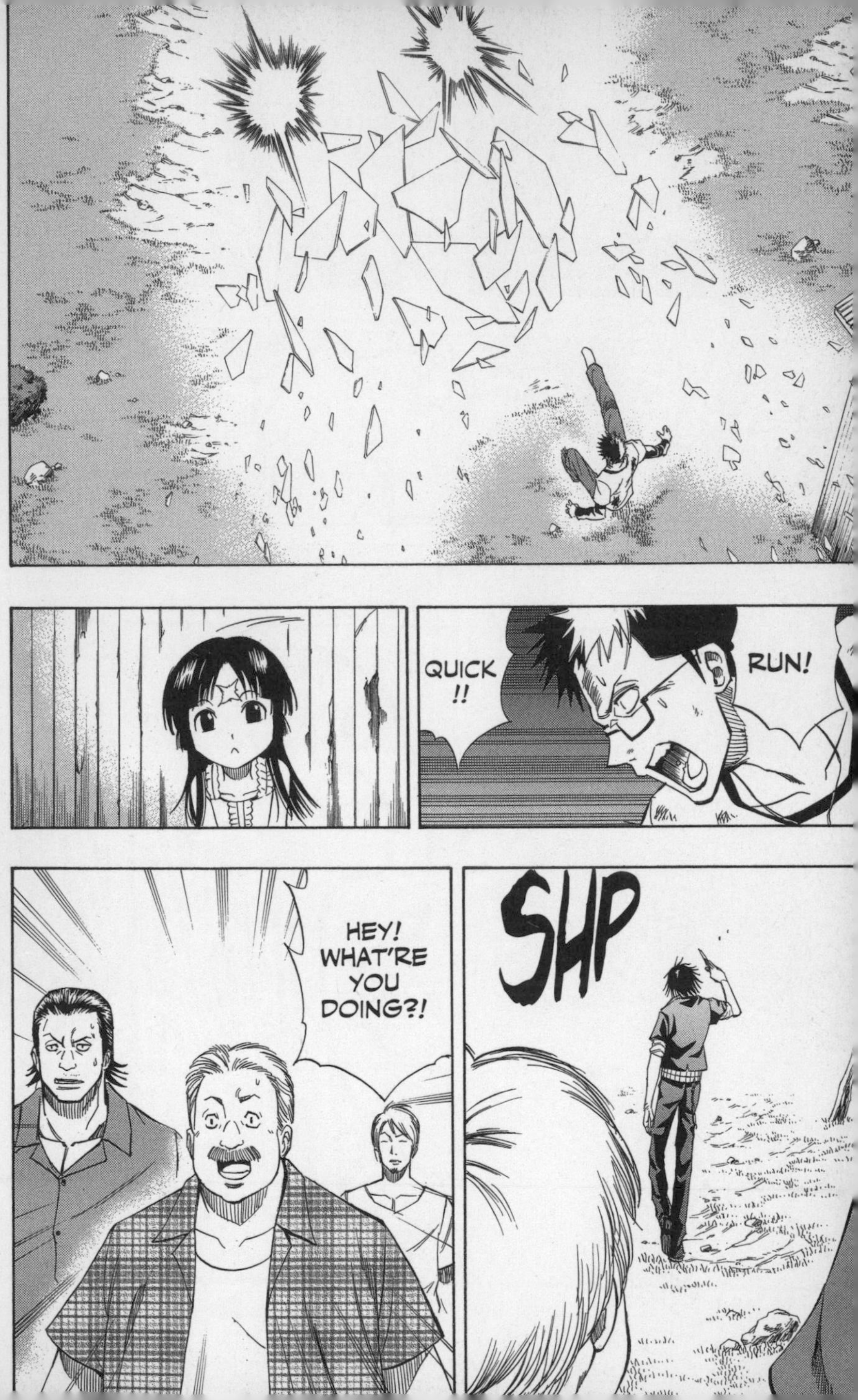
RUN!
QUICK !!
SHP
HEY! WHAT'RE YOU DOING?!

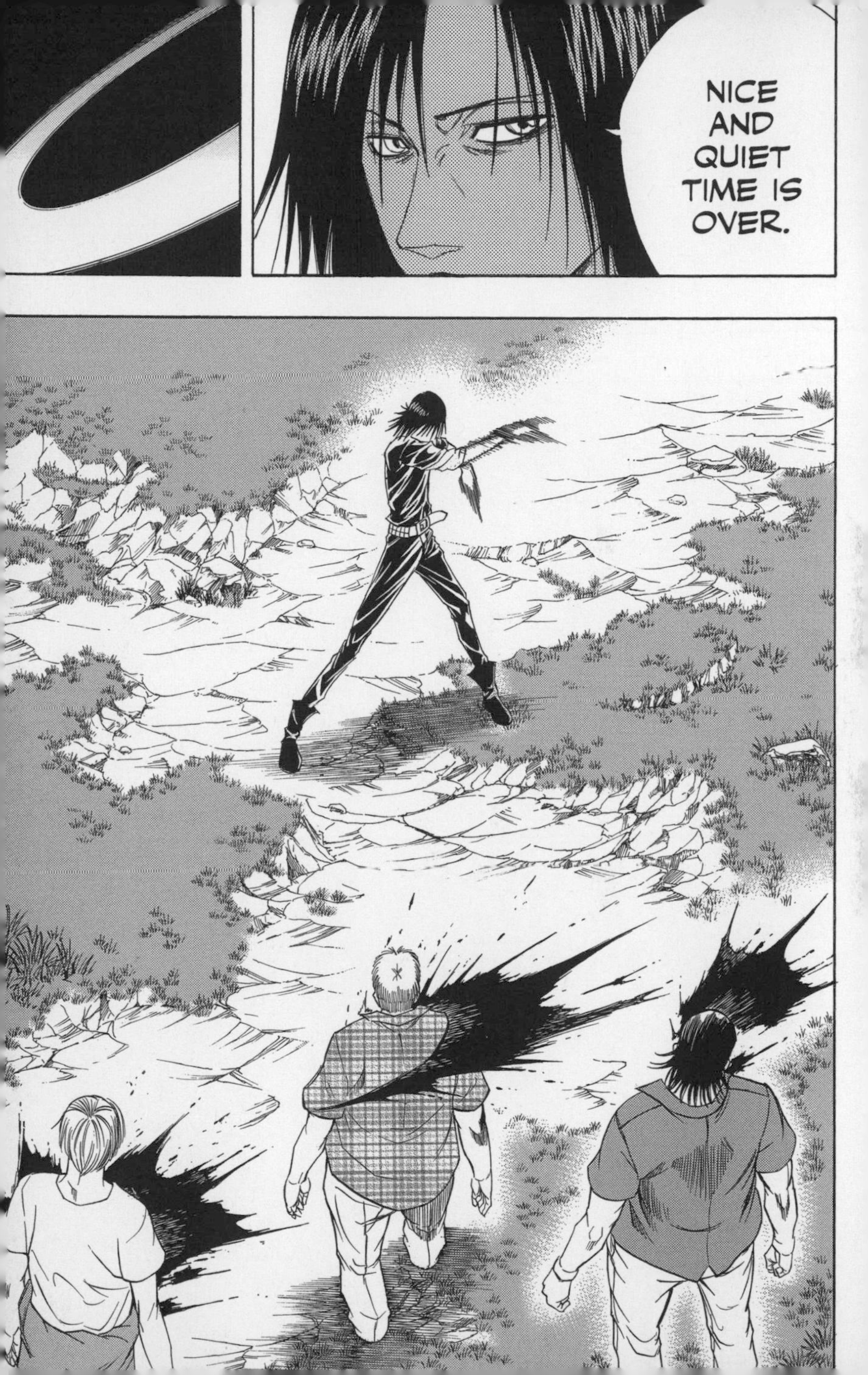
NICE AND QUIET TIME IS OVER.

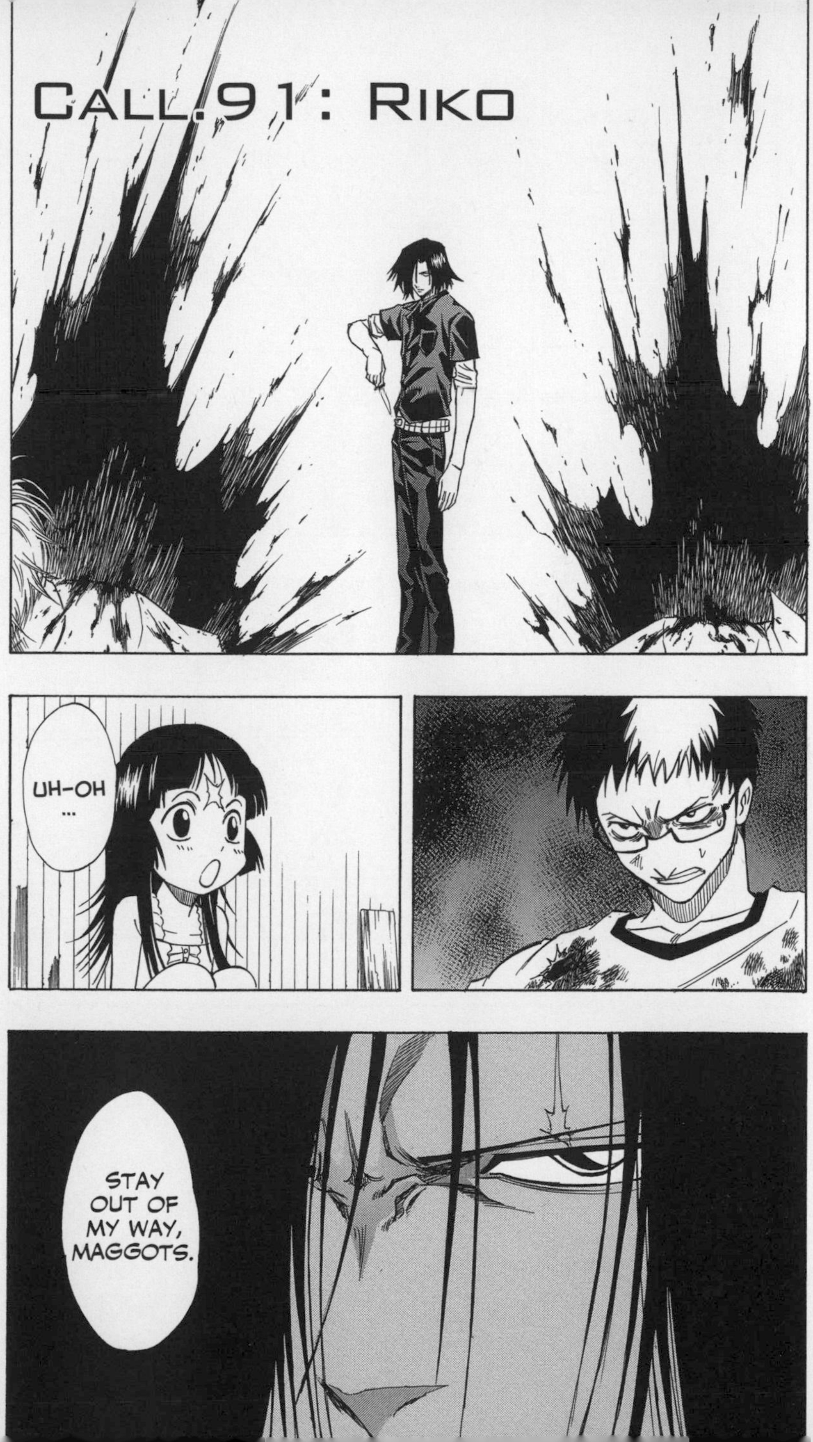
Call.91: Riko
UH-OH ...
STAY OUT OF MY WAY, MAGGOTS.

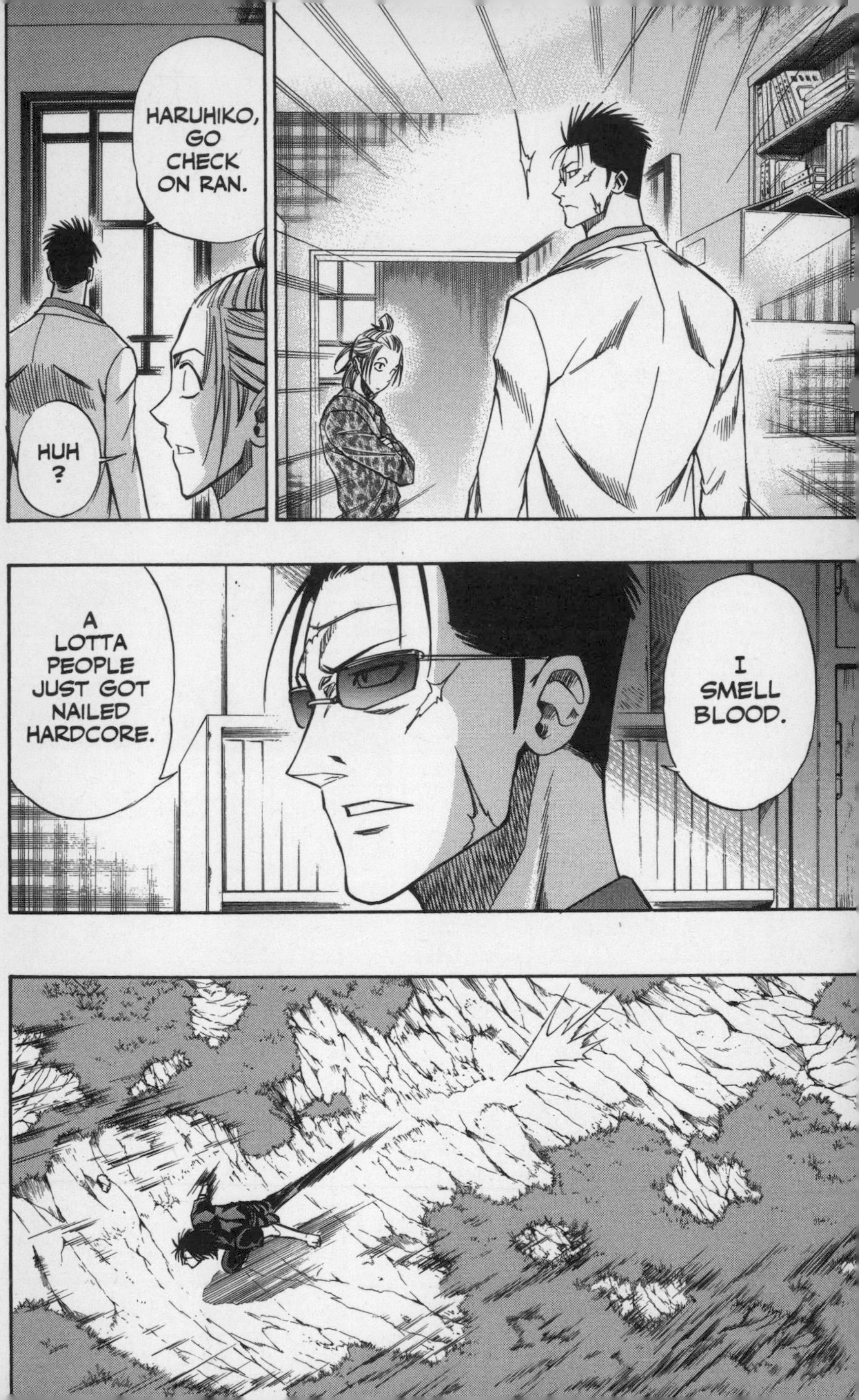
HARUHIKO, GO CHECK ON RAN.
HUH?
I SMELL BLOOD.
A LOTTA PEOPLE JUST GOT NAILED HARDCORE.

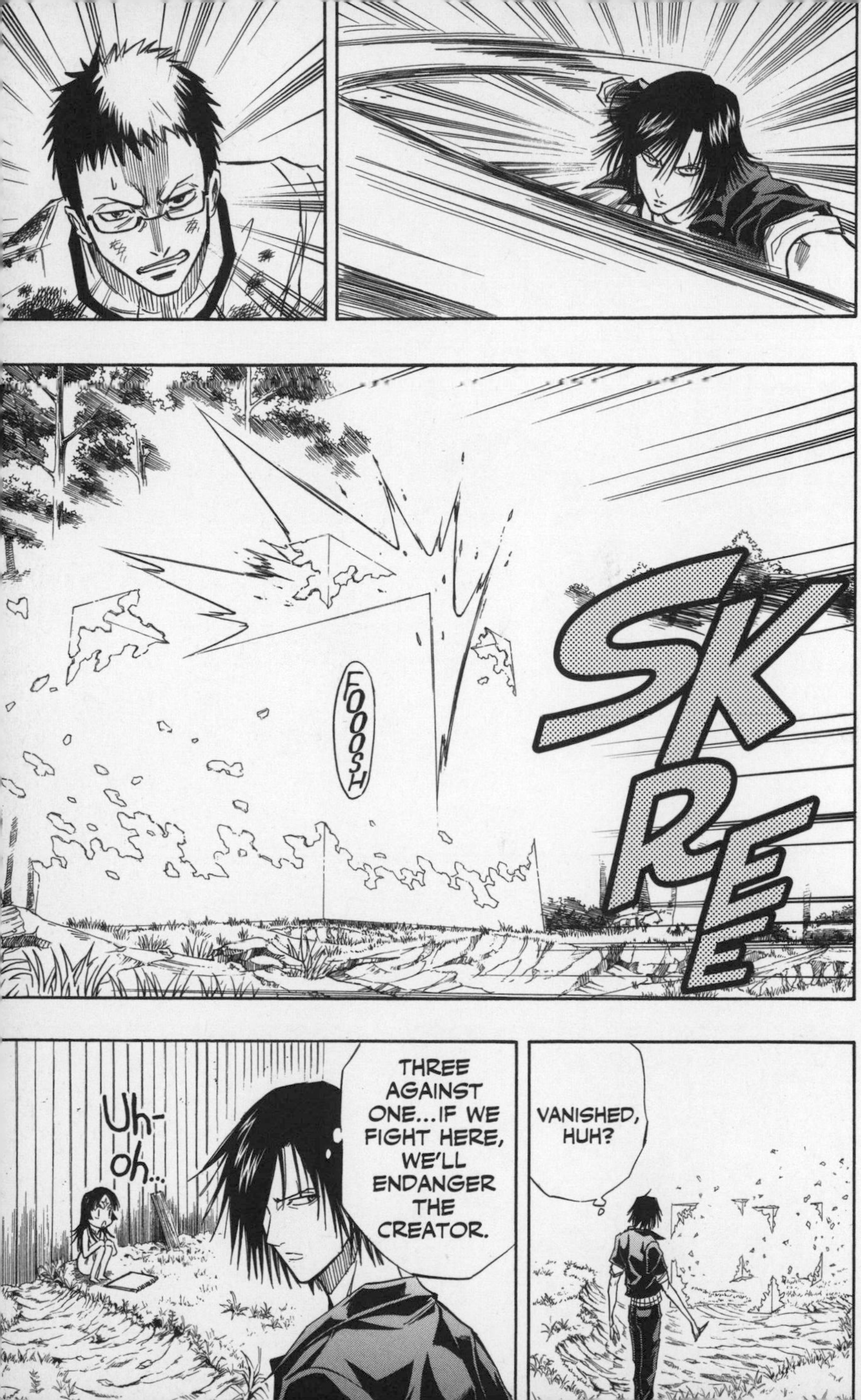
SKREE
FOOOSH
VANISHED, HUH?
THREE AGAINST ONE...IF WE FIGHT HERE, WE'LL ENDANGER THE CREATOR.
Uh-oh...

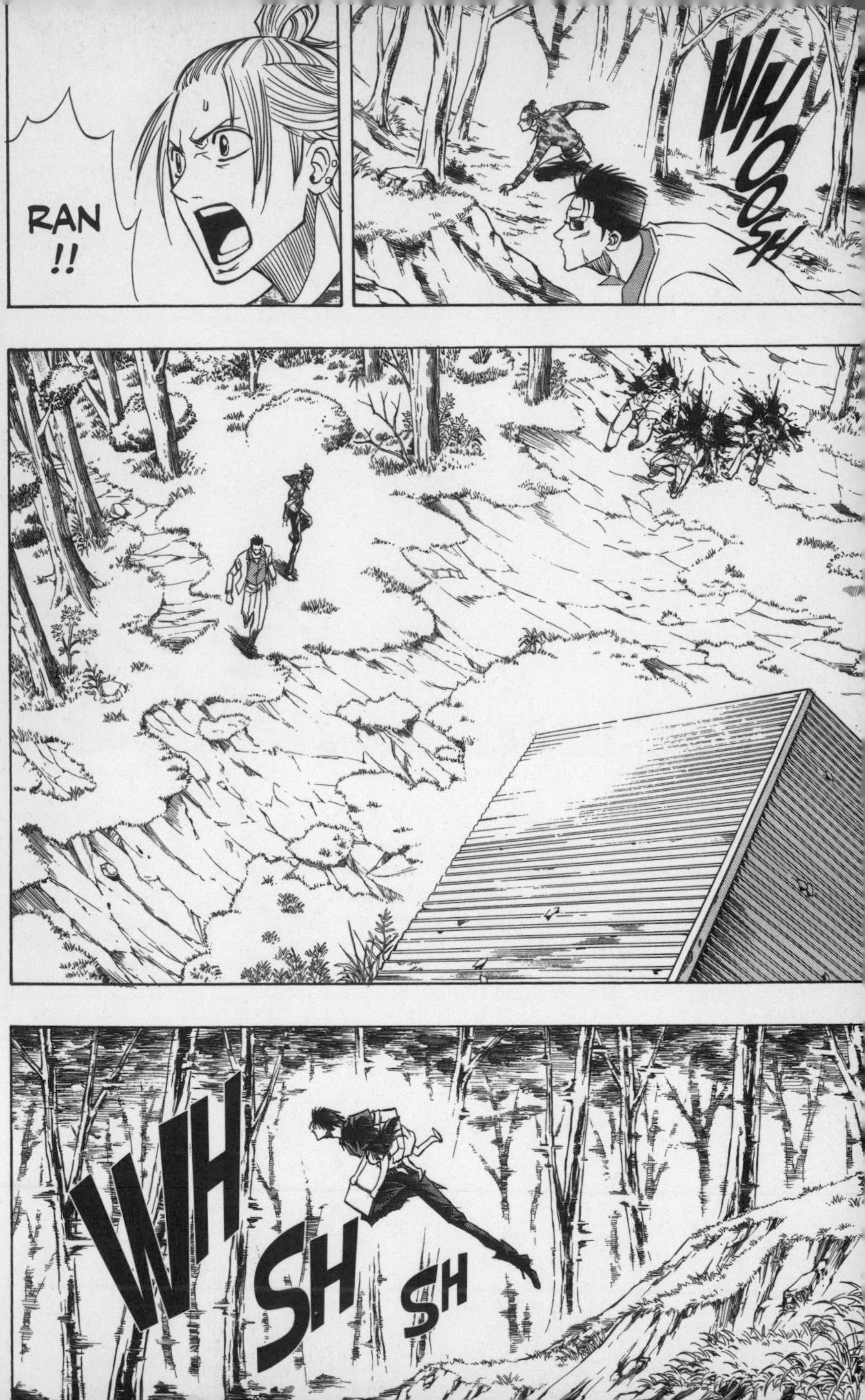
WHOOSH
RAN !!
WHSH SH SH

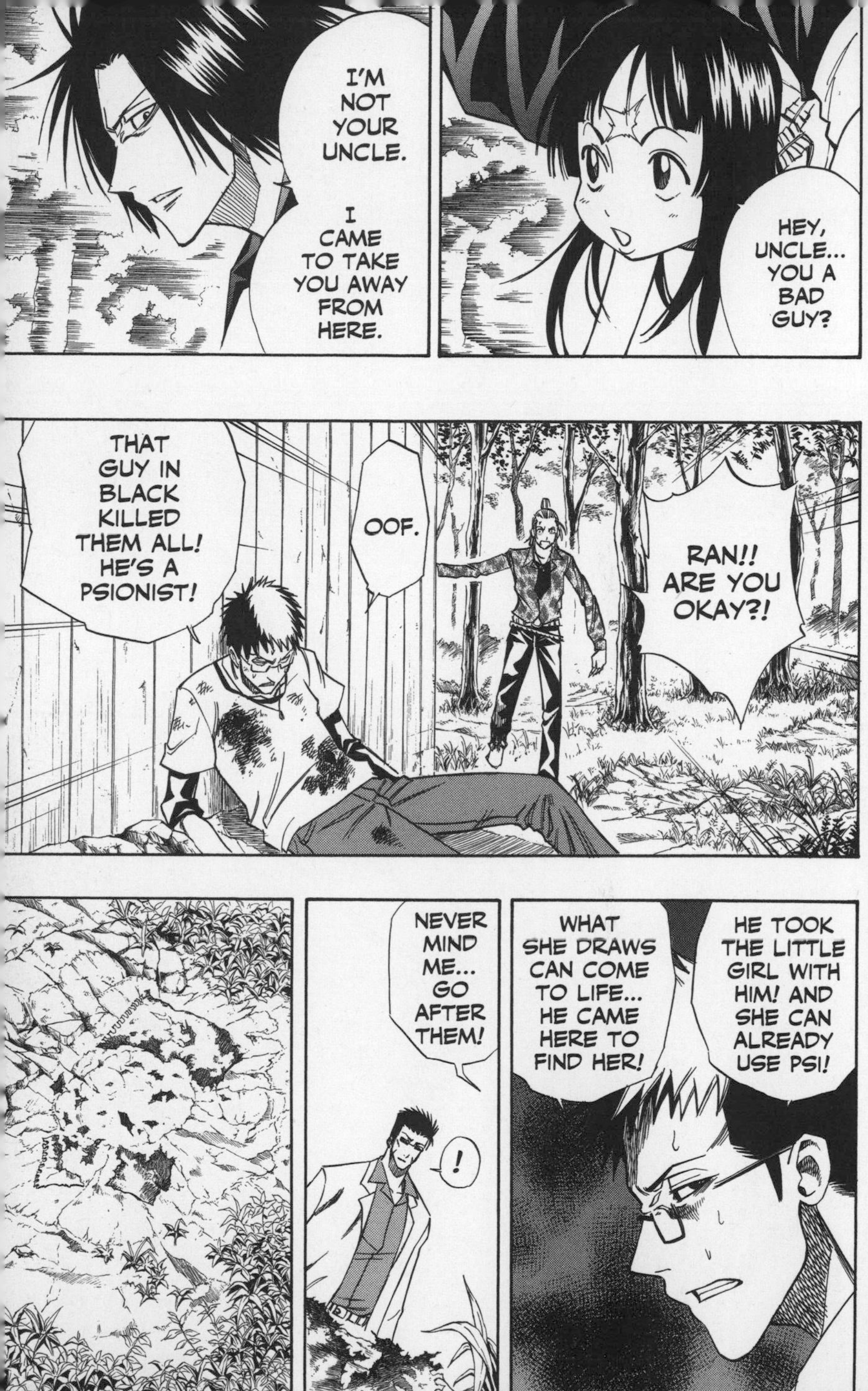
HEY, UNCLE... YOU A BAD GUY?
I'M NOT YOUR UNCLE.
I CAME TO TAKE YOU AWAY FROM HERE.
RAN!! ARE YOU OKAY?!
OOF.
THAT GUY IN BLACK KILLED THEM ALL! HE'S A PSIONIST!
HE TOOK THE LITTLE GIRL WITH HIM! AND SHE CAN ALREADY USE PSI!
WHAT SHE DRAWS CAN COME TO LIFE... HE CAME HERE TO FIND HER!
NEVER MIND ME... GO AFTER THEM!
!

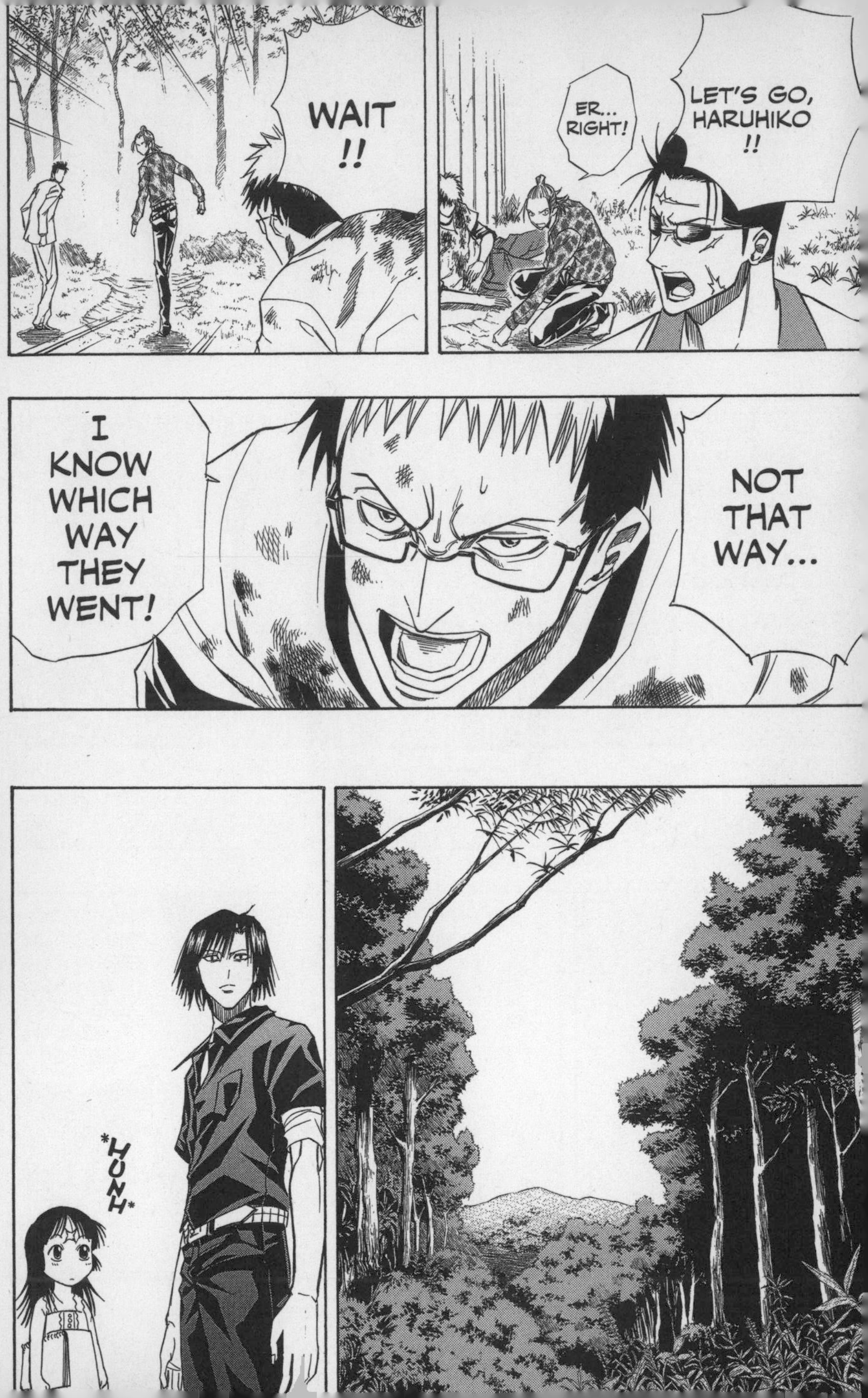
LET'S GO, HARUHIKO !!
ER... RIGHT!
WAIT !!
NOT THAT WAY...
I KNOW WHICH WAY THEY WENT!
HUNH

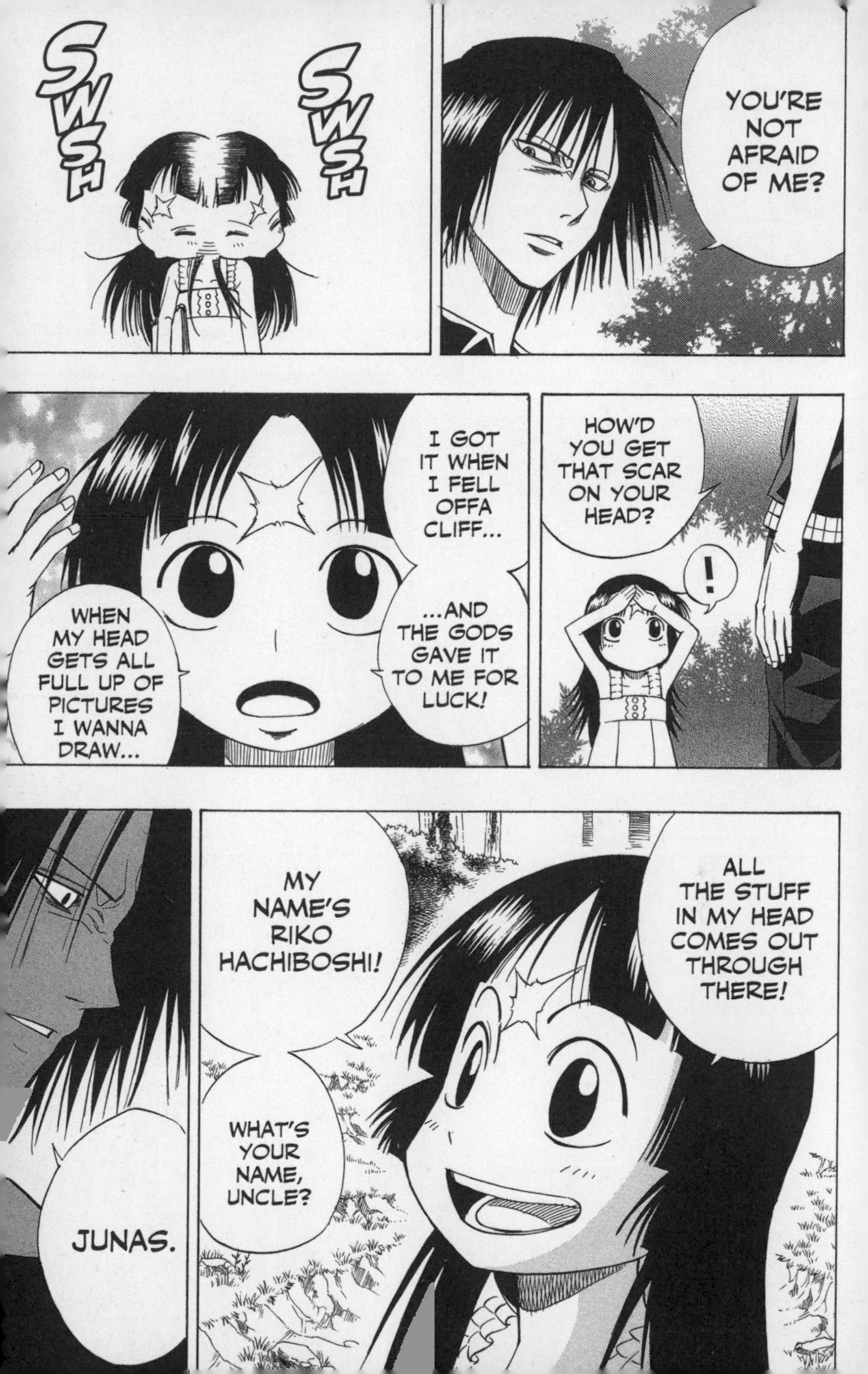
YOU'RE NOT AFRAID OF ME?
SWSH
SWSH
HOW'D YOU GET THAT SCAR ON YOUR HEAD?
!
I GOT IT WHEN I FELL OFFA CLIFF...
...AND THE GODS GAVE IT TO ME FOR LUCK!
WHEN MY HEAD GETS ALL FULL UP OF PICTURES I WANNA DRAW...
ALL THE STUFF IN MY HEAD COMES OUT THROUGH THERE!
MY NAME'S RIKO HACHIBOSHI!
WHAT'S YOUR NAME, UNCLE?
JUNAS.

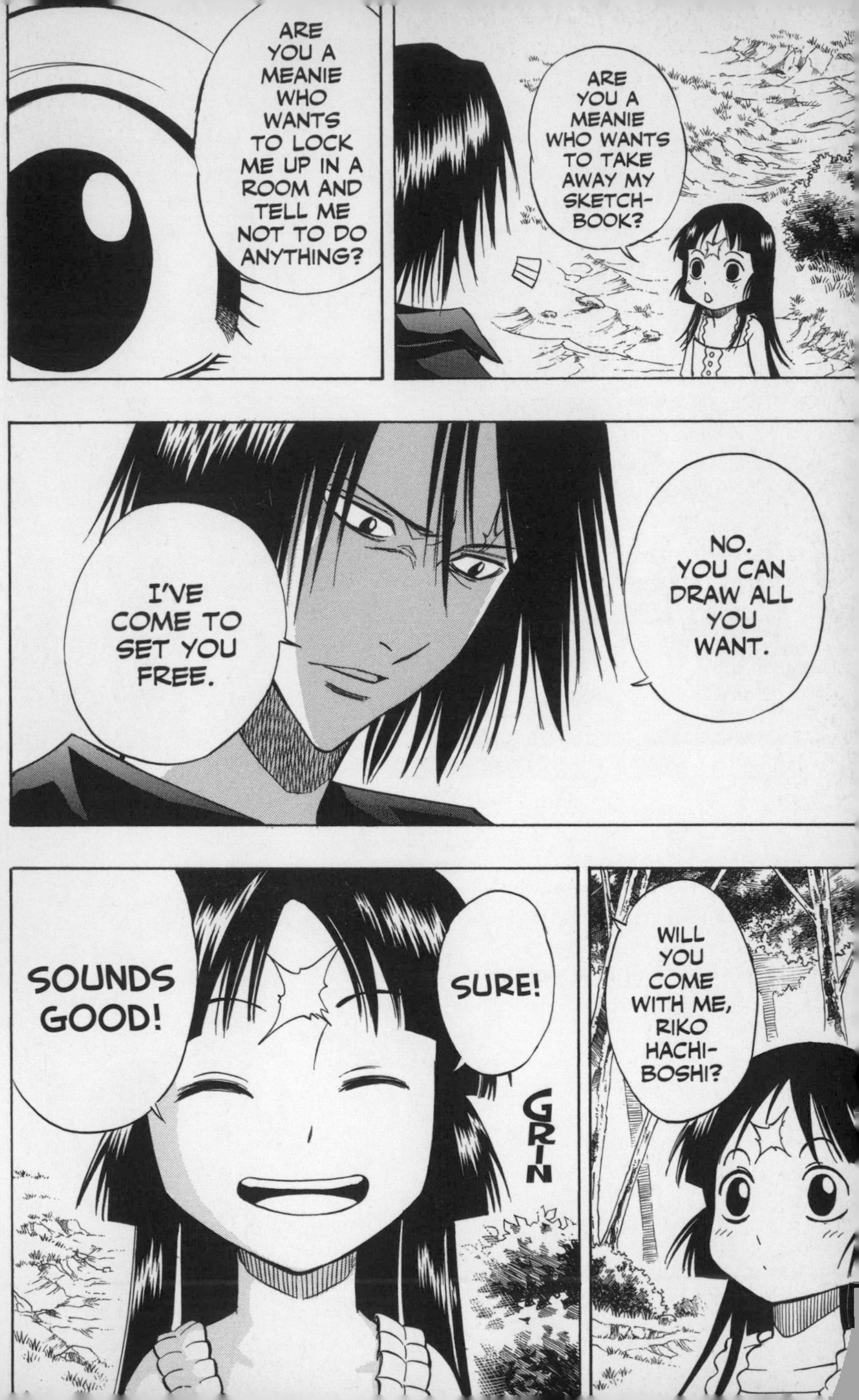
ARE YOU A MEANIE WHO WANTS TO TAKE AWAY MY SKETCH-BOOK?
ARE YOU A MEANIE WHO WANTS TO LOCK ME UP IN A ROOM AND TELL ME NOT TO DO ANYTHING?
NO. YOU CAN DRAW ALL YOU WANT.
I'VE COME TO SET YOU FREE.
WILL YOU COME WITH ME, RIKO HACHI-BOSHI?
SURE!
SOUNDS GOOD!
GRIN

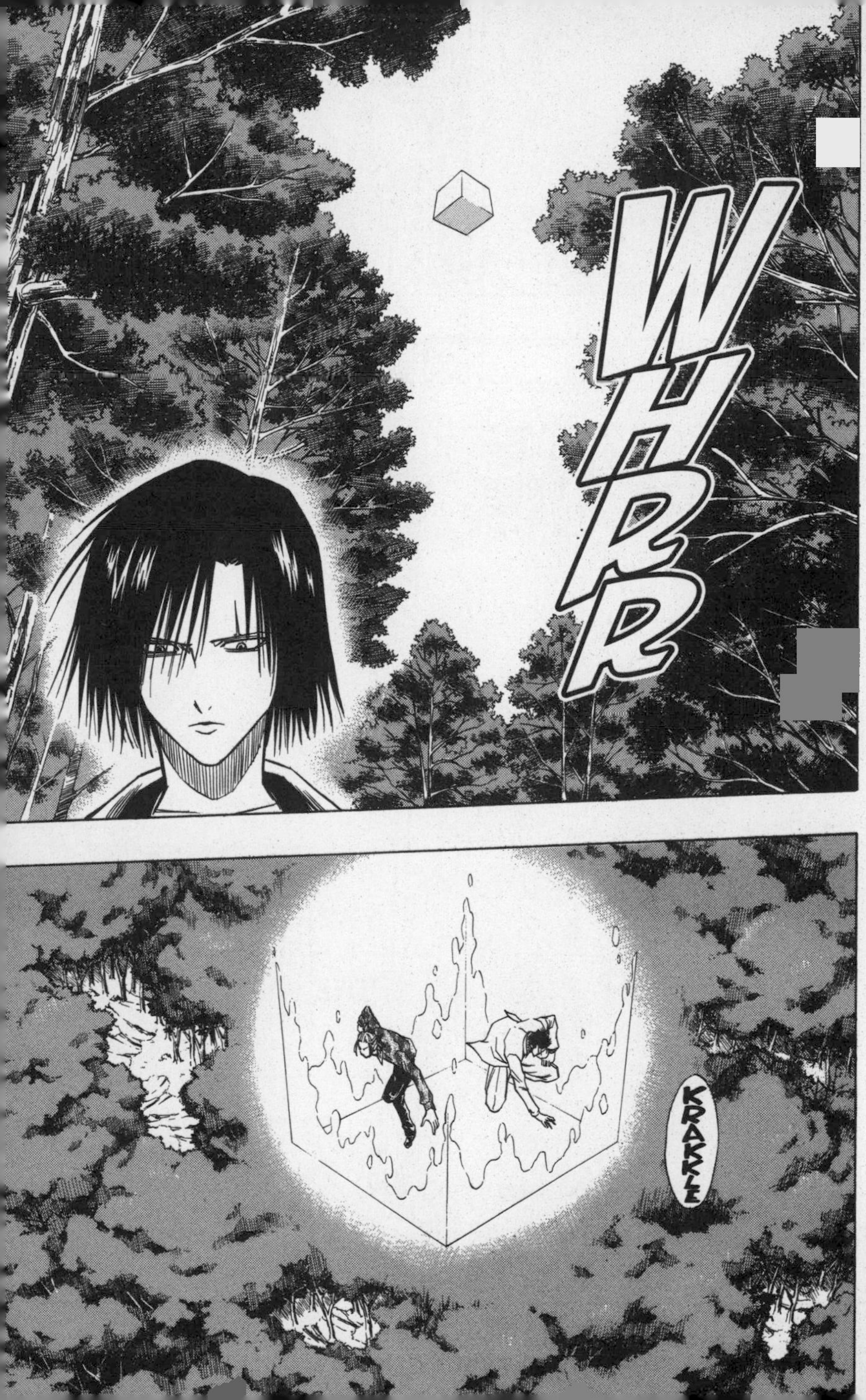
WHRR
KRAKKLE

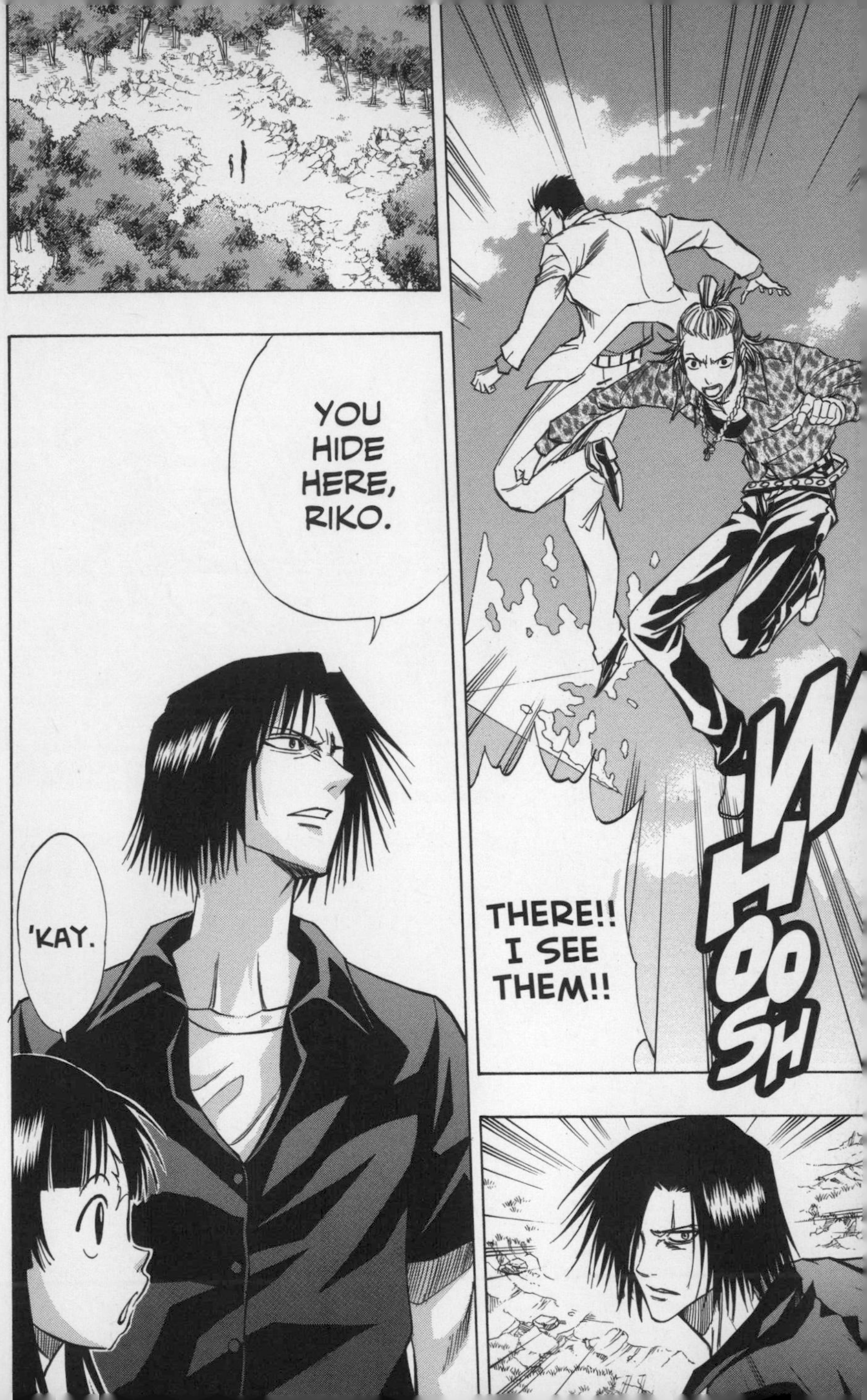
THERE!! I SEE THEM!!
WHOOSH
YOU HIDE HERE, RIKO.
'KAY.

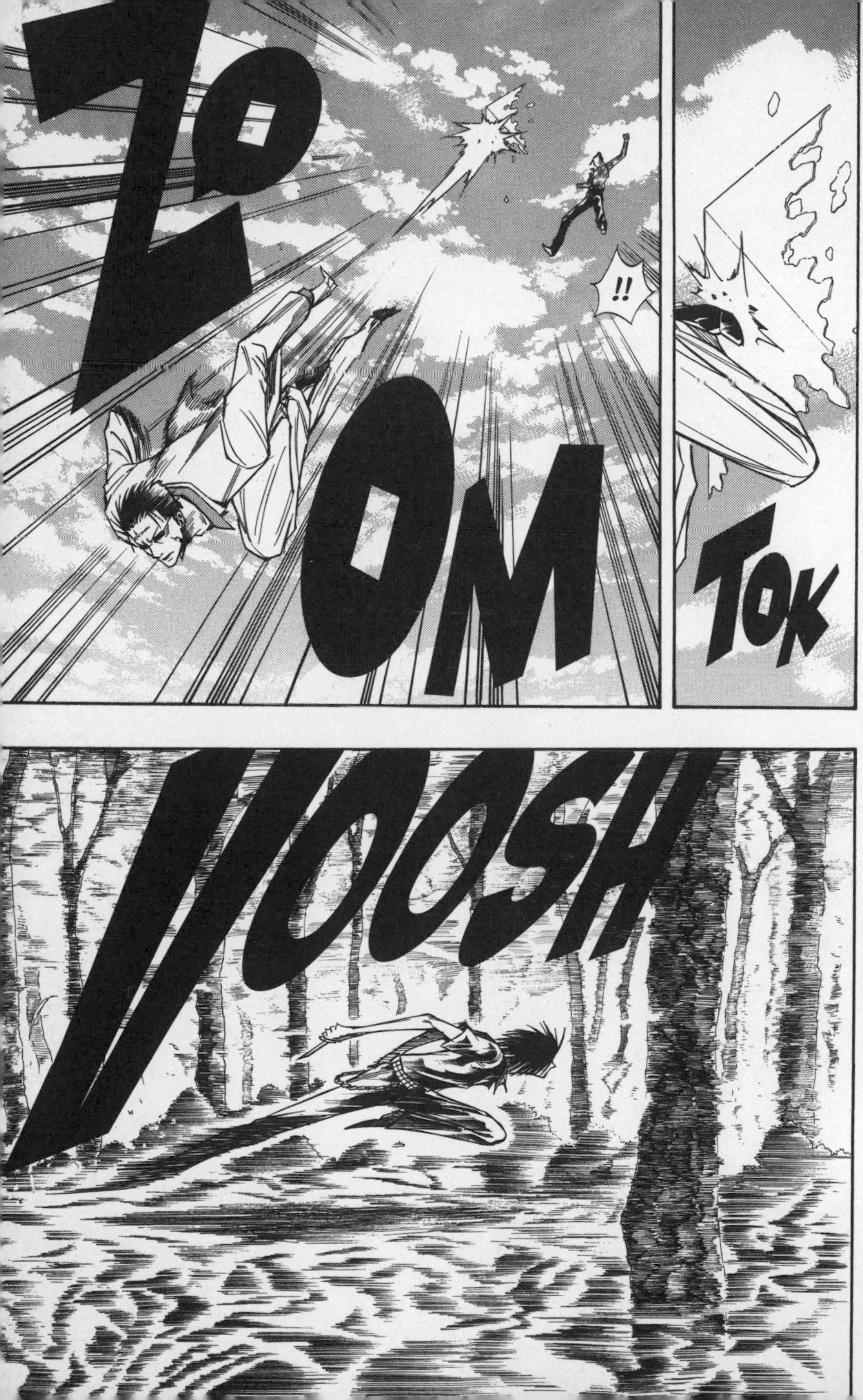
TOK
!!
ZOOM
VOOSH

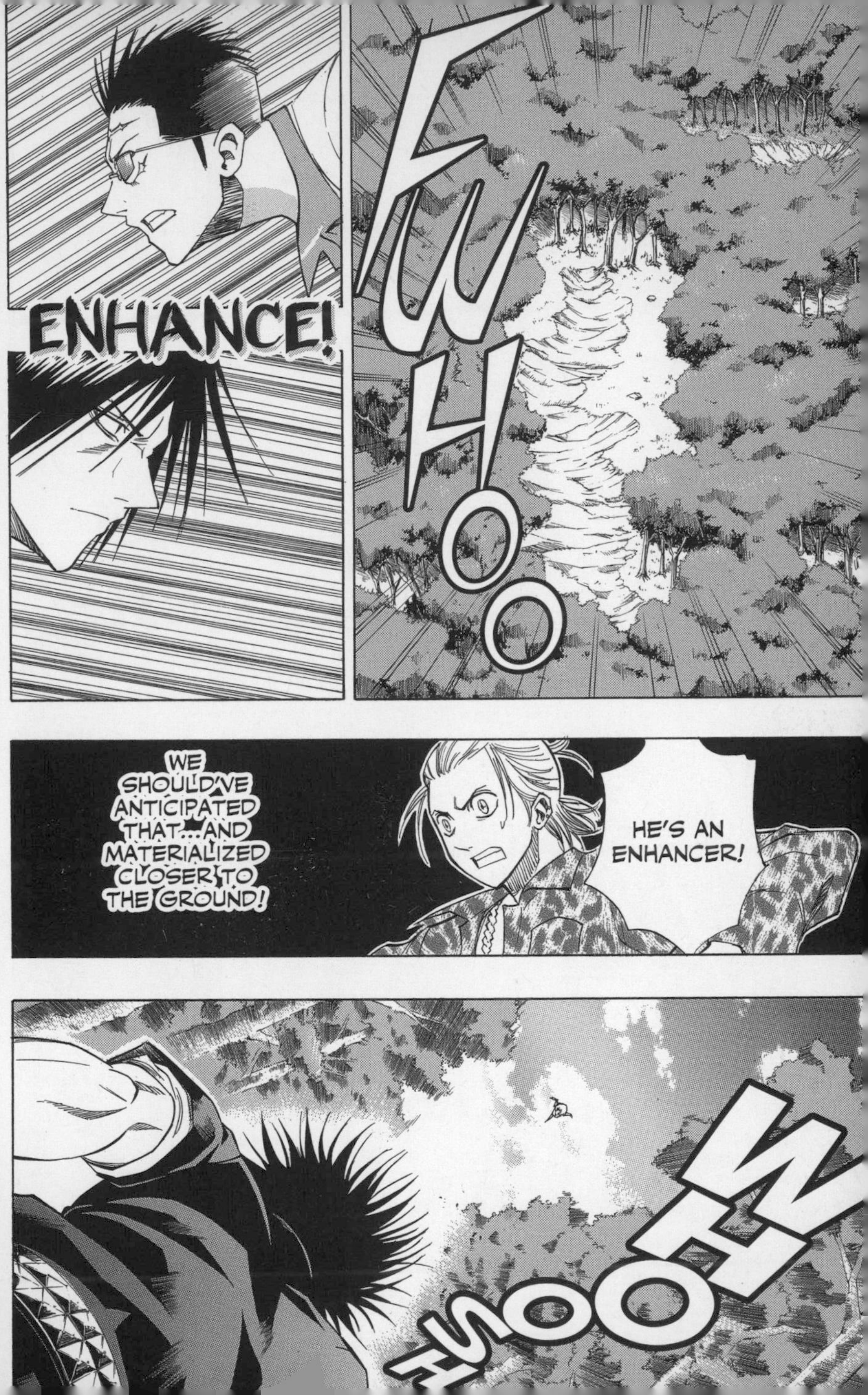
FWHOOO
ENHANCE!
HE'S AN ENHANCER!
WE SHOULD'VE ANTICIPATED THAT...AND MATERIALIZED CLOSER TO THE GROUND!
WHOOSH

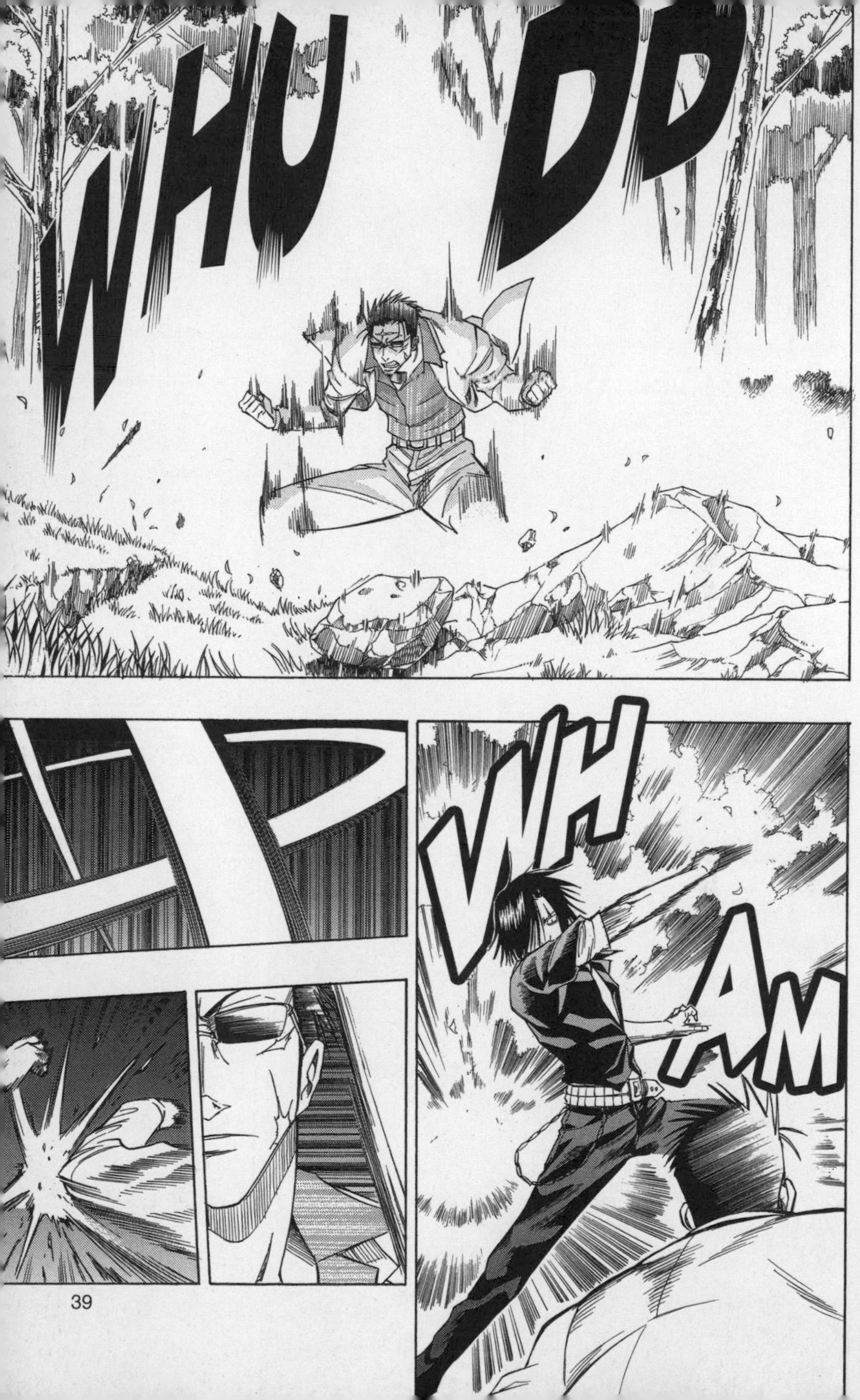
WHUDD
WHAM

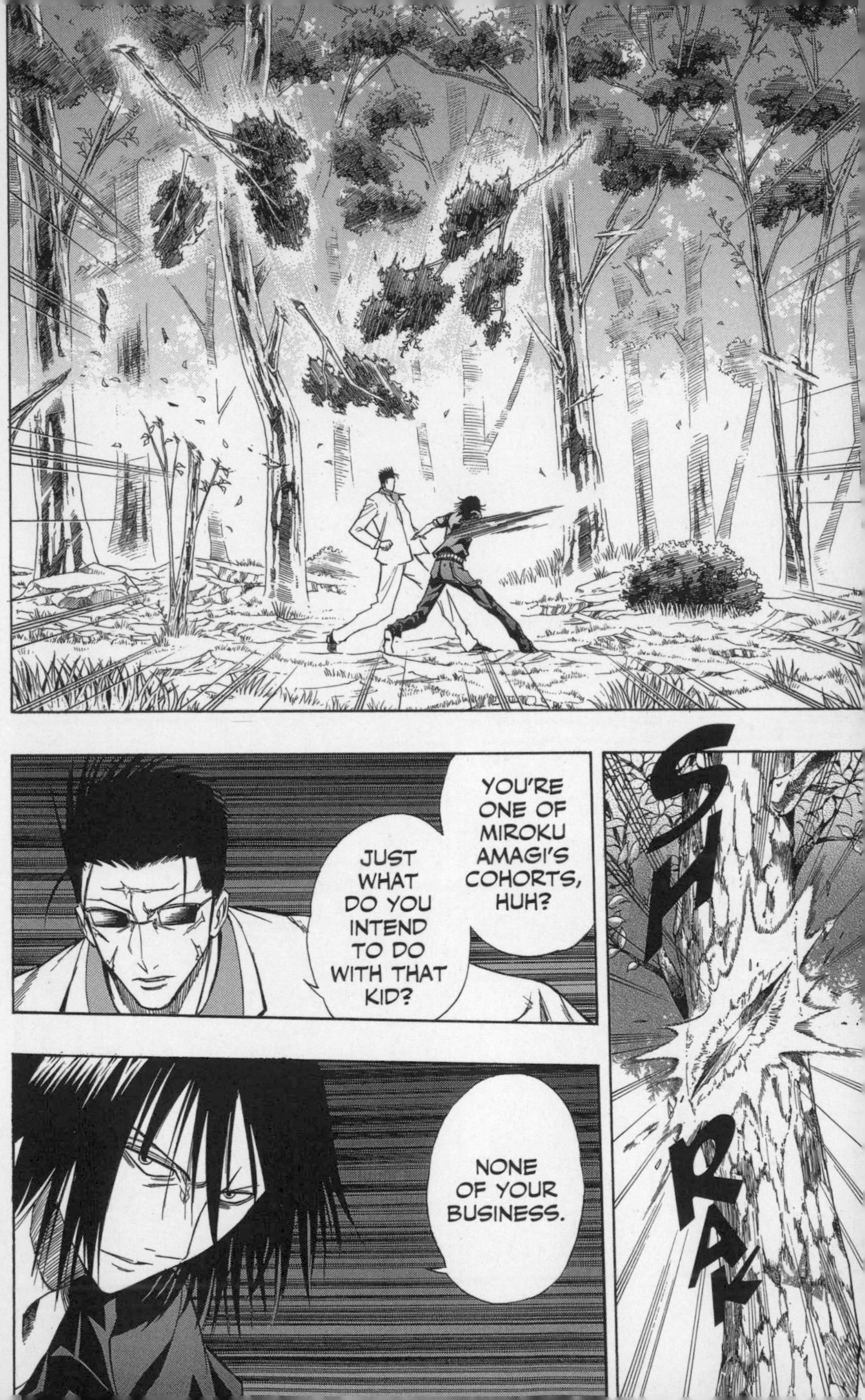
SHHRAK
YOU'RE ONE OF MIROKU AMAGI'S COHORTS, HUH?
JUST WHAT DO YOU INTEND TO DO WITH THAT KID?
NONE OF YOUR BUSINESS.

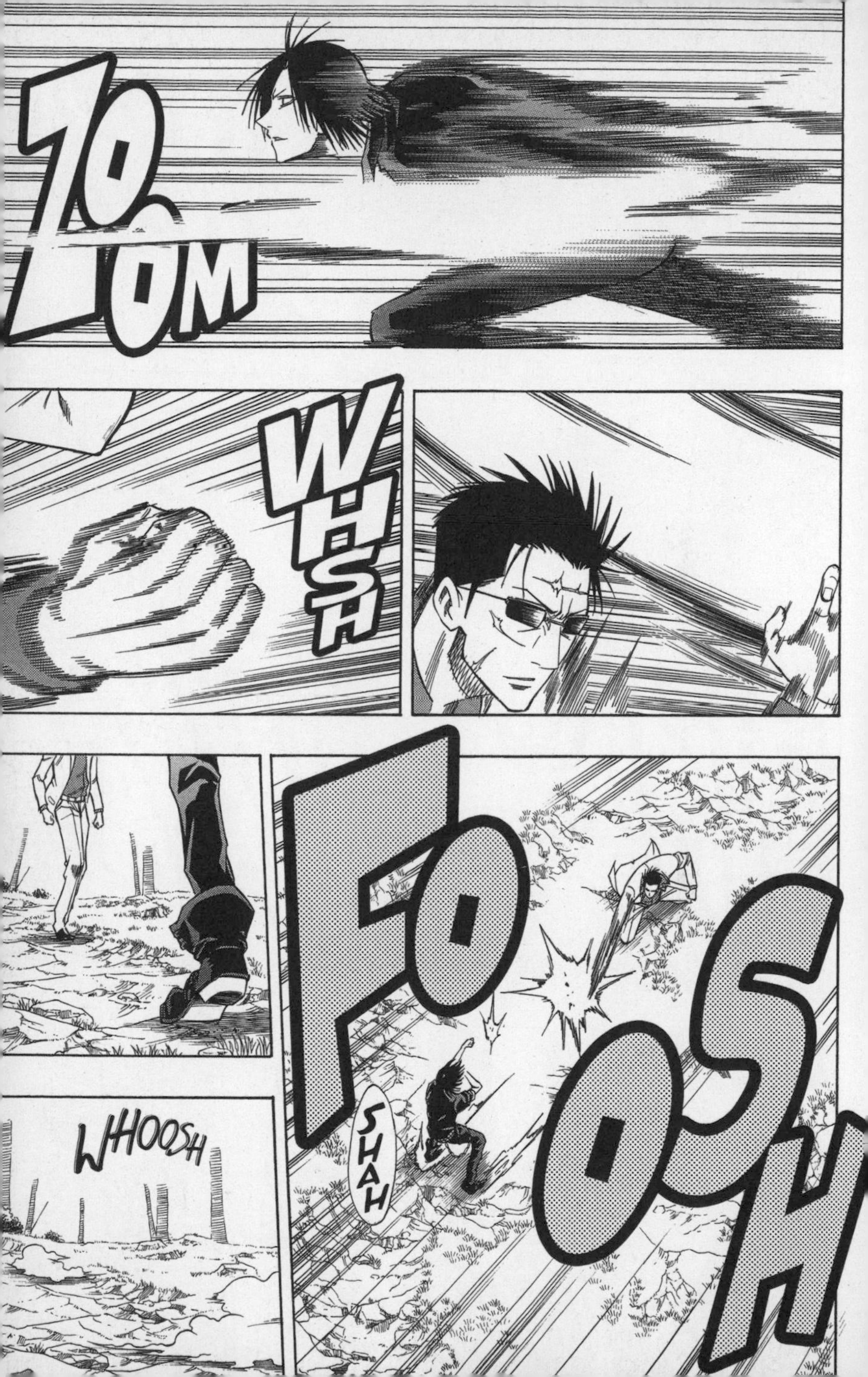
ZOOM
WHSH
FOOSH
SHAH
WHOOSH

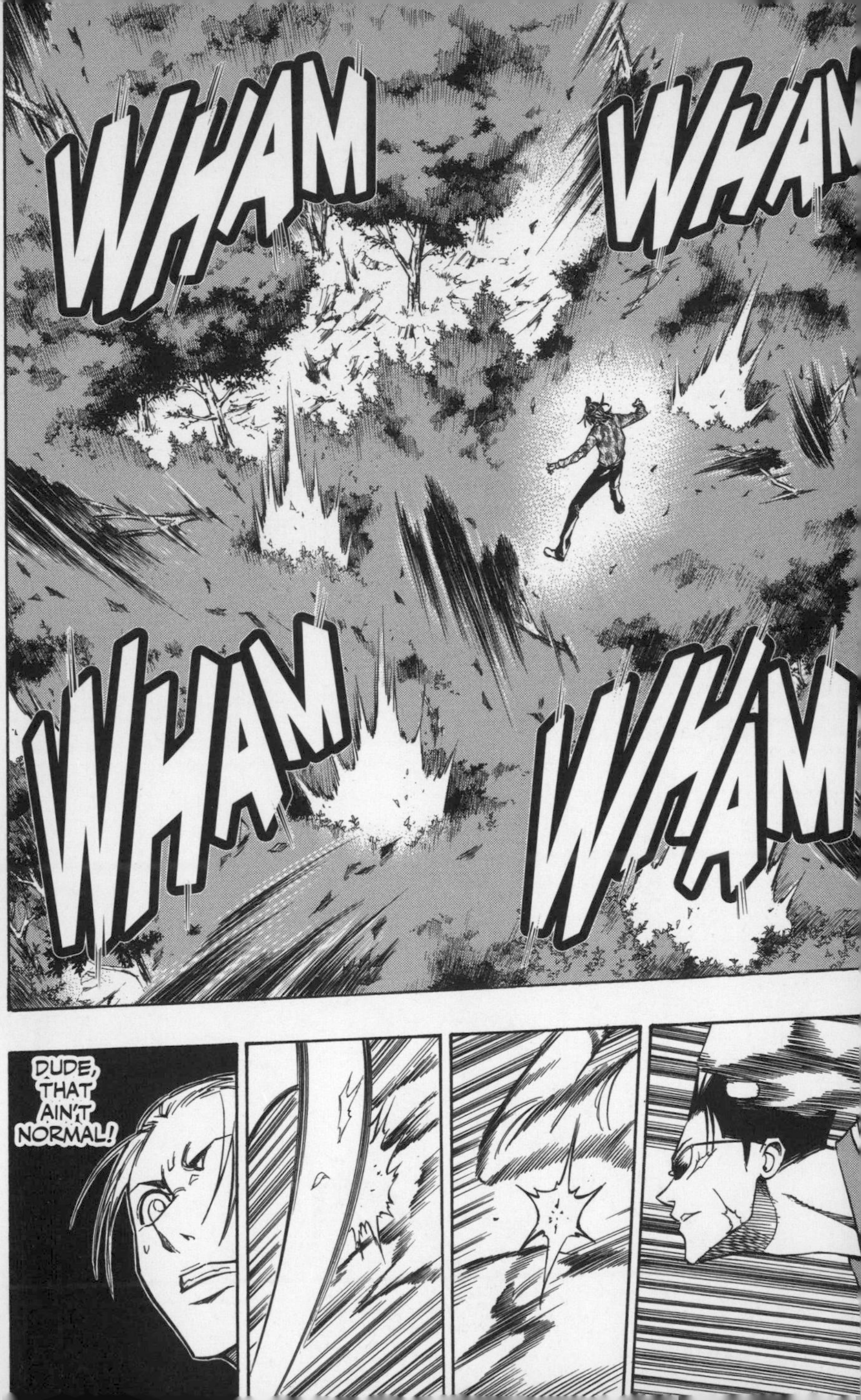
WHAM
WHAM
WHAM
WHAM
DUDE, THAT AIN'T NORMAL!

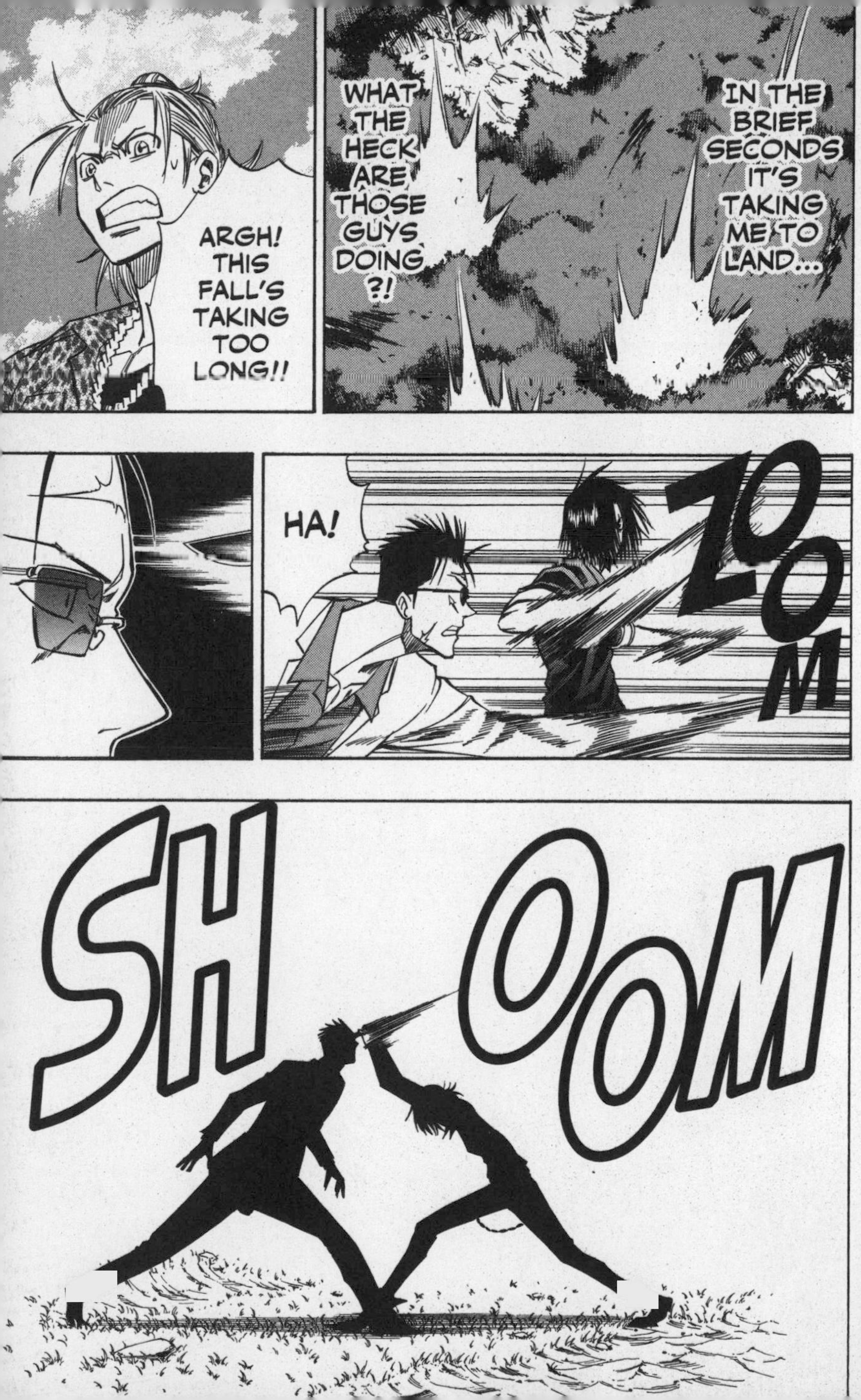
IN THE BRIEF SECONDS IT'S TAKING ME TO LAND...
WHAT THE HECK ARE THOSE GUYS DOING?!
ARGH! THIS FALL'S TAKING TOO LONG!!
ZOOM
HA!
SHOOM

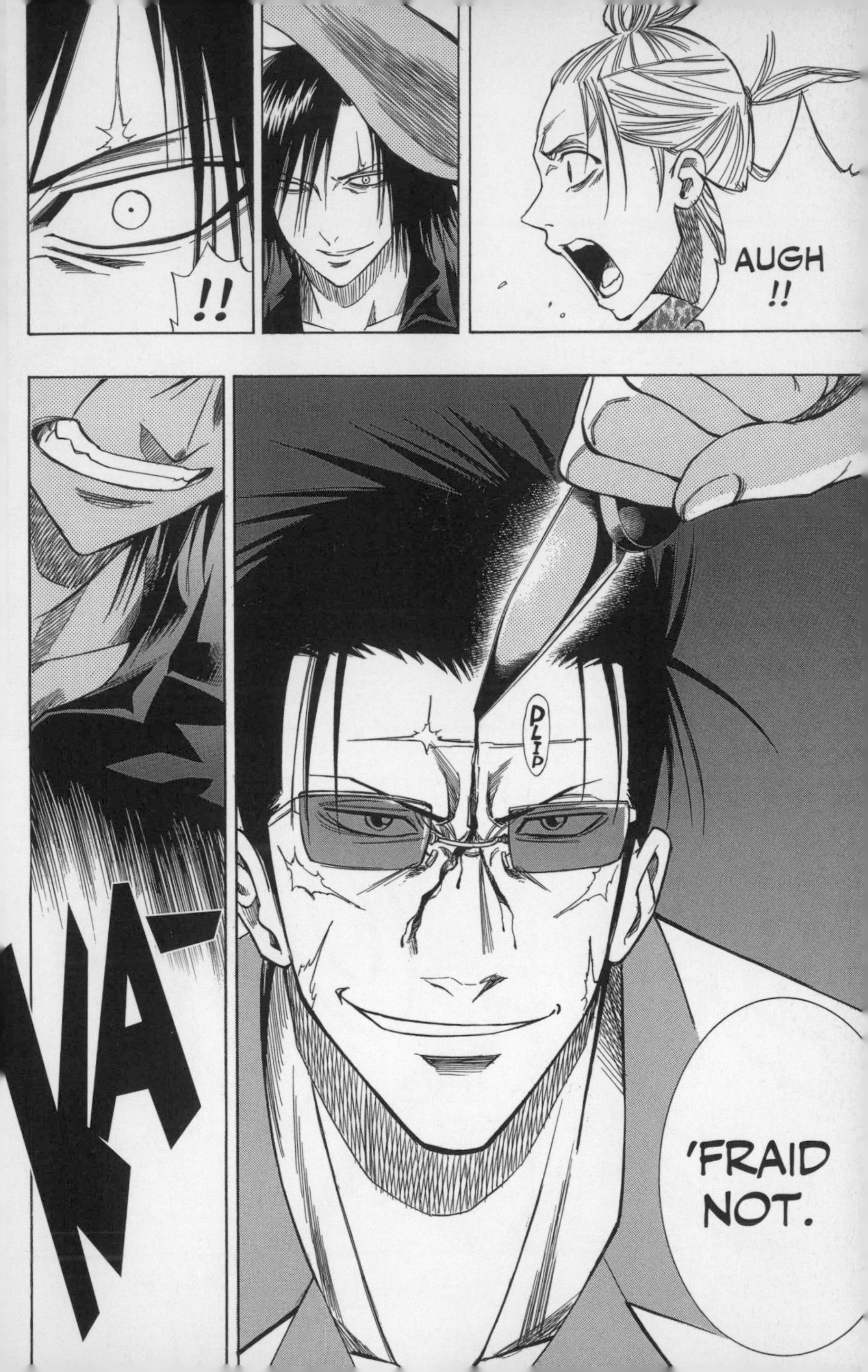
AUGH !!
!!
PLIP
'FRAID NOT.
NA

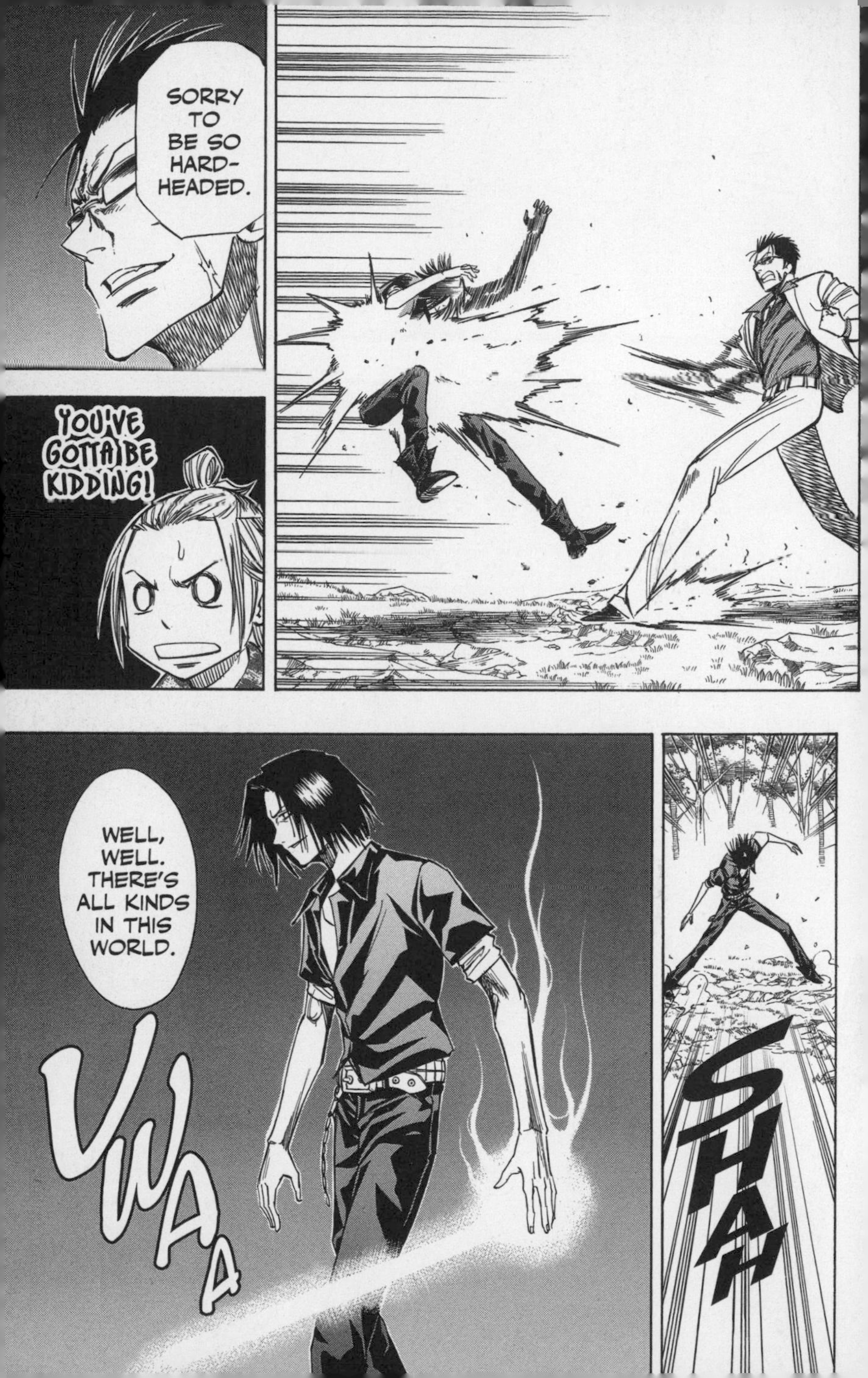
SORRY TO BE SO HARD-HEADED.
YOU'VE GOTTA BE KIDDING!
SHAH
WELL, WELL. THERE'S ALL KINDS IN THIS WORLD.
VWAA

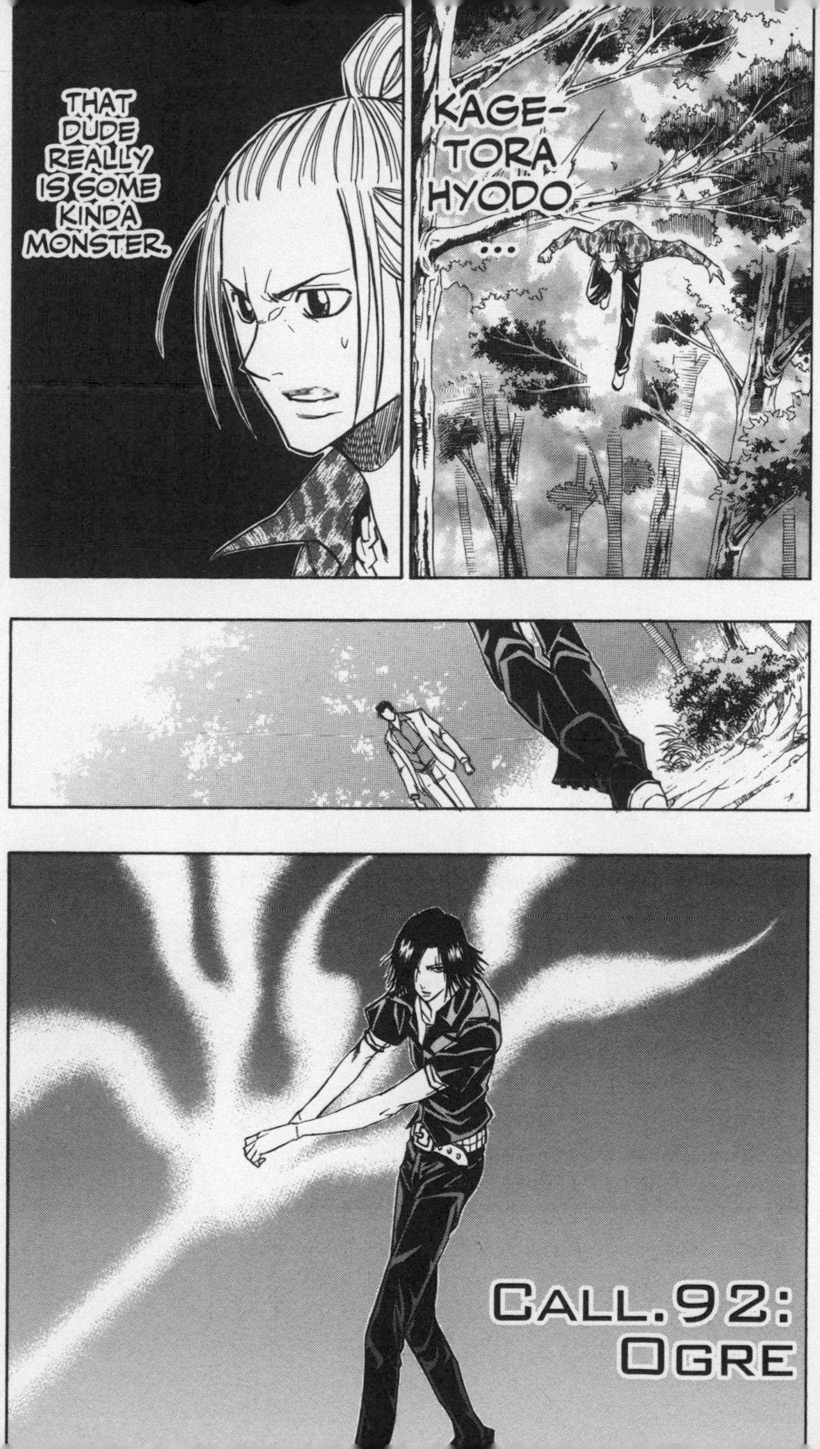
KAGE-TORA HYODO...
THAT DUDE REALLY IS SOME KINDA MONSTER.
CALL.92: OGRE

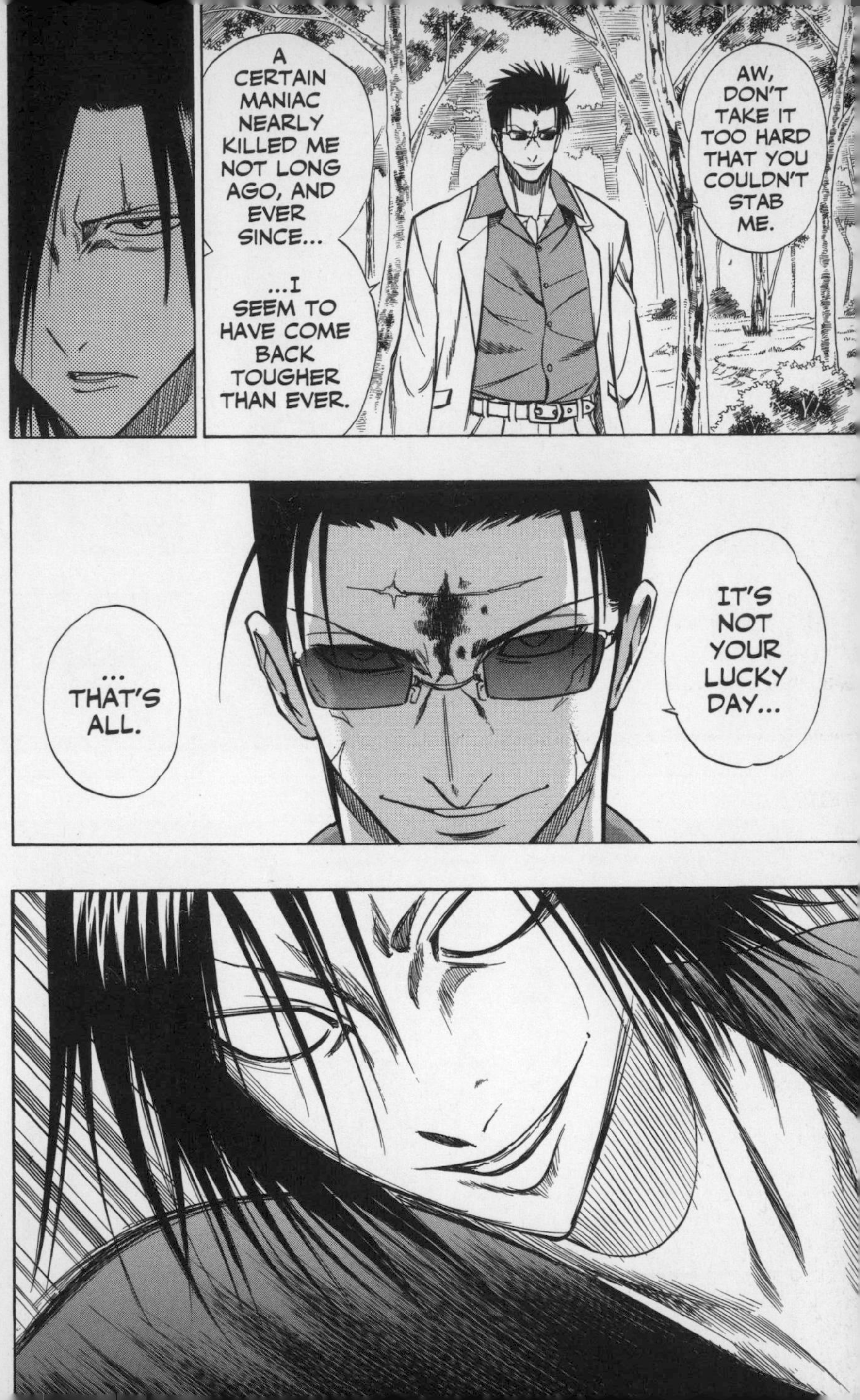
AW, DON'T TAKE IT TOO HARD THAT YOU COULDN'T STAB ME.
A CERTAIN MANIAC NEARLY KILLED ME NOT LONG AGO, AND EVER SINCE...
...I SEEM TO HAVE COME BACK TOUGHER THAN EVER.
IT'S NOT YOUR LUCKY DAY...
...THAT'S ALL.

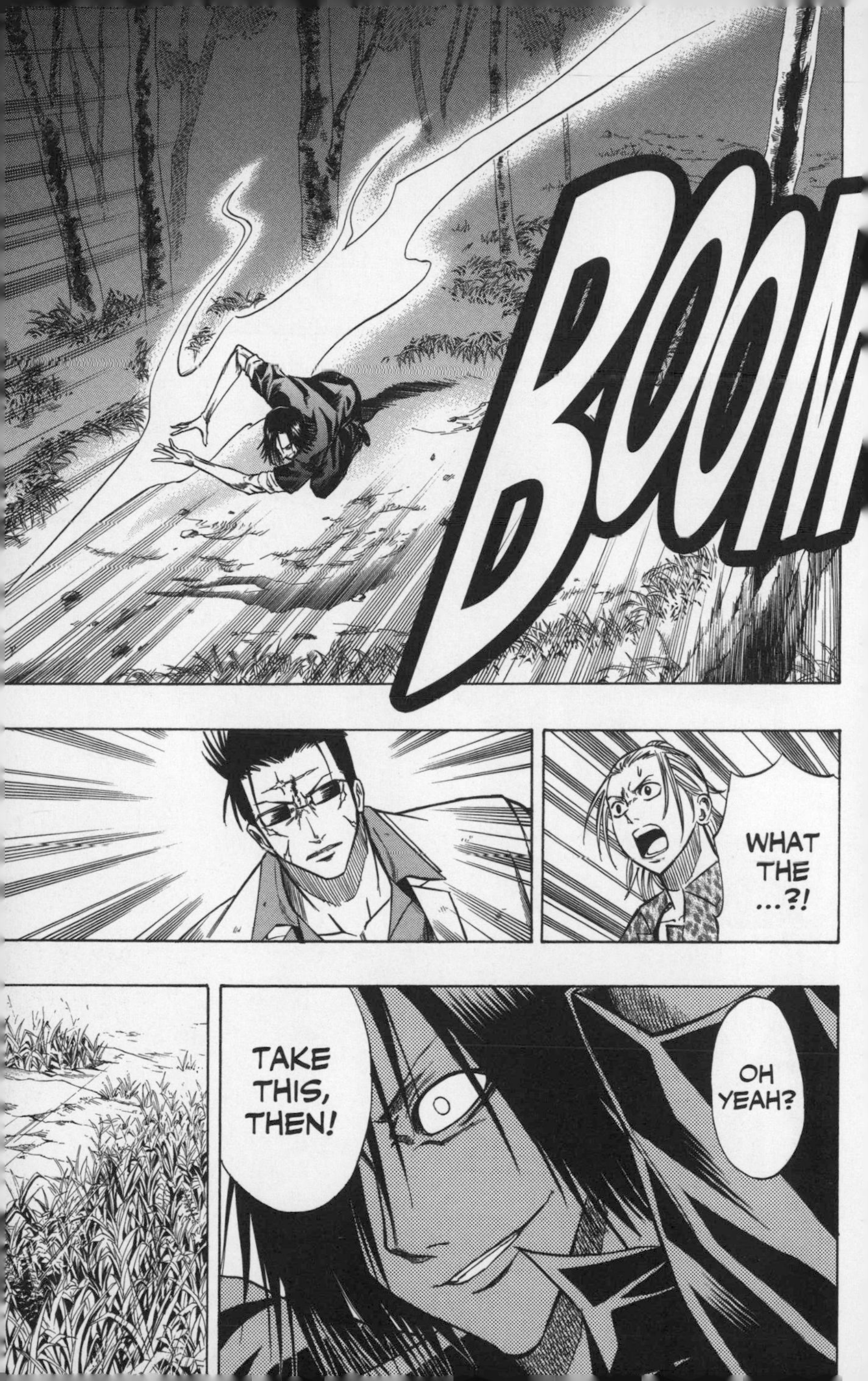
BOOM
WHAT THE ...?!
OH YEAH?
TAKE THIS, THEN!

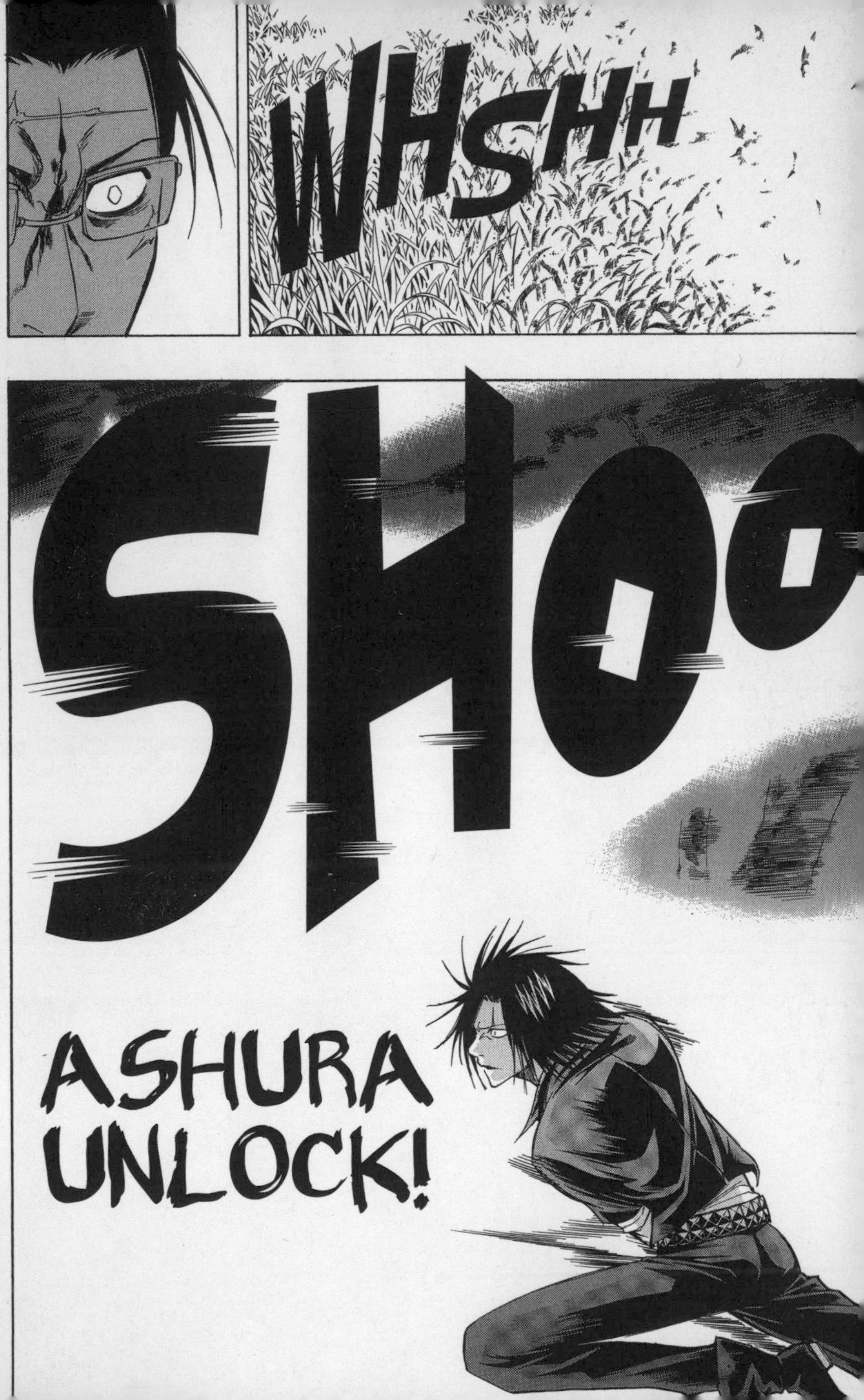
WHSHH
SHOO
ASHURA UNLOCK!

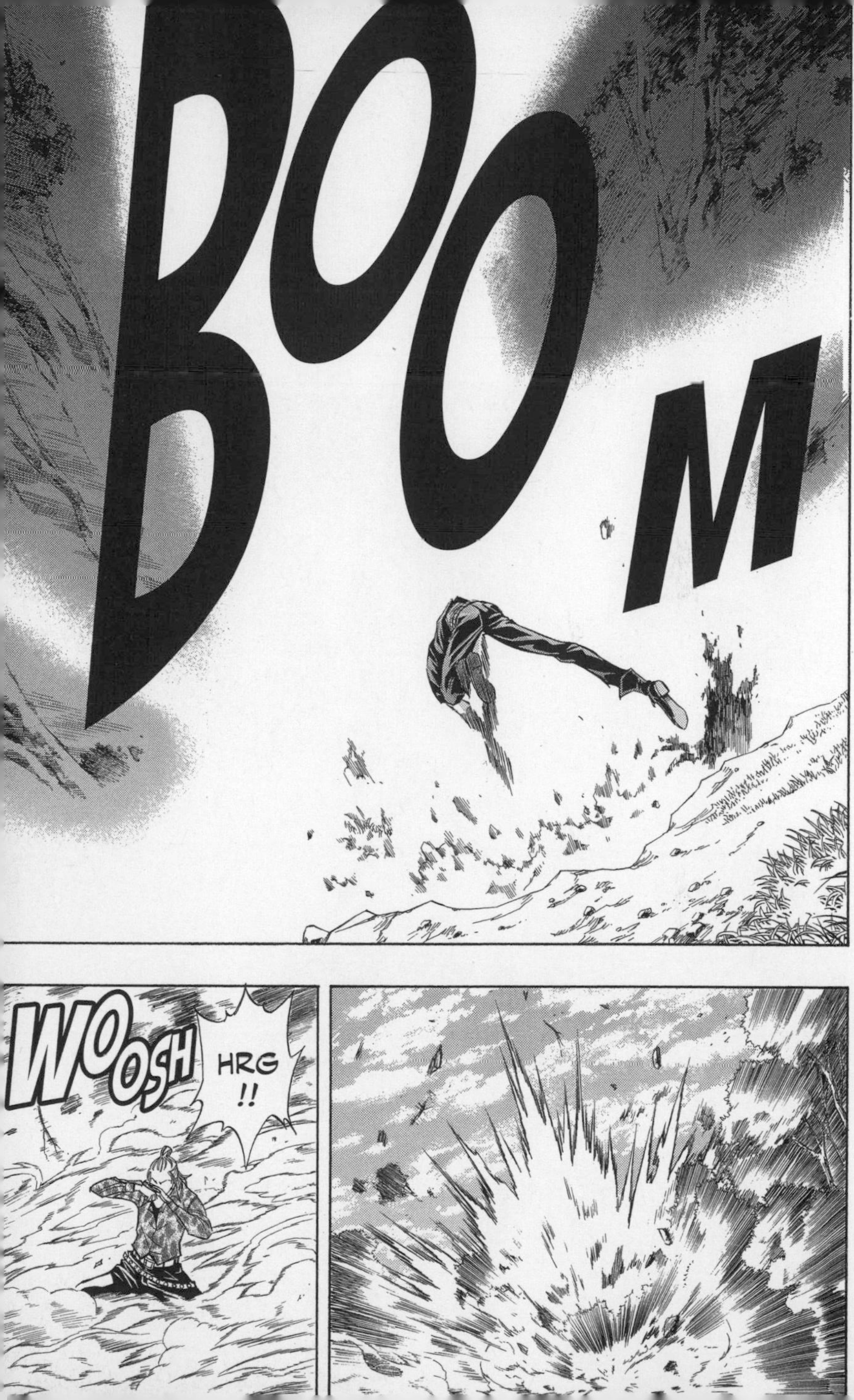
BOOM
HRG !!
WOOSH

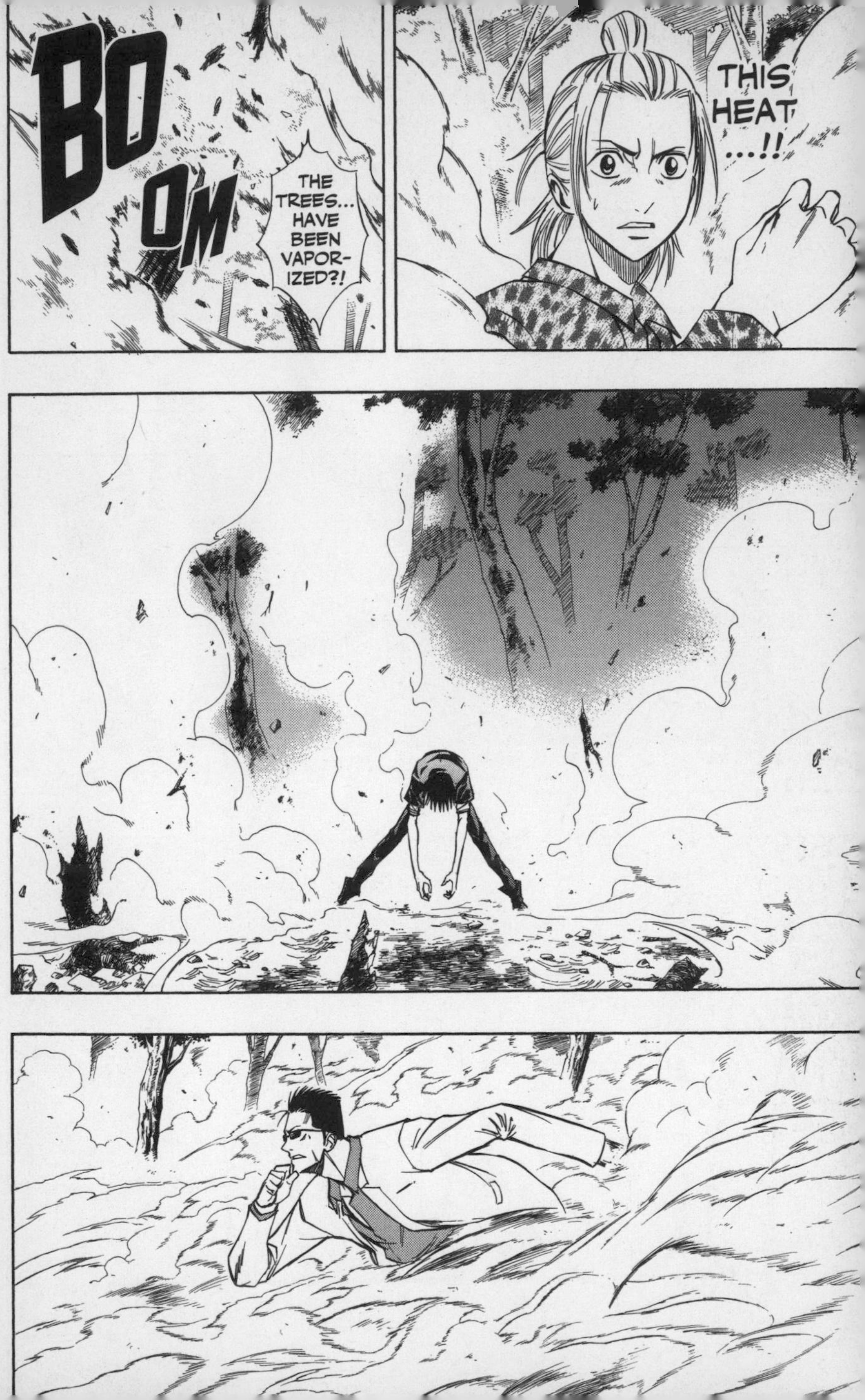
THIS HEAT ...!!
THE TREES... HAVE BEEN VAPORIZED?!
BOOM

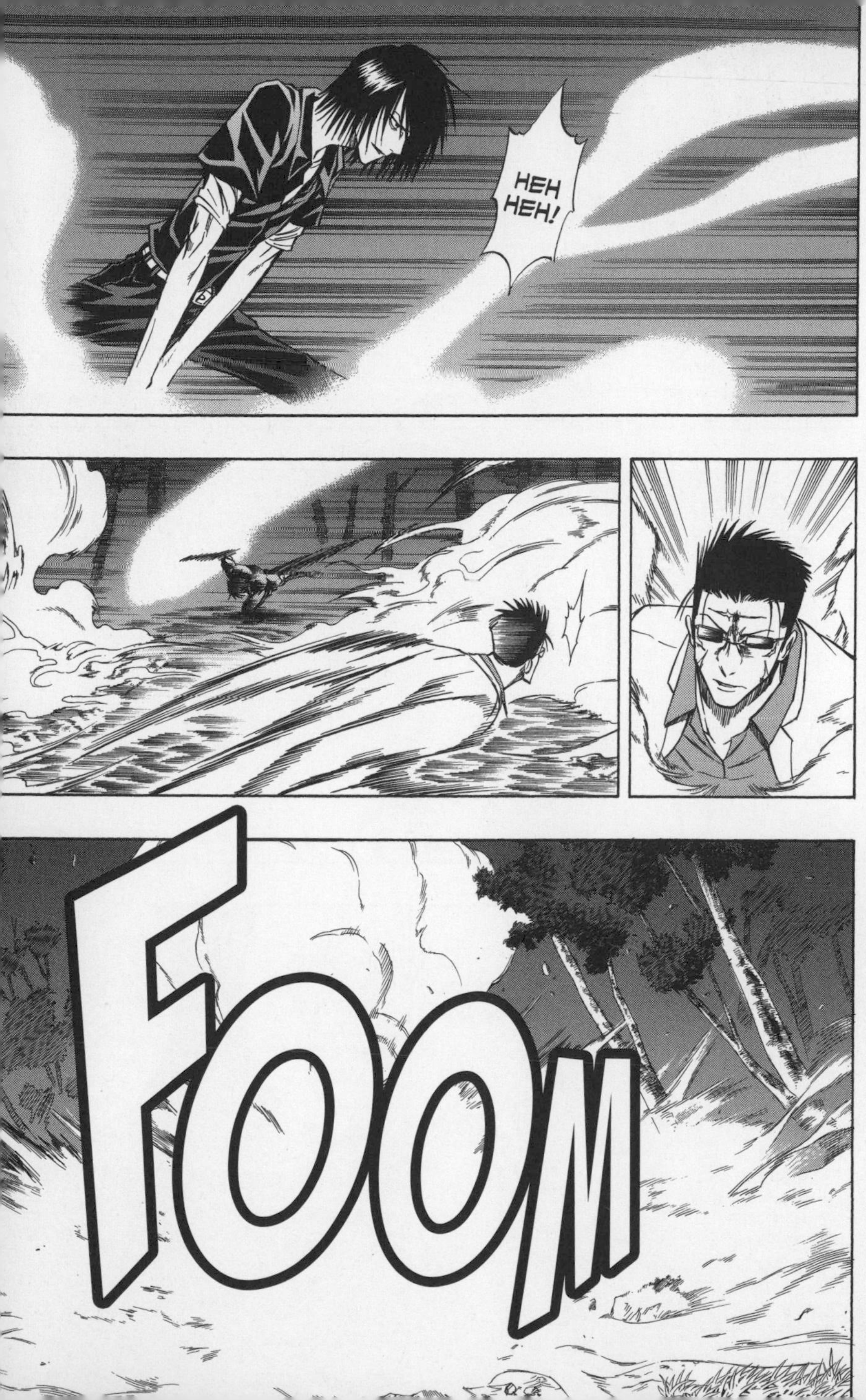
HEH HEH!
FOOM

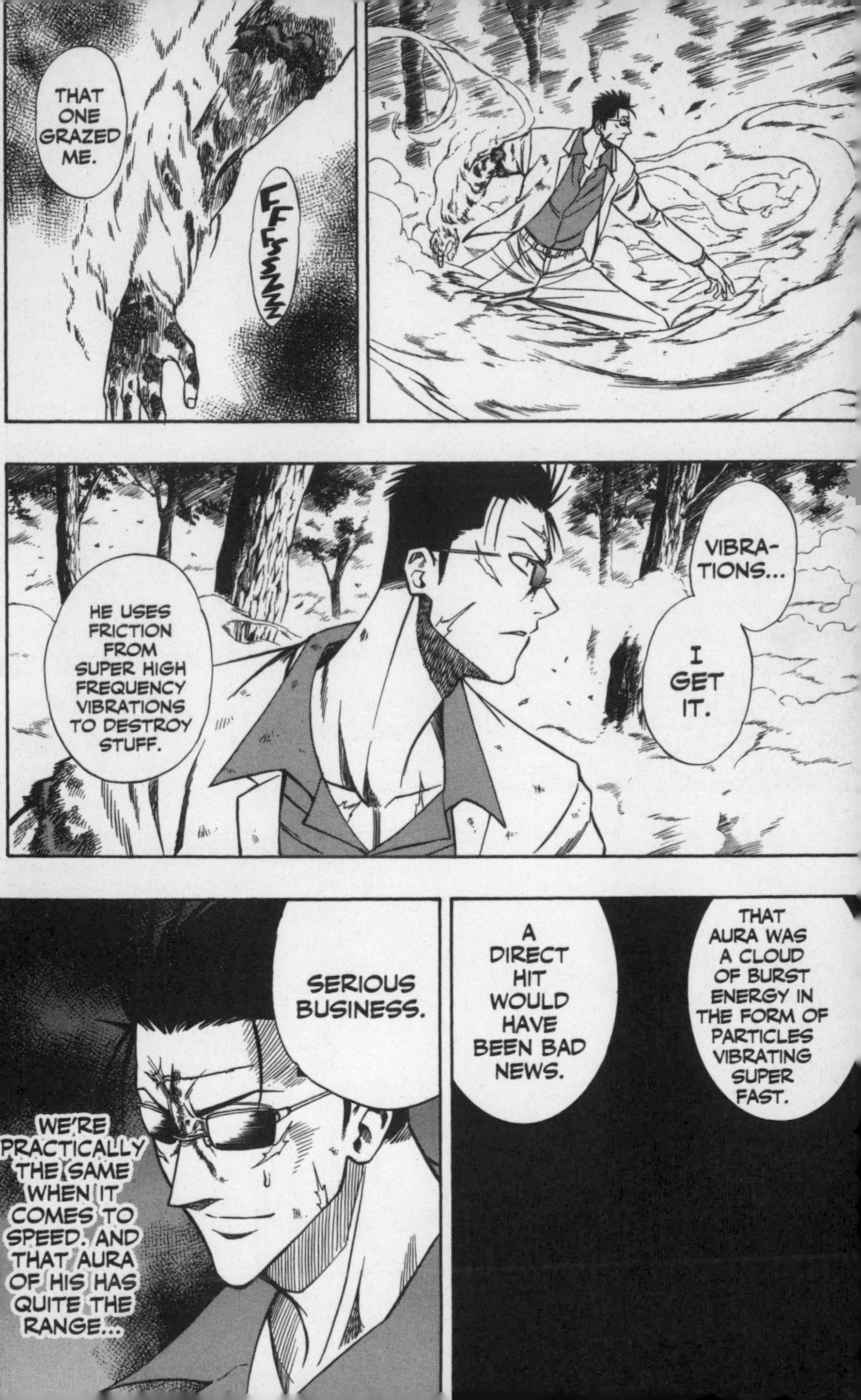
THAT ONE GRAZED ME.
FFFSSZZZZ
VIBRA-TIONS...
I GET IT.
HE USES FRICTION FROM SUPER HIGH FREQUENCY VIBRATIONS TO DESTROY STUFF.
THAT AURA WAS A CLOUD OF BURST ENERGY IN THE FORM OF PARTICLES VIBRATING SUPER FAST.
A DIRECT HIT WOULD HAVE BEEN BAD NEWS.
SERIOUS BUSINESS.
WE'RE PRACTICALLY THE SAME WHEN IT COMES TO SPEED. AND THAT AURA OF HIS HAS QUITE THE RANGE...

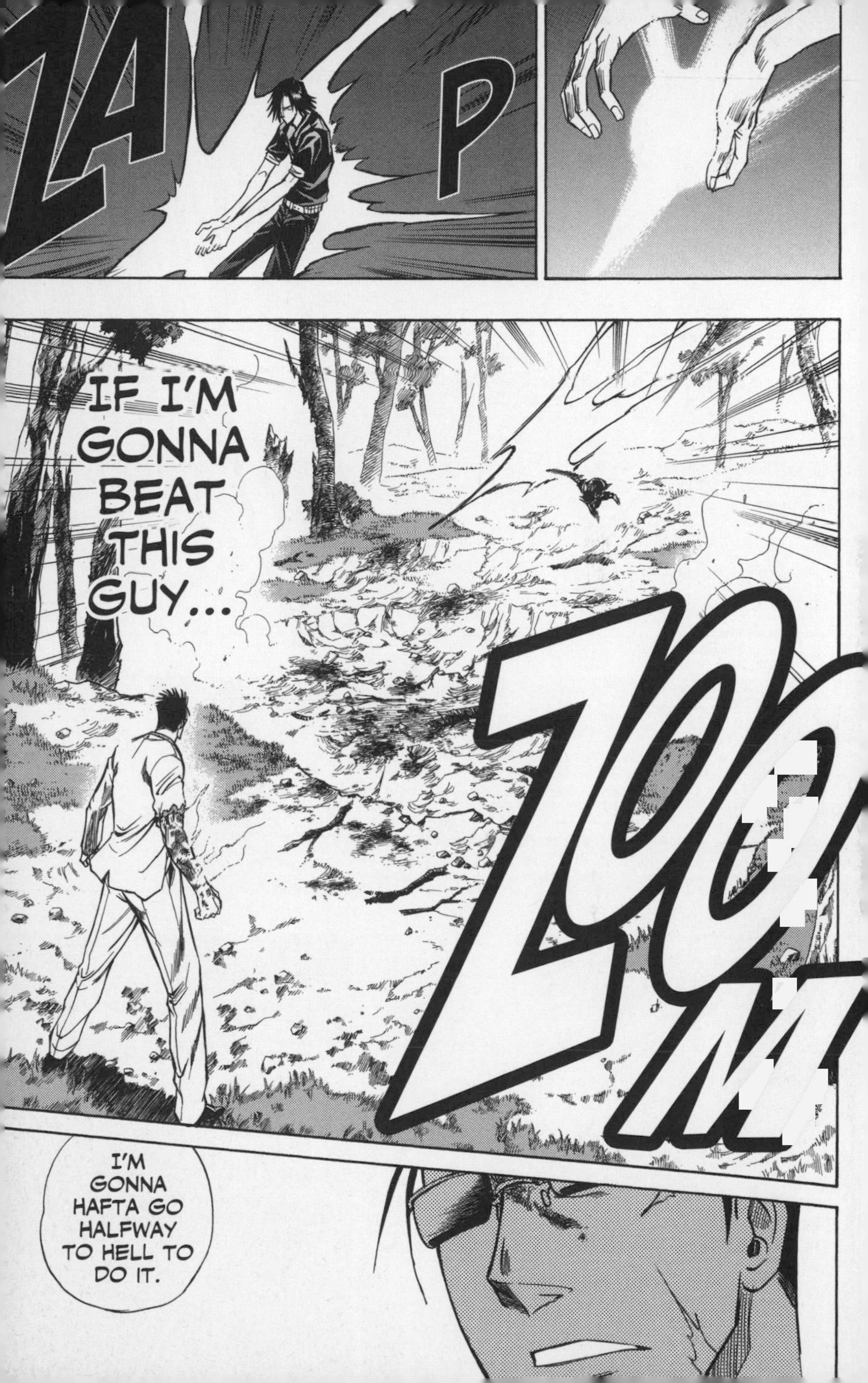

ZAP
IF I'M GONNA BEAT THIS GUY...
ZOOM
I'M GONNA HAFTA GO HALFWAY TO HELL TO DO IT.

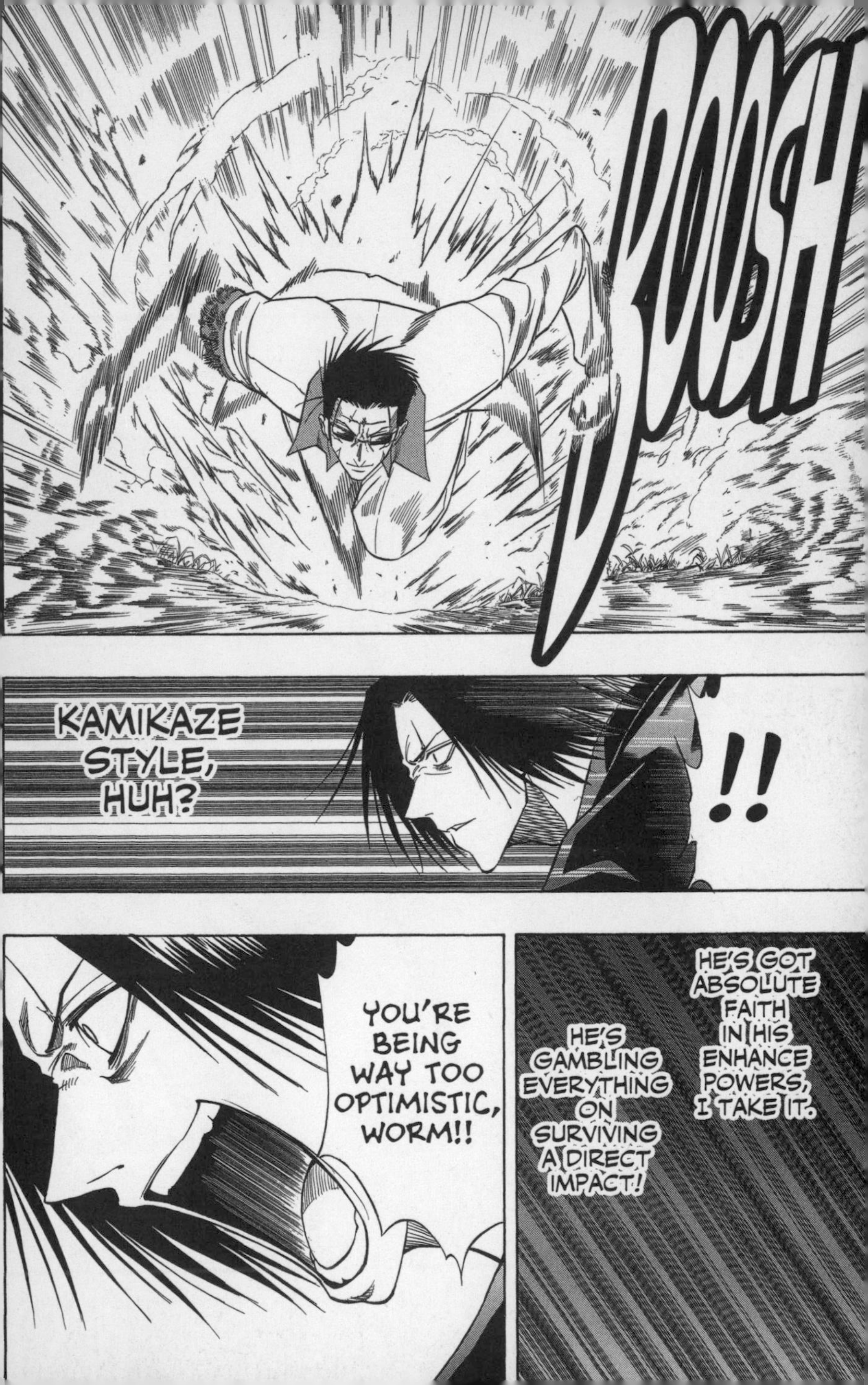
ZOOSH
KAMIKAZE STYLE, HUH?
!!
HE'S GOT ABSOLUTE FAITH IN HIS ENHANCE POWERS, I TAKE IT.
HE'S GAMBLING EVERYTHING ON SURVIVING A DIRECT IMPACT!
YOU'RE BEING WAY TOO OPTIMISTIC, WORM!!

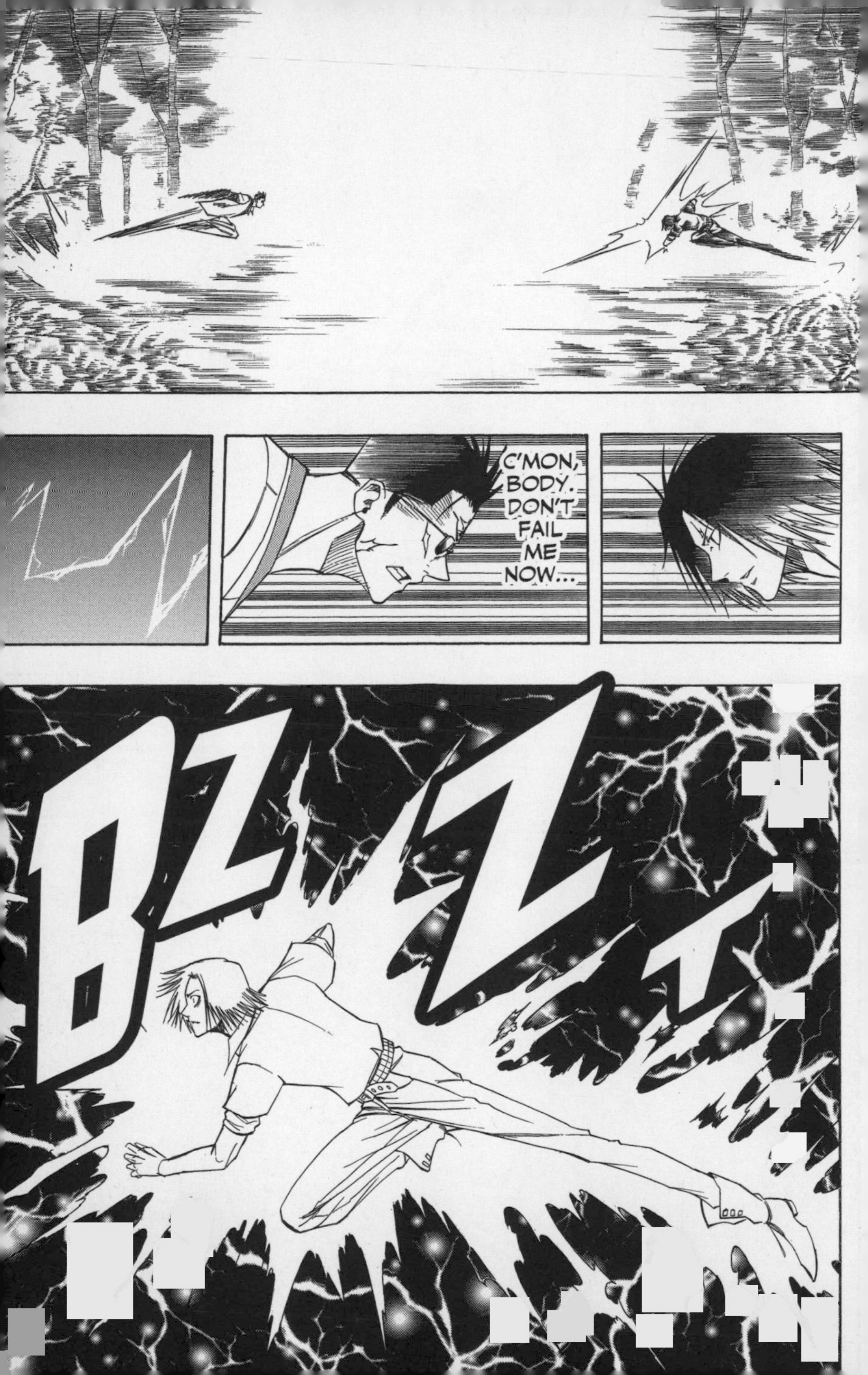
C'MON, BODY. DON'T FAIL ME NOW...

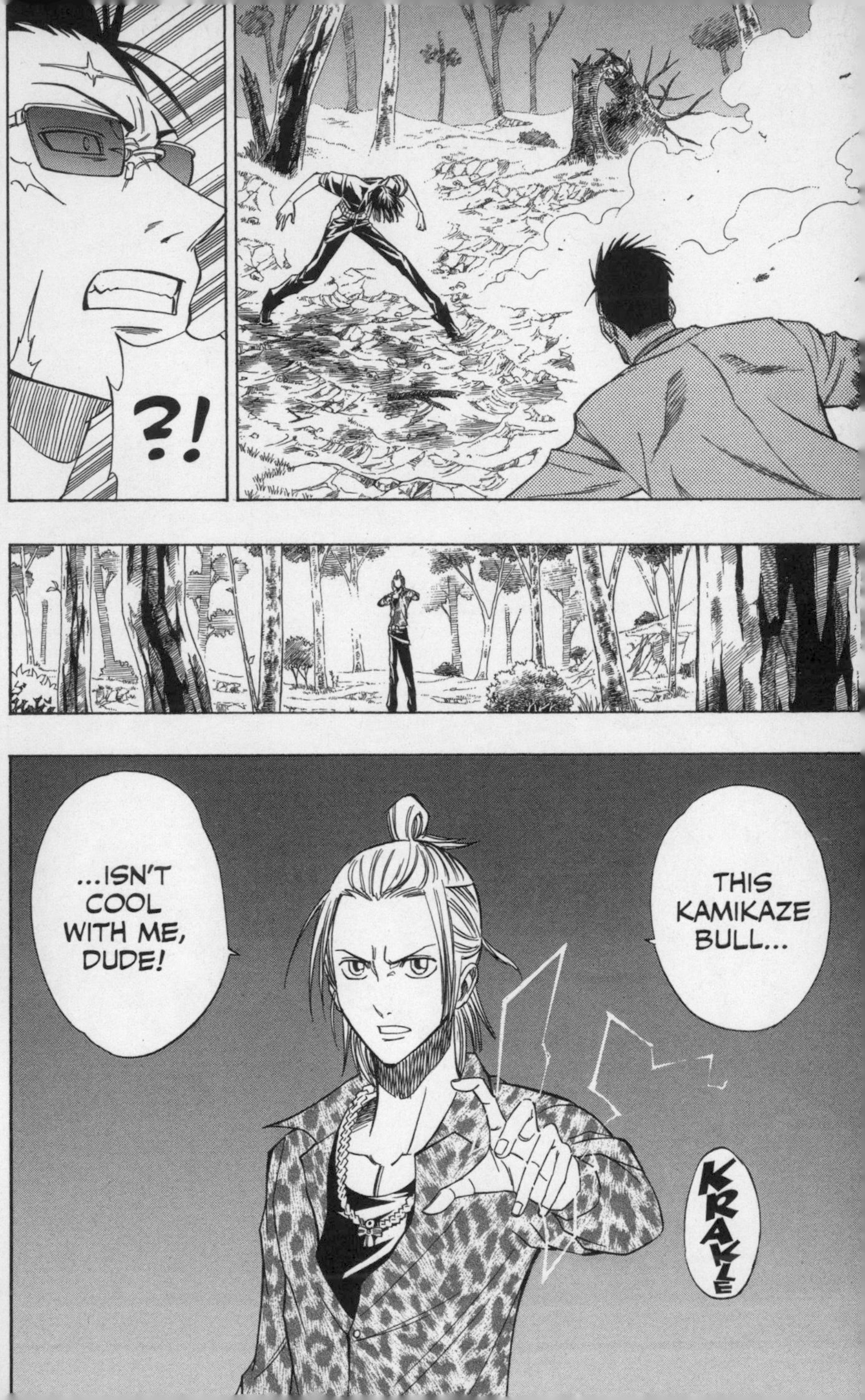
?!
THIS KAMIKAZE BULL...
...ISN'T COOL WITH ME, DUDE!
KRAKLE

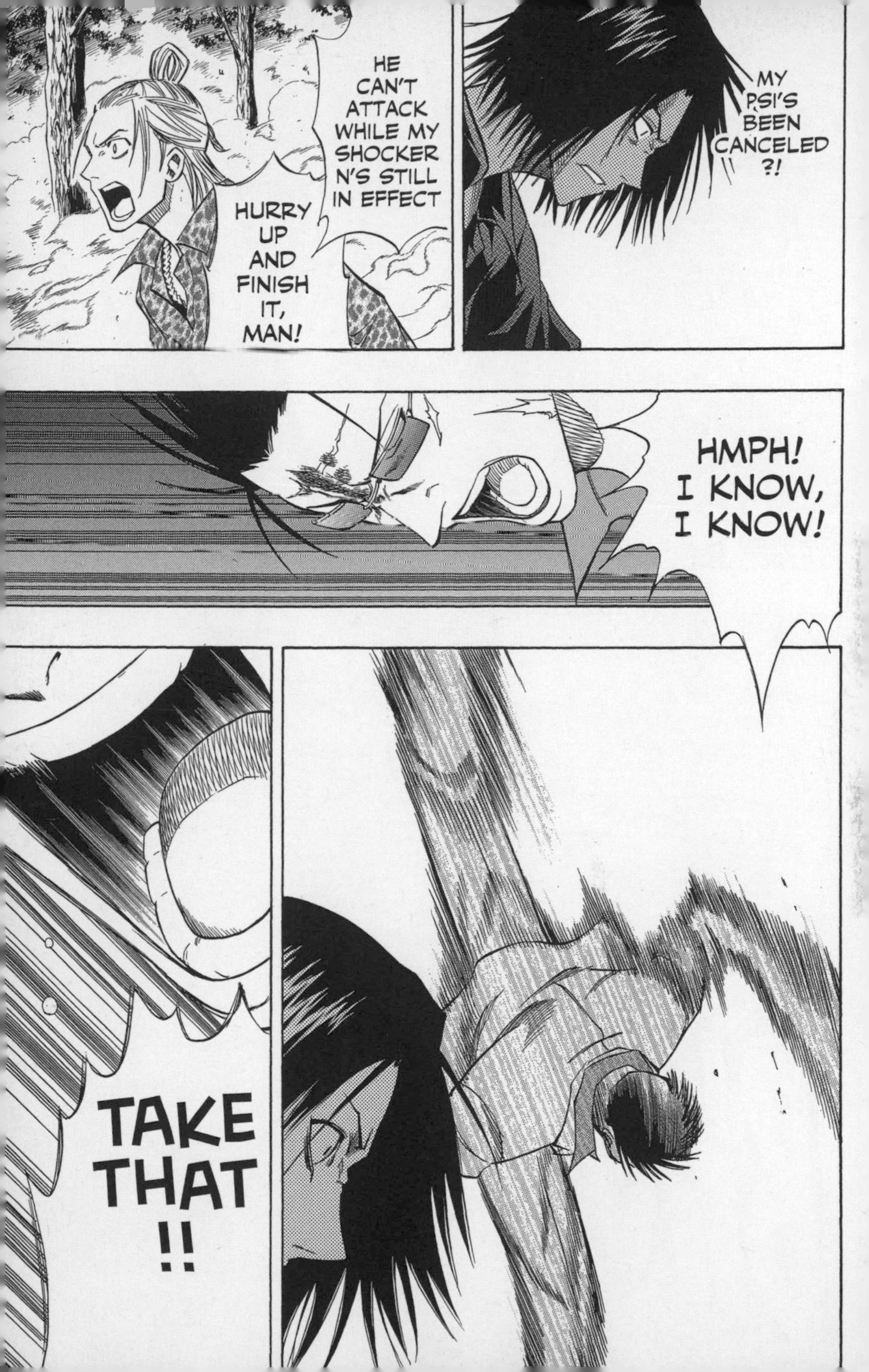
MY PSI'S BEEN CANCELED?!
HE CAN'T ATTACK WHILE MY SHOCKER N'S STILL IN EFFECT
HURRY UP AND FINISH IT, MAN!
HMPH! I KNOW, I KNOW!
TAKE THAT!!

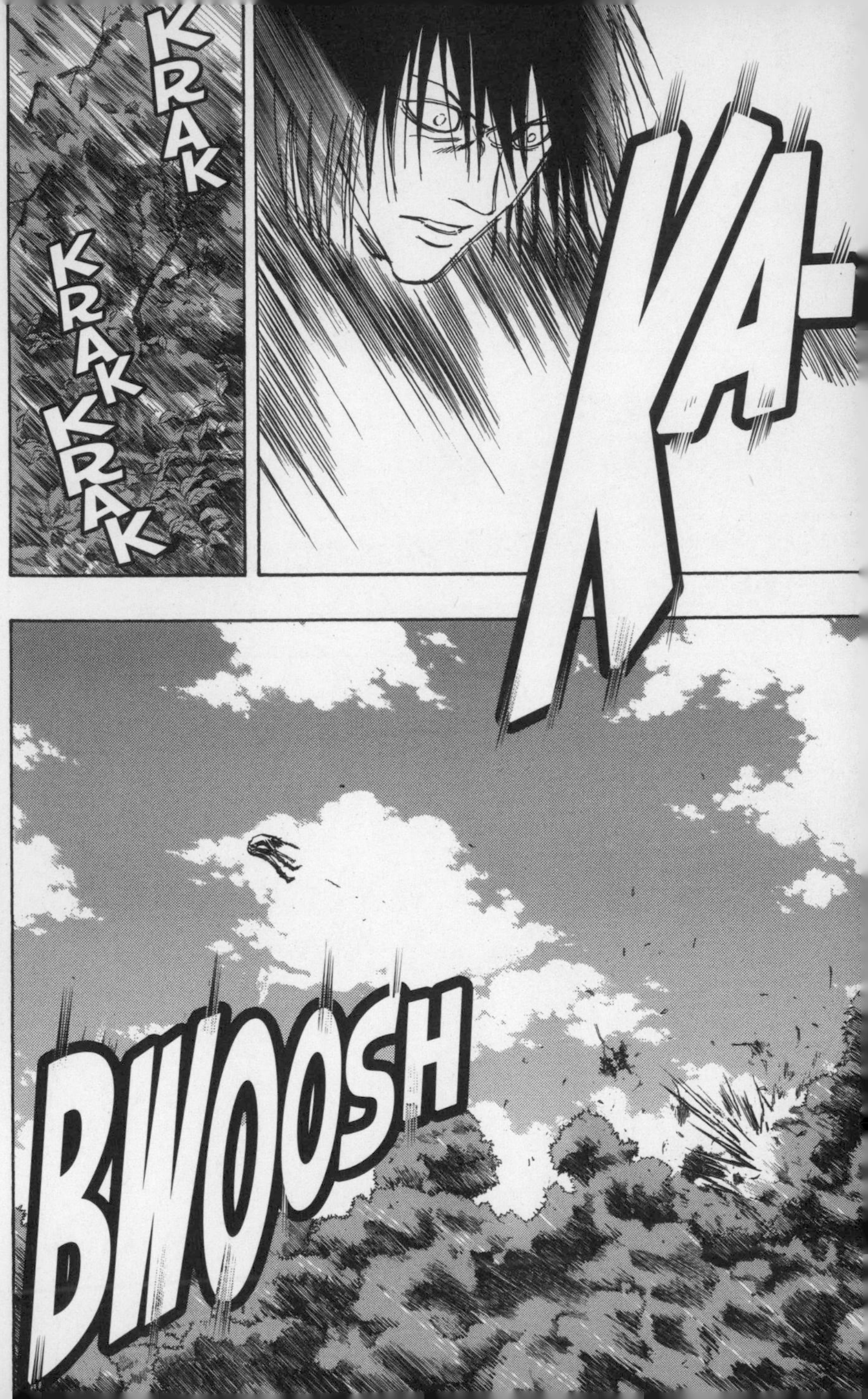
KA-
KRAK
KRAK KRAK
BWOOSH

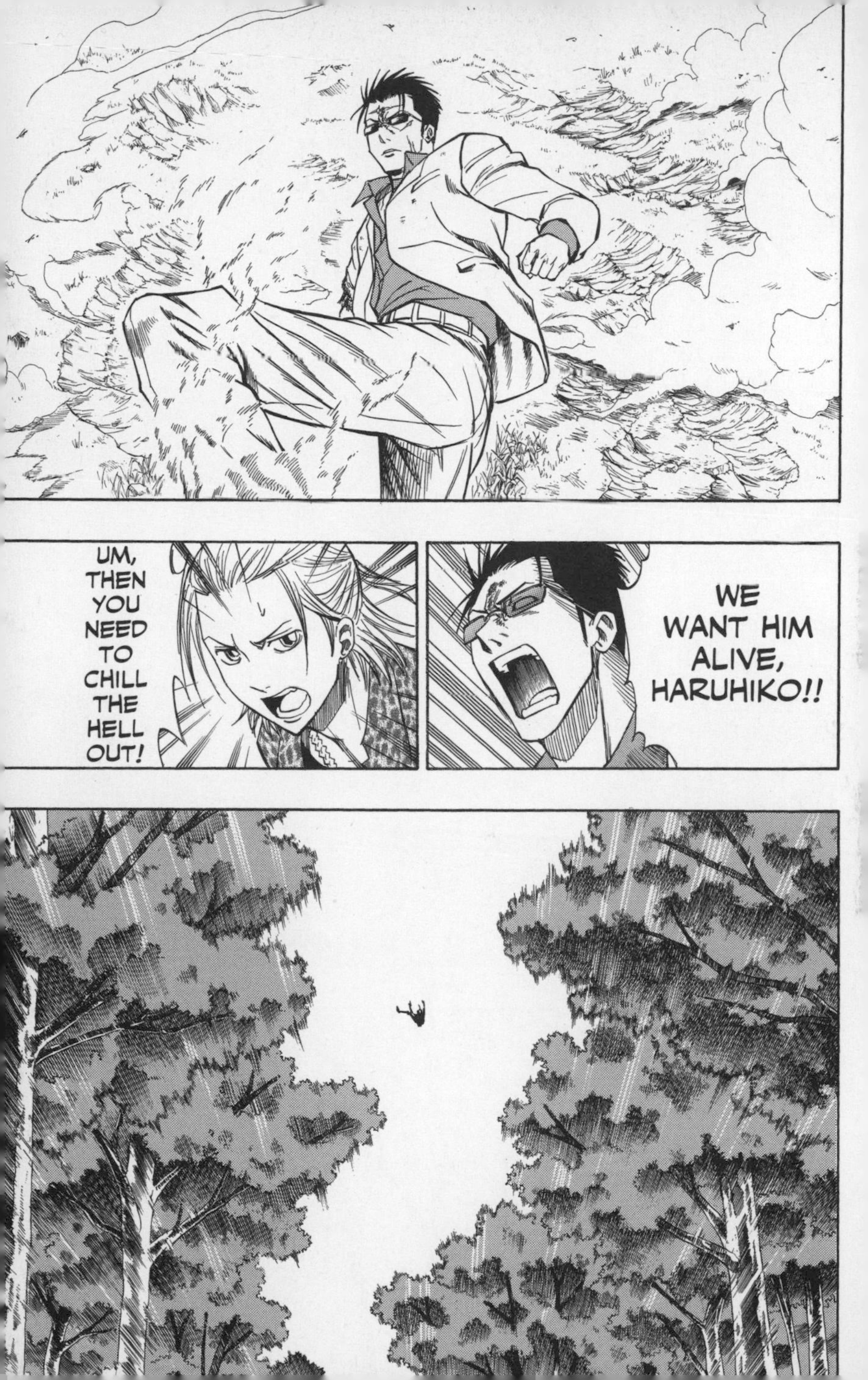
WE WANT HIM ALIVE, HARUHIKO!!
UM, THEN YOU NEED TO CHILL THE HELL OUT!

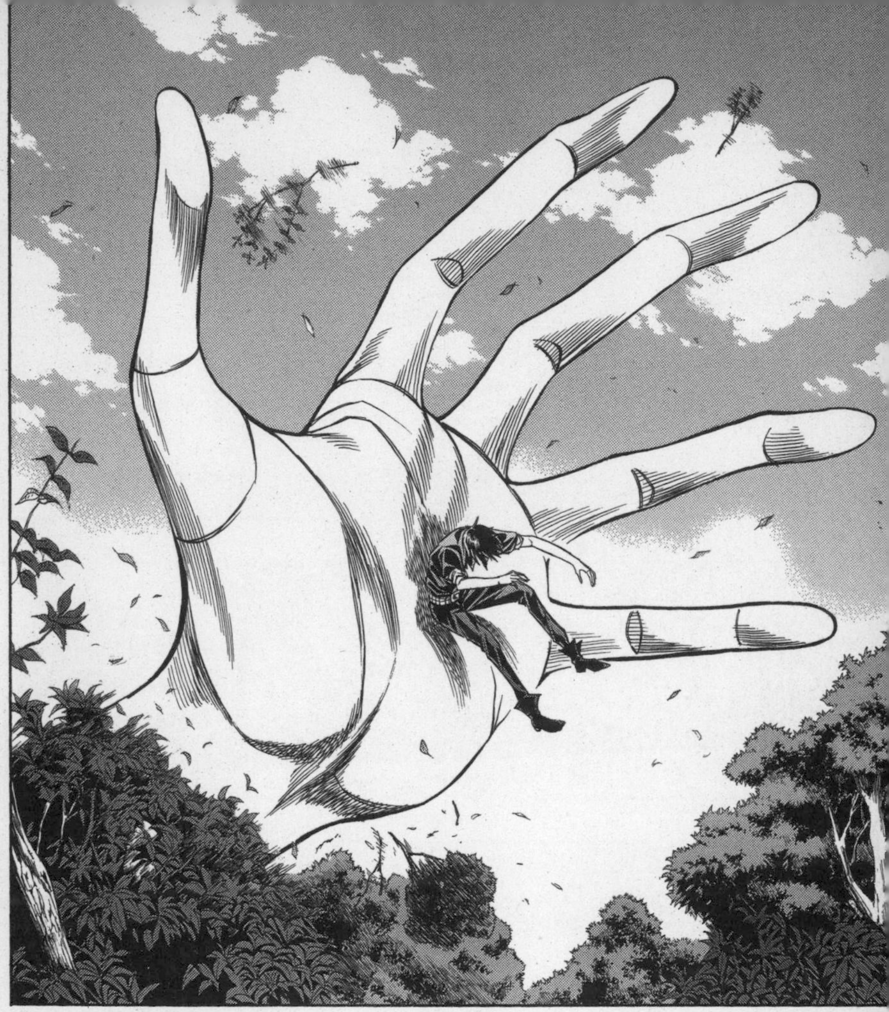
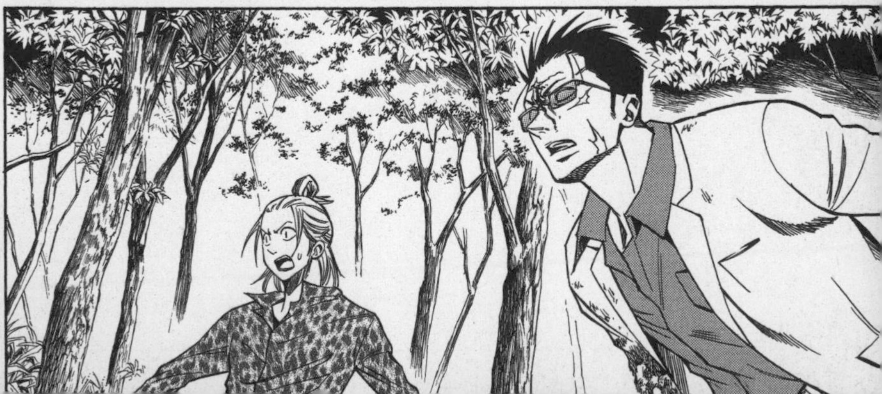

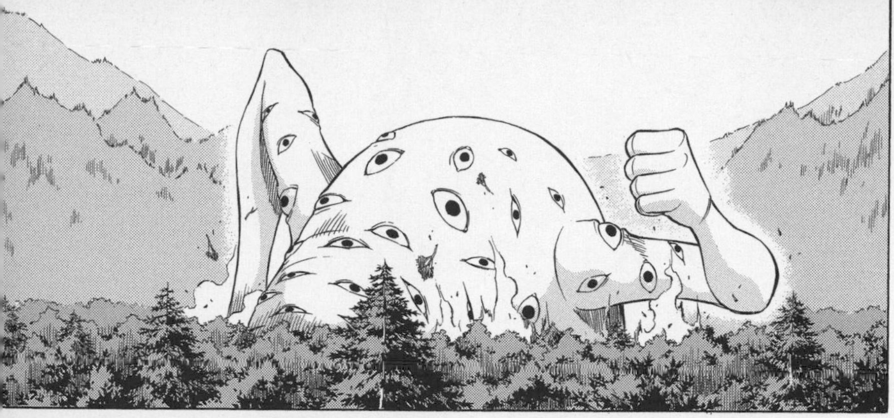

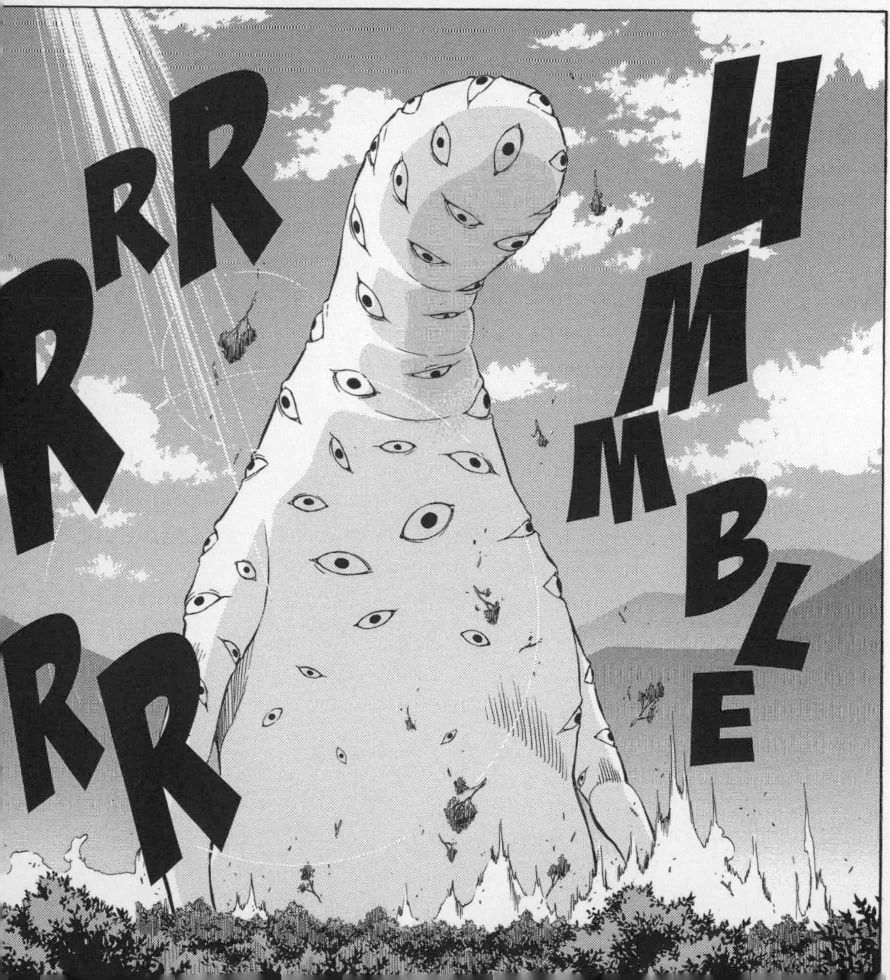
RRRRR
UMMBLE

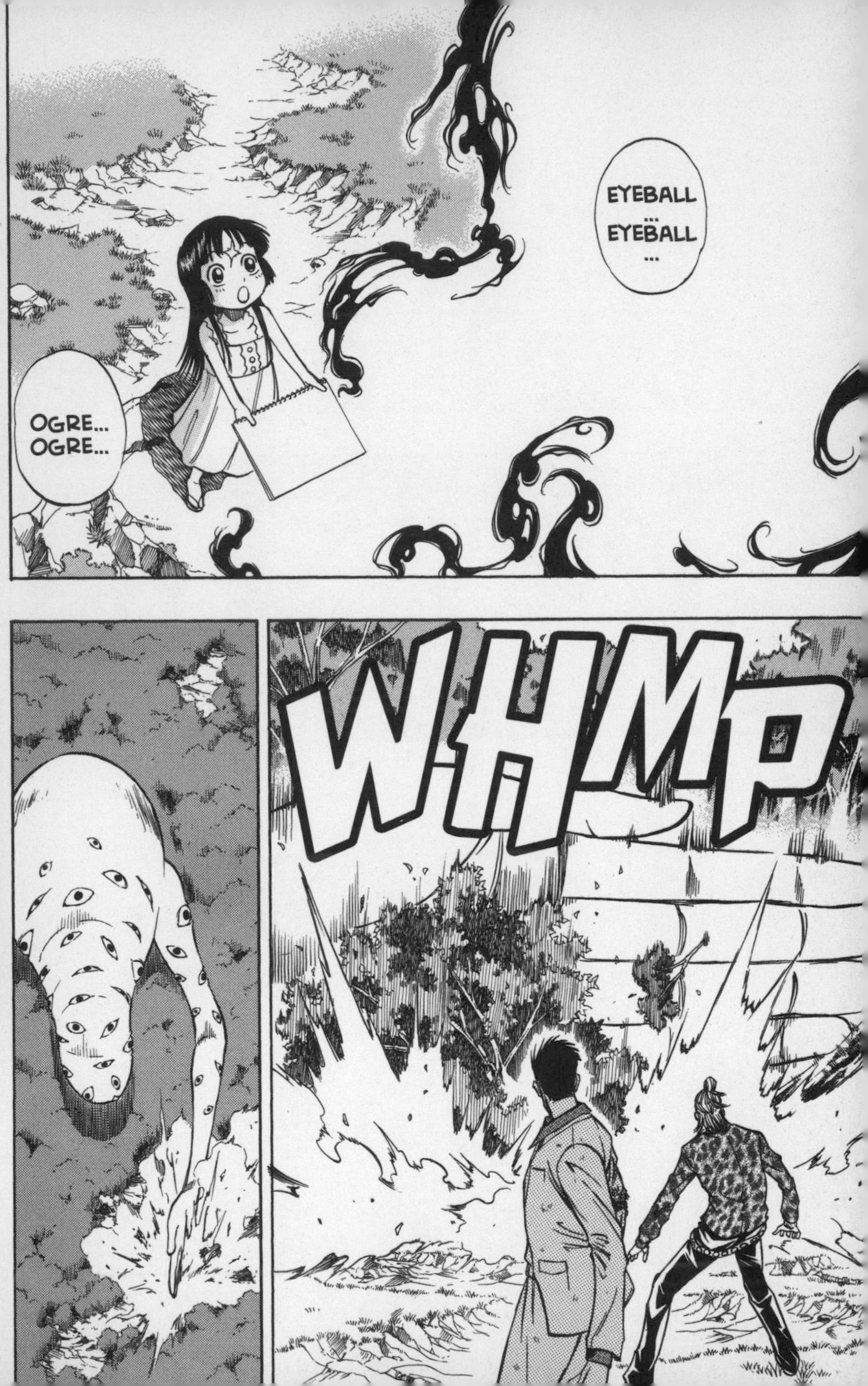
EYEBALL... EYEBALL...
OGRE... OGRE...
WHMP

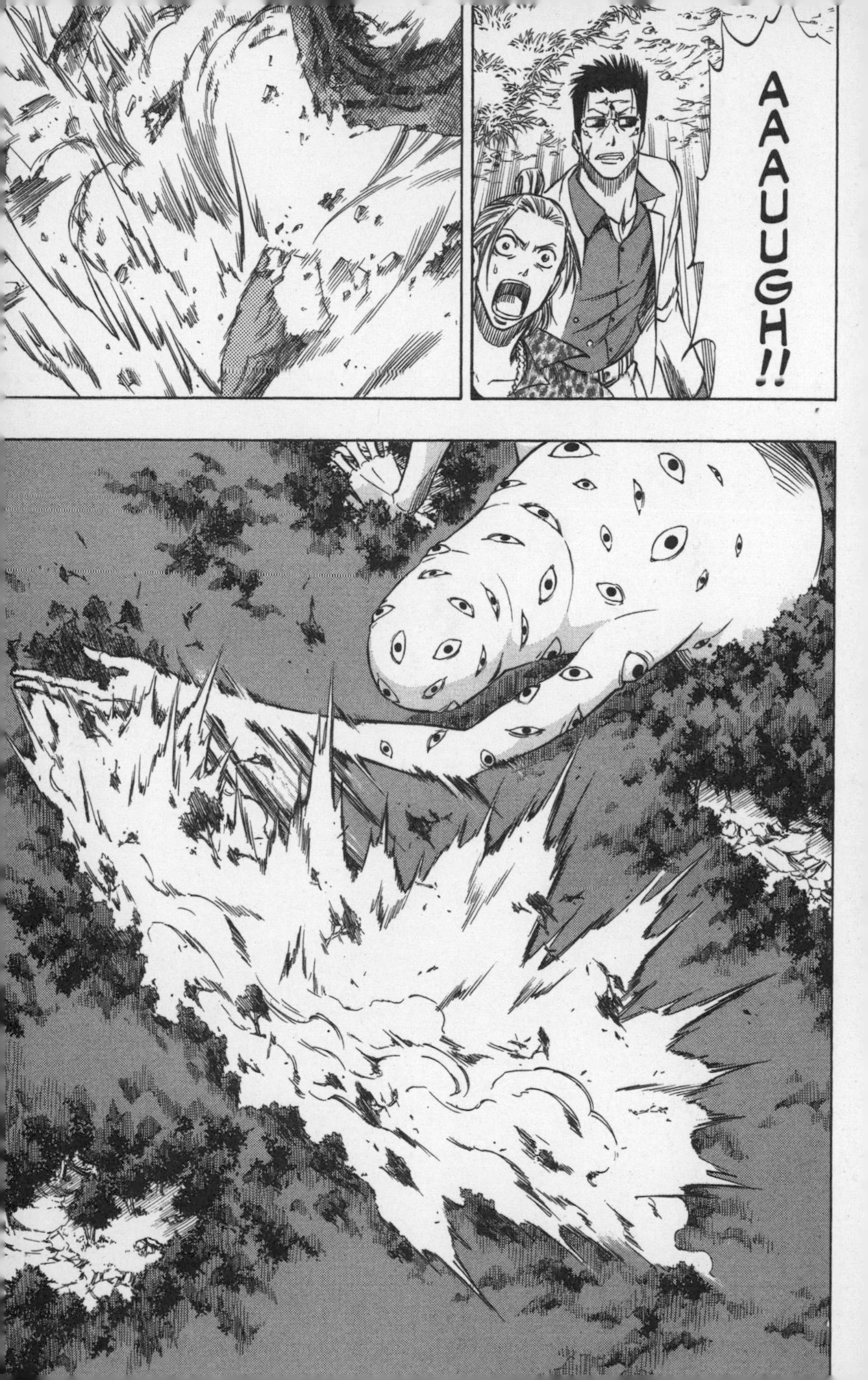
AAAUUGH!!

Mutters and mumblings...

CELL PHONE
THE PHONE I'M USING NOW DOESN'T WORK VERY
WELL ANYMORE, SO I'VE BEEN LOOKING INTO
NEWER MODELS.
I'M INTRIGUED BY THE XPERIA. IT LOOKS
PRETTY FUN.

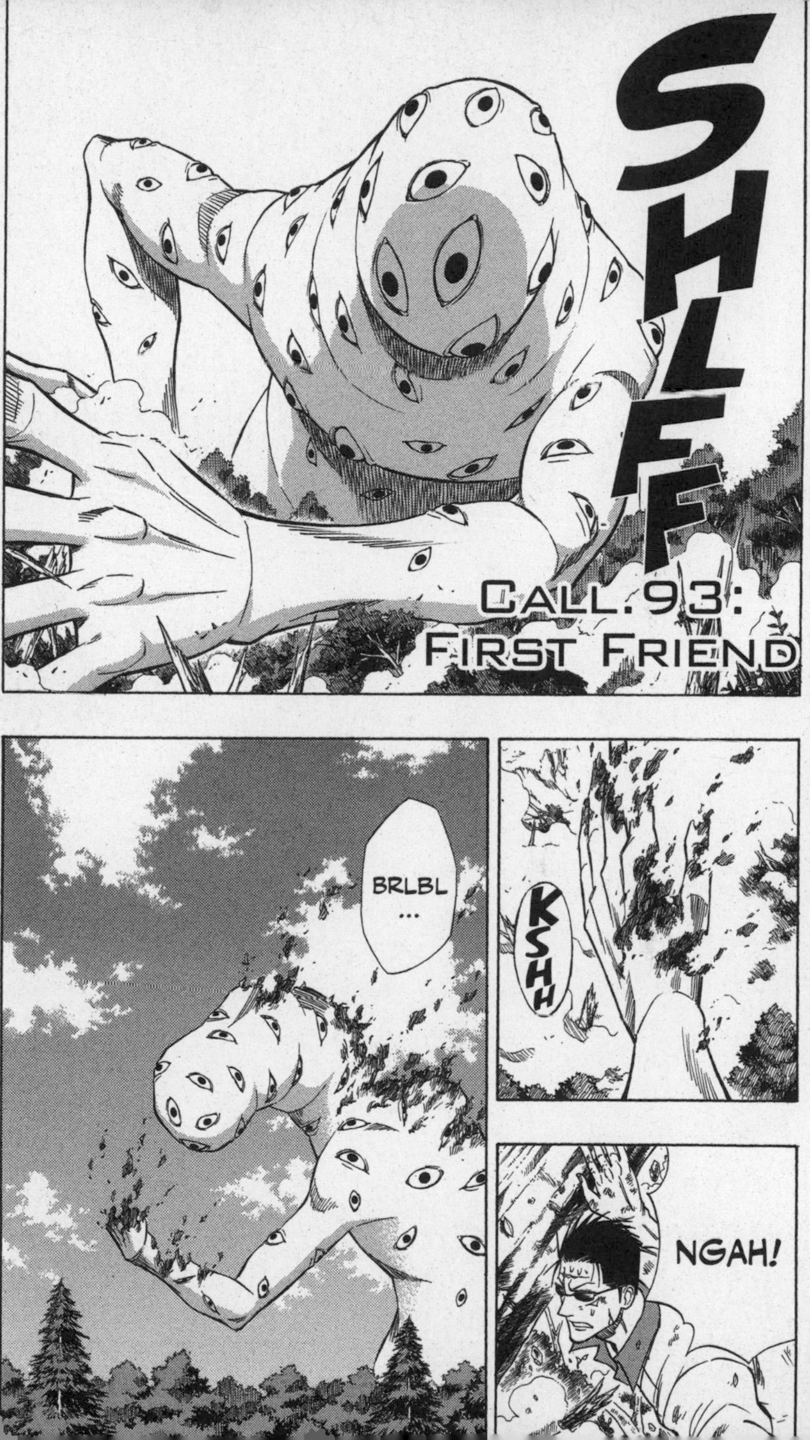
SHLFF
Call. 93: First Friend
KSHH
NGAH!
BRLBL
...

SSSs

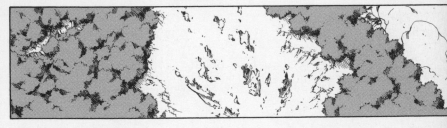

KRUNCH
KRUNCH

GAK!!
KOFF
KOFF

KRASH!

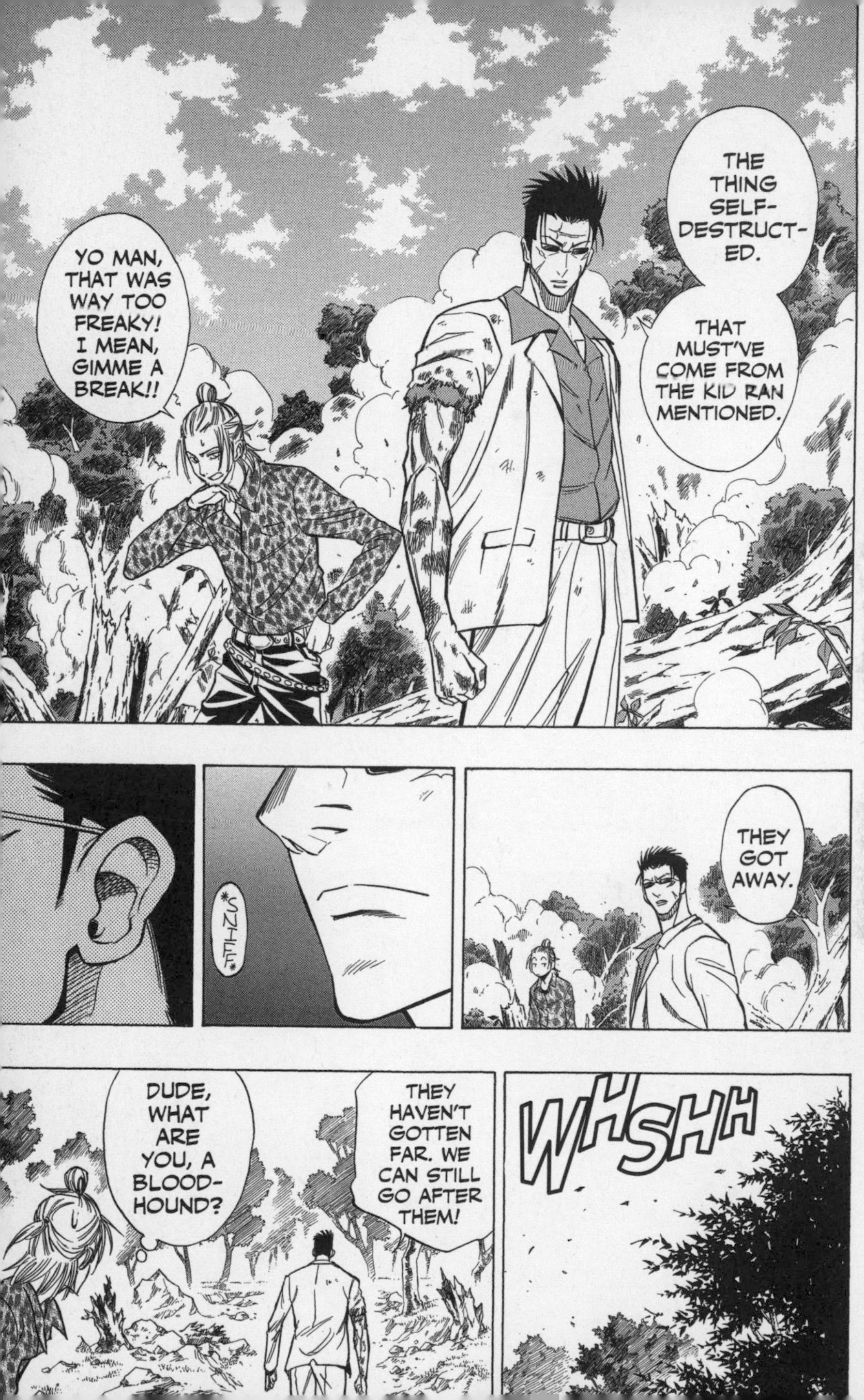
THE THING SELF-DESTRUCT-ED.
THAT MUST'VE COME FROM THE KID RAN MENTIONED.
YO MAN, THAT WAS WAY TOO FREAKY! I MEAN, GIMME A BREAK!!
THEY GOT AWAY.
SNIFF
WHSHH
THEY HAVEN'T GOTTEN FAR. WE CAN STILL GO AFTER THEM!
DUDE, WHAT ARE YOU, A BLOOD-HOUND?

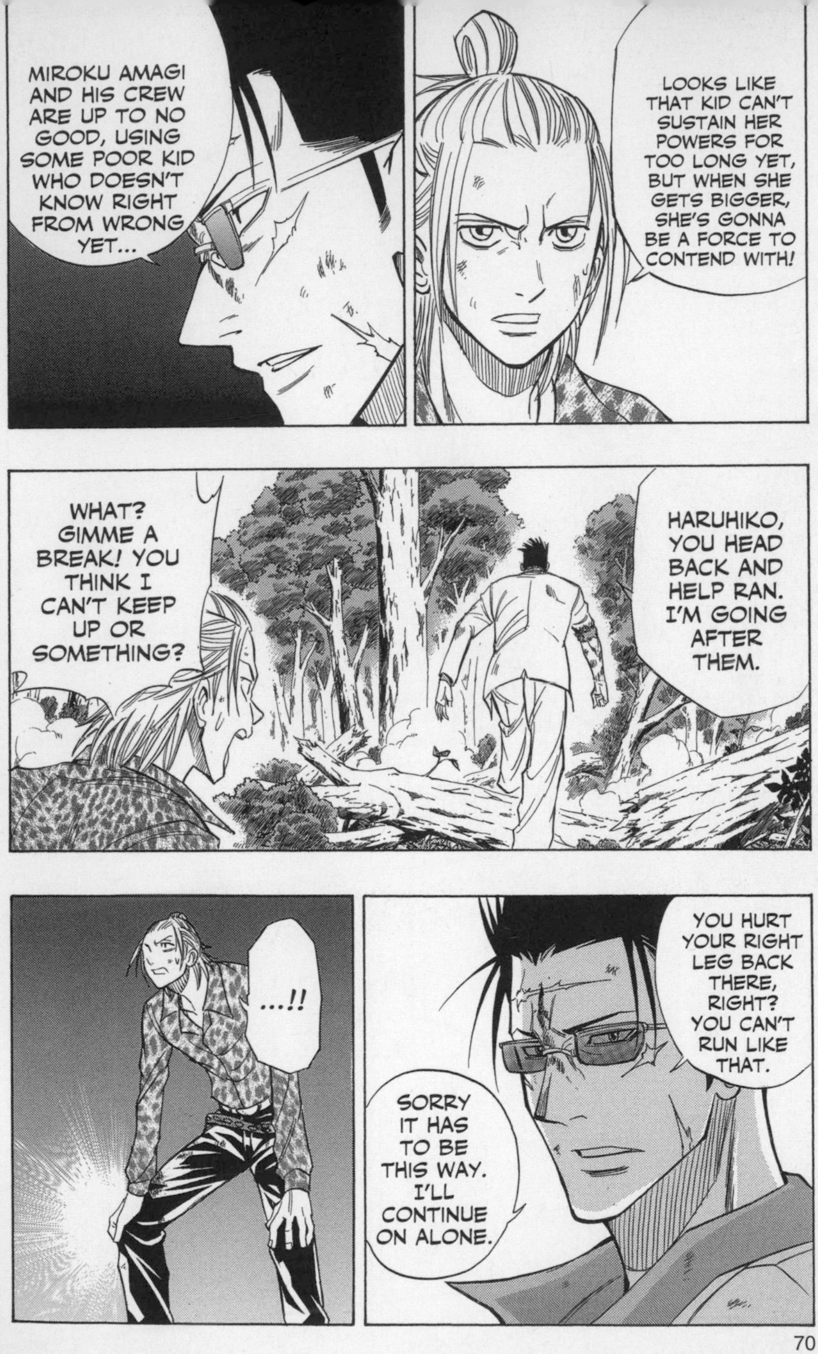
LOOKS LIKE THAT KID CAN'T SUSTAIN HER POWERS FOR TOO LONG YET, BUT WHEN SHE GETS BIGGER, SHE'S GONNA BE A FORCE TO CONTEND WITH!
MIROKU AMAGI AND HIS CREW ARE UP TO NO GOOD, USING SOME POOR KID WHO DOESN'T KNOW RIGHT FROM WRONG YET...
HARUHIKO, YOU HEAD BACK AND HELP RAN. I'M GOING AFTER THEM.
WHAT? GIMME A BREAK! YOU THINK I CAN'T KEEP UP OR SOMETHING?
YOU HURT YOUR RIGHT LEG BACK THERE, RIGHT? YOU CAN'T RUN LIKE THAT.
SORRY IT HAS TO BE THIS WAY. I'LL CONTINUE ON ALONE.
...!!

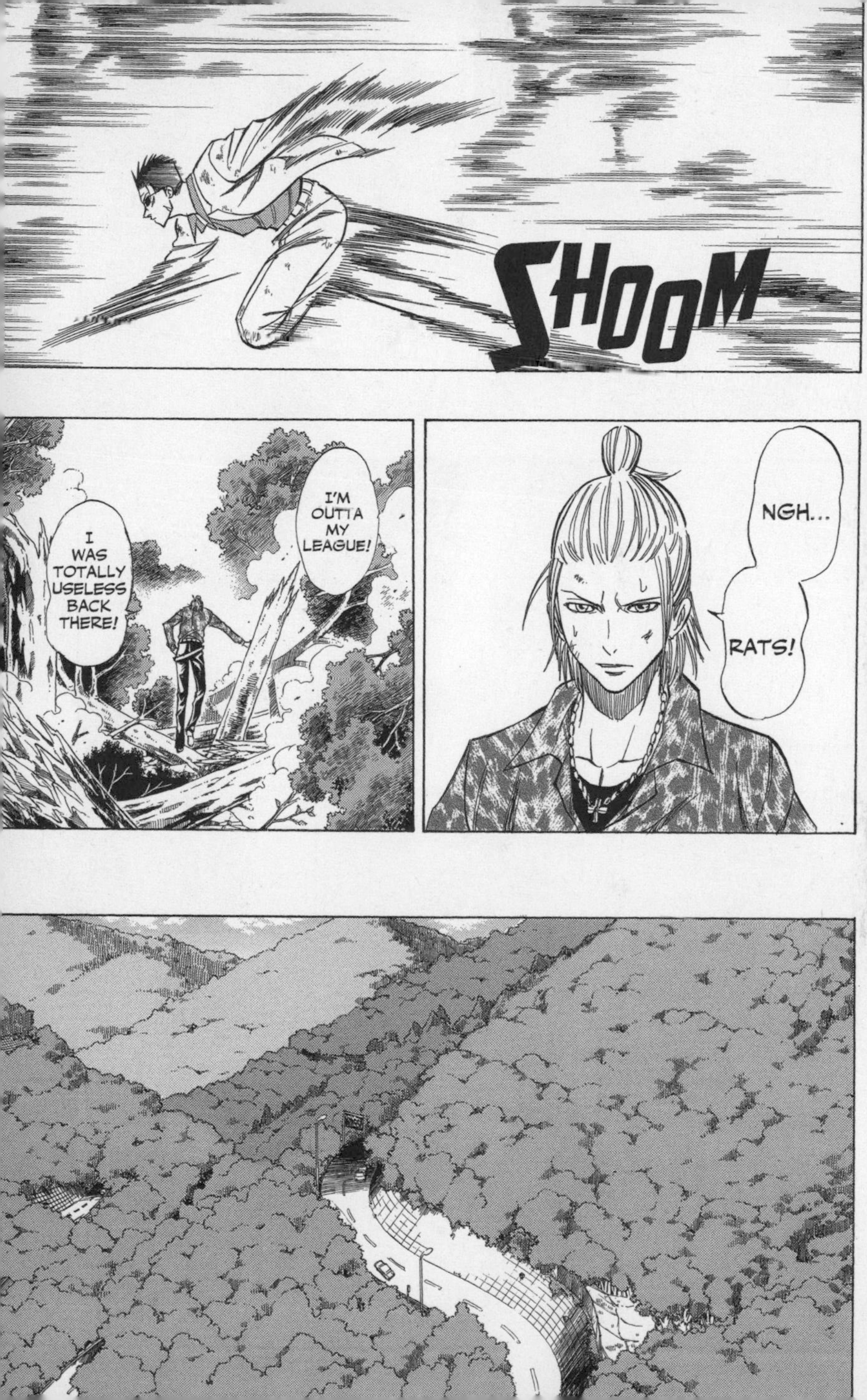
SHOOM
NGH...
RATS!
I'M OUTTA MY LEAGUE!
I WAS TOTALLY USELESS BACK THERE!

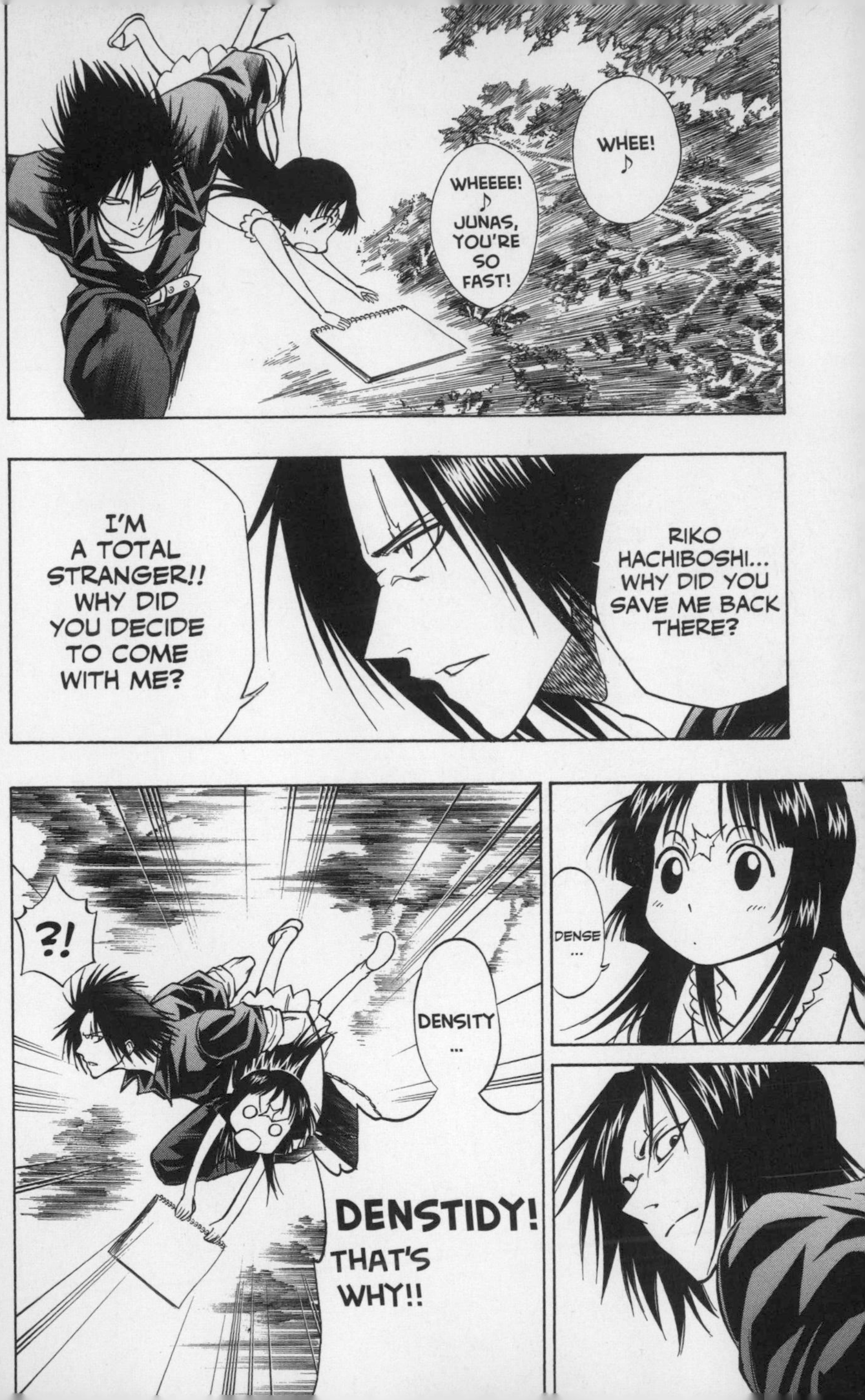
WHEE! ♪
WHEEEE! ♪ JUNAS, YOU'RE SO FAST!
RIKO HACHIBOSHI... WHY DID YOU SAVE ME BACK THERE?
I'M A TOTAL STRANGER!! WHY DID YOU DECIDE TO COME WITH ME?
DENSE...
DENSITY...
DENSTIDY! THAT'S WHY!!
?!

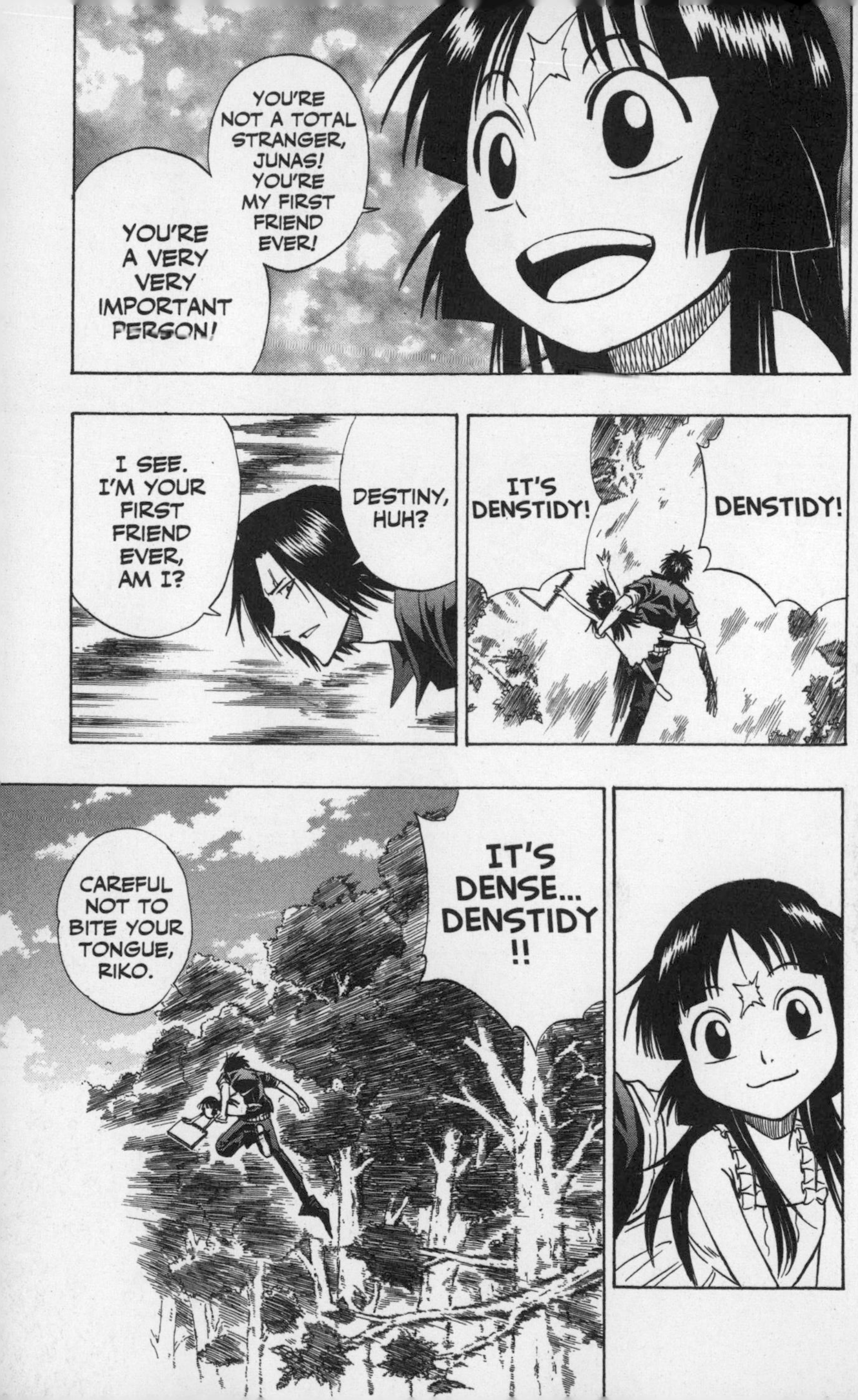
YOU'RE NOT A TOTAL STRANGER, JUNAS! YOU'RE MY FIRST FRIEND EVER!
YOU'RE A VERY VERY IMPORTANT PERSON!
DENSTIDY!
IT'S DENSTIDY!
DESTINY, HUH?
I SEE. I'M YOUR FIRST FRIEND EVER, AM I?
IT'S DENSE... DENSTIDY !!
CAREFUL NOT TO BITE YOUR TONGUE, RIKO.

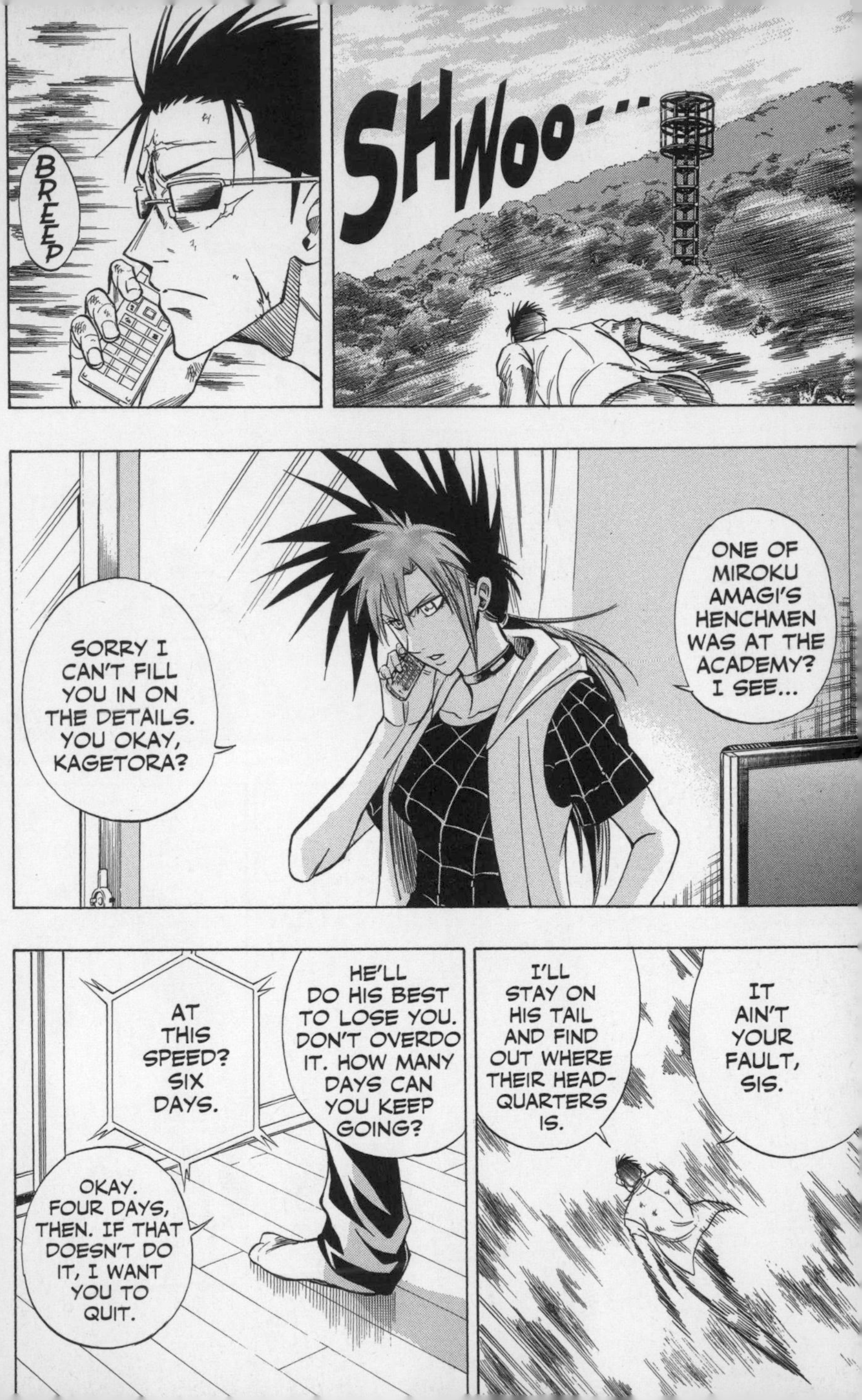
SHWOO...
BREEP
ONE OF MIROKU AMAGI'S HENCHMEN WAS AT THE ACADEMY? I SEE...
SORRY I CAN'T FILL YOU IN ON THE DETAILS. YOU OKAY, KAGETORA?
IT AIN'T YOUR FAULT, SIS.
I'LL STAY ON HIS TAIL AND FIND OUT WHERE THEIR HEAD-QUARTERS IS.
HE'LL DO HIS BEST TO LOSE YOU. DON'T OVERDO IT. HOW MANY DAYS CAN YOU KEEP GOING?
AT THIS SPEED? SIX DAYS.
OKAY. FOUR DAYS, THEN. IF THAT DOESN'T DO IT, I WANT YOU TO QUIT.

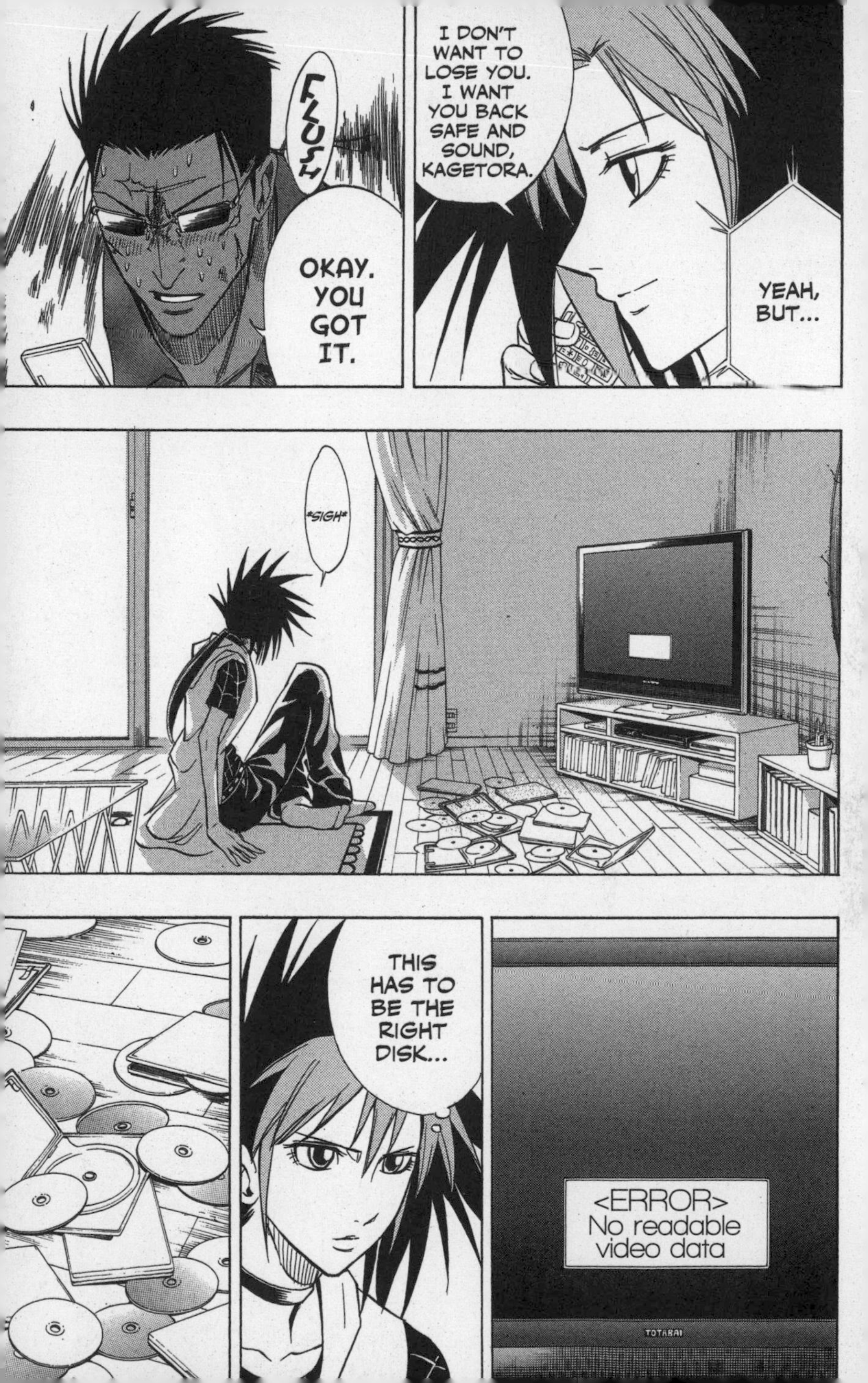
I DON'T WANT TO LOSE YOU. I WANT YOU BACK SAFE AND SOUND, KAGETORA.
YEAH, BUT...
FLUSH
OKAY. YOU GOT IT.
SIGH
<ERROR> No readable video data
TOTABAI
THIS HAS TO BE THE RIGHT DISK...

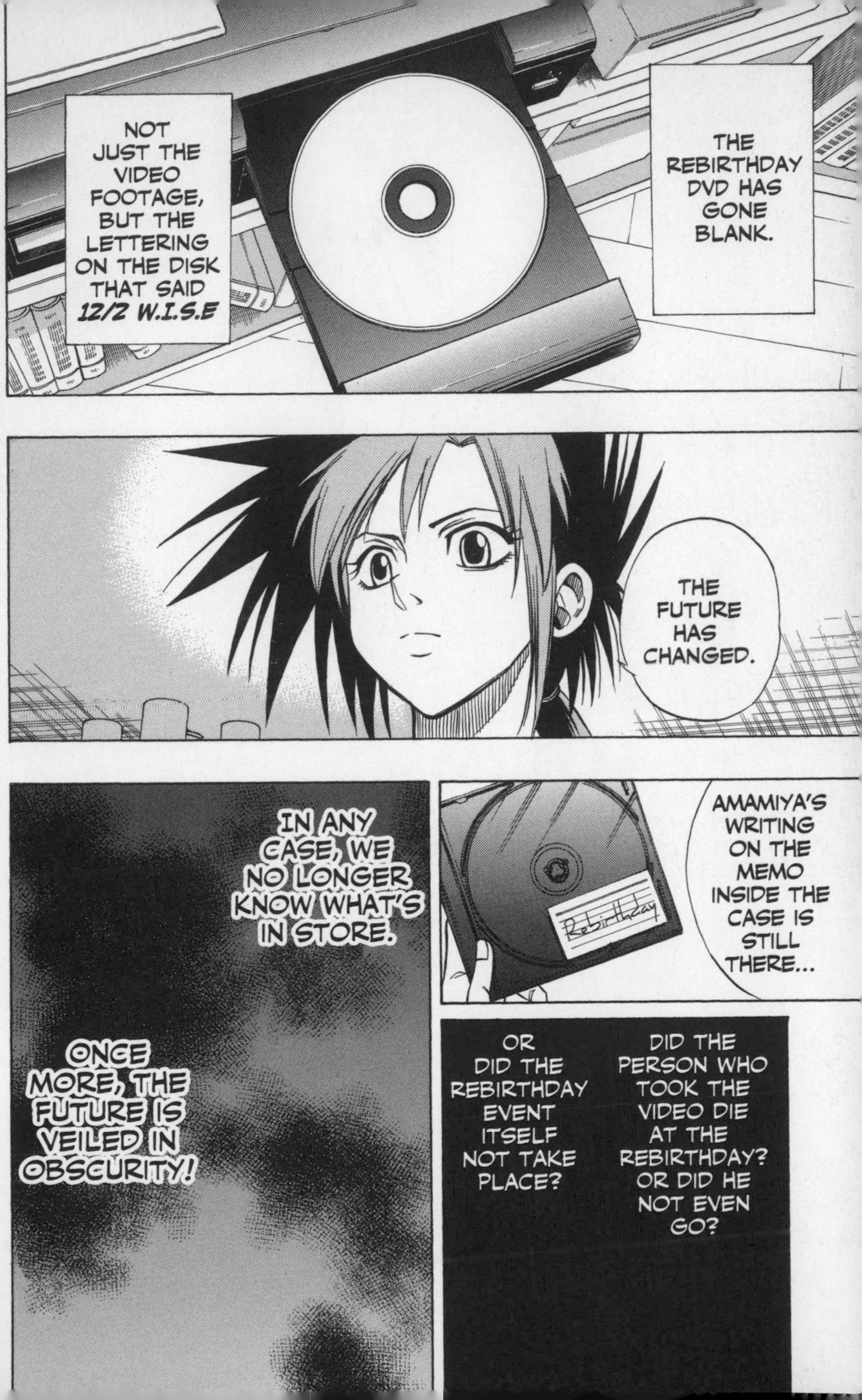
THE REBIRTHDAY DVD HAS GONE BLANK.
NOT JUST THE VIDEO FOOTAGE, BUT THE LETTERING ON THE DISK THAT SAID *12/2 W.I.S.E*
THE FUTURE HAS CHANGED.
AMAMIYA'S WRITING ON THE MEMO INSIDE THE CASE IS STILL THERE...
Rebirthday
DID THE PERSON WHO TOOK THE VIDEO DIE AT THE REBIRTHDAY? OR DID HE NOT EVEN GO?
OR DID THE REBIRTHDAY EVENT ITSELF NOT TAKE PLACE?
IN ANY CASE, WE NO LONGER KNOW WHAT'S IN STORE.
ONCE MORE, THE FUTURE IS VEILED IN OBSCURITY!

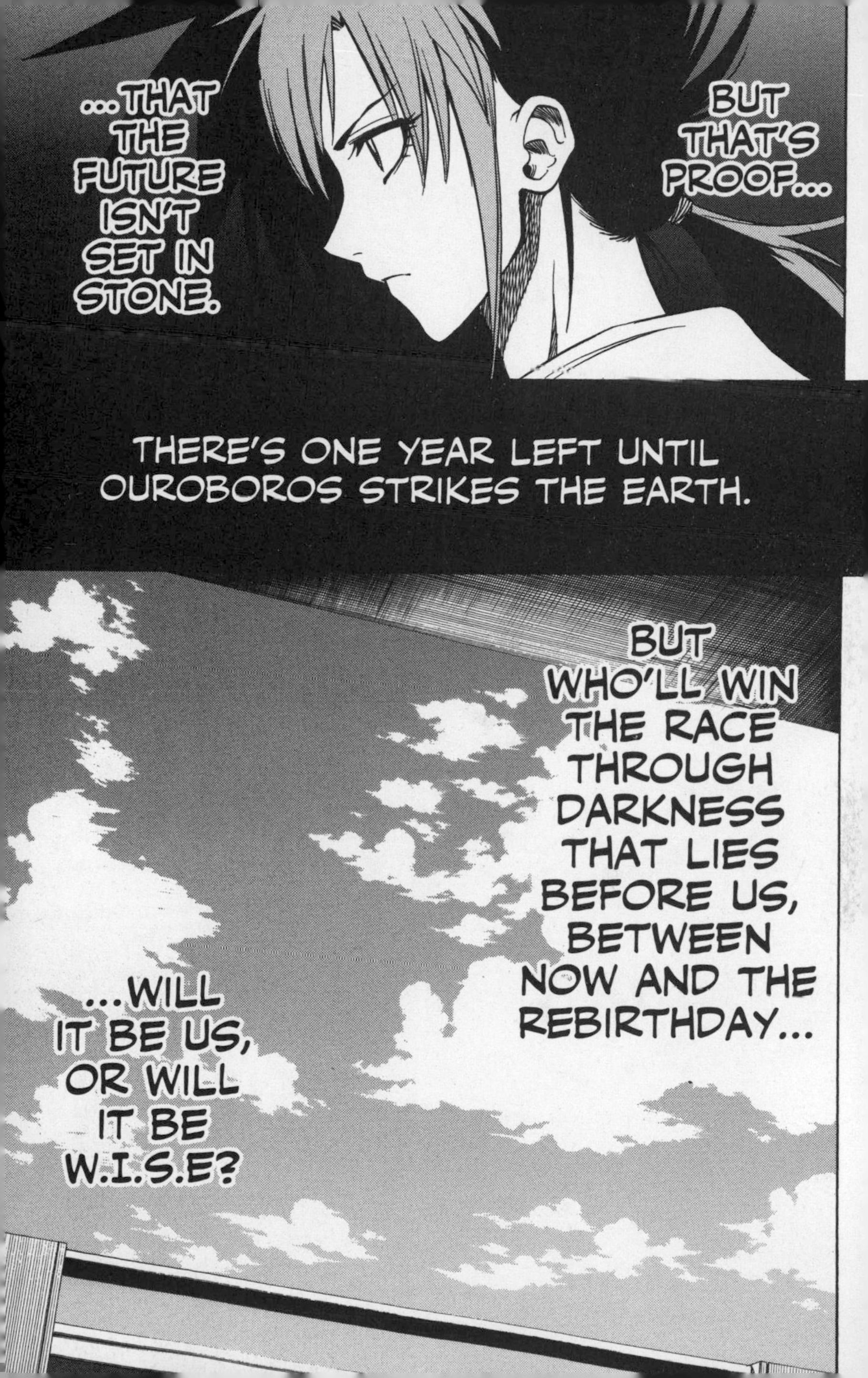
BUT THAT'S PROOF...
...THAT THE FUTURE ISN'T SET IN STONE.
THERE'S ONE YEAR LEFT UNTIL OUROBOROS STRIKES THE EARTH.
BUT WHO'LL WIN THE RACE THROUGH DARKNESS THAT LIES BEFORE US, BETWEEN NOW AND THE REBIRTHDAY...
...WILL IT BE US, OR WILL IT BE W.I.S.E?

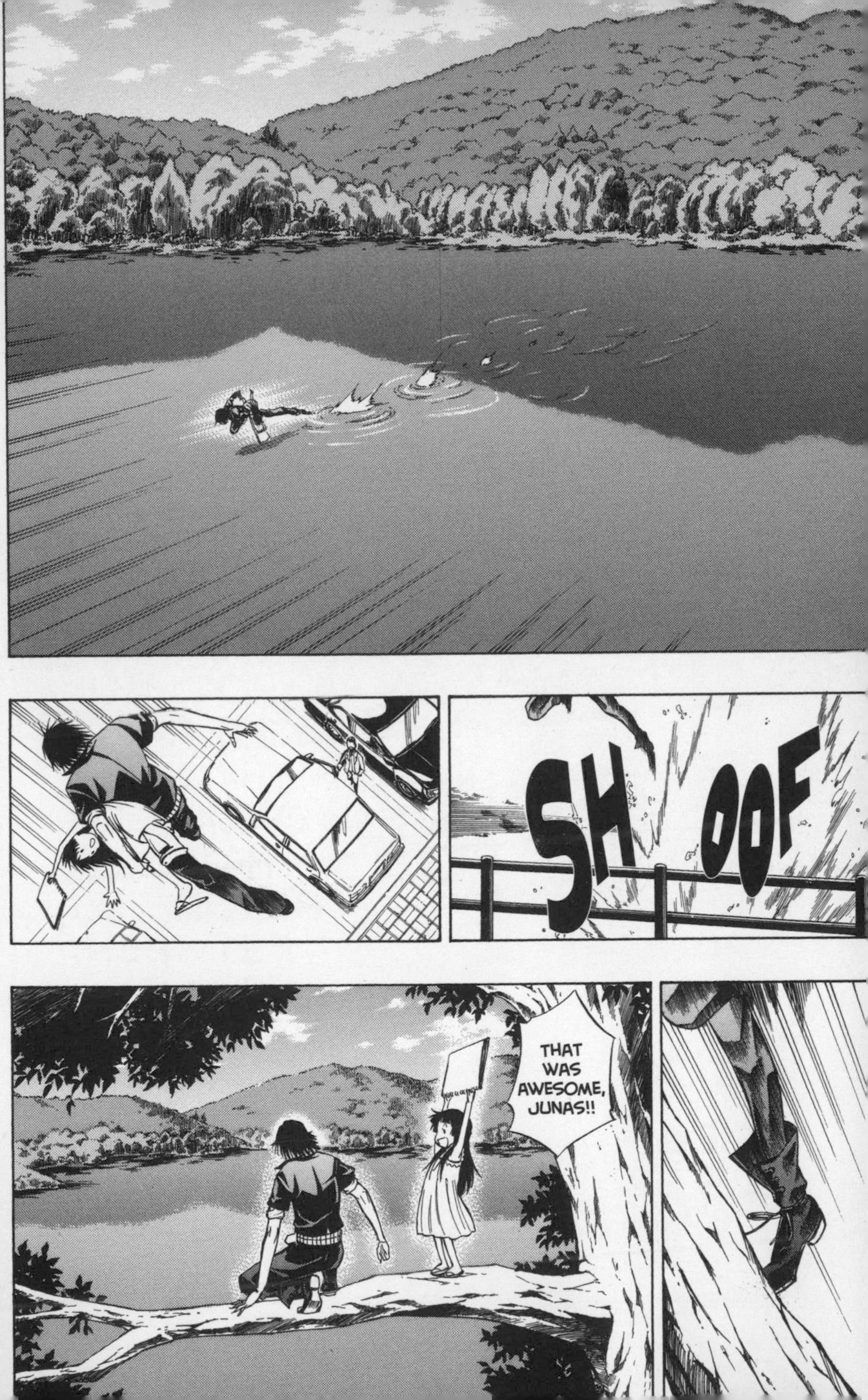
SH OOF
THAT WAS AWESOME, JUNAS!!

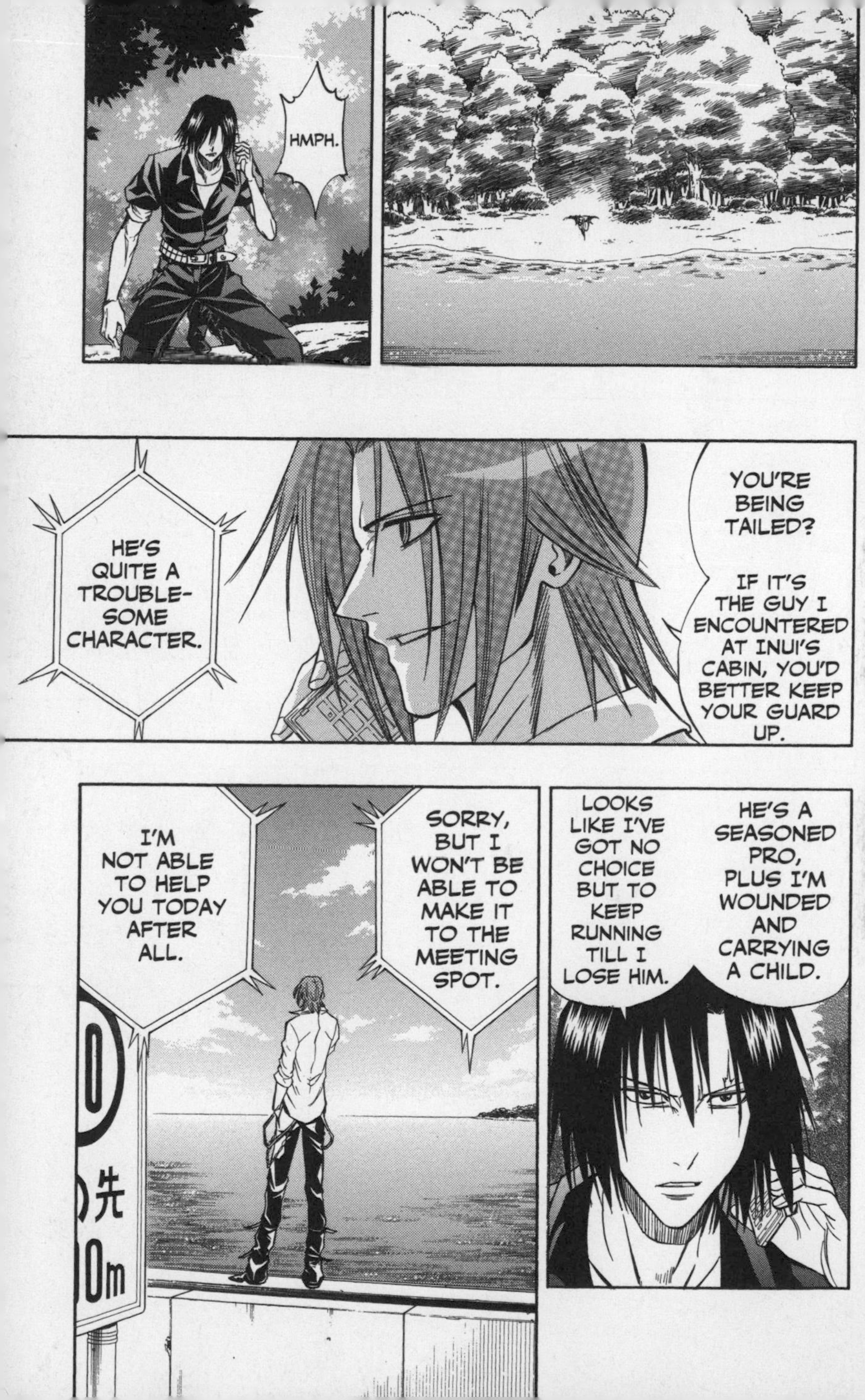
HMPH.
YOU'RE BEING TAILED?
IF IT'S THE GUY I ENCOUNTERED AT INUI'S CABIN, YOU'D BETTER KEEP YOUR GUARD UP.
HE'S QUITE A TROUBLE-SOME CHARACTER.
HE'S A SEASONED PRO, PLUS I'M WOUNDED AND CARRYING A CHILD.
LOOKS LIKE I'VE GOT NO CHOICE BUT TO KEEP RUNNING TILL I LOSE HIM.
SORRY, BUT I WON'T BE ABLE TO MAKE IT TO THE MEETING SPOT.
I'M NOT ABLE TO HELP YOU TODAY AFTER ALL.

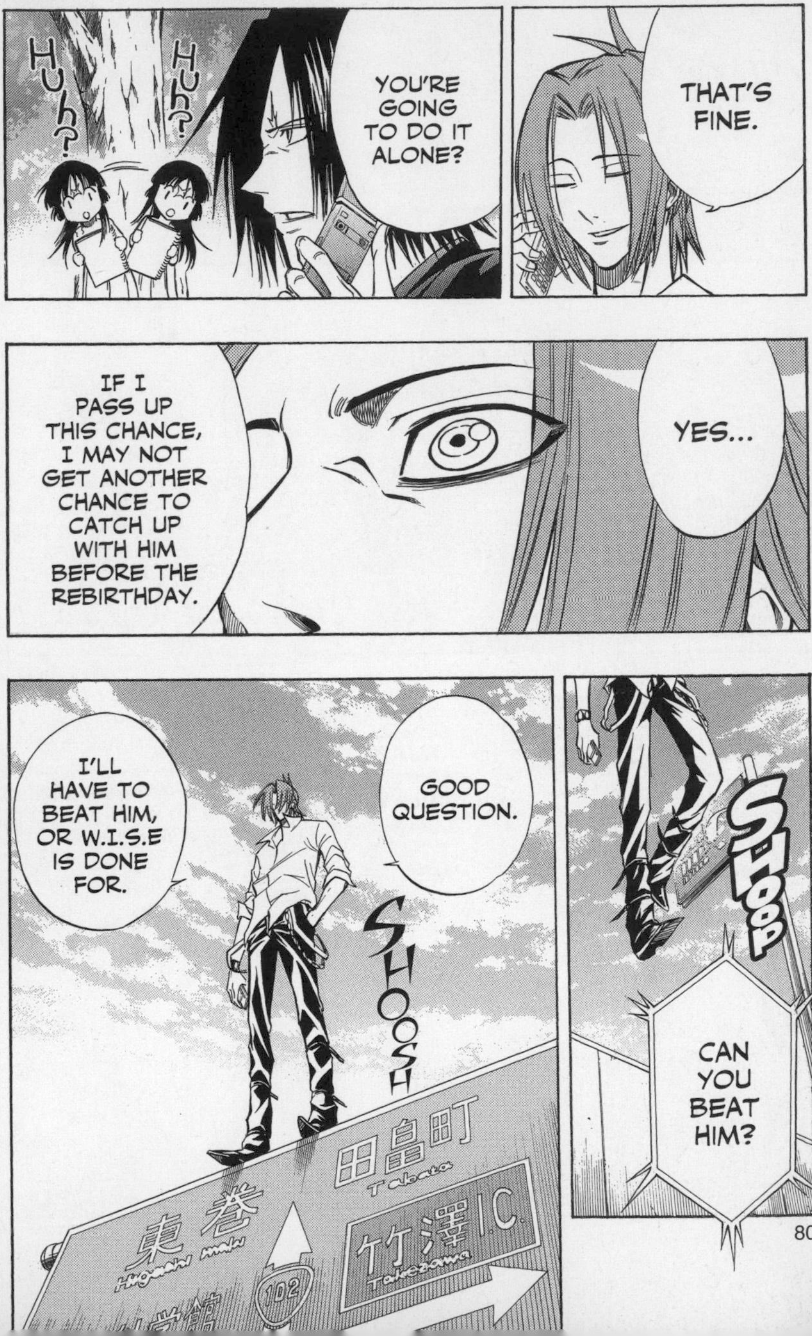
THAT'S FINE.
YOU'RE GOING TO DO IT ALONE?
HUh?
HUh?
YES...
IF I PASS UP THIS CHANCE, I MAY NOT GET ANOTHER CHANCE TO CATCH UP WITH HIM BEFORE THE REBIRTHDAY.
SHOOP
CAN YOU BEAT HIM?
GOOD QUESTION.
SHOOSH
I'LL HAVE TO BEAT HIM, OR W.I.S.E IS DONE FOR.
田畠町
Tabata
東巻
Higashi maki
竹澤 I.C.
Takezawa
102

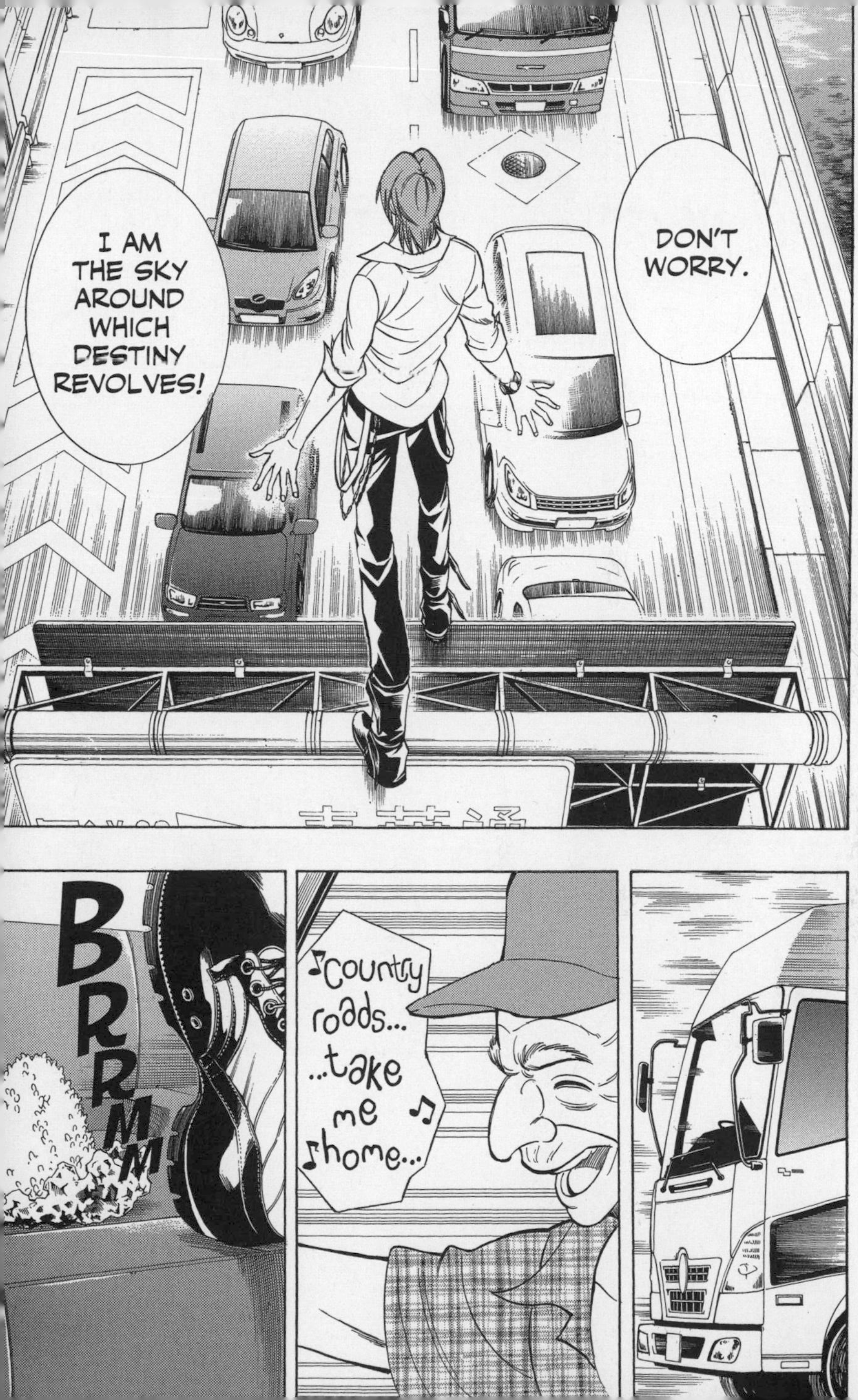
DON'T WORRY.
I AM THE SKY AROUND WHICH DESTINY REVOLVES!
♪Country roads... ...take me ♪ ♪home...
BRRMM

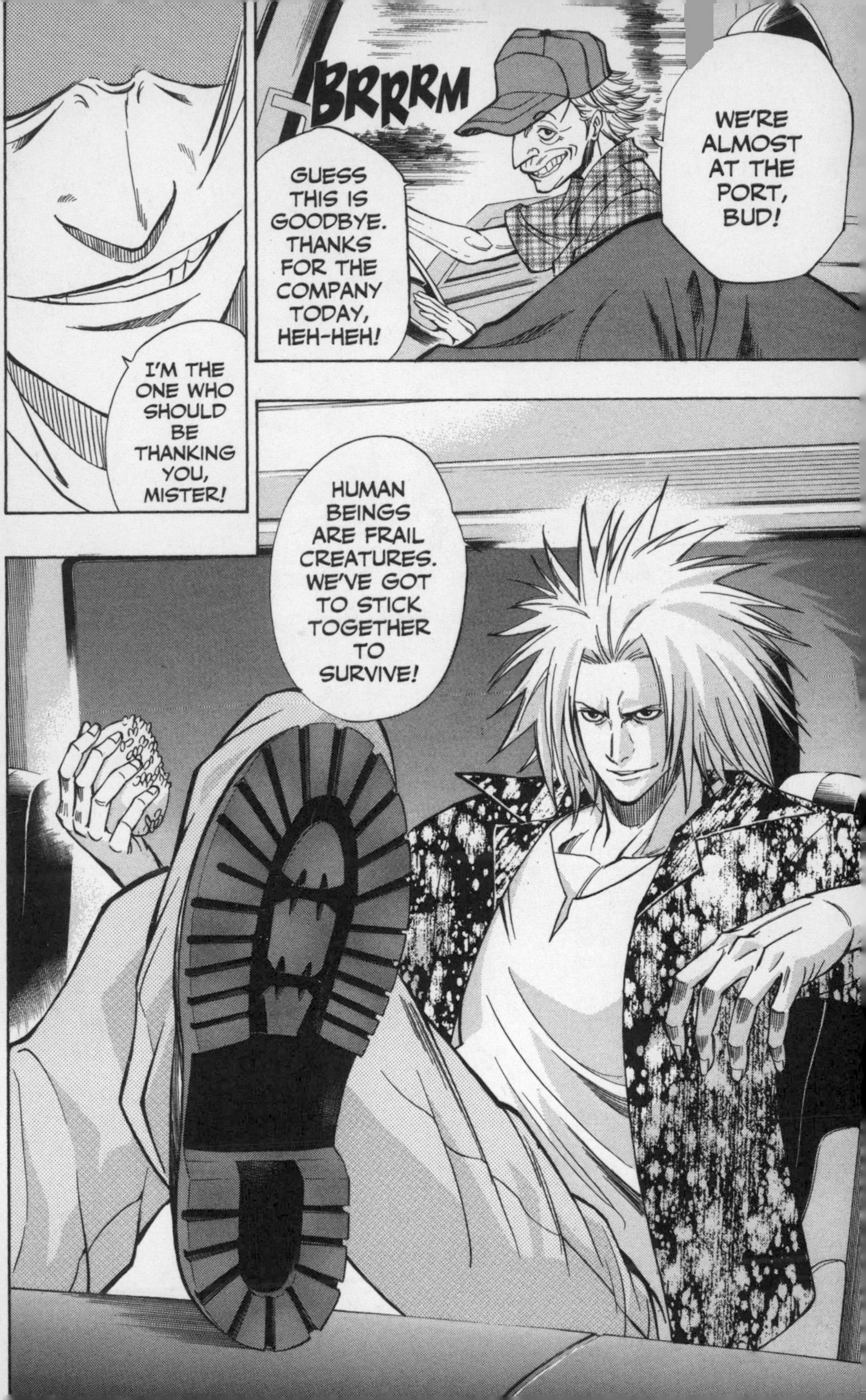
BRRRM
WE'RE ALMOST AT THE PORT, BUD!
GUESS THIS IS GOODBYE. THANKS FOR THE COMPANY TODAY, HEH-HEH!
I'M THE ONE WHO SHOULD BE THANKING YOU, MISTER!
HUMAN BEINGS ARE FRAIL CREATURES. WE'VE GOT TO STICK TOGETHER TO SURVIVE!

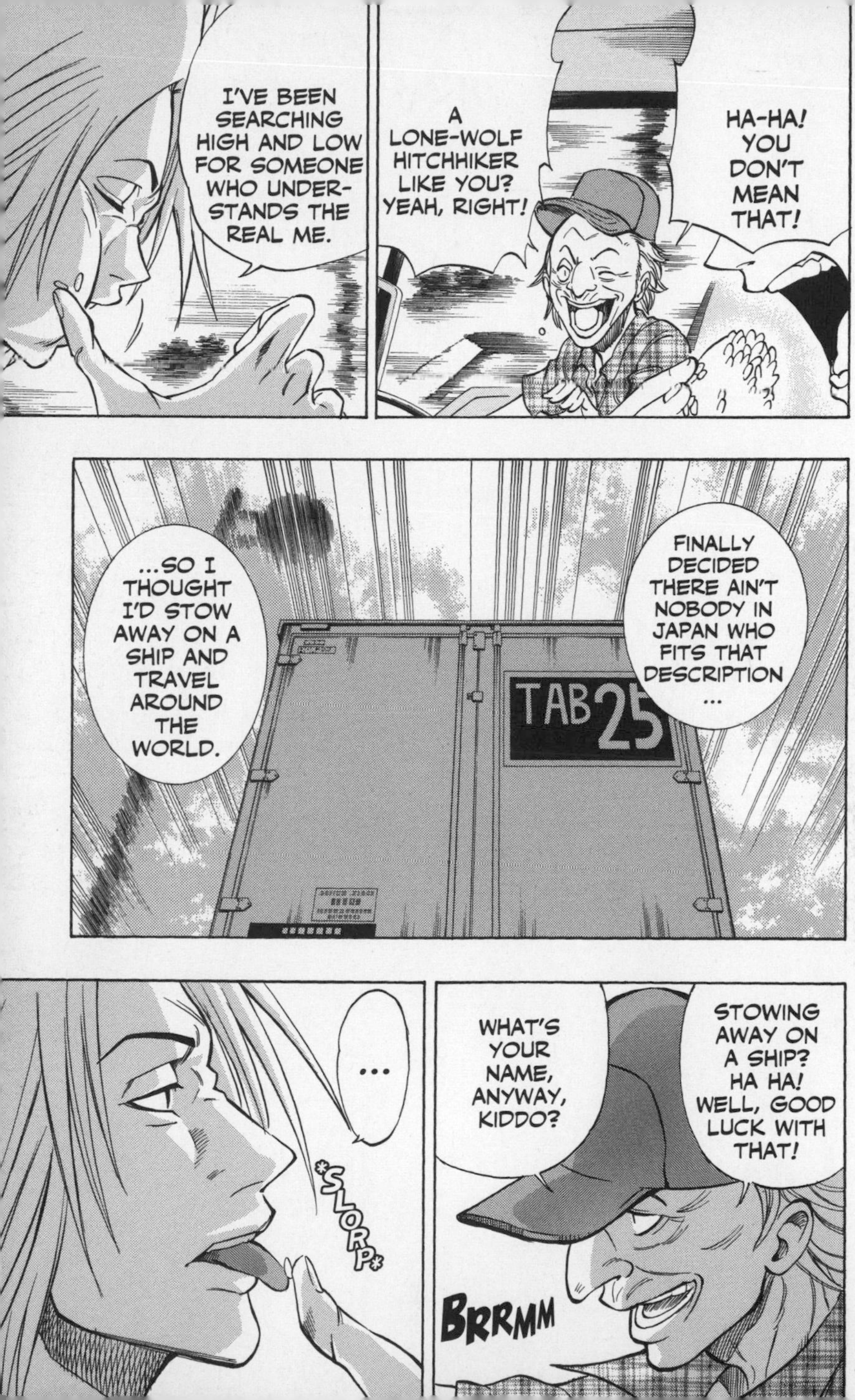
HA-HA! YOU DON'T MEAN THAT!
A LONE-WOLF HITCHHIKER LIKE YOU? YEAH, RIGHT!
I'VE BEEN SEARCHING HIGH AND LOW FOR SOMEONE WHO UNDER-STANDS THE REAL ME.
FINALLY DECIDED THERE AIN'T NOBODY IN JAPAN WHO FITS THAT DESCRIPTION ...
TAB 25
...SO I THOUGHT I'D STOW AWAY ON A SHIP AND TRAVEL AROUND THE WORLD.
STOWING AWAY ON A SHIP? HA HA! WELL, GOOD LUCK WITH THAT!
WHAT'S YOUR NAME, ANYWAY, KIDDO?
BRRMM
...
SLORP

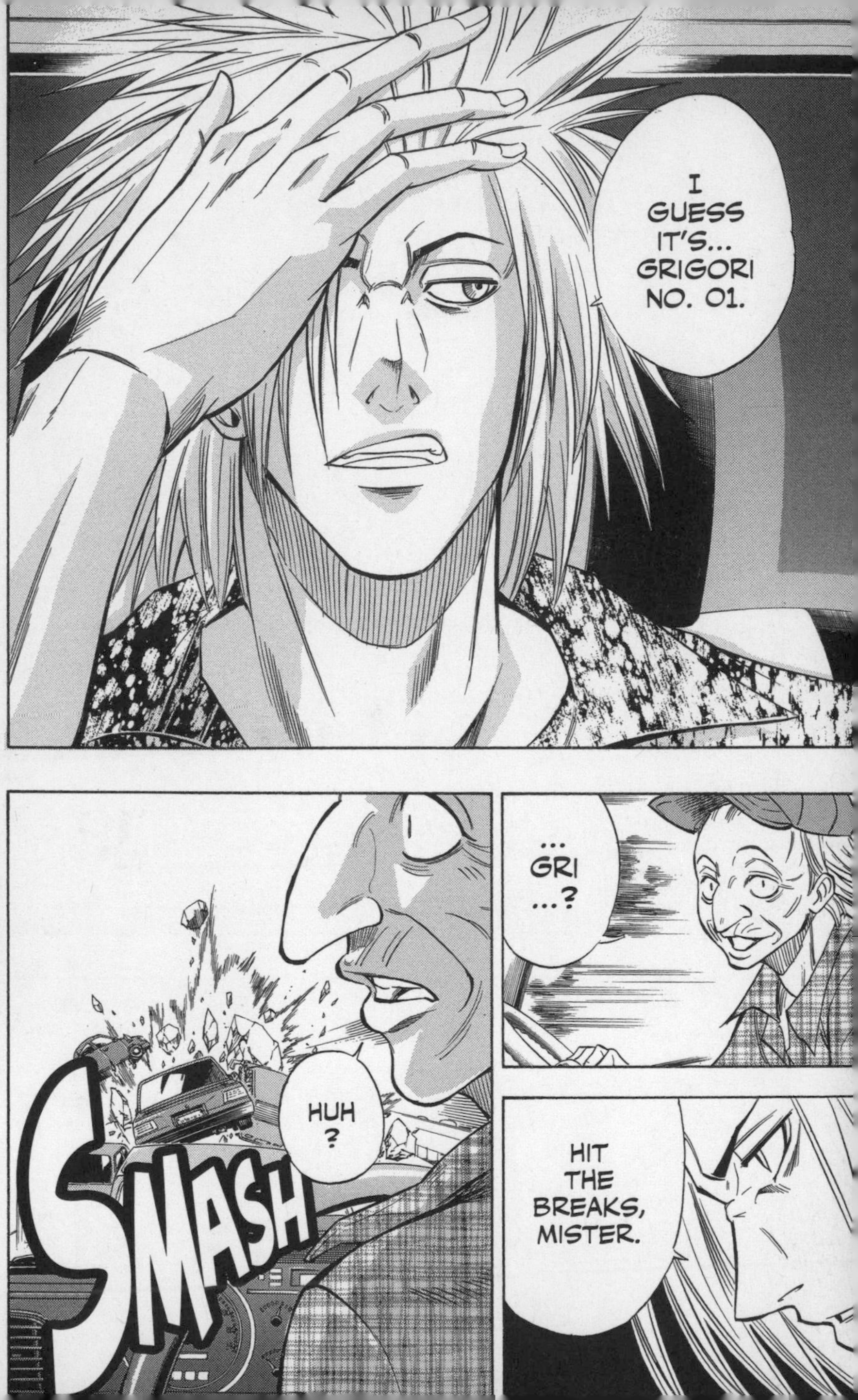
I GUESS IT'S... GRIGORI NO. 01.
... GRI ...?
HIT THE BREAKS, MISTER.
HUH ?
SMASH

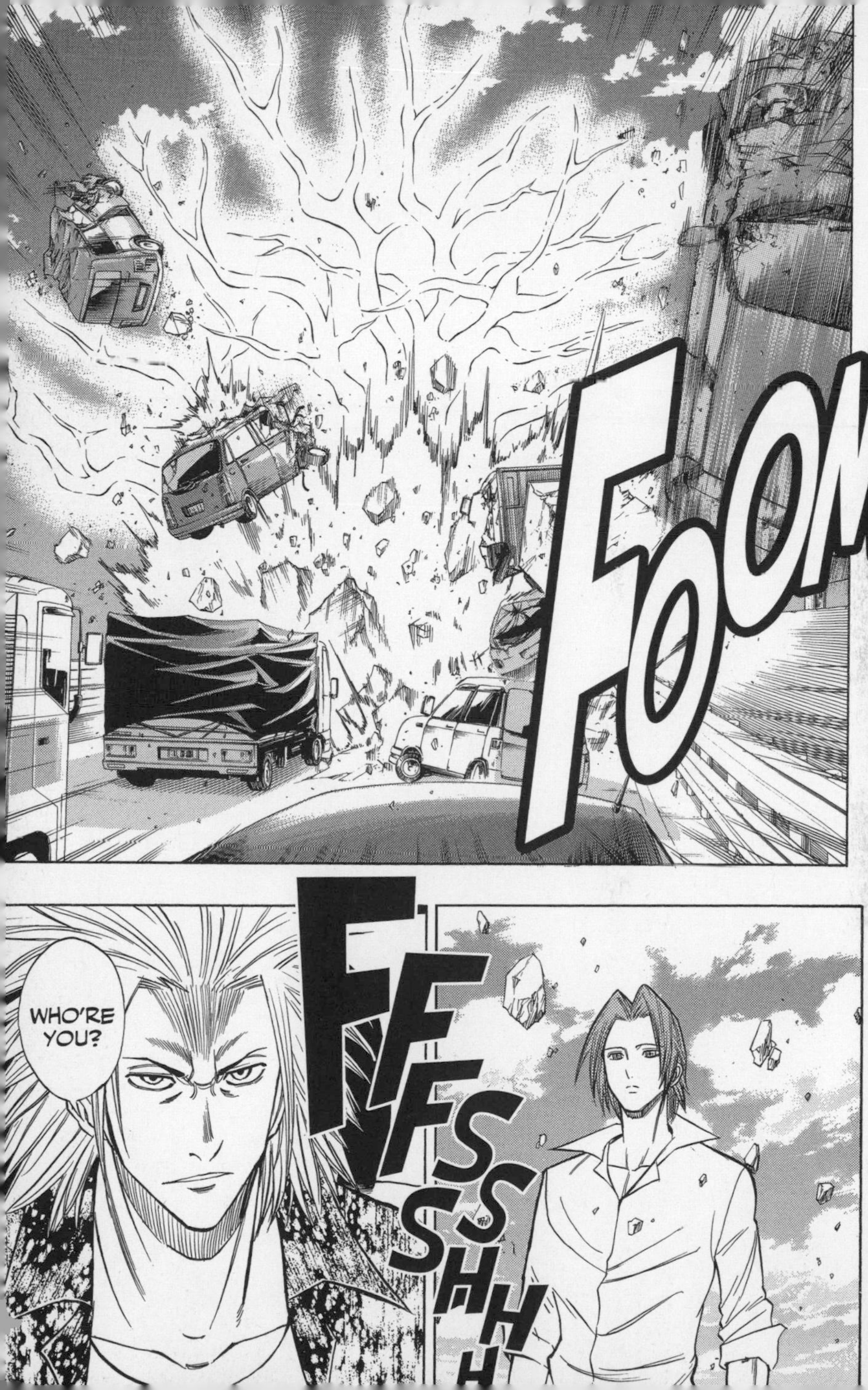
FOOM
FFFSSSHHHH
WHO'RE YOU?

Hip
hip
hooray!

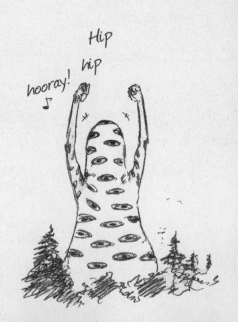

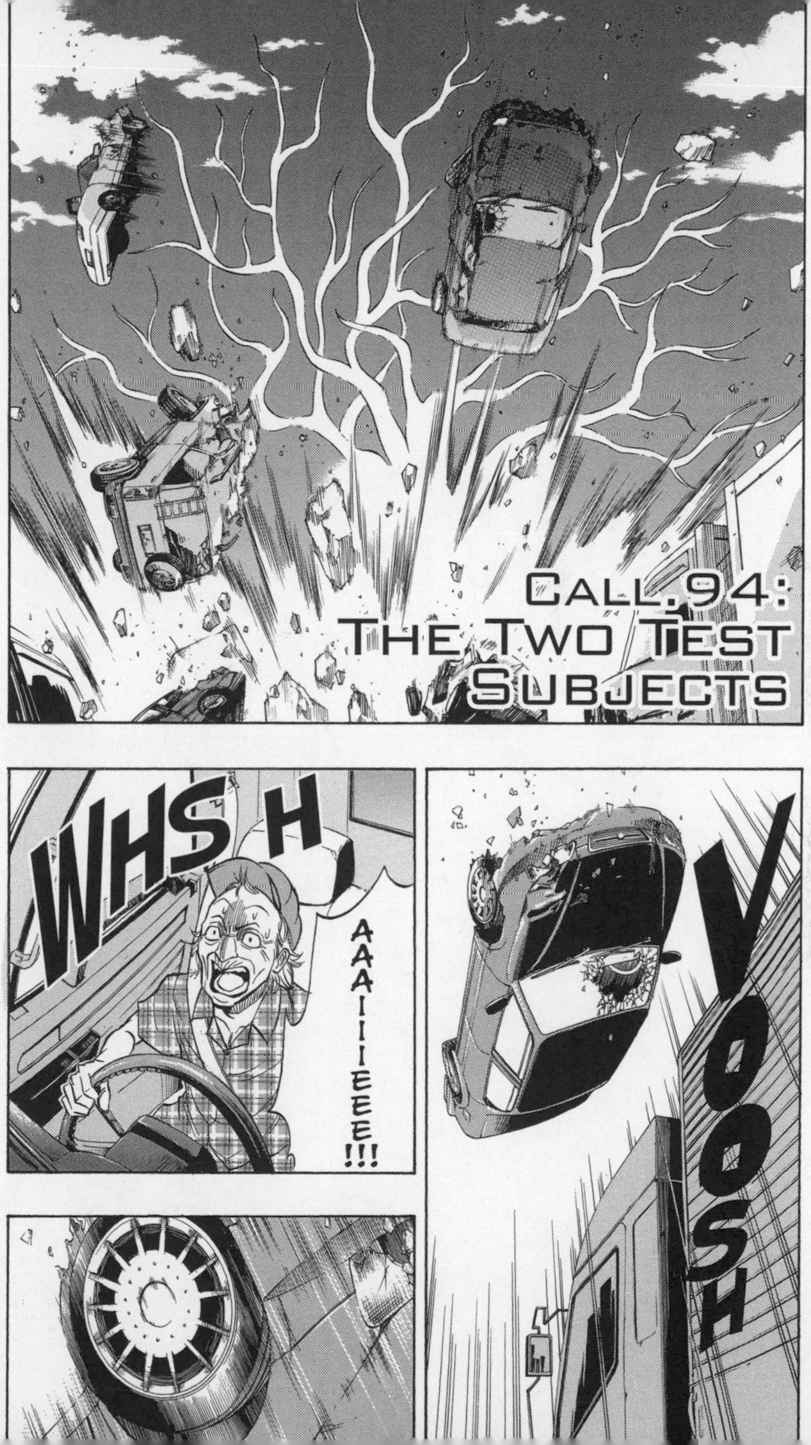
CALL.94:
THE TWO TEST SUBJECTS
VOOSH
WHSH
AAAIIIIEEEE!!!

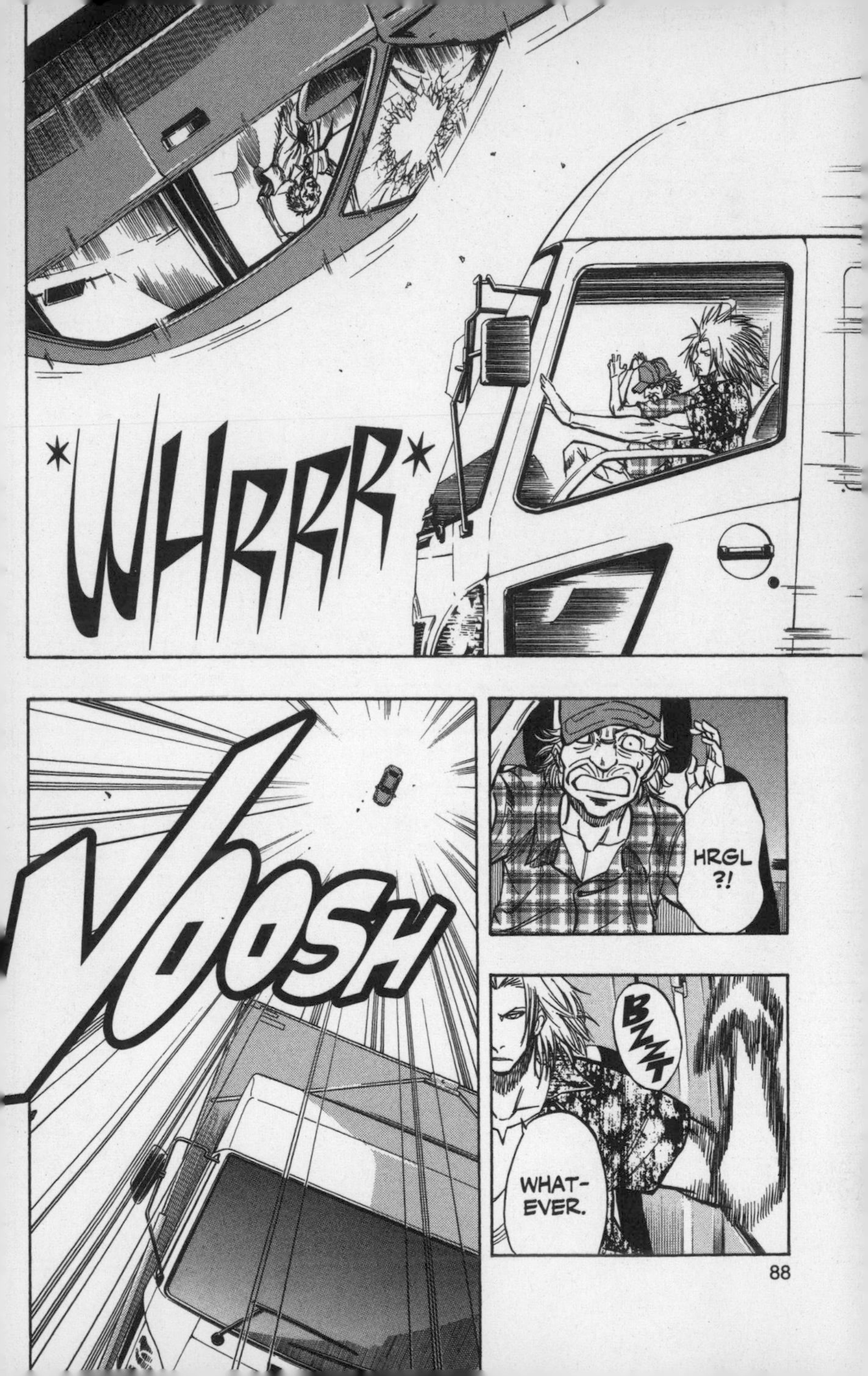
WHRRR
HRGL ?!
BZZT
WHAT-EVER.
VOOSH

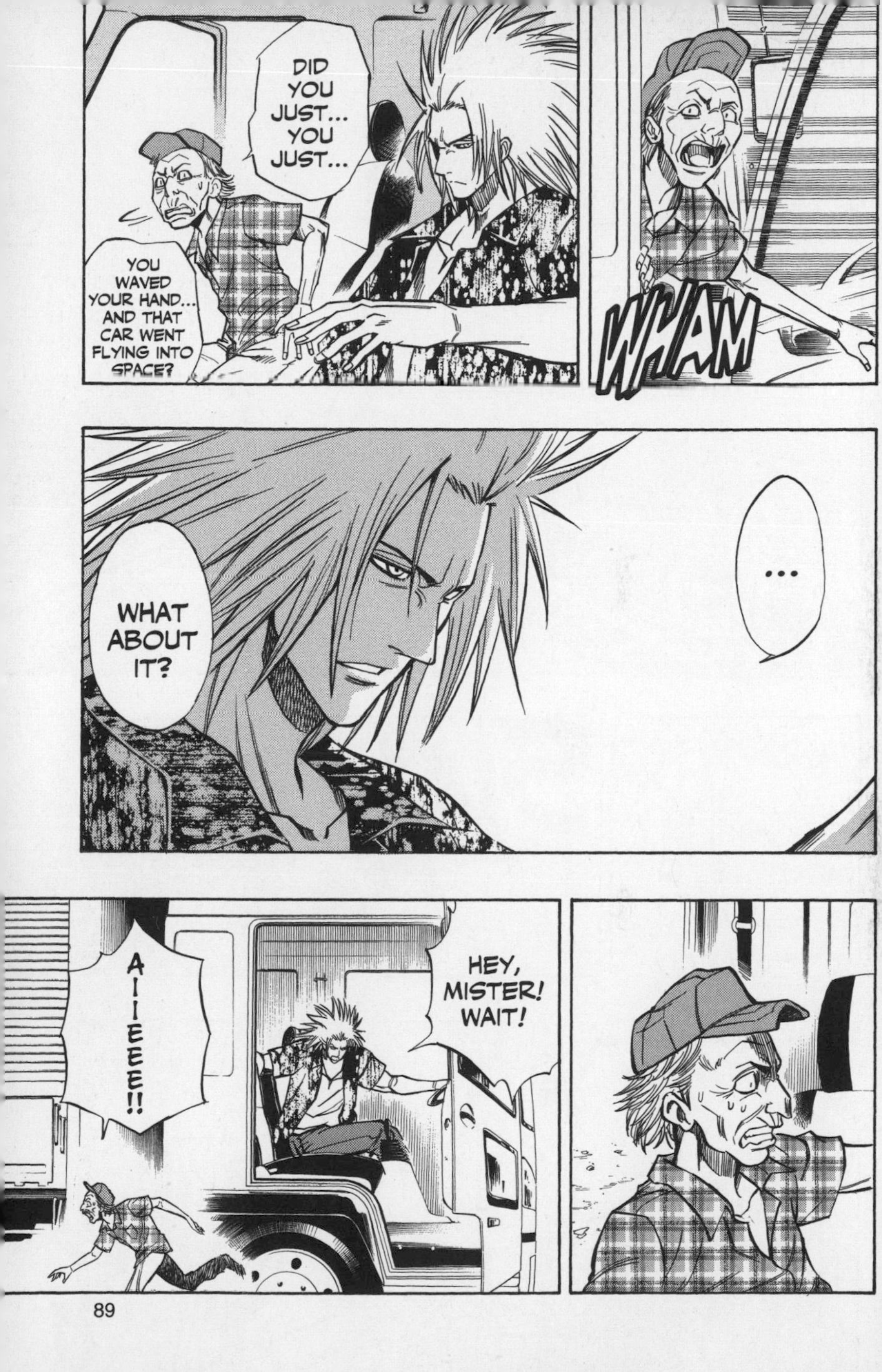

WHAM
DID YOU JUST... YOU JUST...
YOU WAVED YOUR HAND... AND THAT CAR WENT FLYING INTO SPACE?
...
WHAT ABOUT IT?
HEY, MISTER! WAIT!
AIIEEE!!

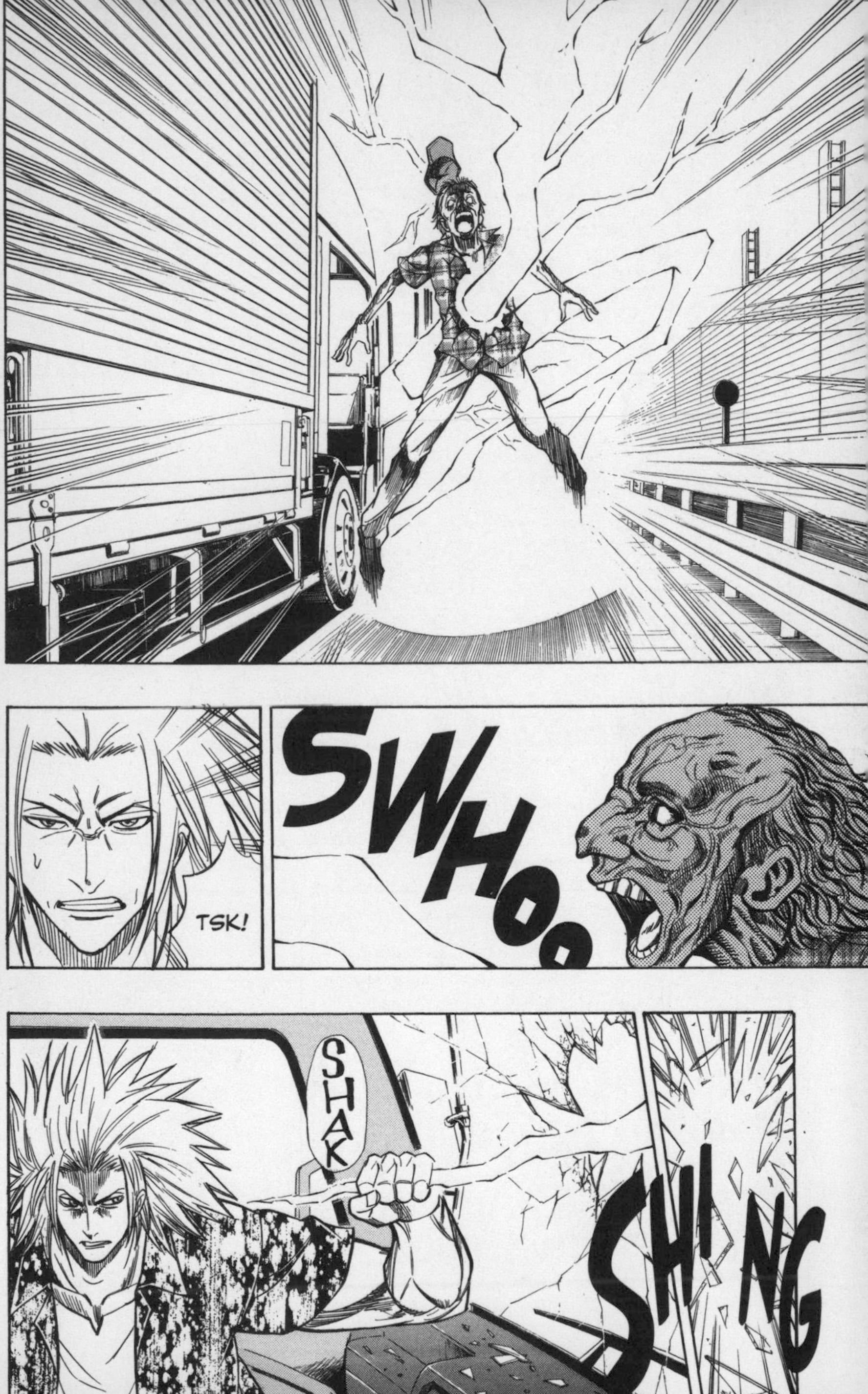
SWHOO
TSK!
SHING
SHAK

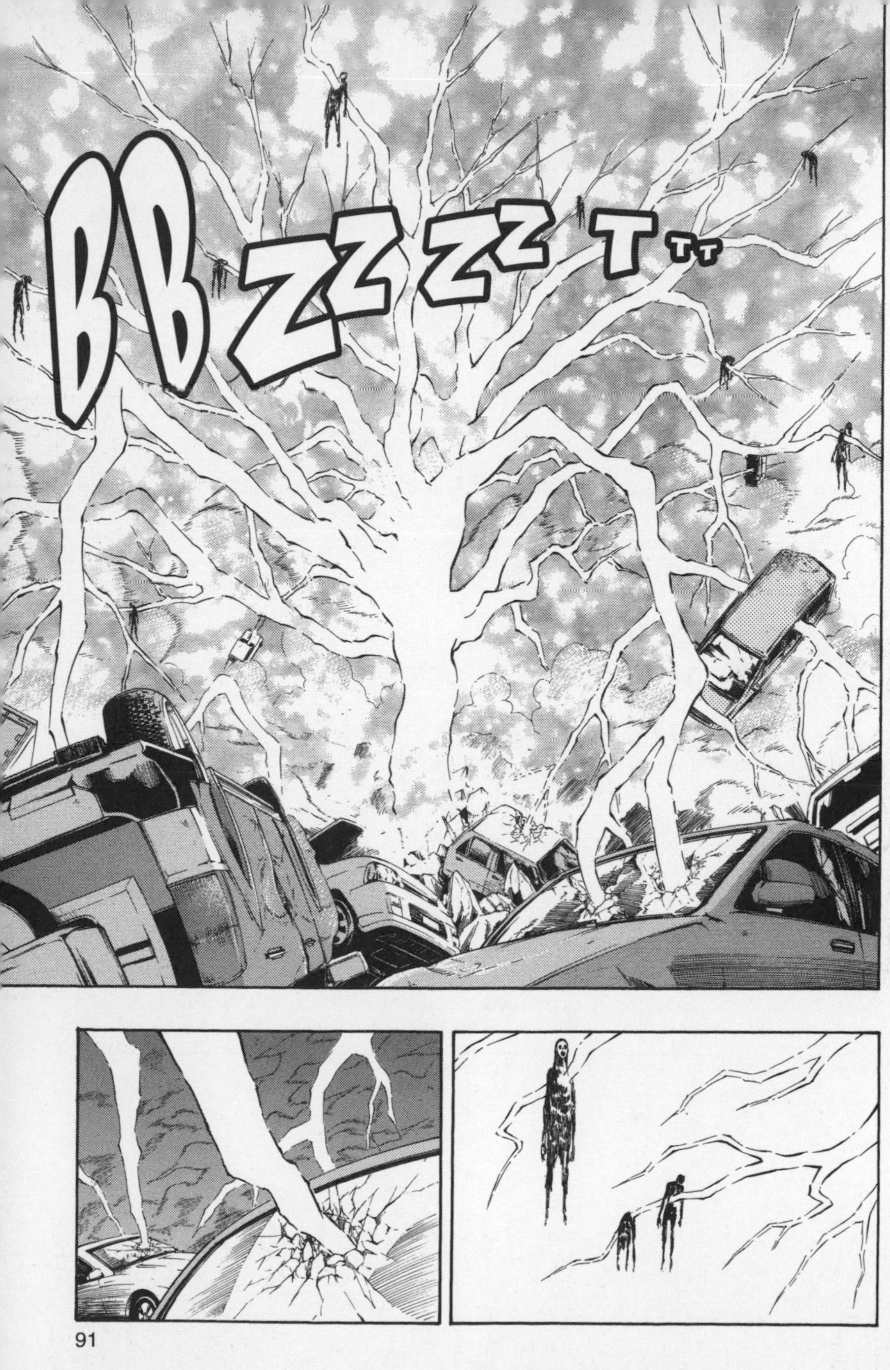
BBZZZZTTT

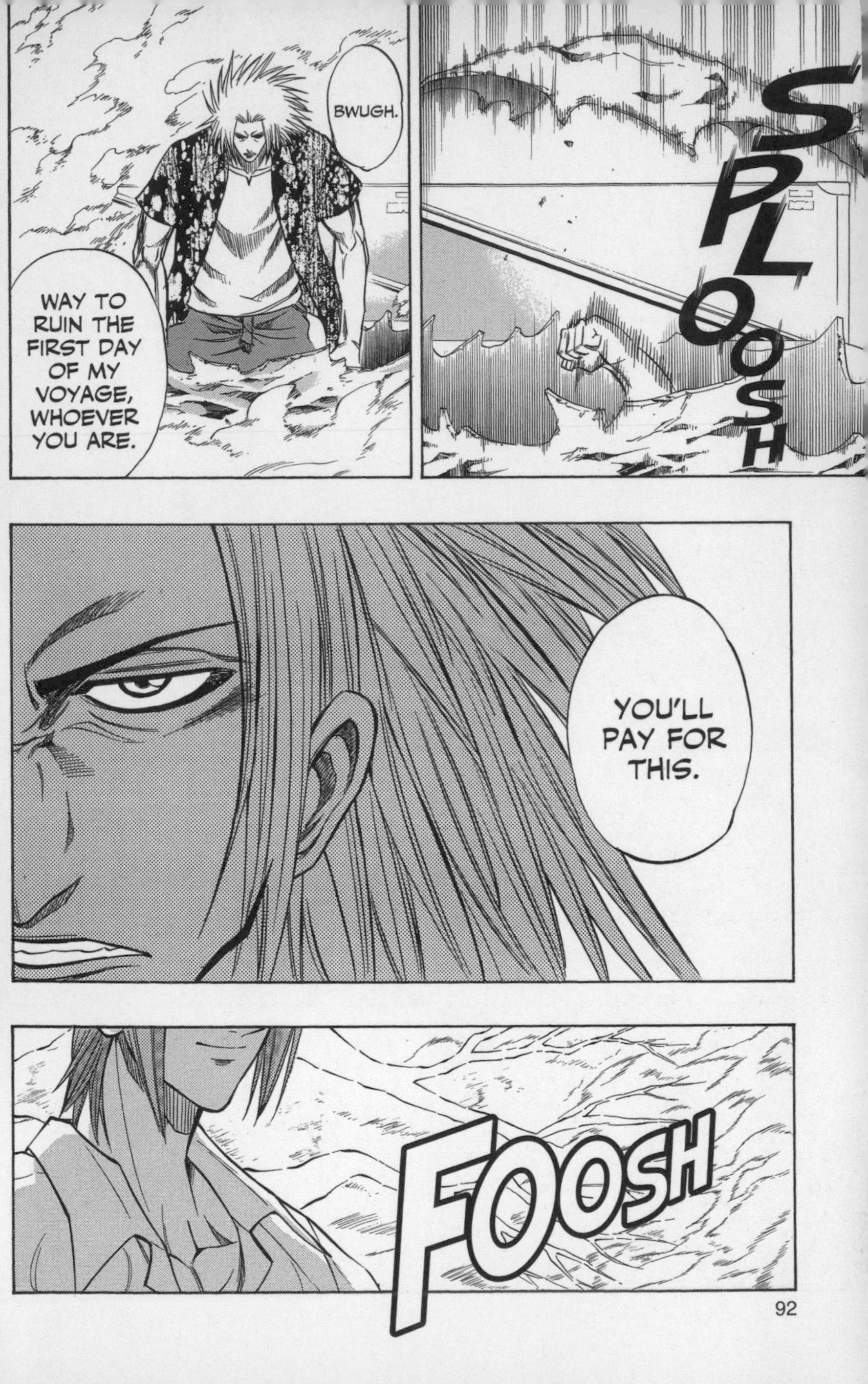
SPLOOSH
BWUGH.
WAY TO RUIN THE FIRST DAY OF MY VOYAGE, WHOEVER YOU ARE.
YOU'LL PAY FOR THIS.
FOOSH

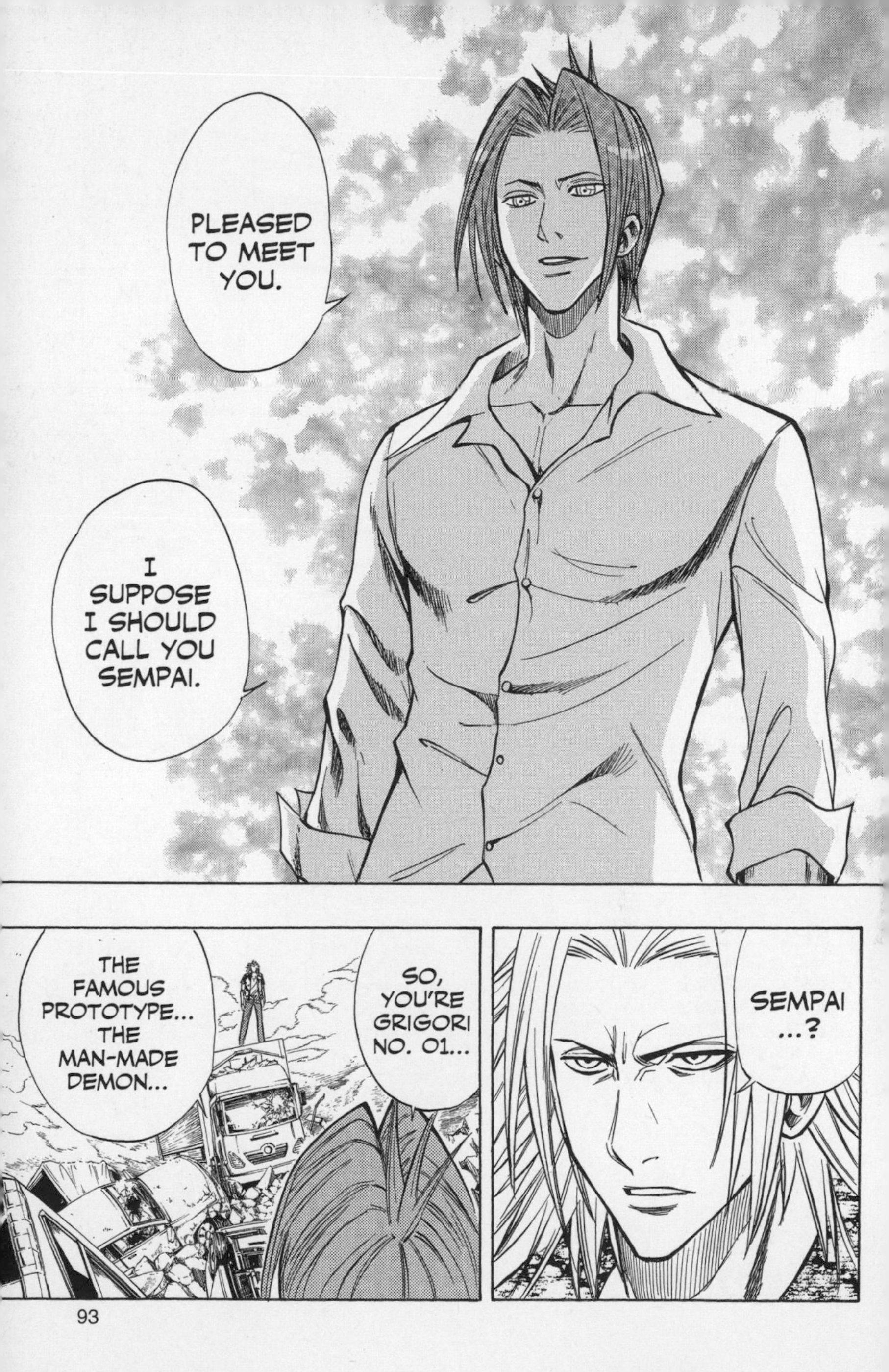
PLEASED TO MEET YOU.
I SUPPOSE I SHOULD CALL YOU SEMPAI.
SEMPAI ...?
SO, YOU'RE GRIGORI NO. 01...
THE FAMOUS PROTOTYPE... THE MAN-MADE DEMON...

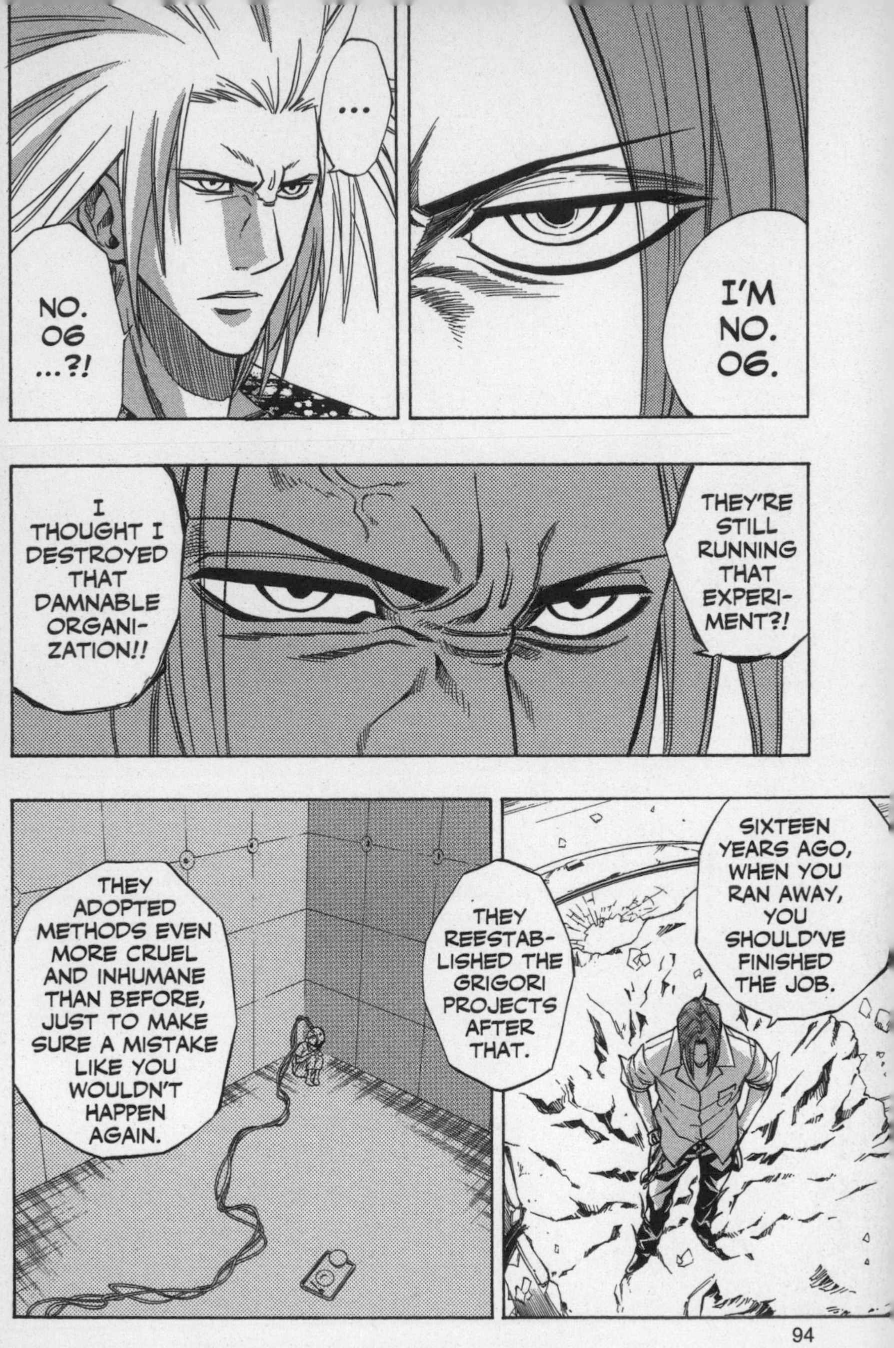
I'M NO. 06.
...
NO. 06 ...?!
THEY'RE STILL RUNNING THAT EXPERIMENT?!
I THOUGHT I DESTROYED THAT DAMNABLE ORGANIZATION!!
SIXTEEN YEARS AGO, WHEN YOU RAN AWAY, YOU SHOULD'VE FINISHED THE JOB.
THEY REESTABLISHED THE GRIGORI PROJECTS AFTER THAT.
THEY ADOPTED METHODS EVEN MORE CRUEL AND INHUMANE THAN BEFORE, JUST TO MAKE SURE A MISTAKE LIKE YOU WOULDN'T HAPPEN AGAIN.

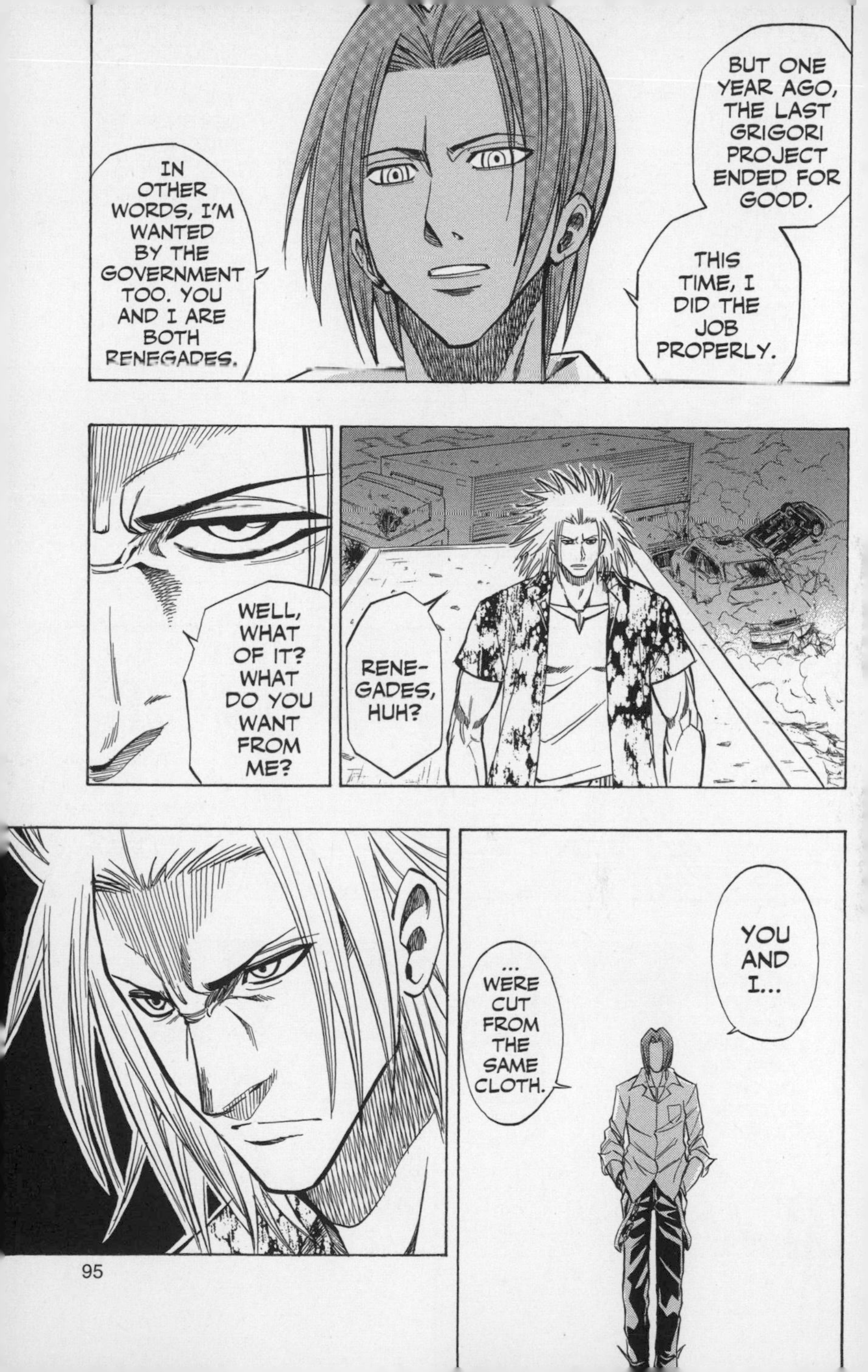
BUT ONE YEAR AGO, THE LAST GRIGORI PROJECT ENDED FOR GOOD.
THIS TIME, I DID THE JOB PROPERLY.
IN OTHER WORDS, I'M WANTED BY THE GOVERNMENT TOO. YOU AND I ARE BOTH RENEGADES.
RENE-GADES, HUH?
WELL, WHAT OF IT? WHAT DO YOU WANT FROM ME?
YOU AND I...
...WERE CUT FROM THE SAME CLOTH.

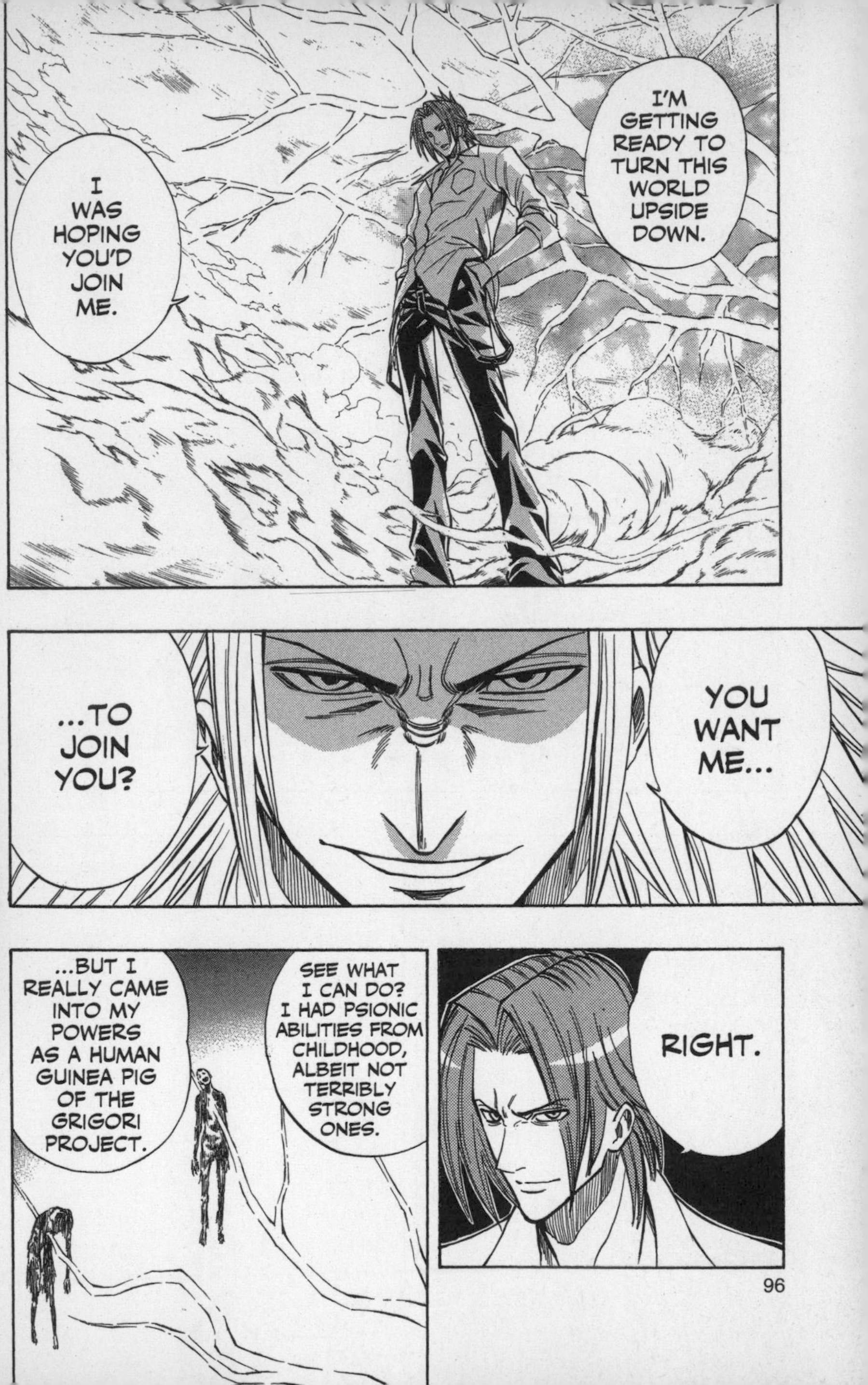

I'M GETTING READY TO TURN THIS WORLD UPSIDE DOWN.
I WAS HOPING YOU'D JOIN ME.
YOU WANT ME...
...TO JOIN YOU?
RIGHT.
SEE WHAT I CAN DO? I HAD PSIONIC ABILITIES FROM CHILDHOOD, ALBEIT NOT TERRIBLY STRONG ONES.
...BUT I REALLY CAME INTO MY POWERS AS A HUMAN GUINEA PIG OF THE GRIGORI PROJECT.

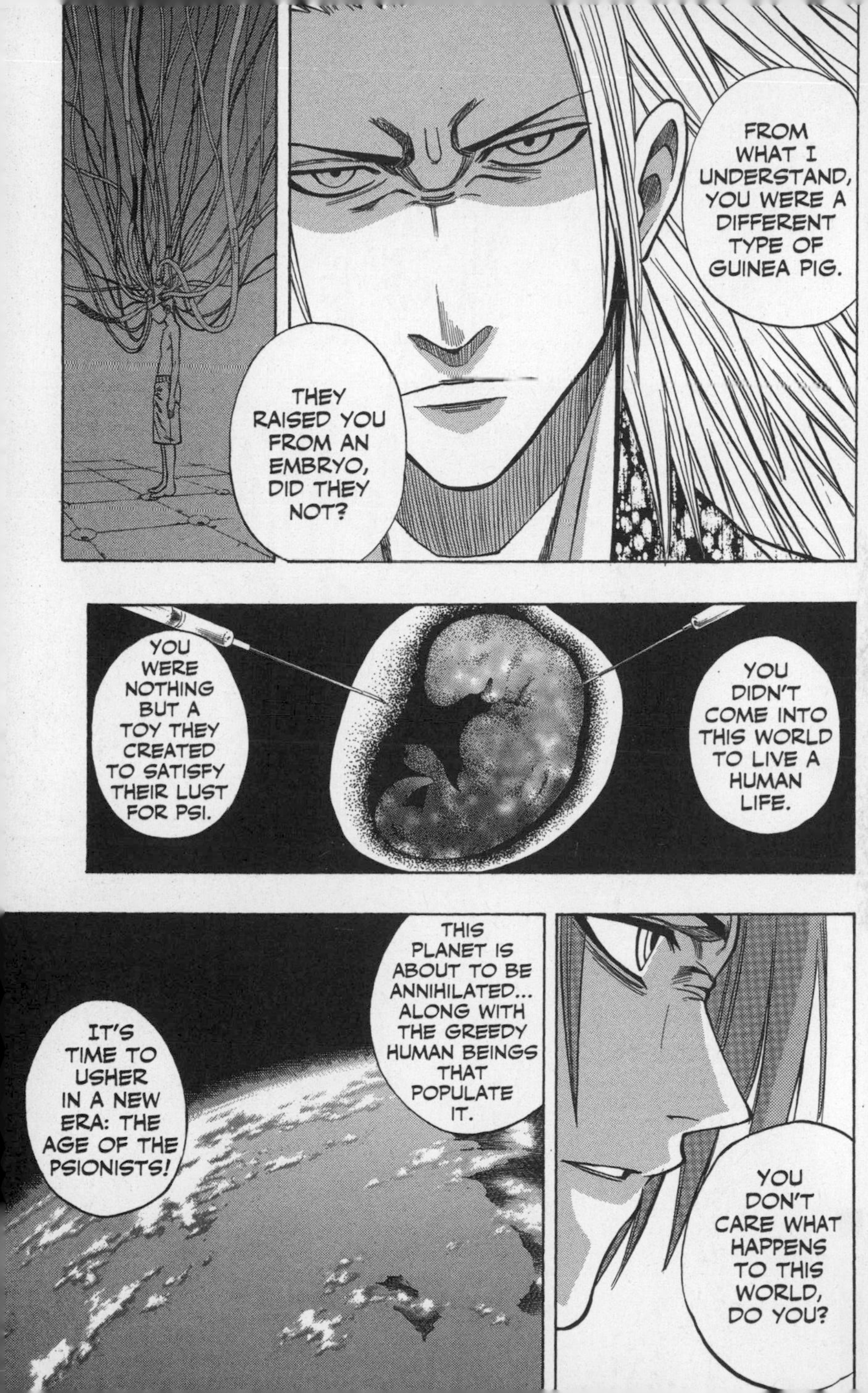
FROM WHAT I UNDERSTAND, YOU WERE A DIFFERENT TYPE OF GUINEA PIG.
THEY RAISED YOU FROM AN EMBRYO, DID THEY NOT?
YOU DIDN'T COME INTO THIS WORLD TO LIVE A HUMAN LIFE.
YOU WERE NOTHING BUT A TOY THEY CREATED TO SATISFY THEIR LUST FOR PSI.
YOU DON'T CARE WHAT HAPPENS TO THIS WORLD, DO YOU?
THIS PLANET IS ABOUT TO BE ANNIHILATED... ALONG WITH THE GREEDY HUMAN BEINGS THAT POPULATE IT.
IT'S TIME TO USHER IN A NEW ERA: THE AGE OF THE PSIONISTS!

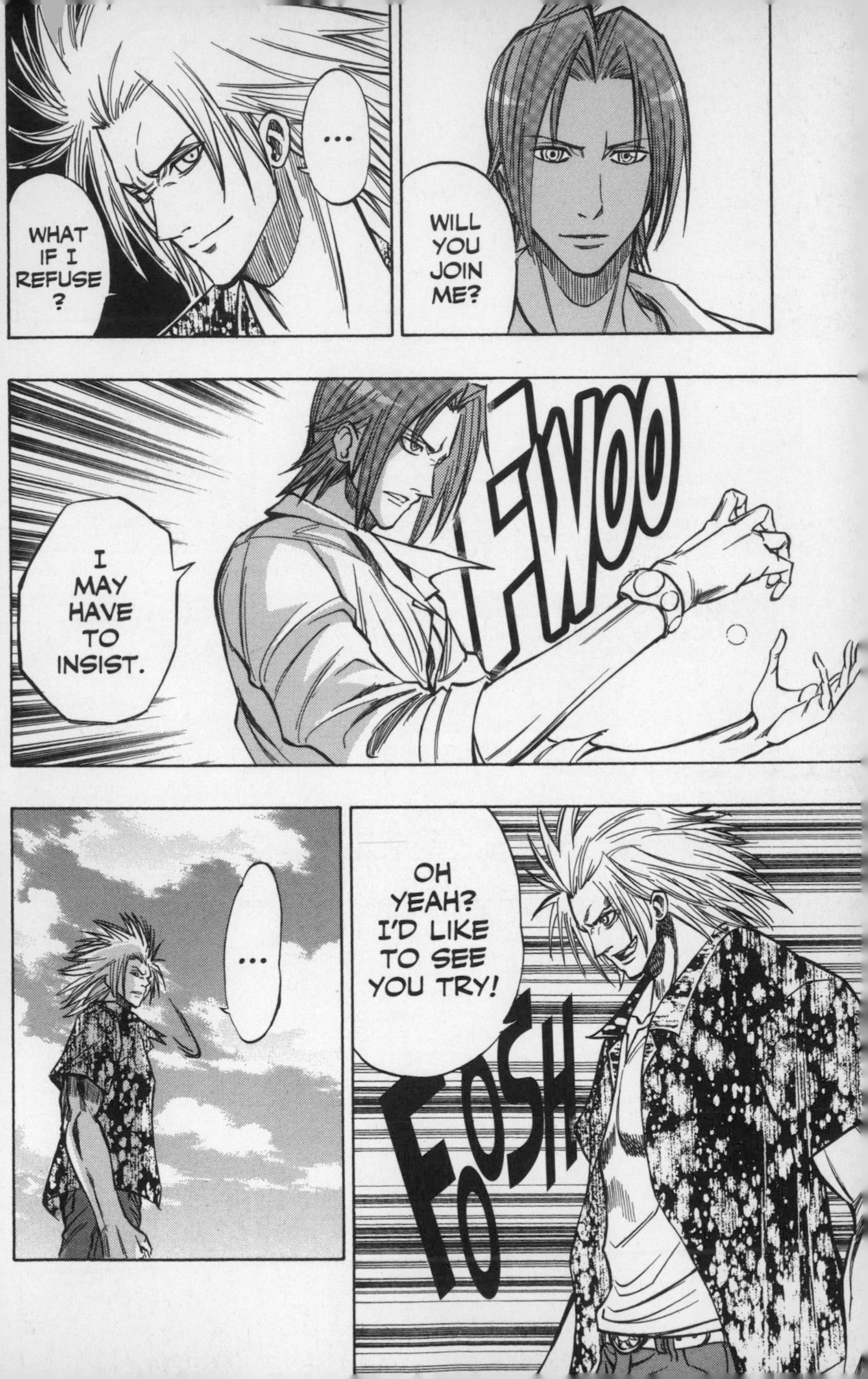
WILL YOU JOIN ME?
...
WHAT IF I REFUSE?
FWOO
I MAY HAVE TO INSIST.
OH YEAH? I'D LIKE TO SEE YOU TRY!
FOOSH
...

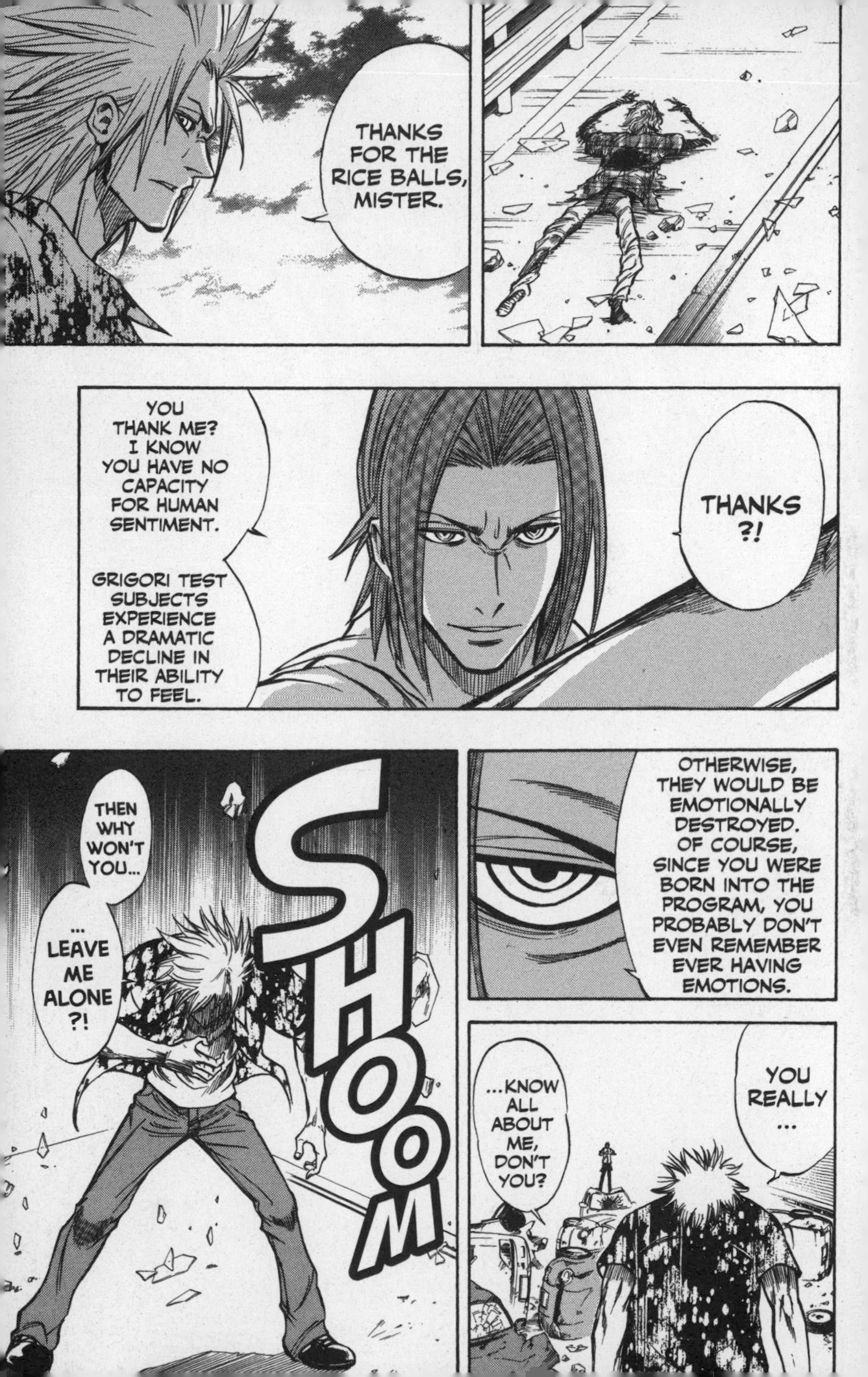
THANKS FOR THE RICE BALLS, MISTER.
THANKS ?!
YOU THANK ME? I KNOW YOU HAVE NO CAPACITY FOR HUMAN SENTIMENT.
GRIGORI TEST SUBJECTS EXPERIENCE A DRAMATIC DECLINE IN THEIR ABILITY TO FEEL.
OTHERWISE, THEY WOULD BE EMOTIONALLY DESTROYED. OF COURSE, SINCE YOU WERE BORN INTO THE PROGRAM, YOU PROBABLY DON'T EVEN REMEMBER EVER HAVING EMOTIONS.
YOU REALLY ...
...KNOW ALL ABOUT ME, DON'T YOU?
THEN WHY WON'T YOU...
... LEAVE ME ALONE ?!
SHOOOM

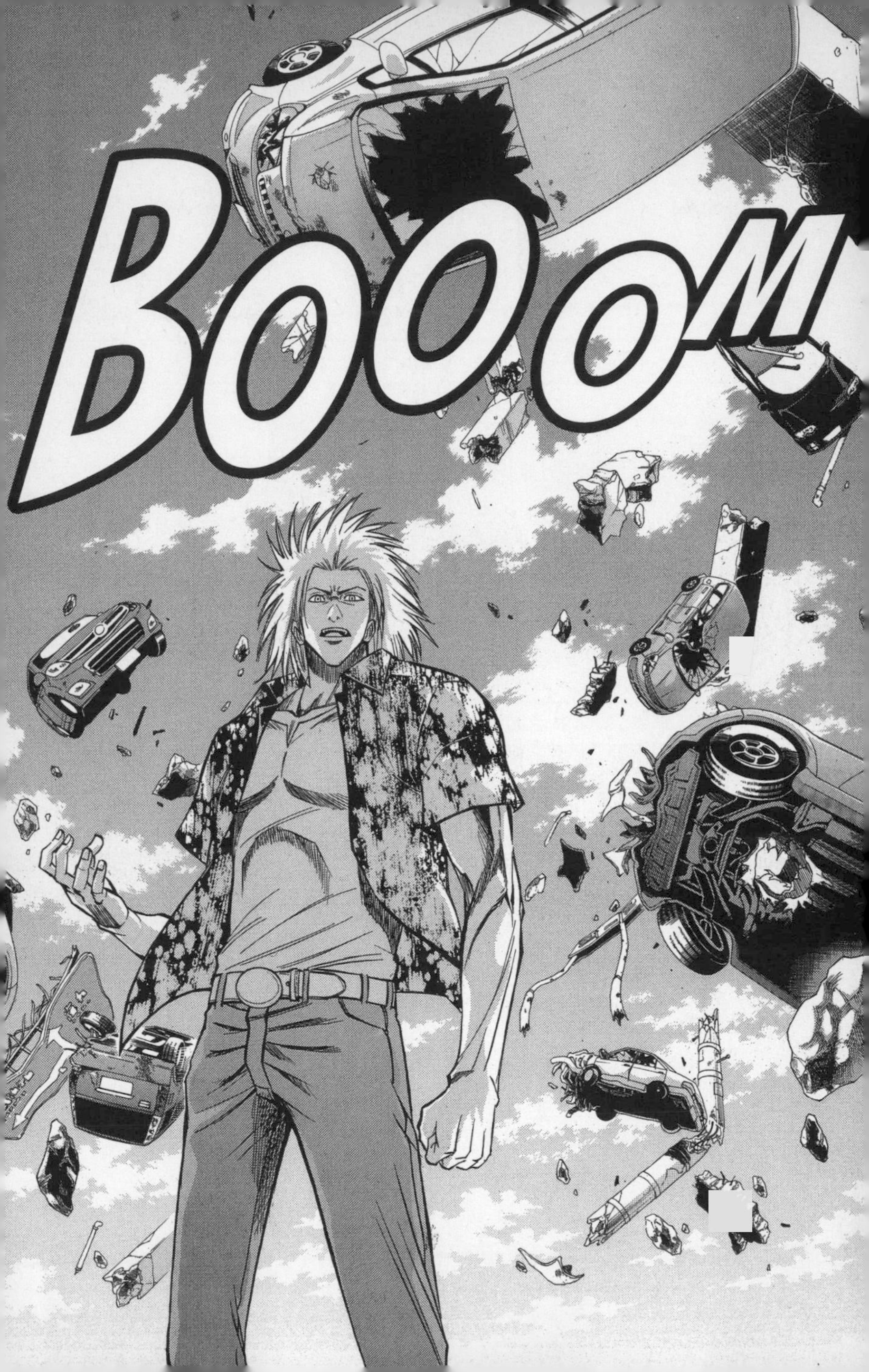
BOOOM

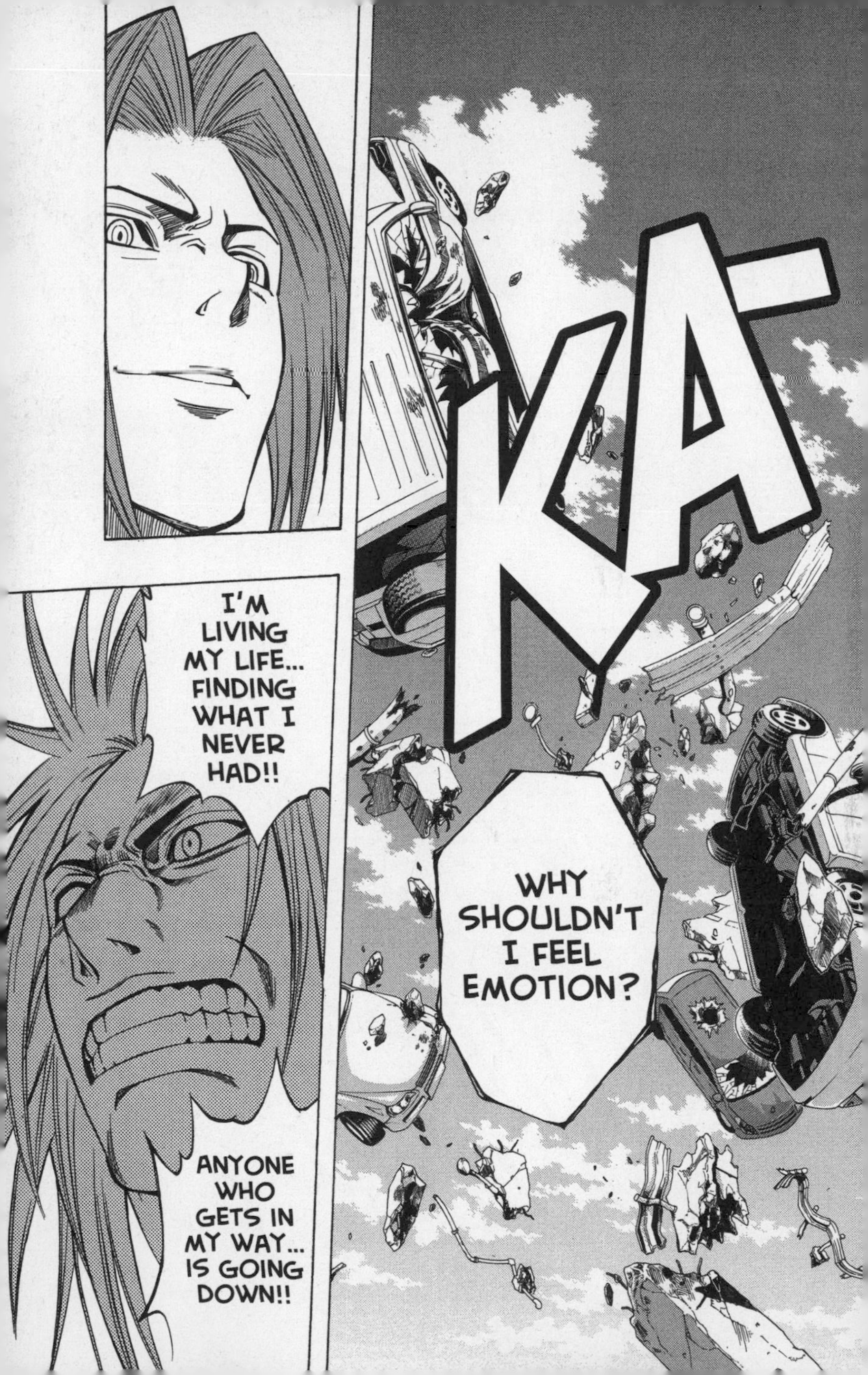
KA
WHY SHOULDN'T I FEEL EMOTION?
I'M LIVING MY LIFE... FINDING WHAT I NEVER HAD!!
ANYONE WHO GETS IN MY WAY... IS GOING DOWN!!

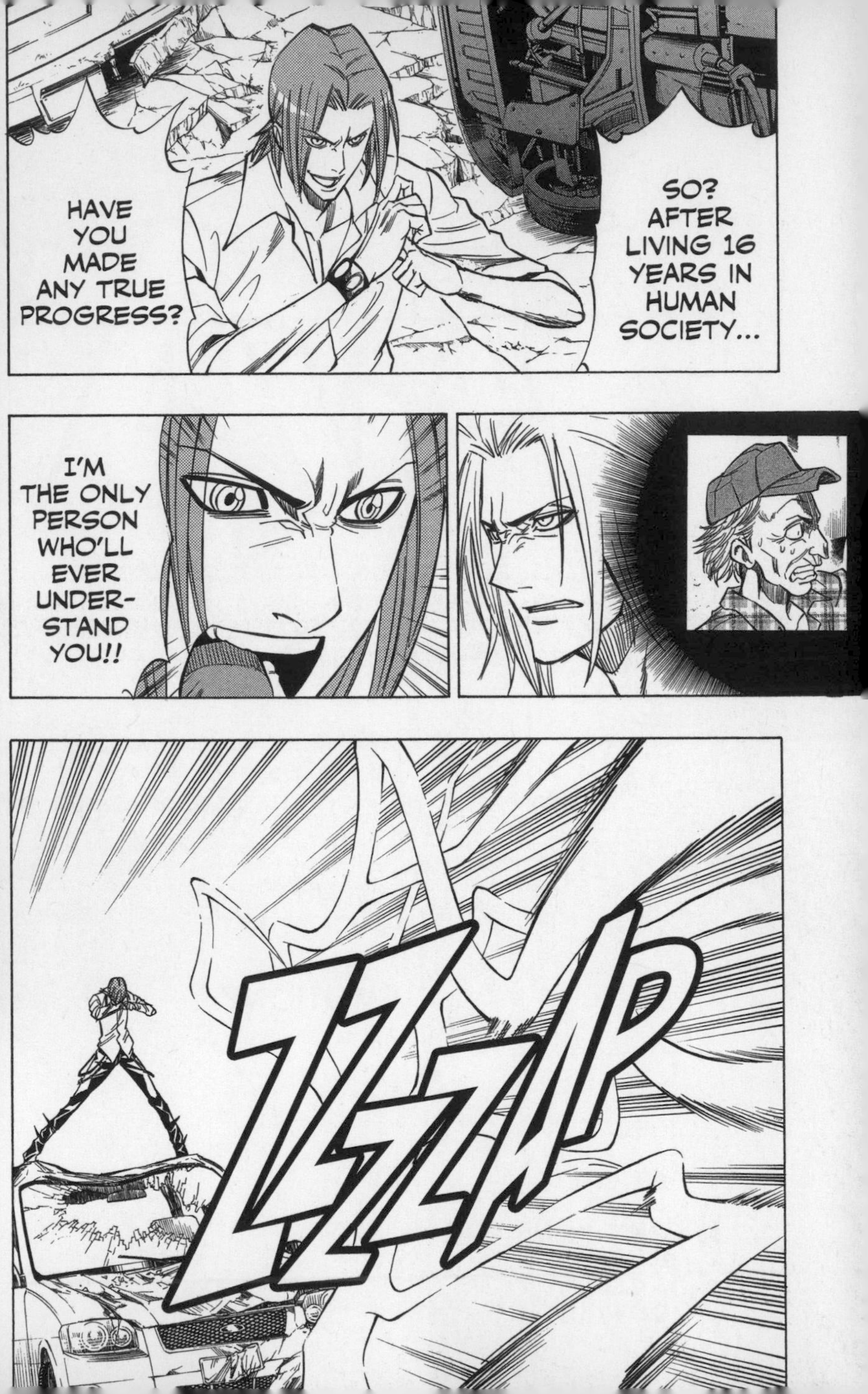
SO? AFTER LIVING 16 YEARS IN HUMAN SOCIETY...
HAVE YOU MADE ANY TRUE PROGRESS?
I'M THE ONLY PERSON WHO'LL EVER UNDER-STAND YOU!!
ZZZAP

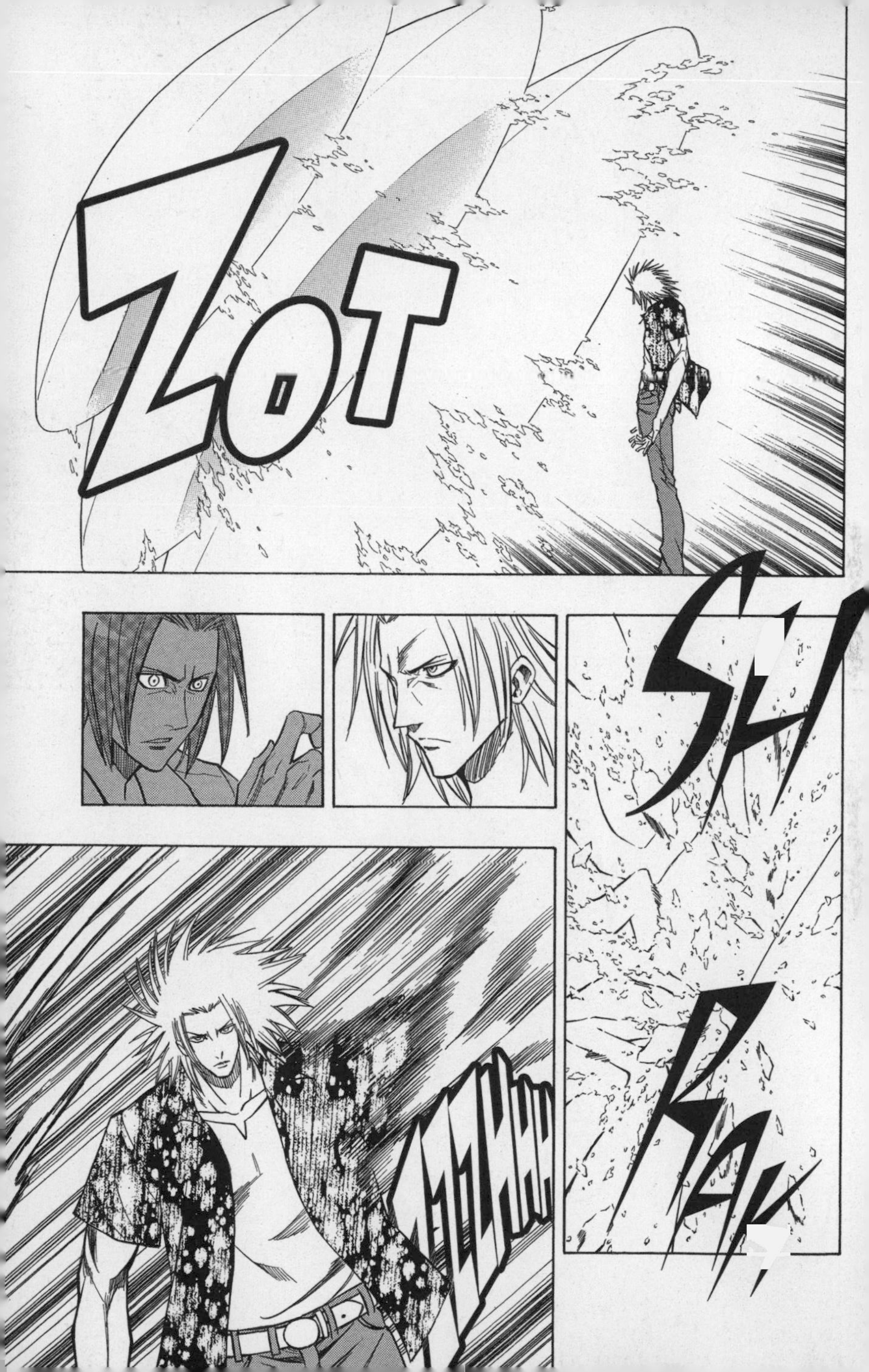
ZOT
SHRAK

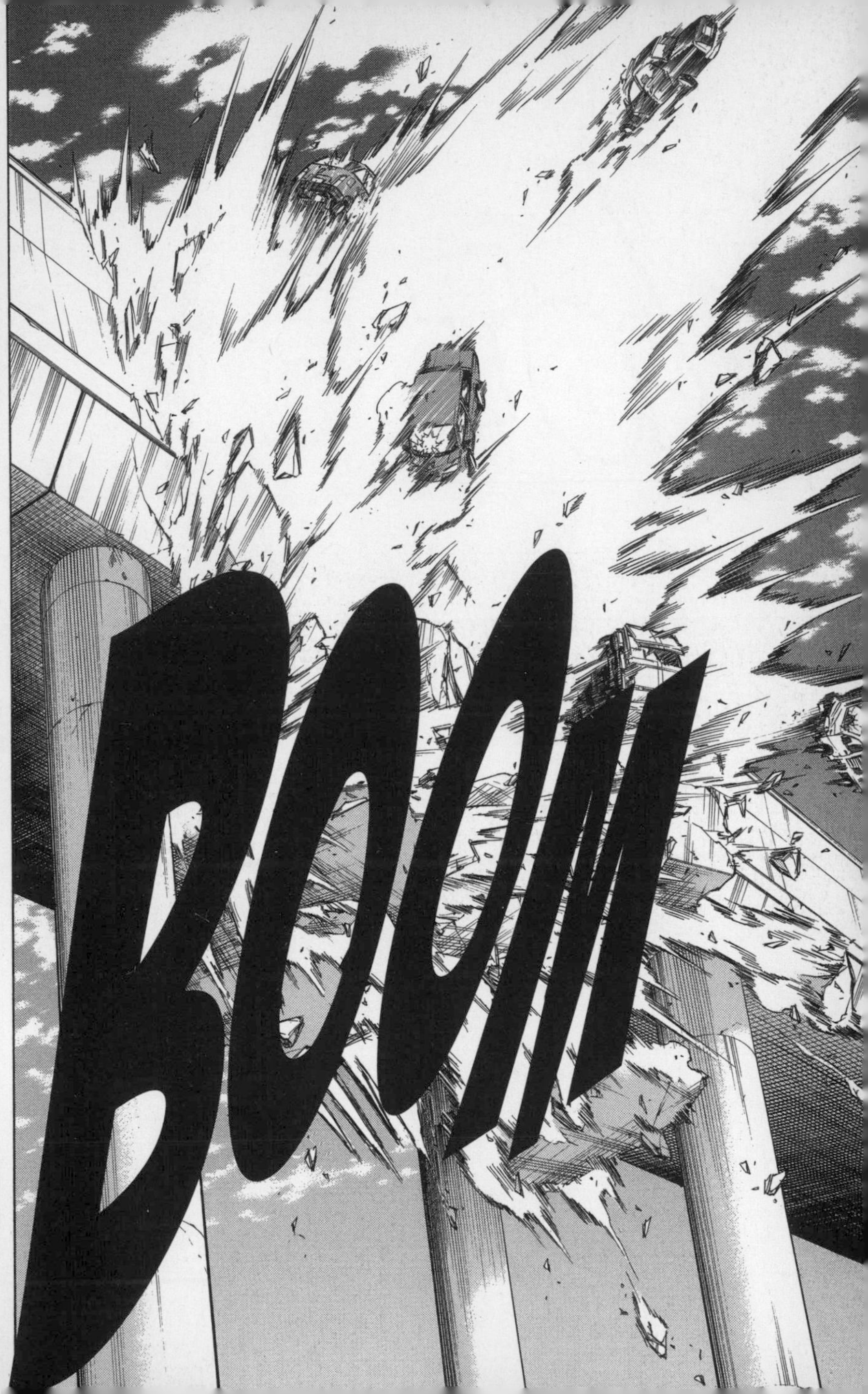
BOOM

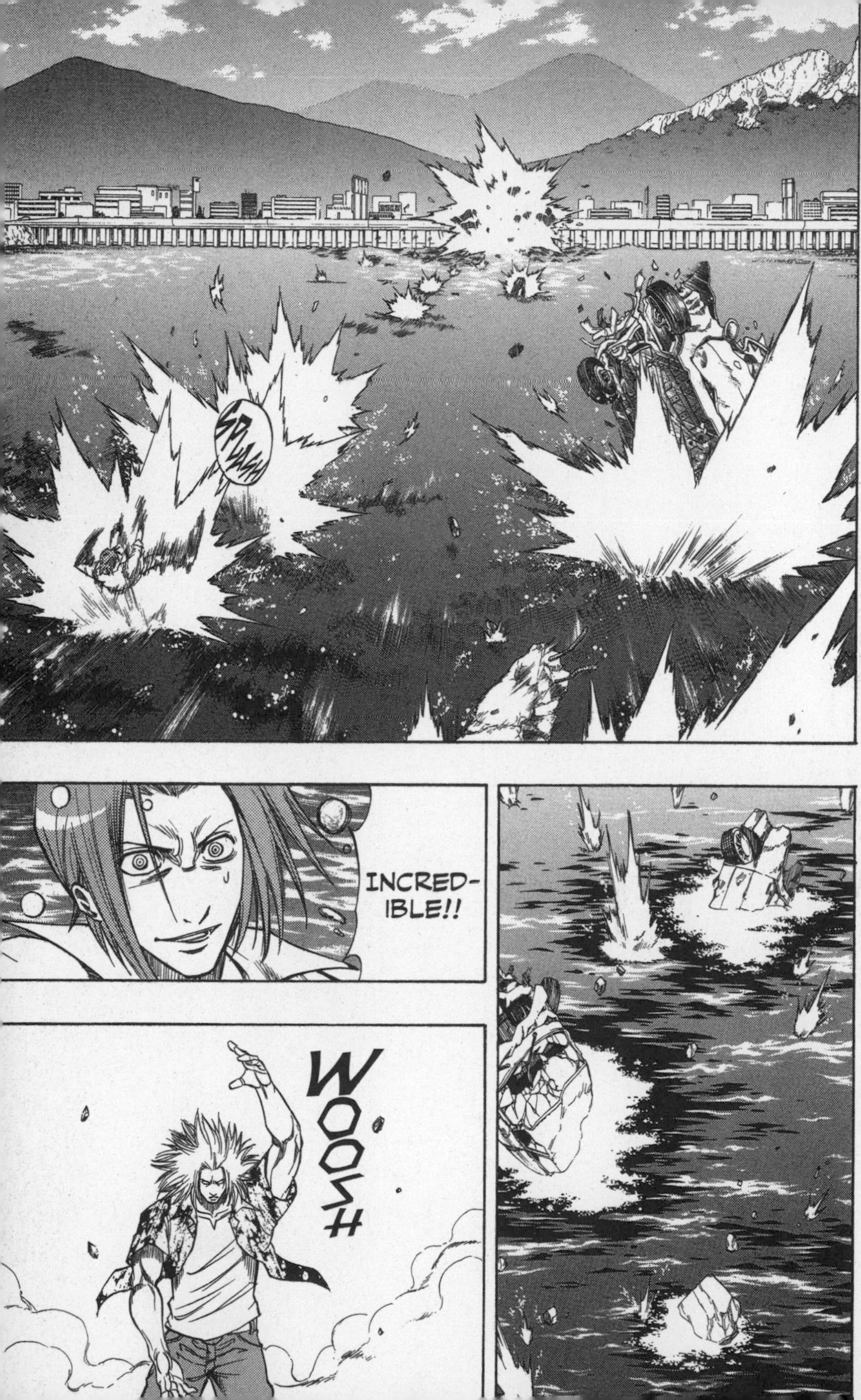
SPLASH
INCRED-
IBLE!!
WOOSH

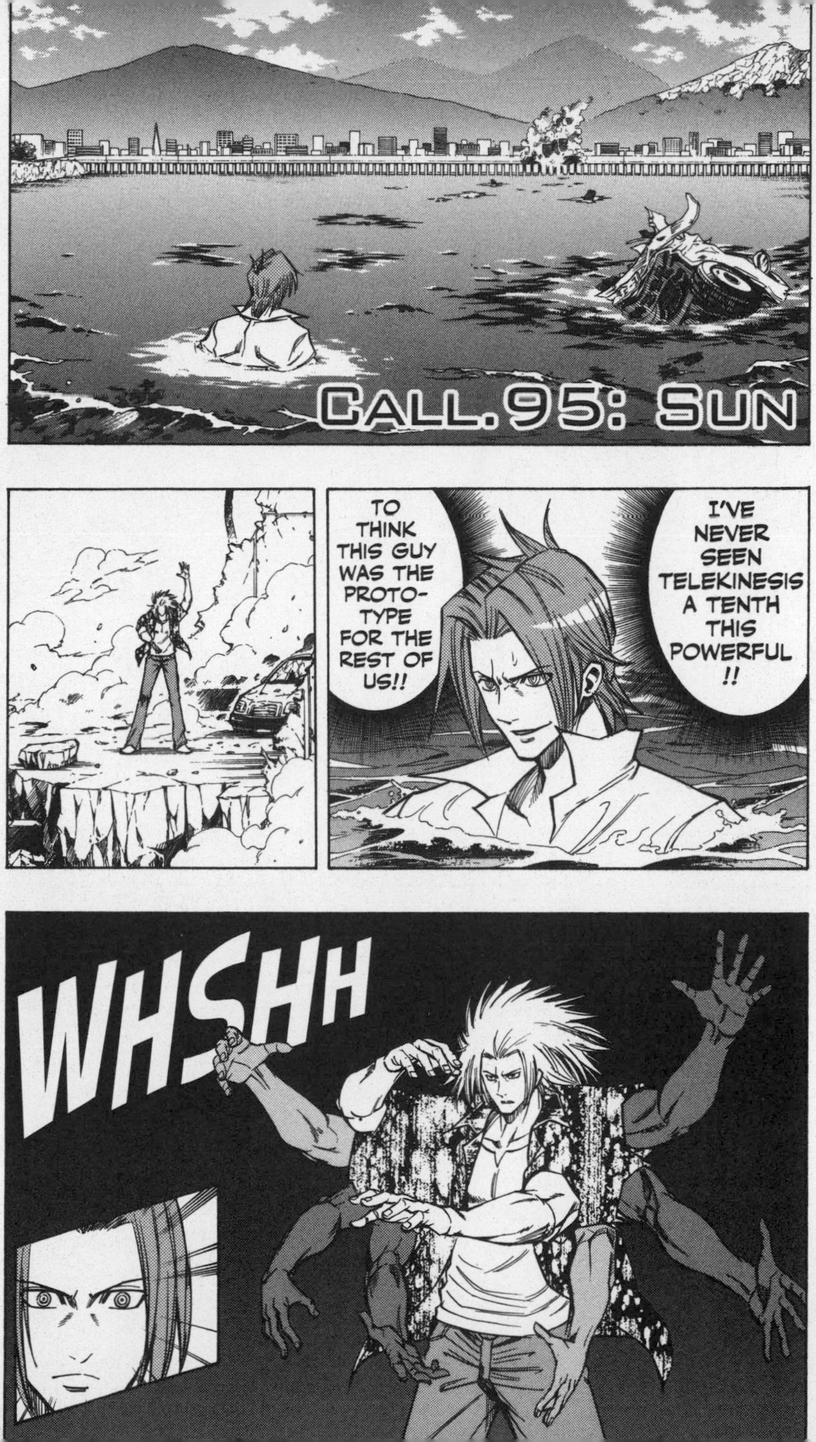
CALL.95: SUN
I'VE NEVER SEEN TELEKINESIS A TENTH THIS POWERFUL!!
TO THINK THIS GUY WAS THE PROTO-TYPE FOR THE REST OF US!!
WHSHH

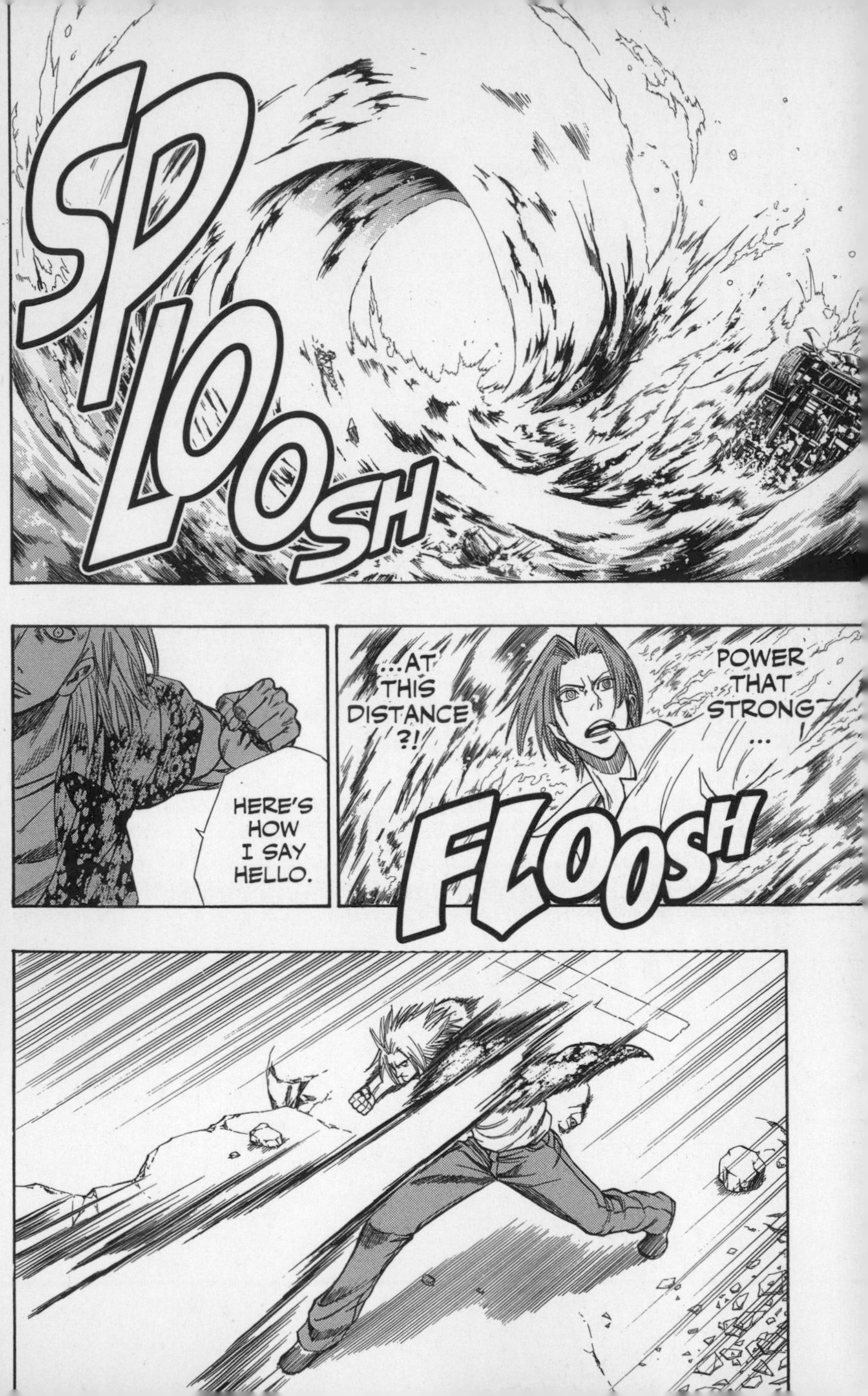
SPLOOSH
POWER THAT STRONG...
...AT THIS DISTANCE?!
FLOOSH
HERE'S HOW I SAY HELLO.

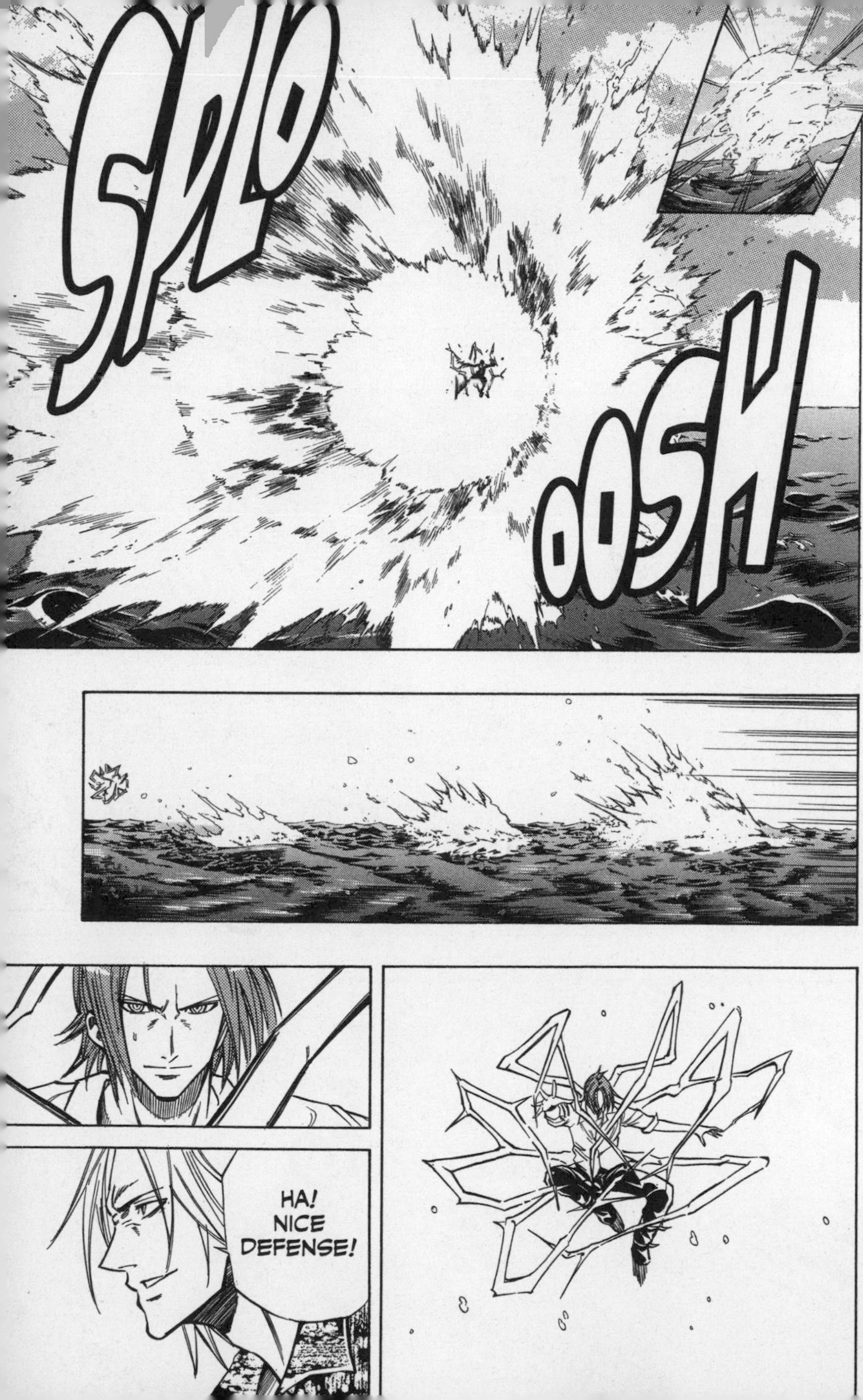
SPLO
OOSH
HA! NICE DEFENSE!

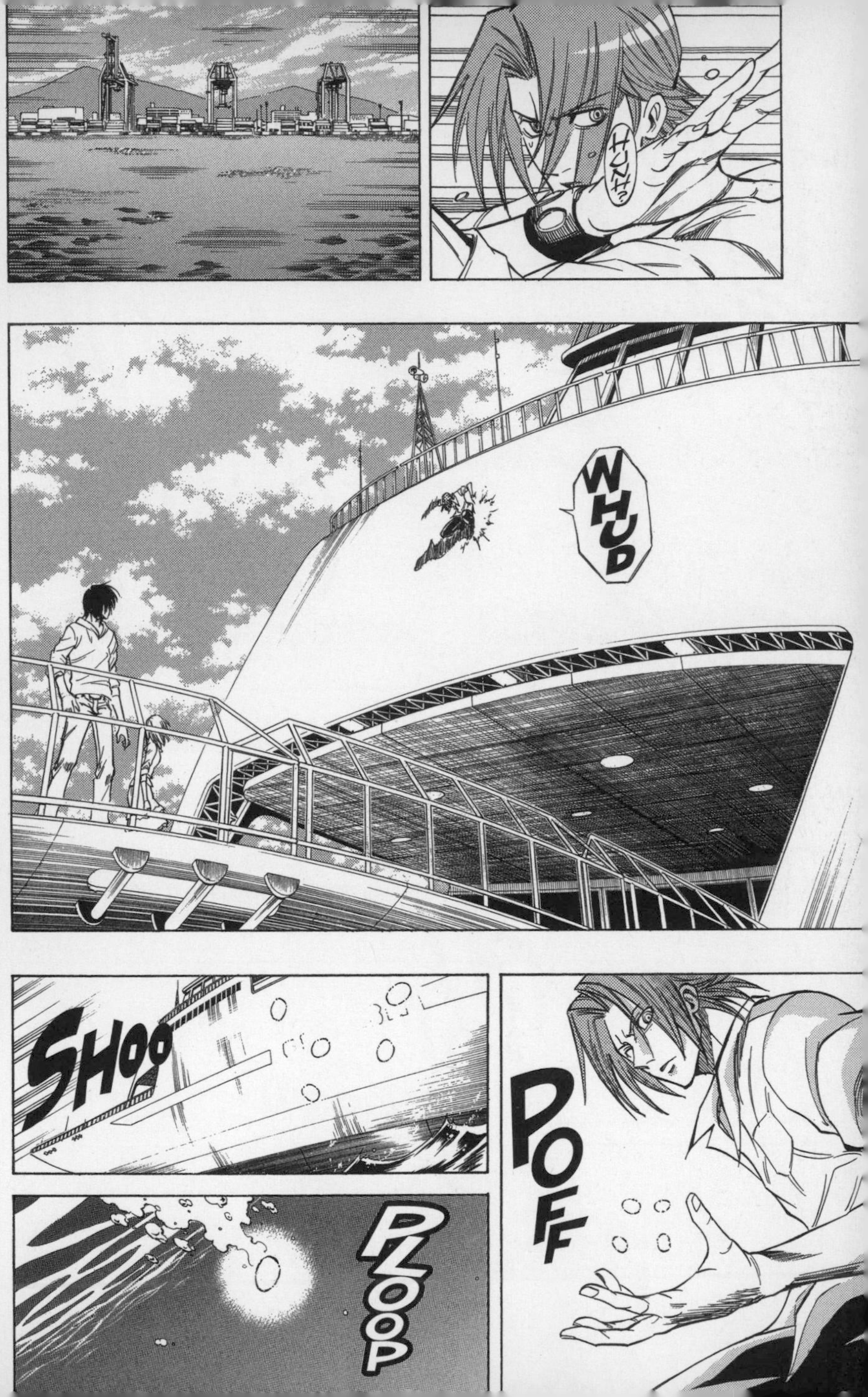
HUNH?
WHUD
POFF
SHOO
PLOOP

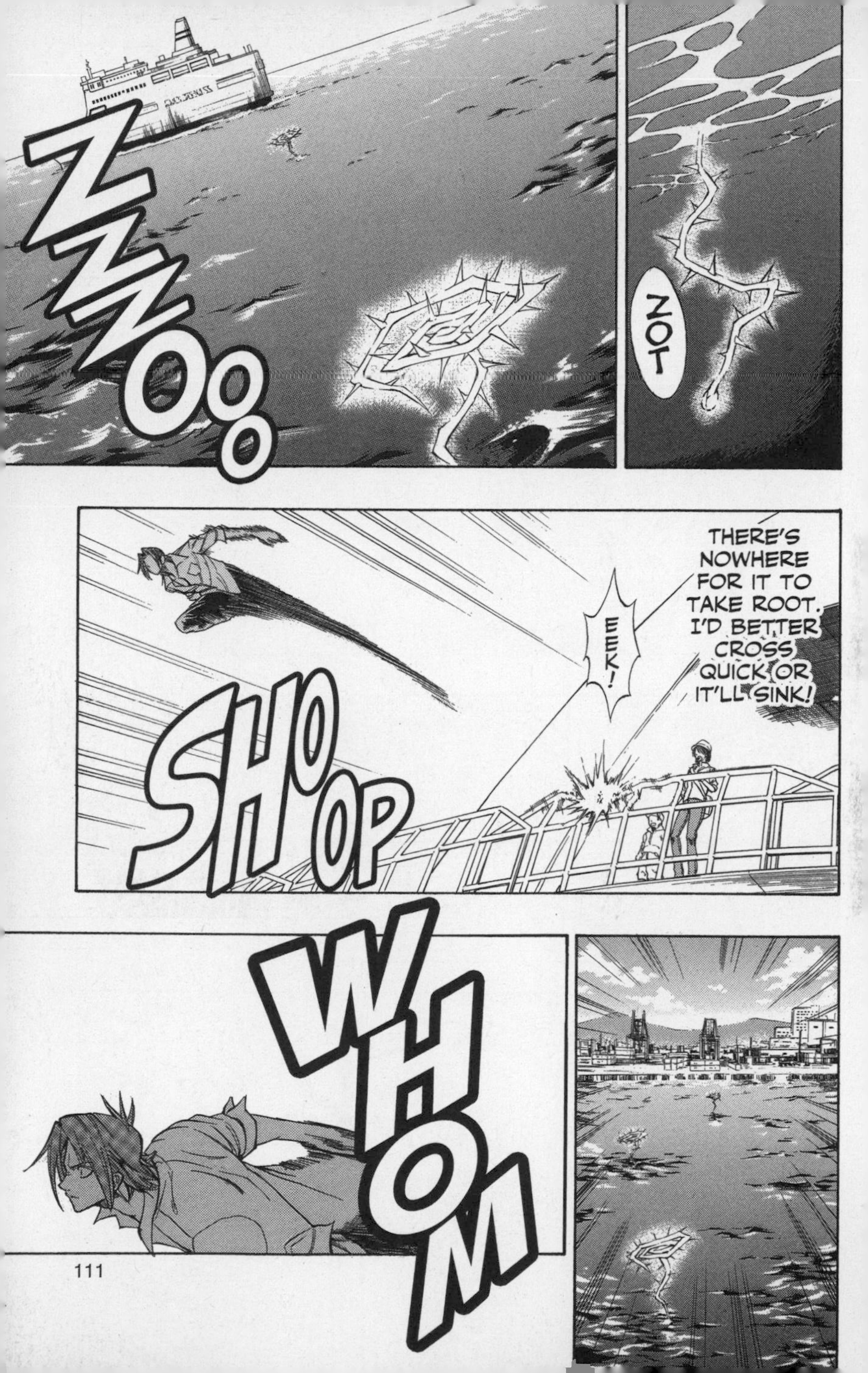
ZOT
ZZZOOO
THERE'S NOWHERE FOR IT TO TAKE ROOT. I'D BETTER CROSS QUICK OR IT'LL SINK!
EEK!
SHOOP
WHOM

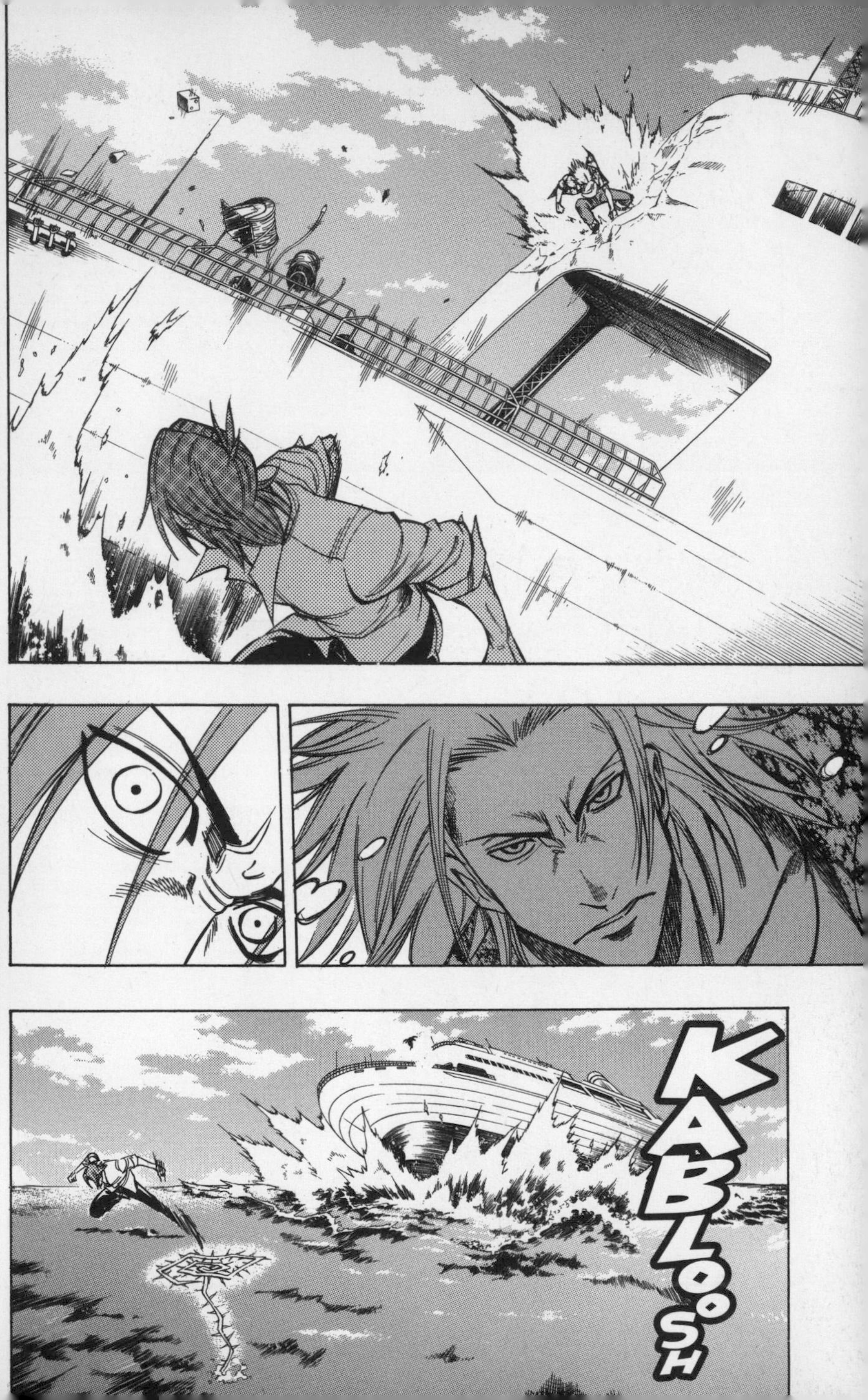
KABLOOSH

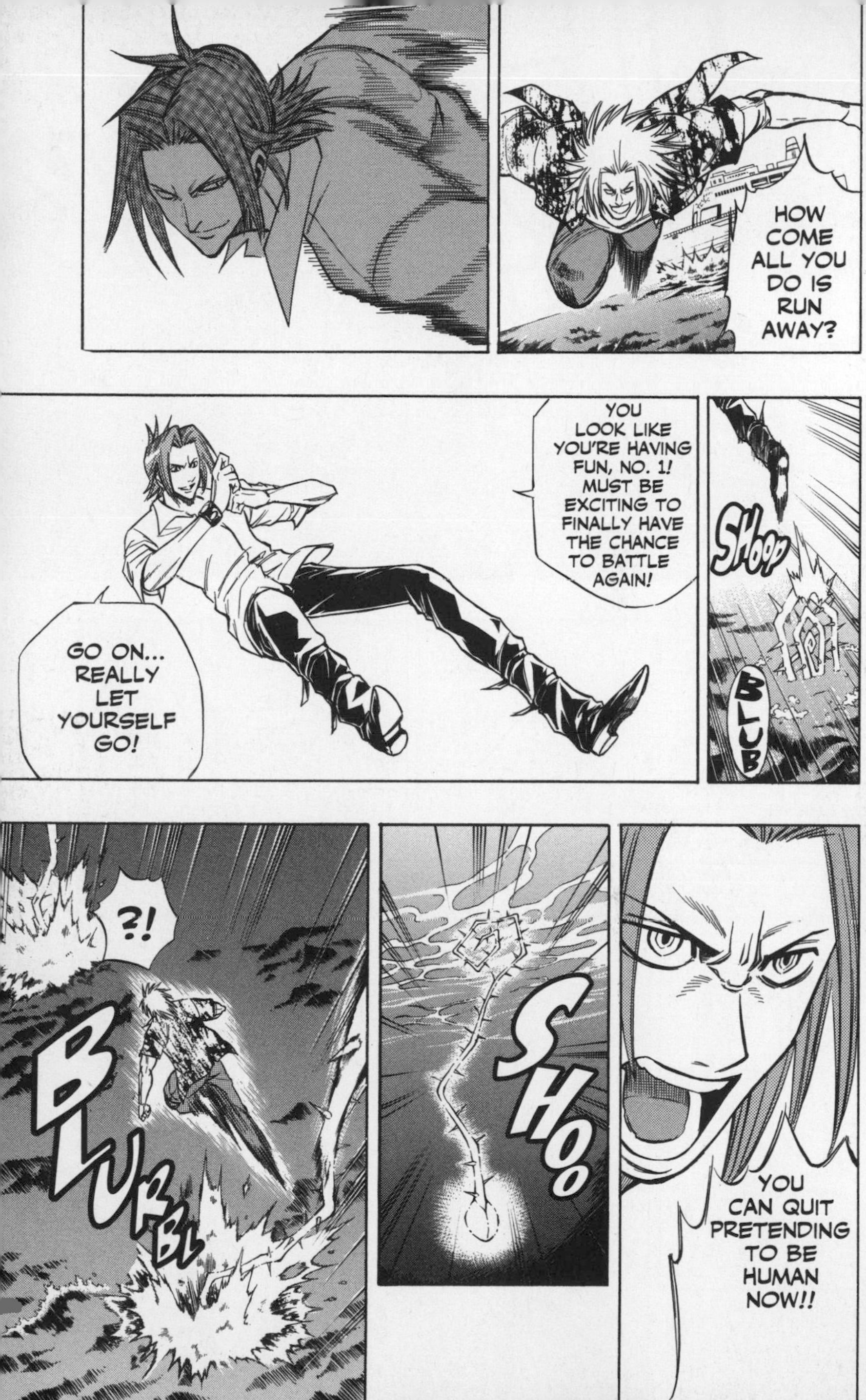
HOW COME ALL YOU DO IS RUN AWAY?
SHOOP
BLUB
YOU LOOK LIKE YOU'RE HAVING FUN, NO. 1! MUST BE EXCITING TO FINALLY HAVE THE CHANCE TO BATTLE AGAIN!
GO ON... REALLY LET YOURSELF GO!
YOU CAN QUIT PRETENDING TO BE HUMAN NOW!!
SHOO
?!
BLUBBL

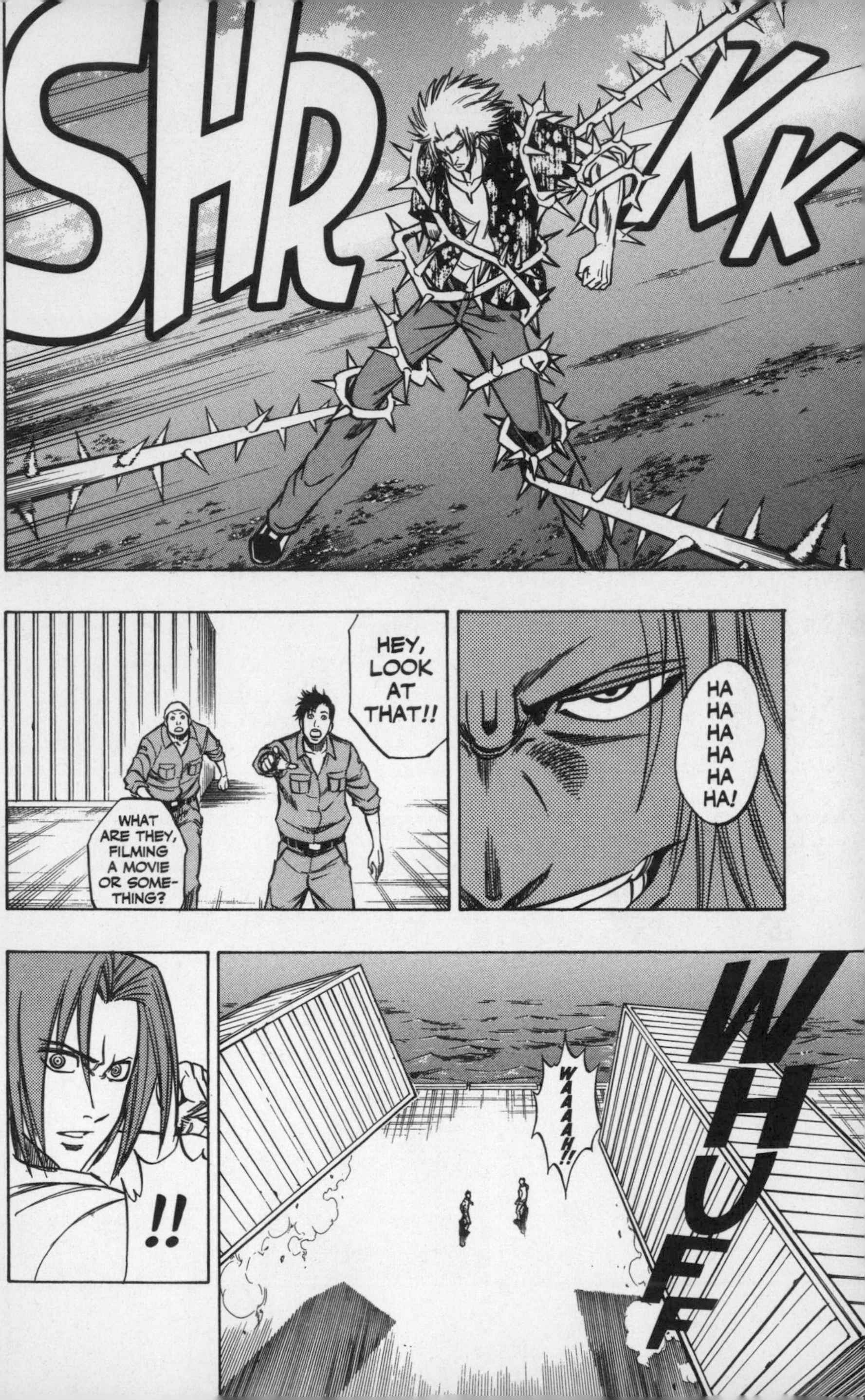
SHRKK
HA HA HA HA HA HA!
HEY, LOOK AT THAT!!
WHAT ARE THEY, FILMING A MOVIE OR SOME-THING?
WHUFF
WAAAAAH!!
!!

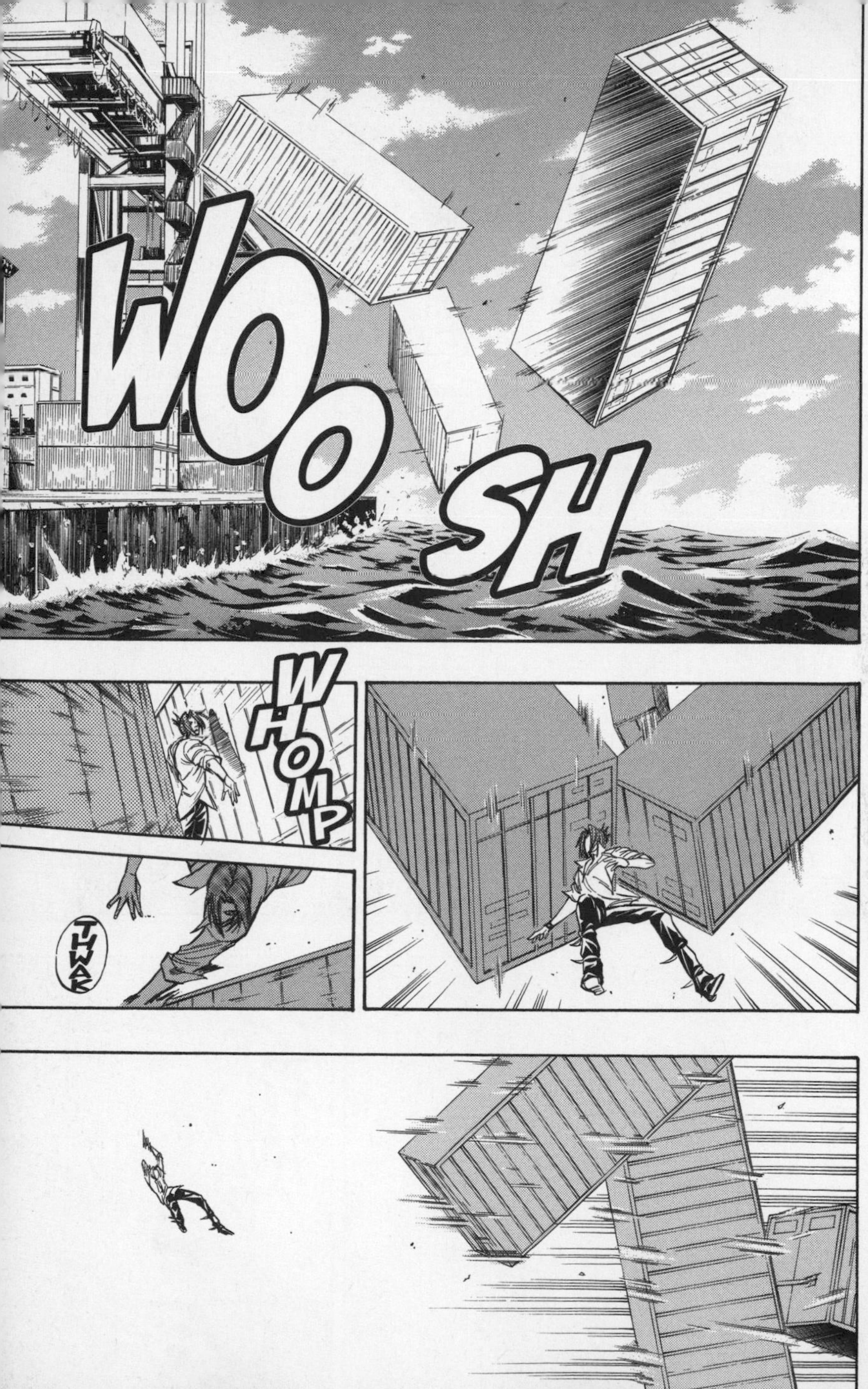
WOOSH
WHOMP
THWAK

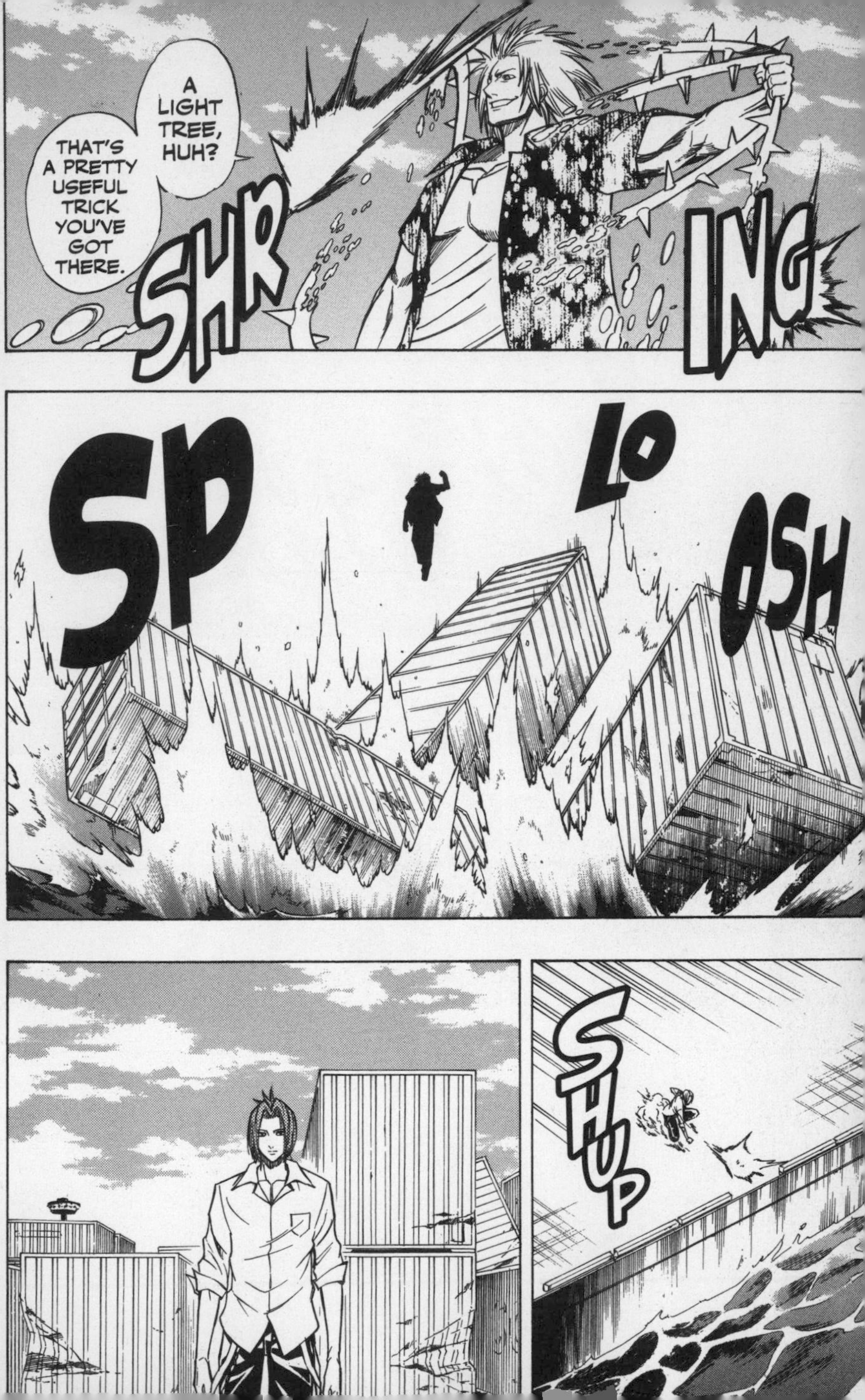
A LIGHT TREE, HUH?
THAT'S A PRETTY USEFUL TRICK YOU'VE GOT THERE.
SHRING
SPLOOSH
SHUP

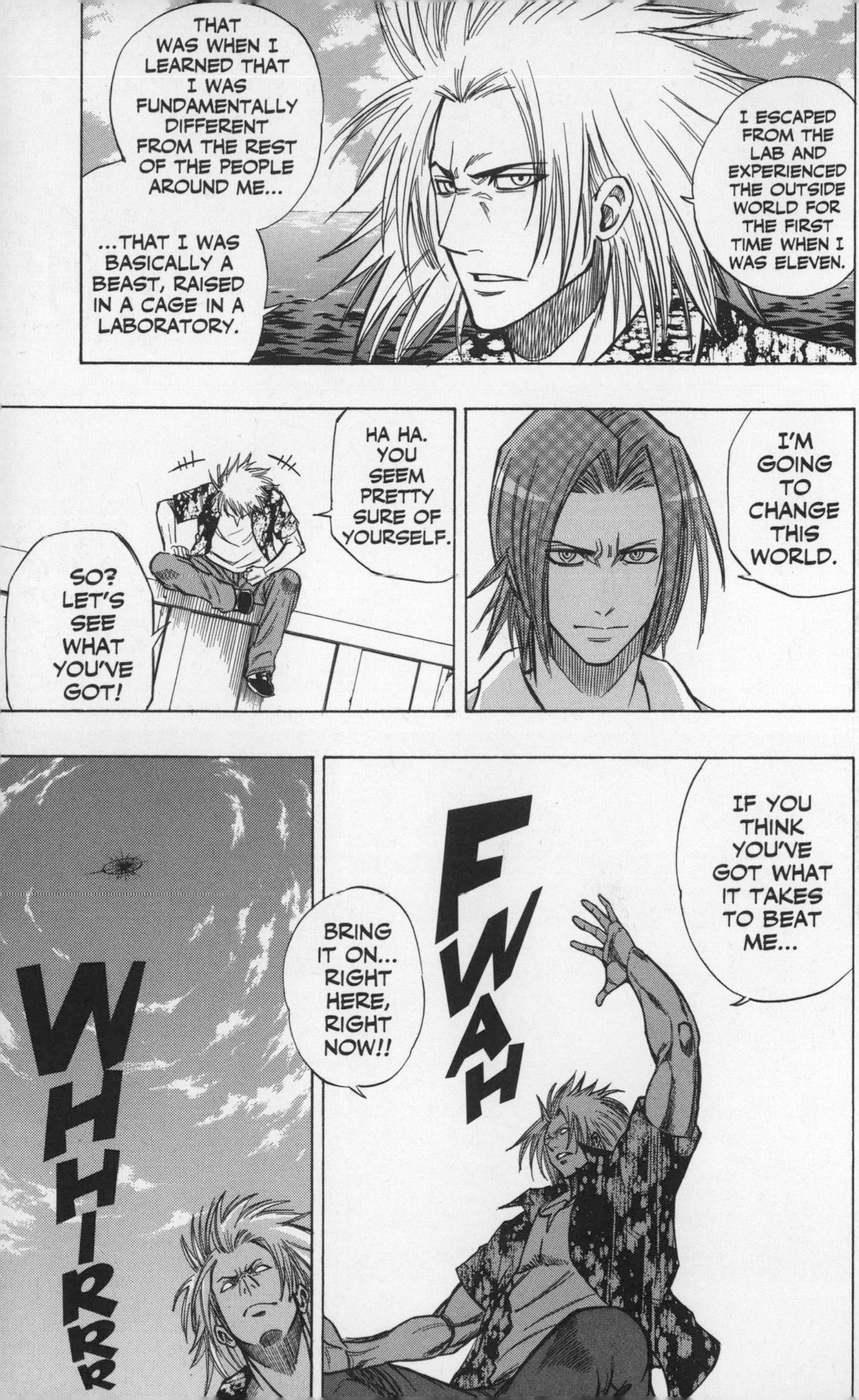
I ESCAPED FROM THE LAB AND EXPERIENCED THE OUTSIDE WORLD FOR THE FIRST TIME WHEN I WAS ELEVEN.
THAT WAS WHEN I LEARNED THAT I WAS FUNDAMENTALLY DIFFERENT FROM THE REST OF THE PEOPLE AROUND ME...
...THAT I WAS BASICALLY A BEAST, RAISED IN A CAGE IN A LABORATORY.
I'M GOING TO CHANGE THIS WORLD.
HA HA. YOU SEEM PRETTY SURE OF YOURSELF.
SO? LET'S SEE WHAT YOU'VE GOT!
IF YOU THINK YOU'VE GOT WHAT IT TAKES TO BEAT ME...
BRING IT ON... RIGHT HERE, RIGHT NOW!!
FWAH
WHHIRRR

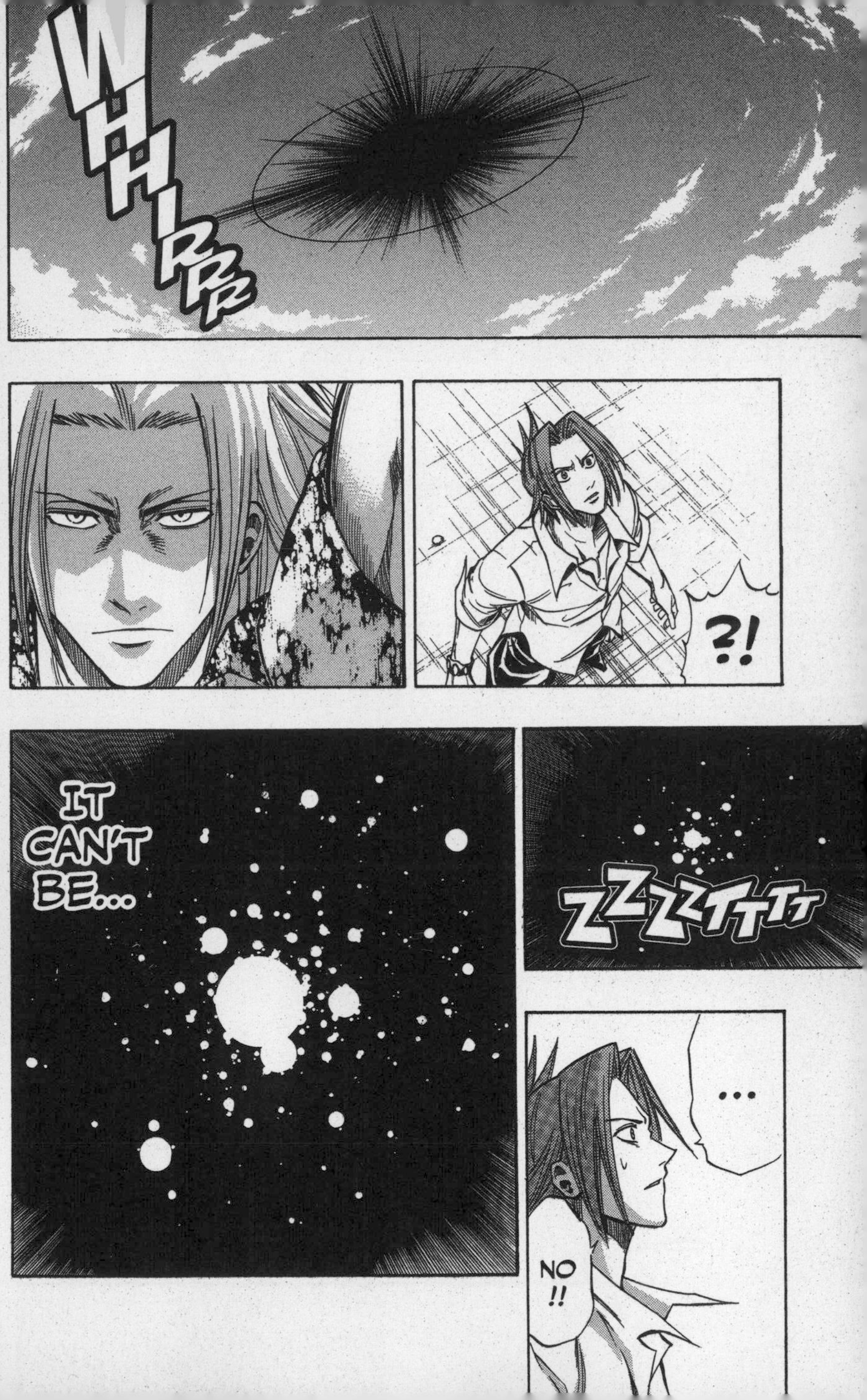
WHHIRRR
?!
ZZZZTTTT
...
NO!!
IT CAN'T BE...

HE'S WARPING THE SUN'S RAYS?!

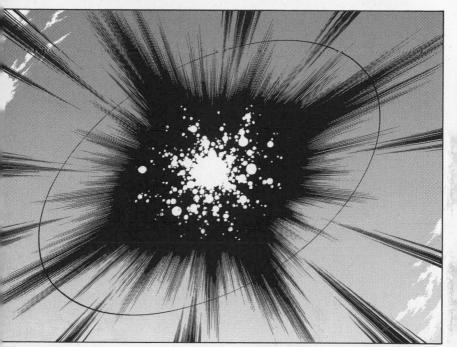

DYING SUN!

I DIDN'T THINK...

...TELEKINESIS OF THIS LEVEL EVEN EXISTED!!

119

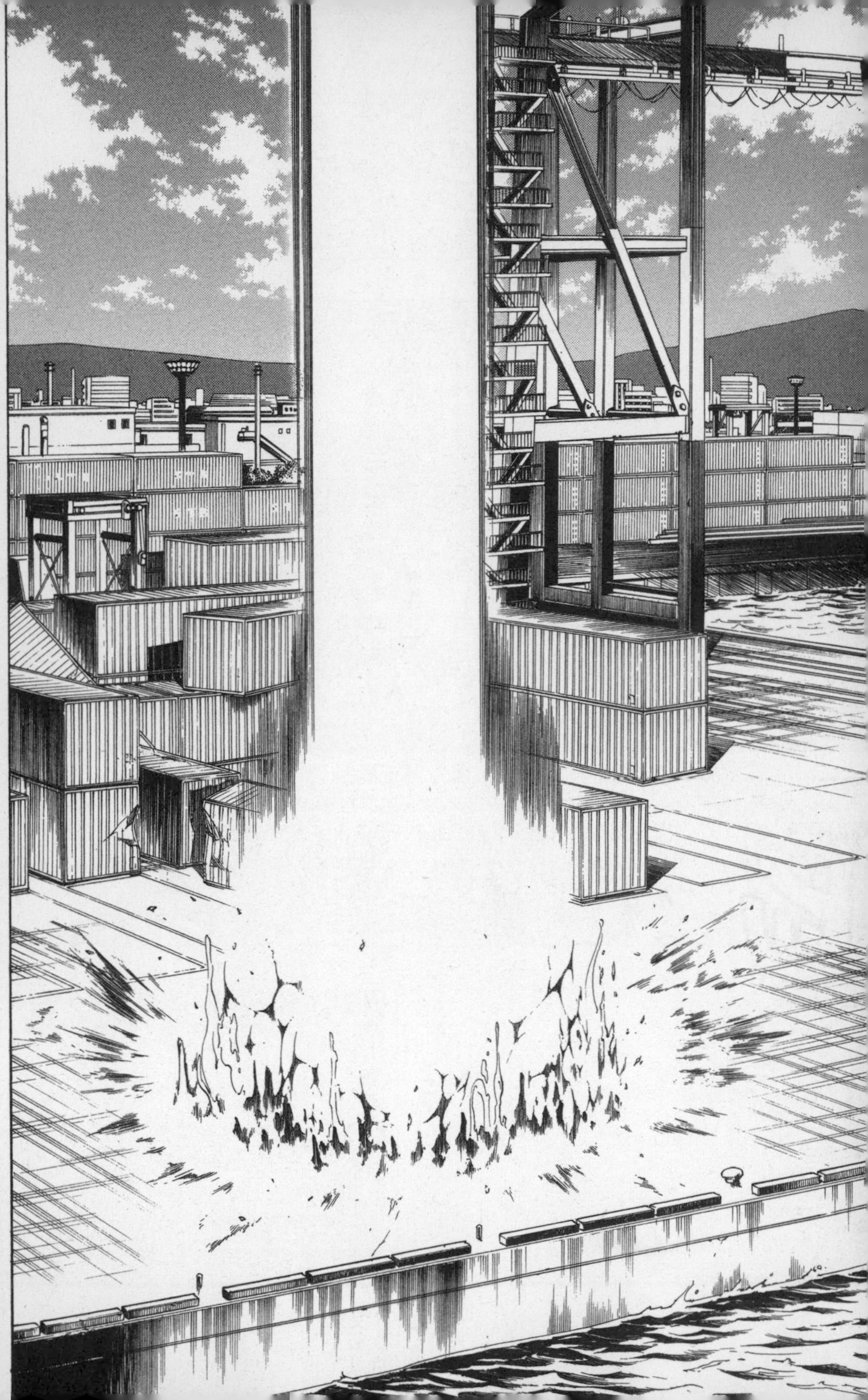

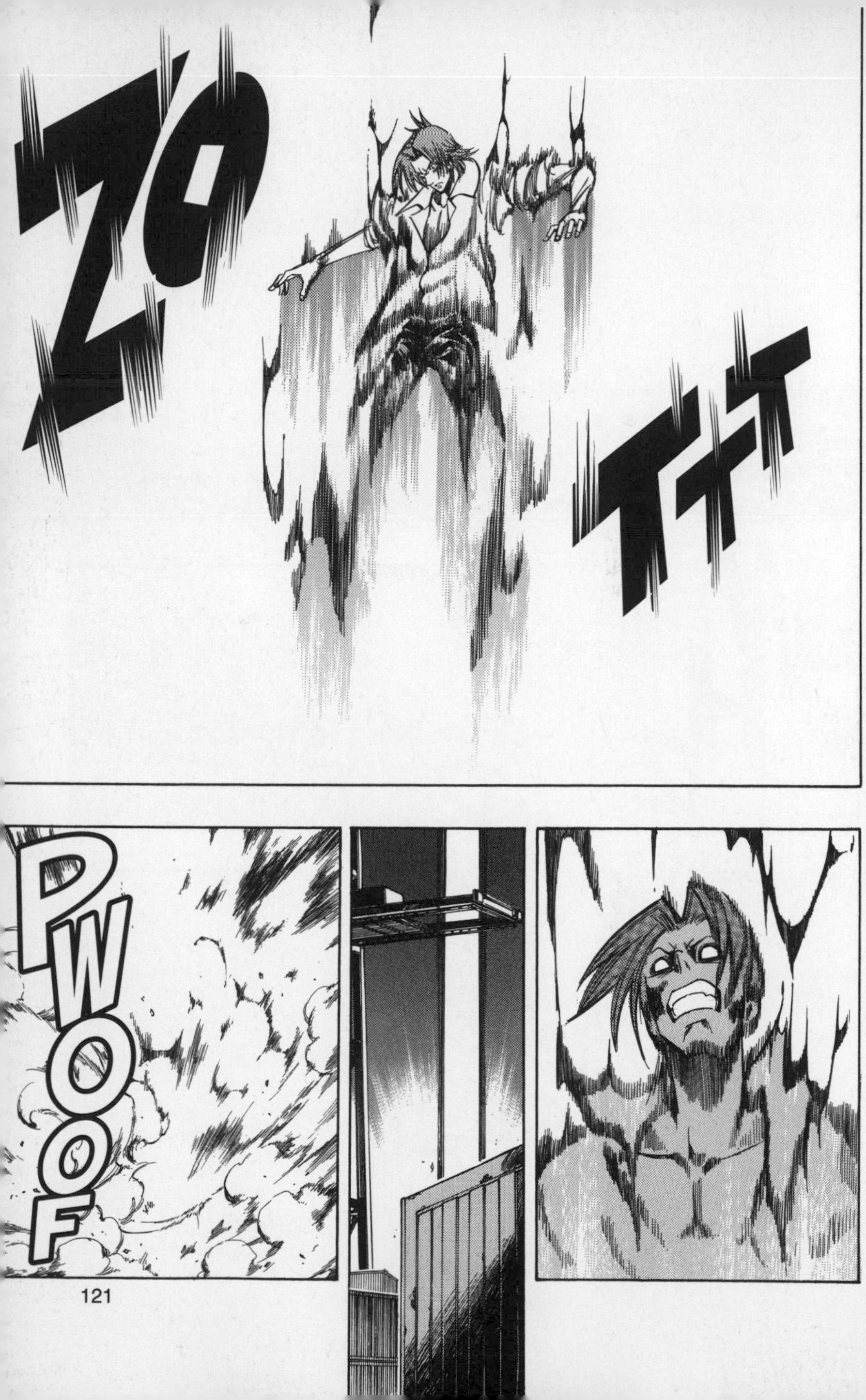
ZO
PWOOF

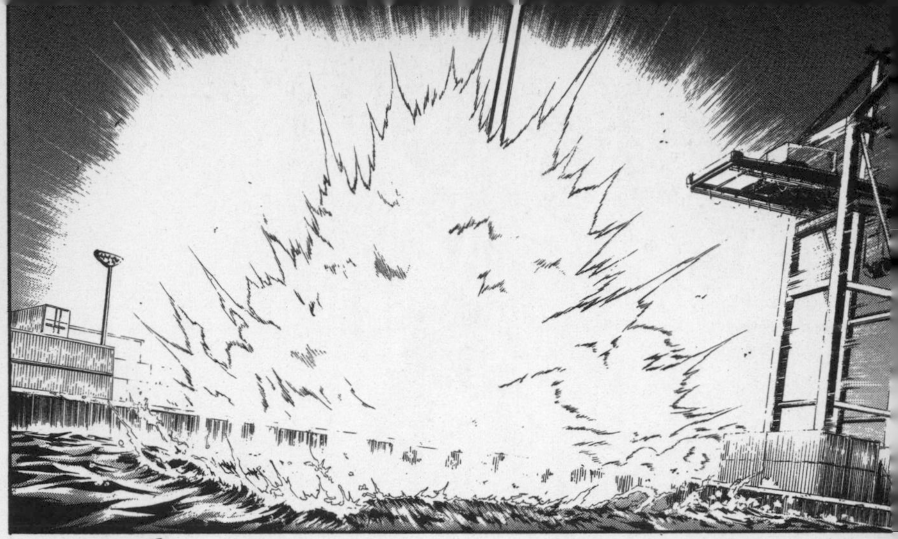

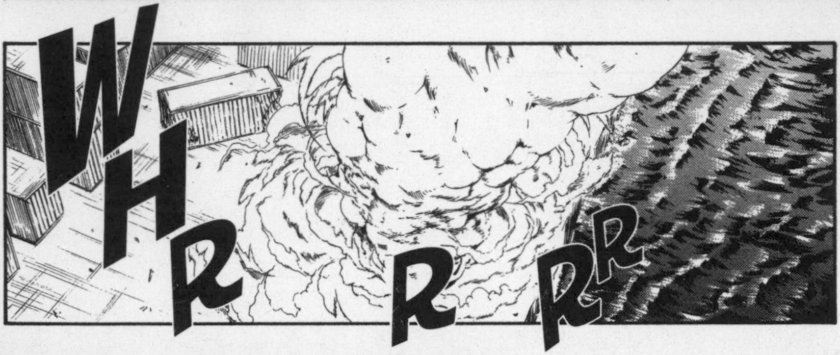
WHRRRR

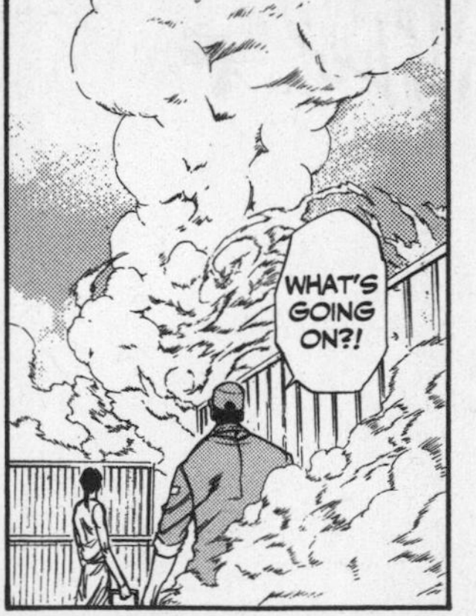
WHAT'S GOING ON?!

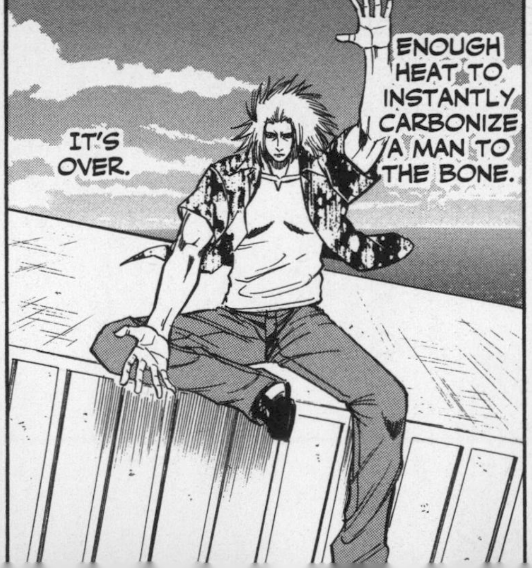
ENOUGH HEAT TO INSTANTLY CARBONIZE A MAN TO THE BONE.
IT'S OVER.

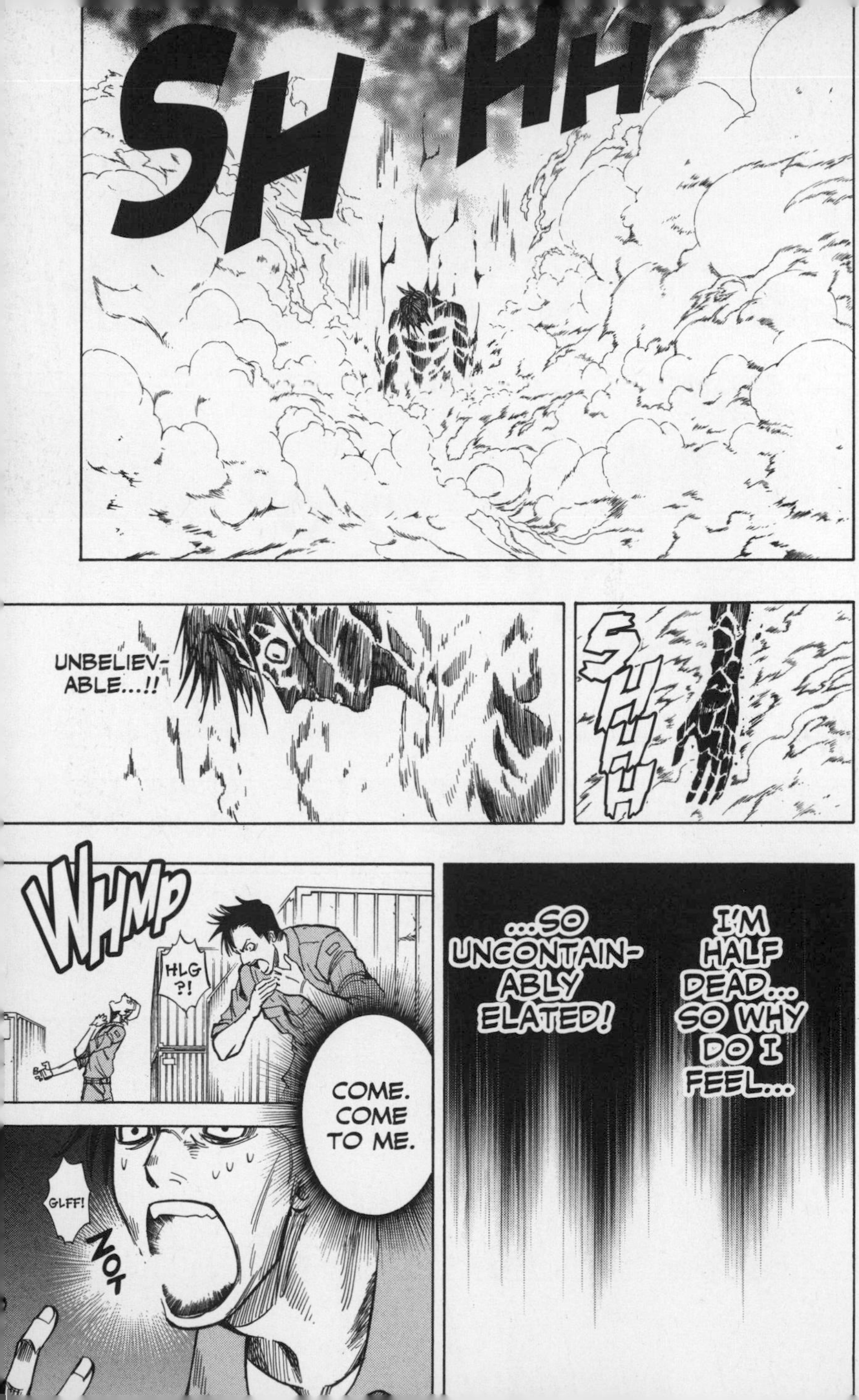
SHHH
SHUHH
UNBELIEVABLE...!!
I'M HALF DEAD... SO WHY DO I FEEL...
...SO UNCONTAINABLY ELATED!
WHUMP
HLG ?!
COME. COME TO ME.
GLFF!
NOT

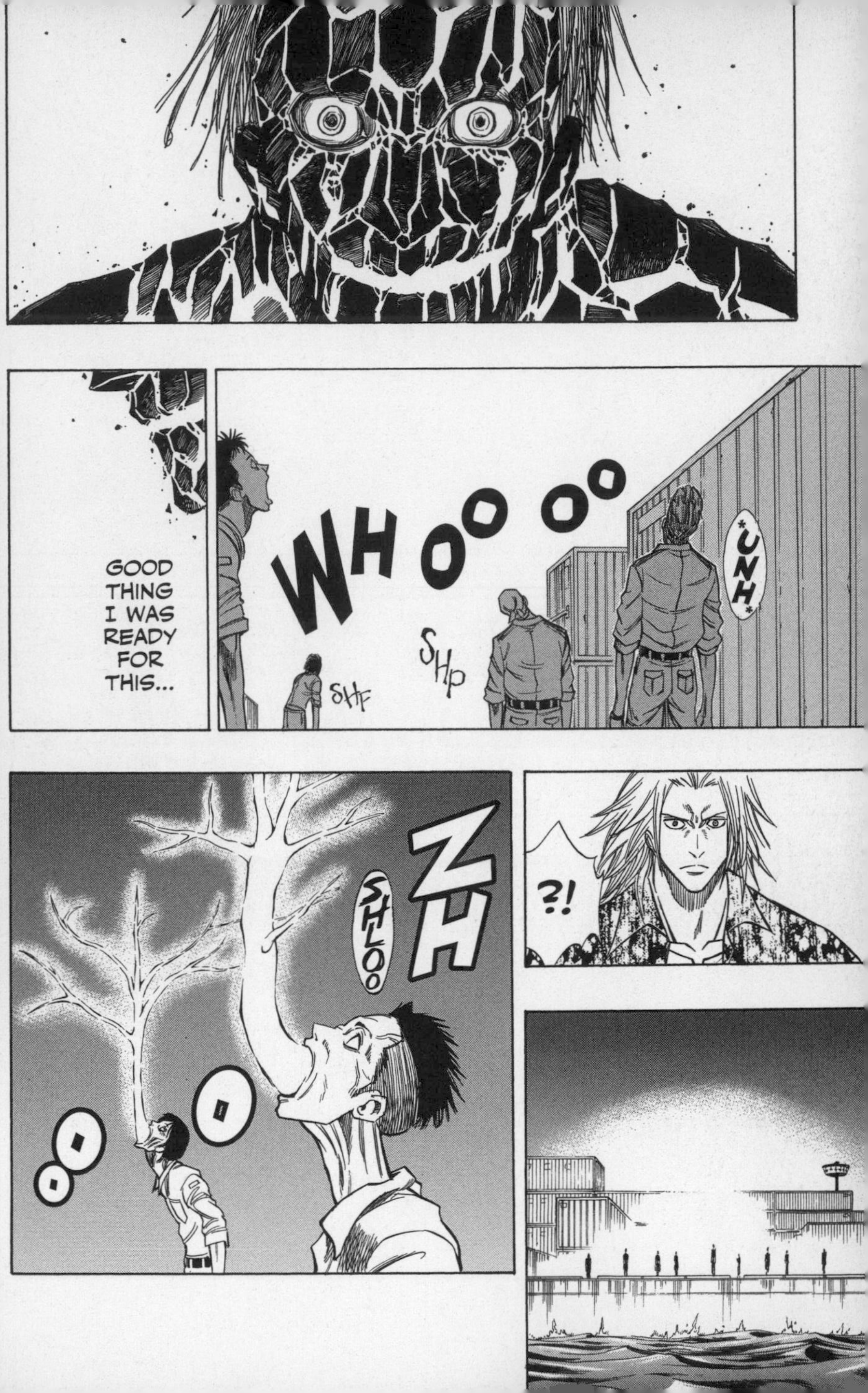

UNH
WHOOOO
SHp
SHF
GOOD THING I WAS READY FOR THIS...
?!
ZH
SHLOOO

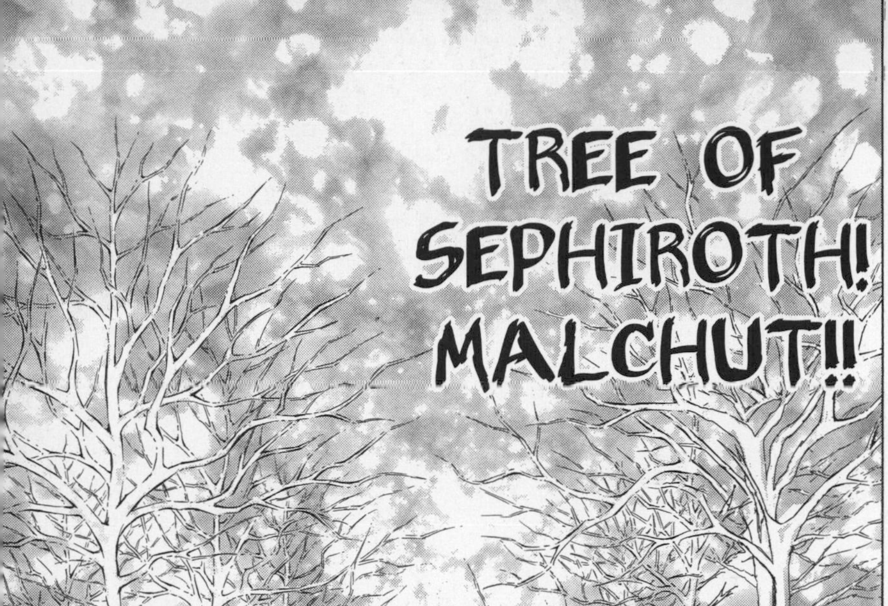
TREE OF SEPHIROTH! MALCHUT!!
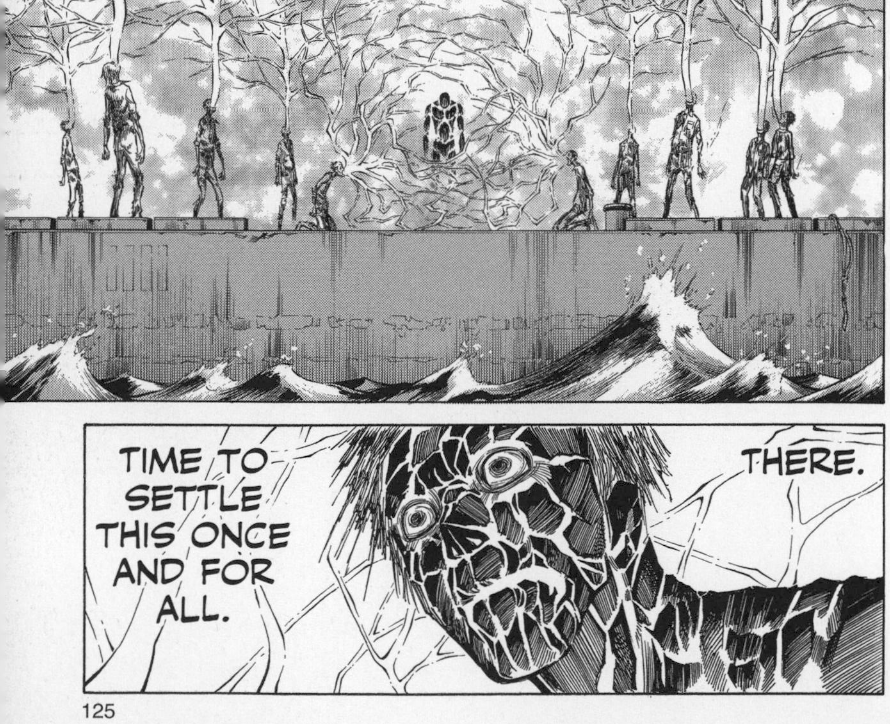
THERE.
TIME TO SETTLE THIS ONCE AND FOR ALL.

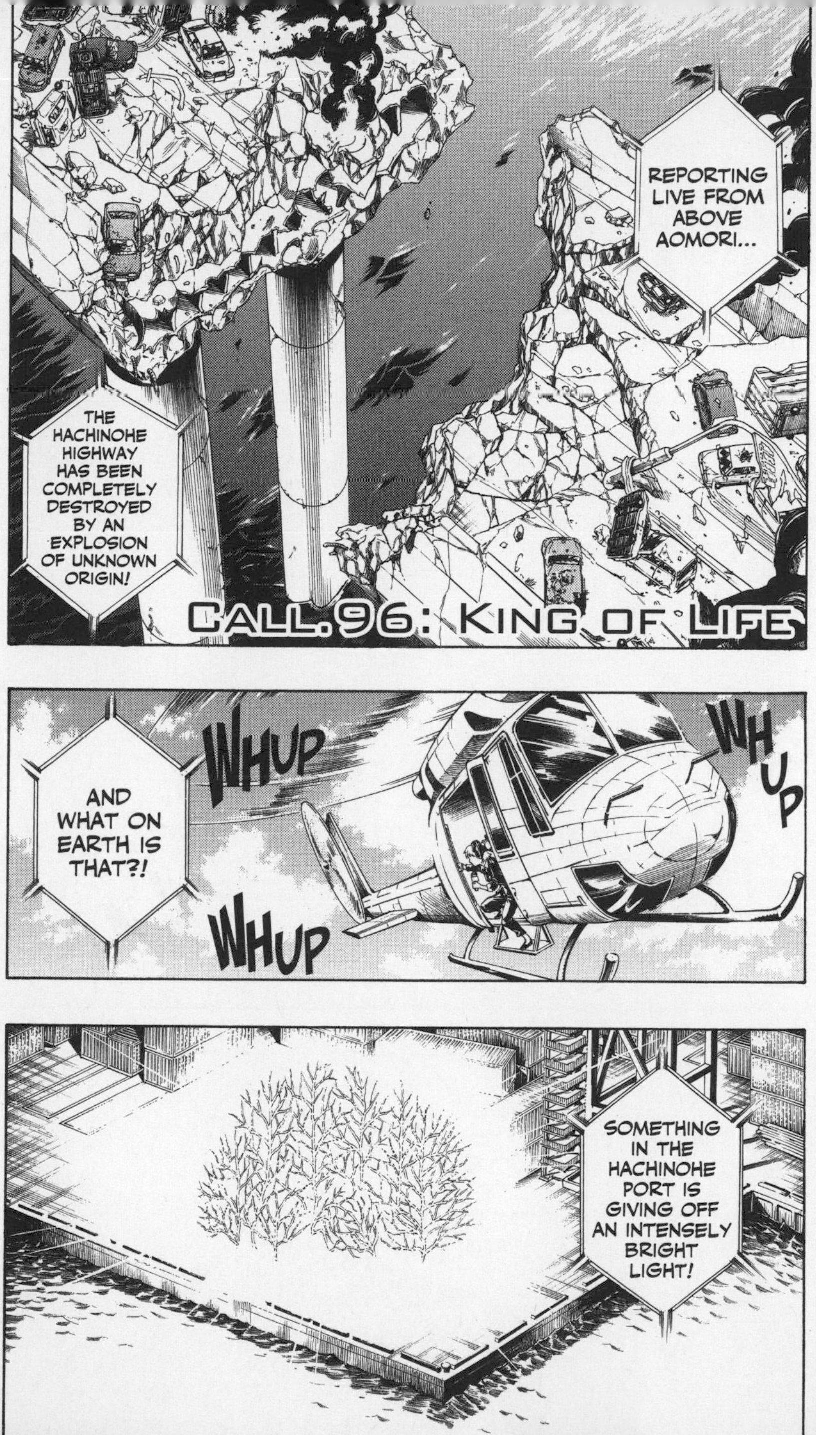
REPORTING LIVE FROM ABOVE AOMORI...
THE HACHINOHE HIGHWAY HAS BEEN COMPLETELY DESTROYED BY AN EXPLOSION OF UNKNOWN ORIGIN!
CALL.96: KING OF LIFE
WHUP
WHUP
AND WHAT ON EARTH IS THAT?!
WHUP
SOMETHING IN THE HACHINOHE PORT IS GIVING OFF AN INTENSELY BRIGHT LIGHT!

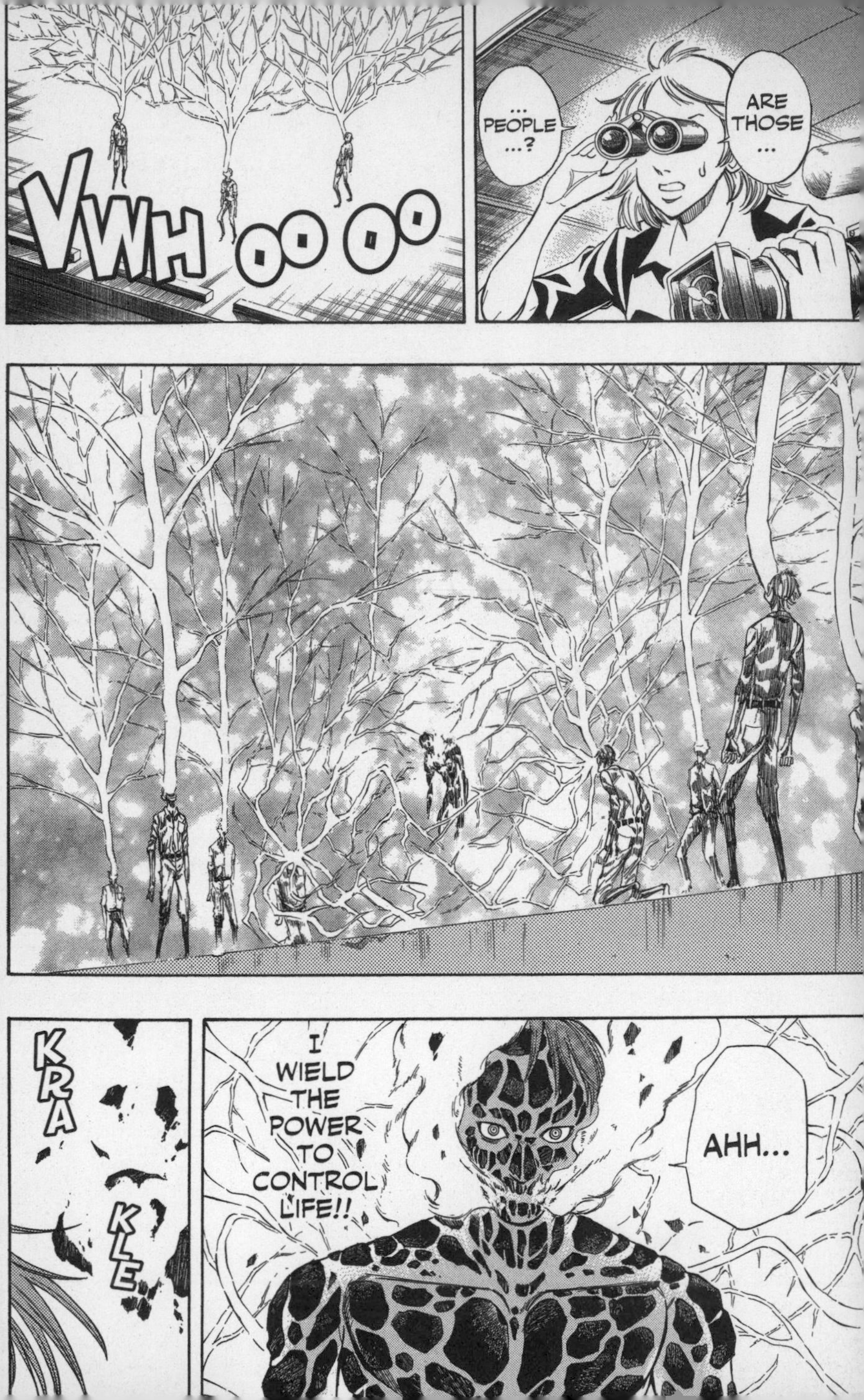
ARE THOSE ...
... PEOPLE ...?
VWHOOOO
AHH...
I WIELD THE POWER TO CONTROL LIFE!!
KRAKLE

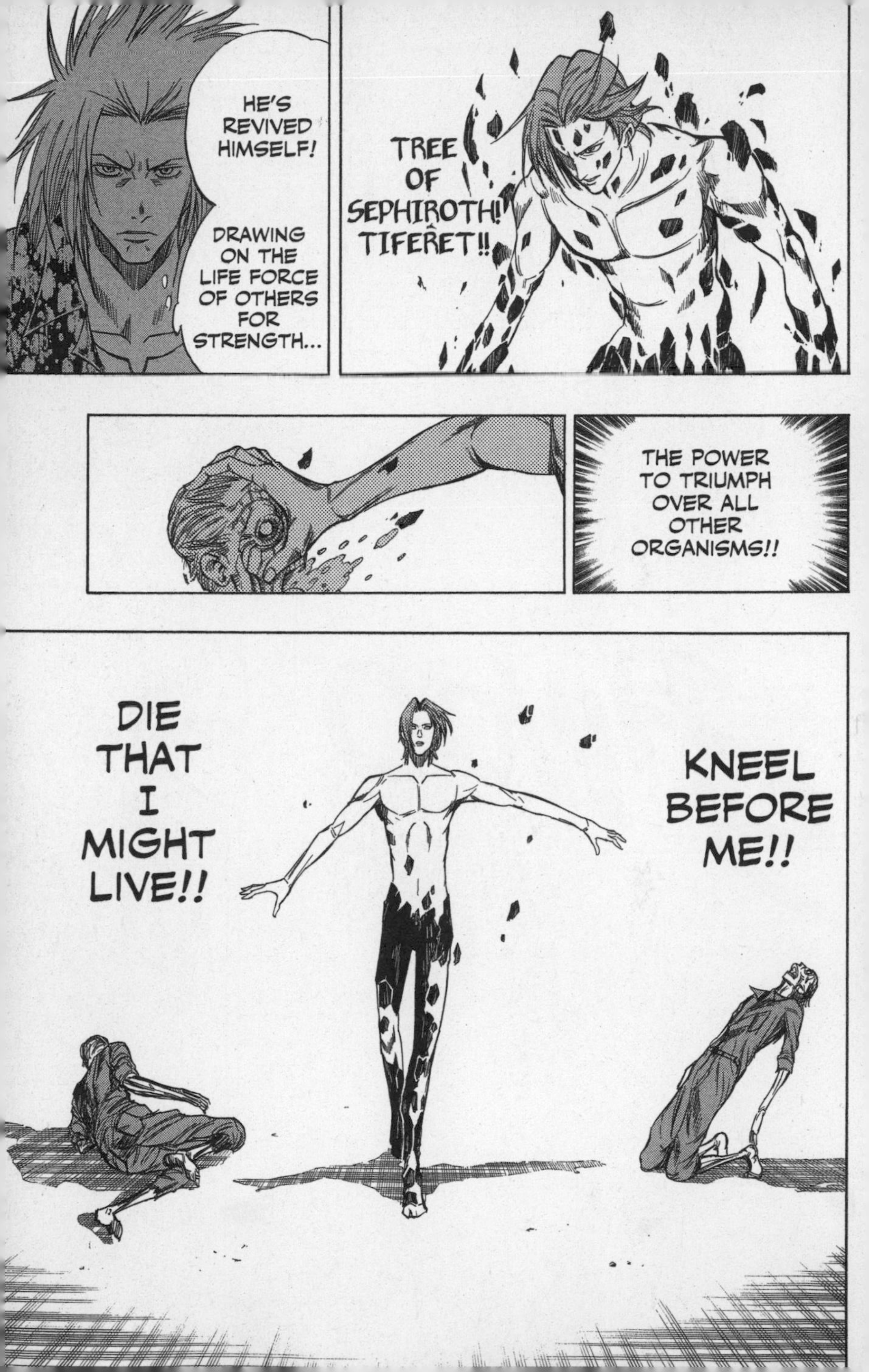
TREE OF SEPHIROTH! TIFERET!!
HE'S REVIVED HIMSELF!
DRAWING ON THE LIFE FORCE OF OTHERS FOR STRENGTH...
THE POWER TO TRIUMPH OVER ALL OTHER ORGANISMS!!
KNEEL BEFORE ME!!
DIE THAT I MIGHT LIVE!!

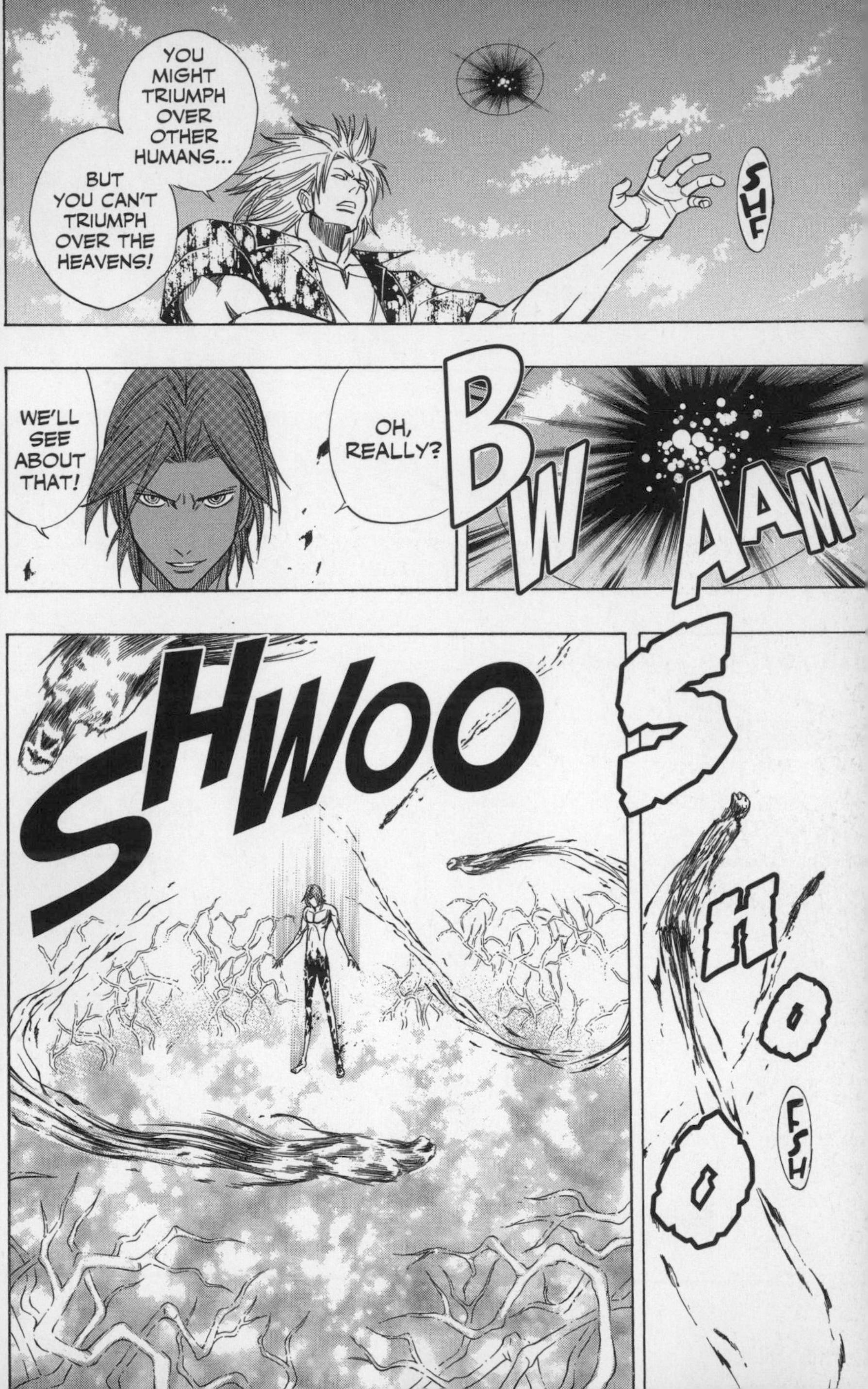
YOU MIGHT TRIUMPH OVER OTHER HUMANS...
BUT YOU CAN'T TRIUMPH OVER THE HEAVENS!
SHF
BWAAM
OH, REALLY?
WE'LL SEE ABOUT THAT!
SHOO
FSH
SHWOO

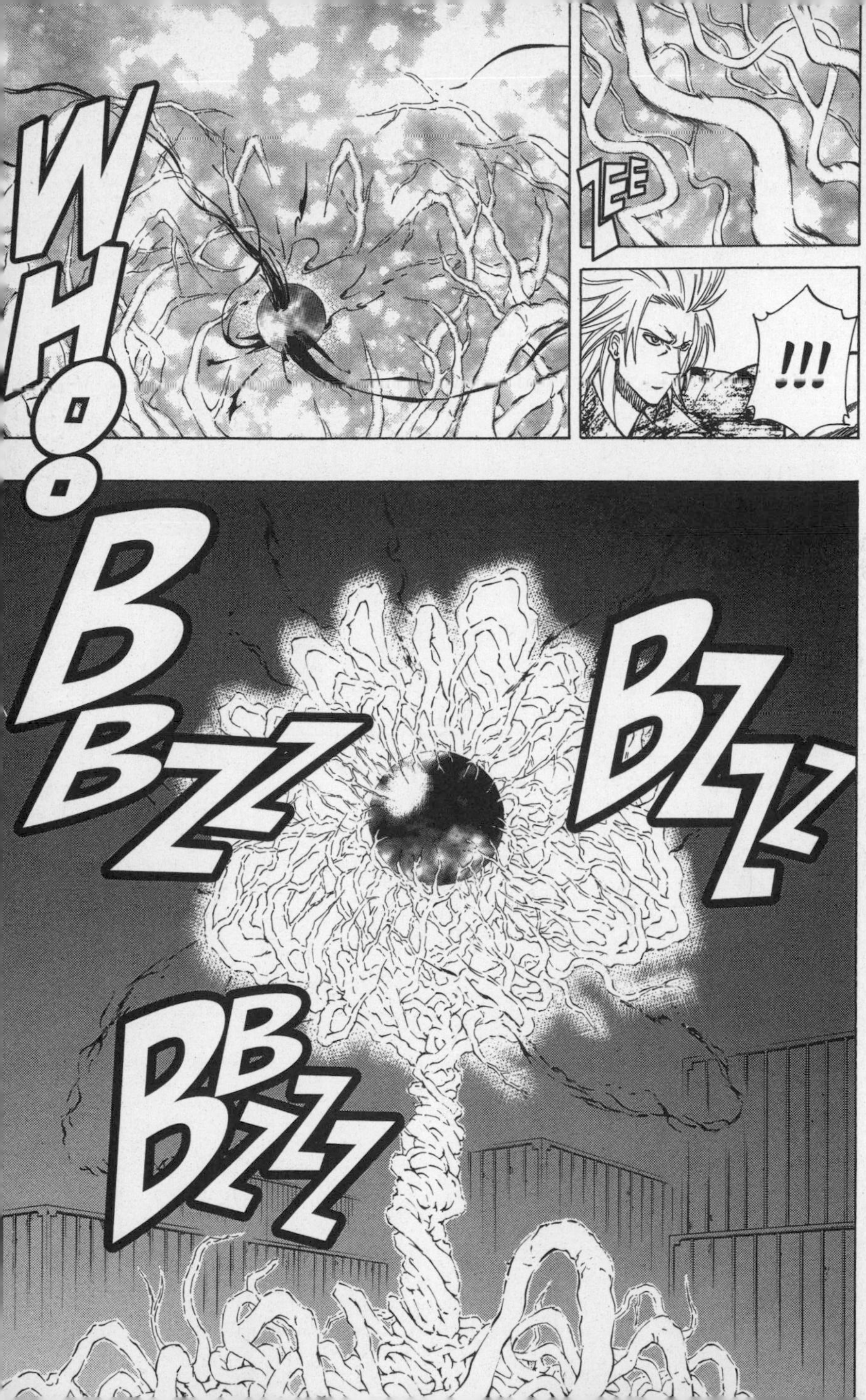
ZEE
!!!
WHOO
BZZZ
BBZZ
BBZZZ

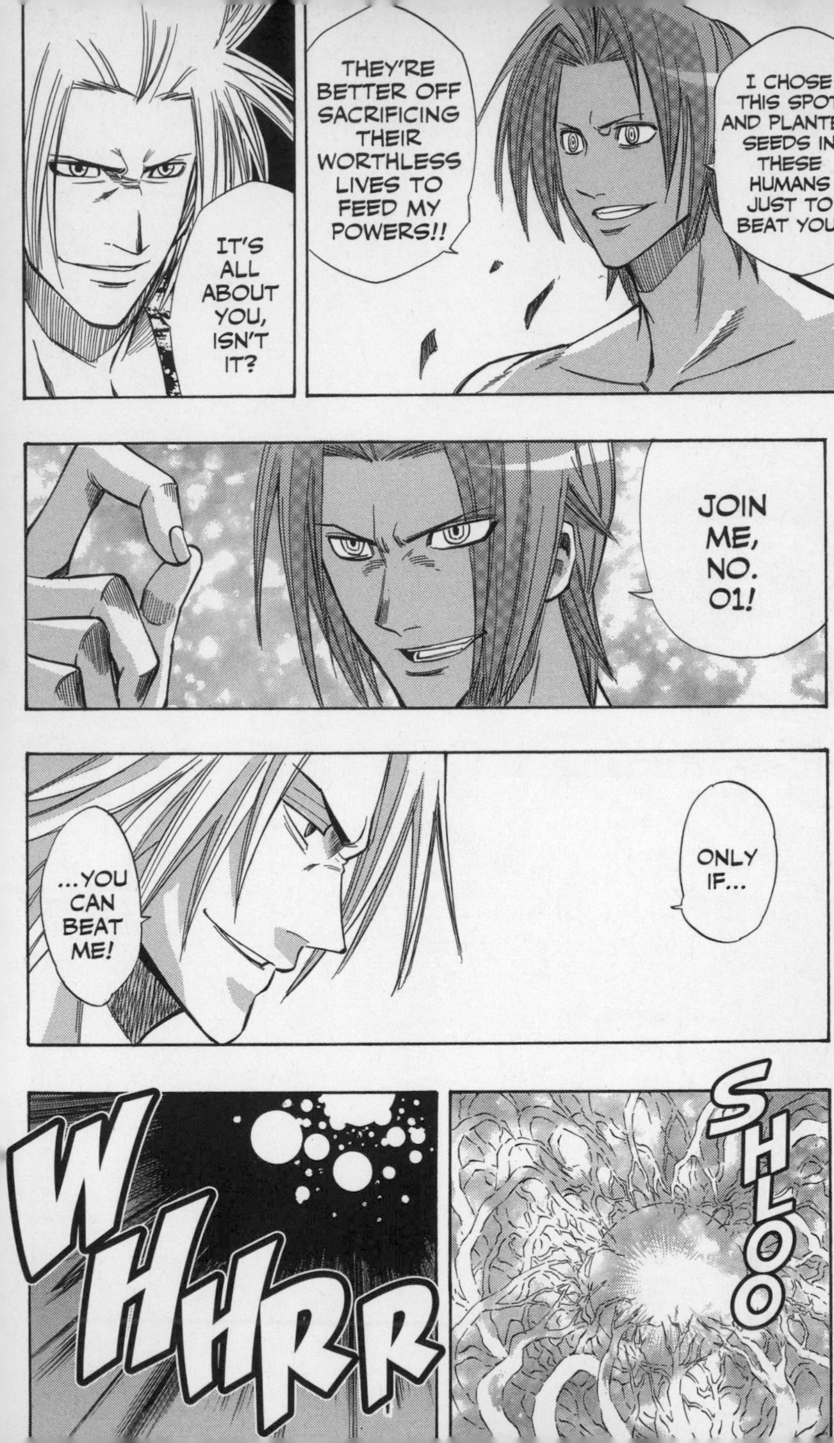
I CHOSE THIS SPOT AND PLANTED SEEDS IN THESE HUMANS JUST TO BEAT YOU.
THEY'RE BETTER OFF SACRIFICING THEIR WORTHLESS LIVES TO FEED MY POWERS!!
IT'S ALL ABOUT YOU, ISN'T IT?
JOIN ME, NO. 01!
ONLY IF...
...YOU CAN BEAT ME!
SHLOO
WHHRR

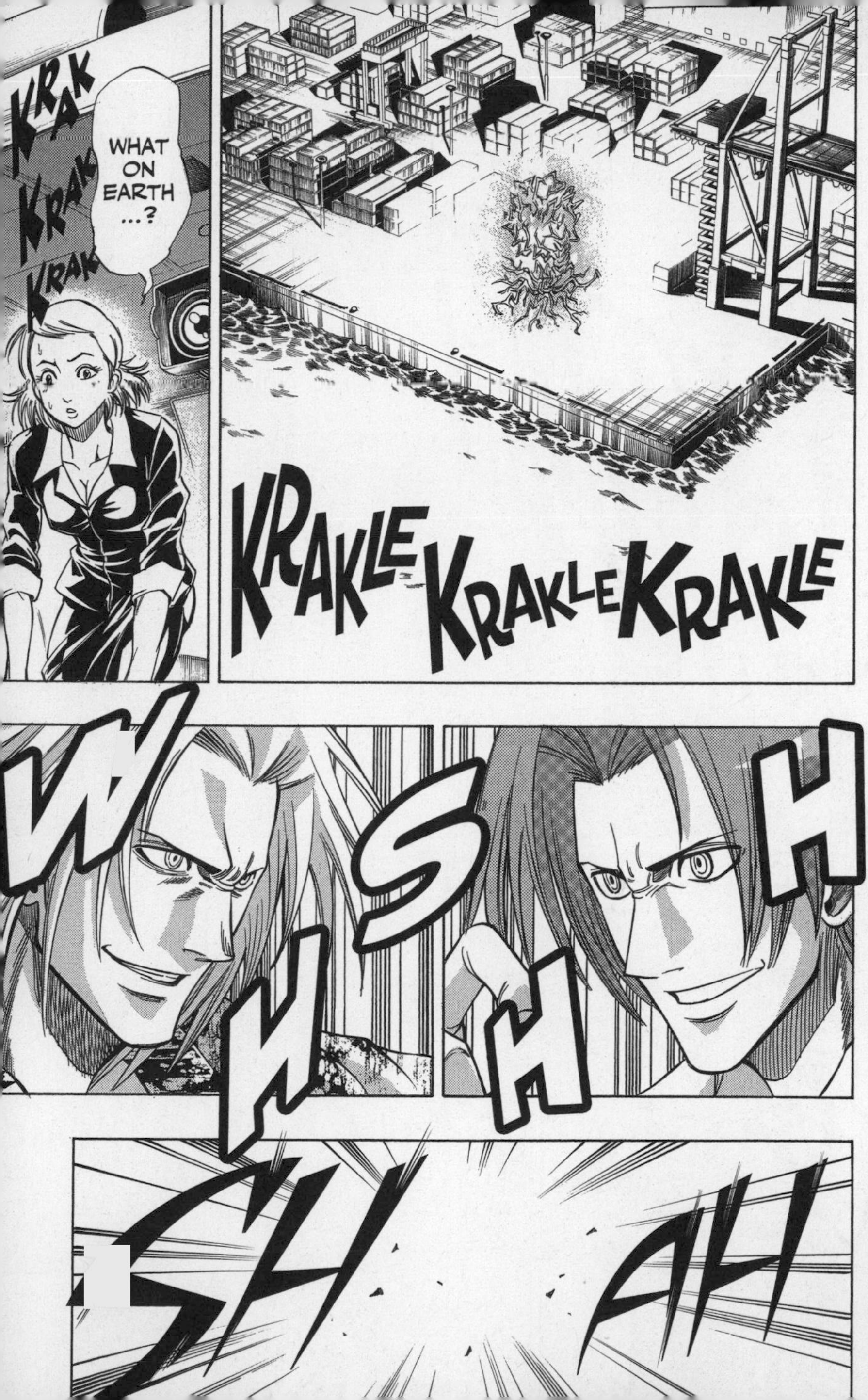
KRAKLE KRAKLE KRAKLE
KRAK KRAK KRAK
WHAT ON EARTH ...?
WSHHH
SHAH

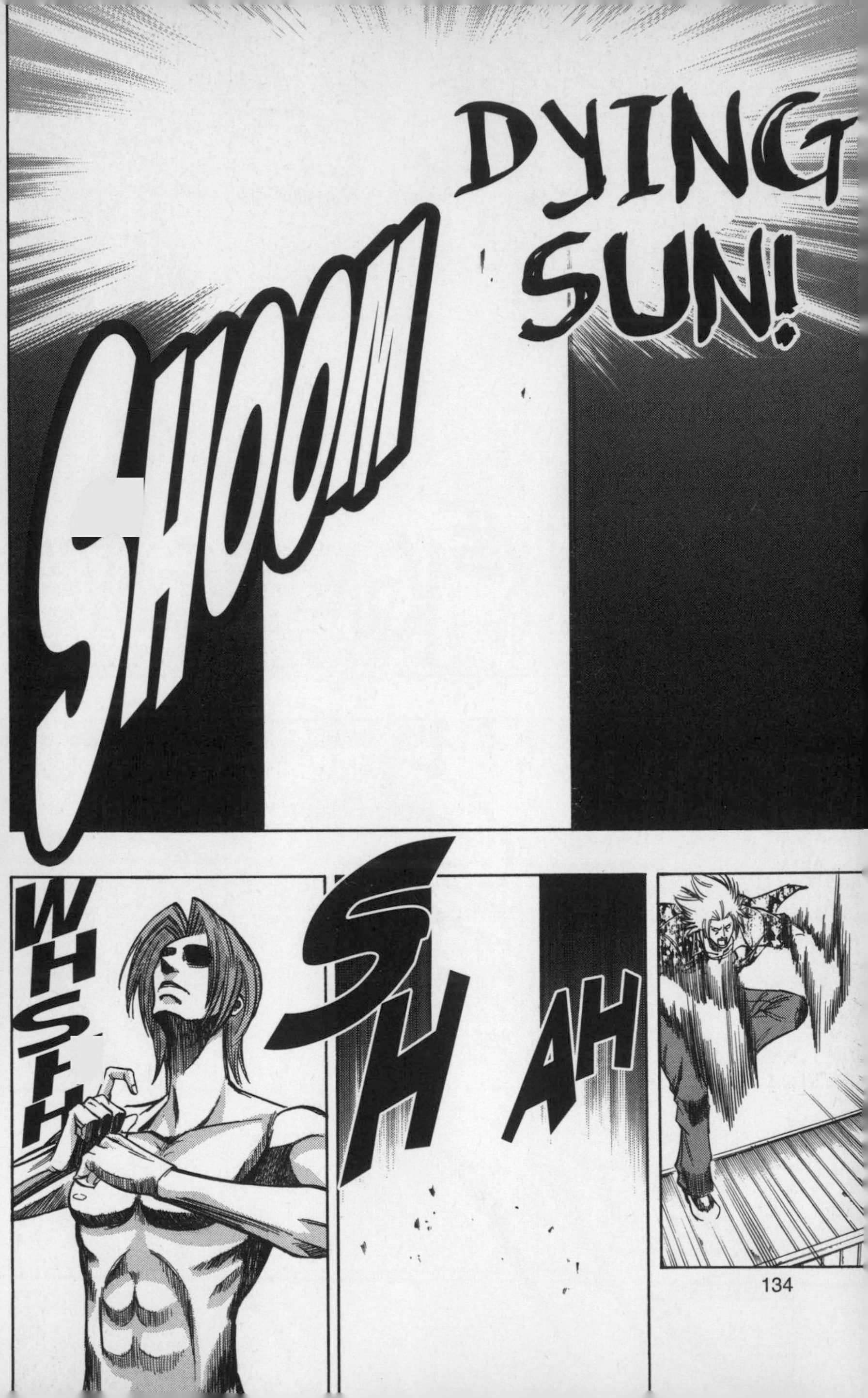
DYING SUN!
SHOOM
SHHAH
WHSHH

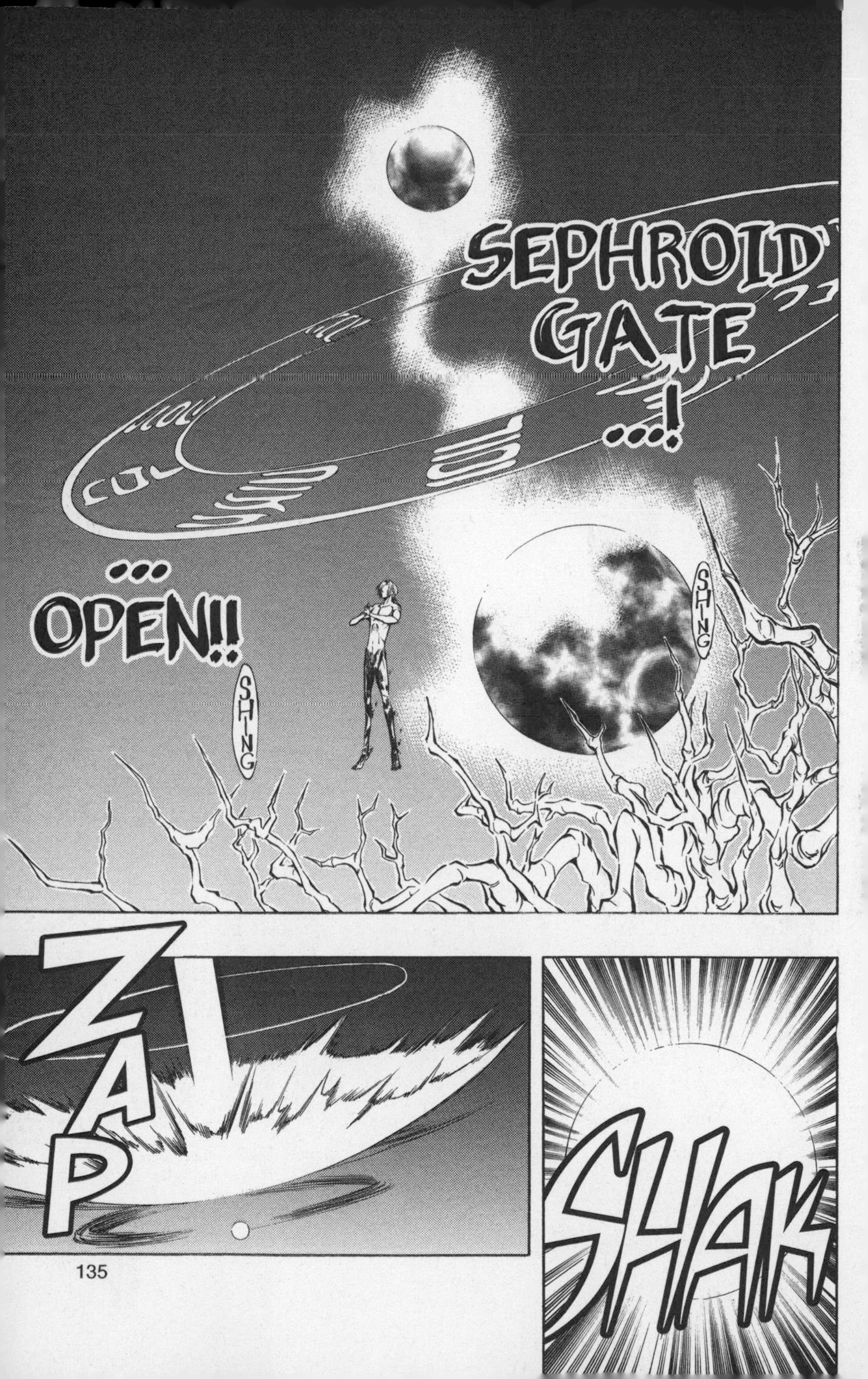
SEPHROID GATE ...!
...OPEN!!
SHING
SHING
SHAK
ZAP

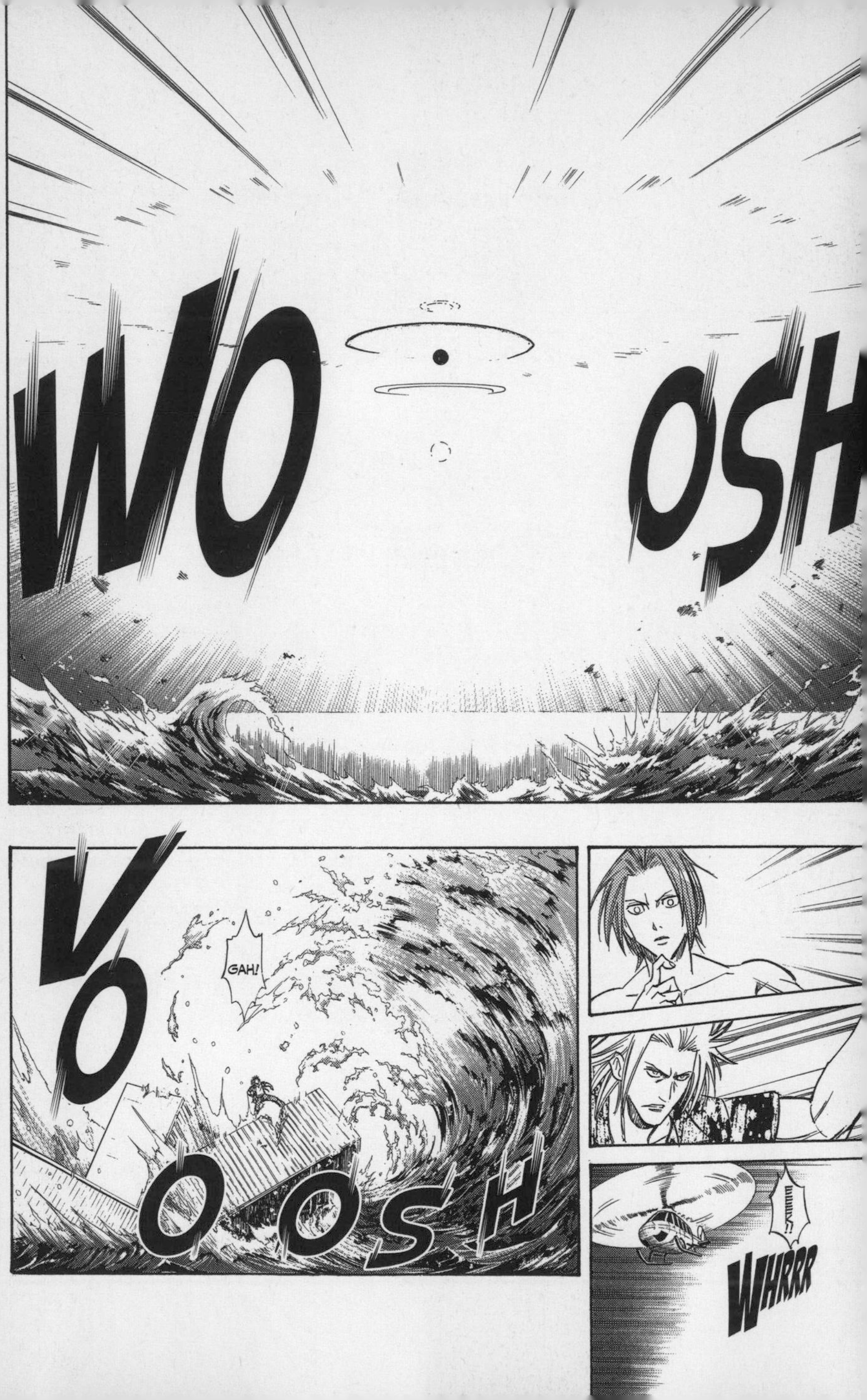
WO OSH
EEK!
WHRRR
GAH!
VOOOSH

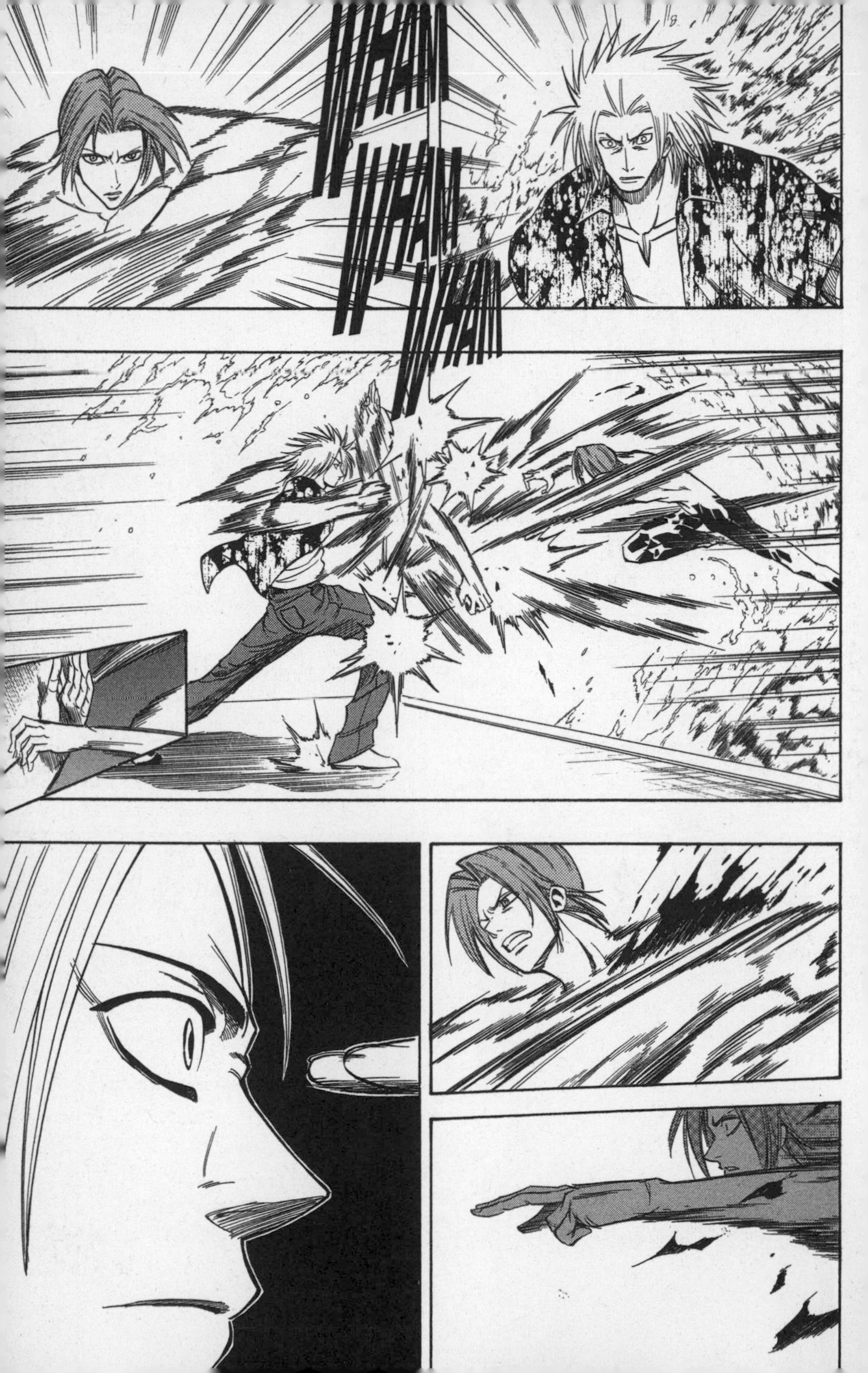
WHAM
WHAM
WHAM
WHAM

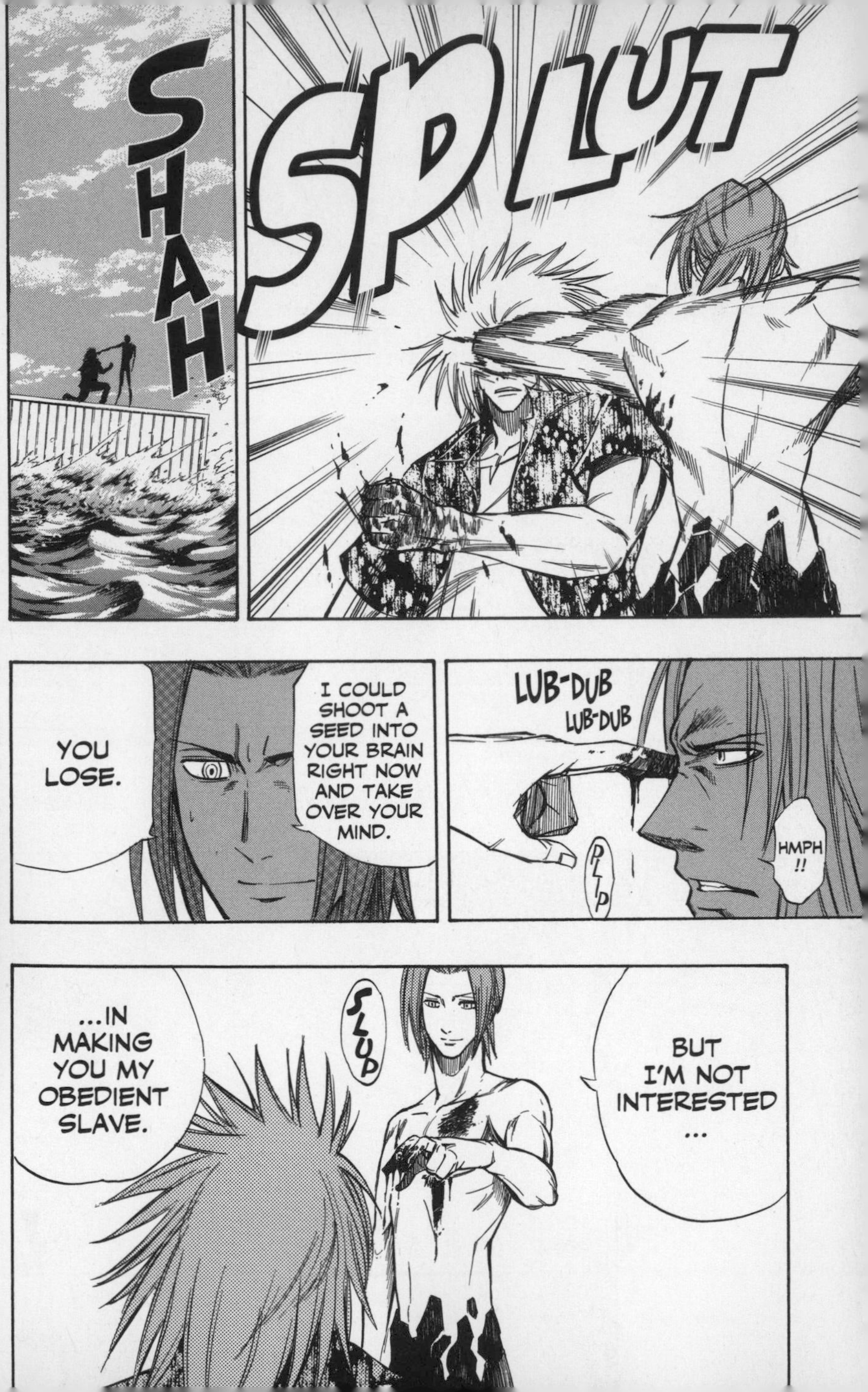
SPLUT
SHAH
LUB-DUB
LUB-DUB
HMPH !!
PLIP
I COULD SHOOT A SEED INTO YOUR BRAIN RIGHT NOW AND TAKE OVER YOUR MIND.
YOU LOSE.
BUT I'M NOT INTERESTED ...
SLUP
...IN MAKING YOU MY OBEDIENT SLAVE.

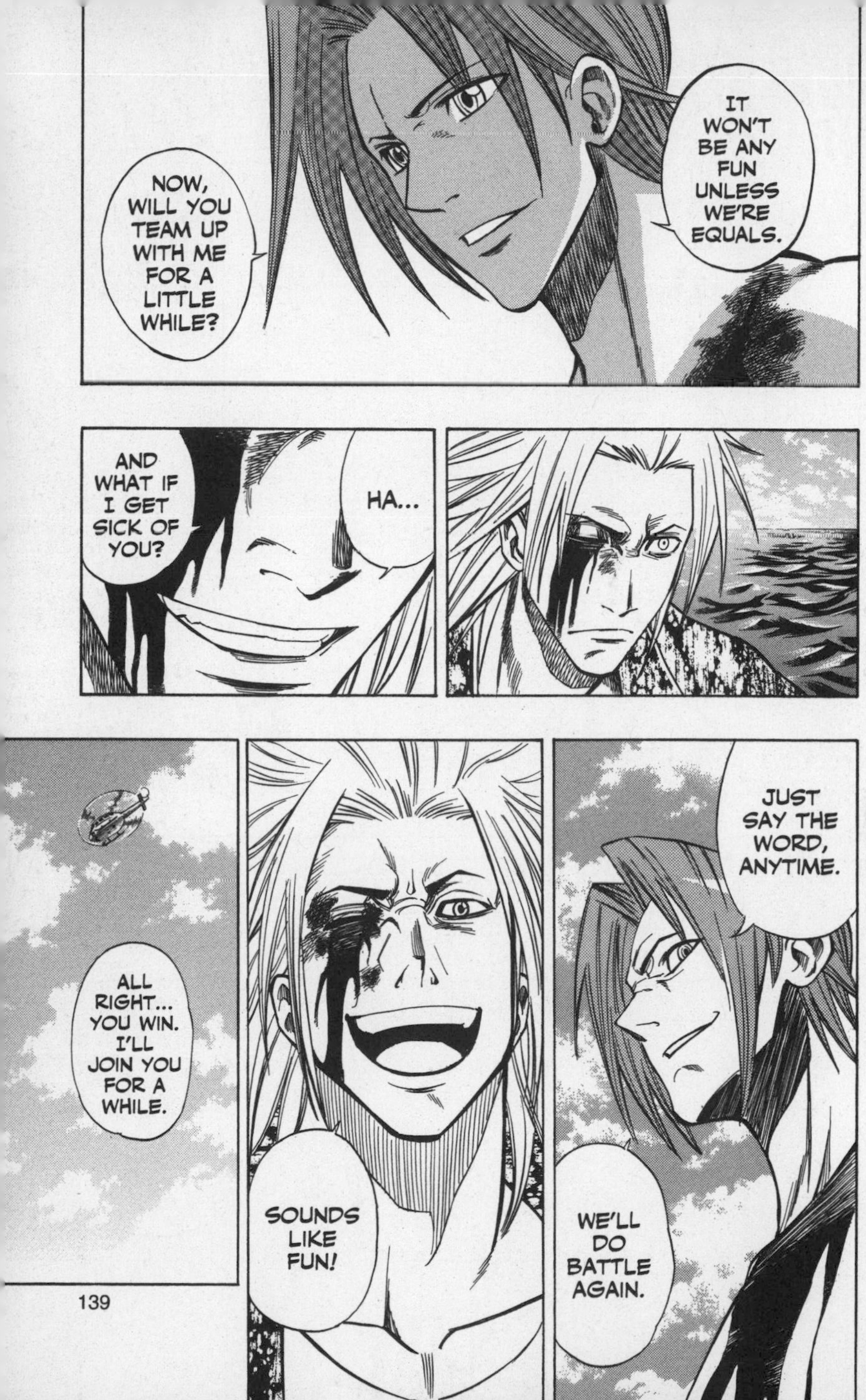
IT WON'T BE ANY FUN UNLESS WE'RE EQUALS.
NOW, WILL YOU TEAM UP WITH ME FOR A LITTLE WHILE?
HA...
AND WHAT IF I GET SICK OF YOU?
JUST SAY THE WORD, ANYTIME.
WE'LL DO BATTLE AGAIN.
SOUNDS LIKE FUN!
ALL RIGHT... YOU WIN. I'LL JOIN YOU FOR A WHILE.

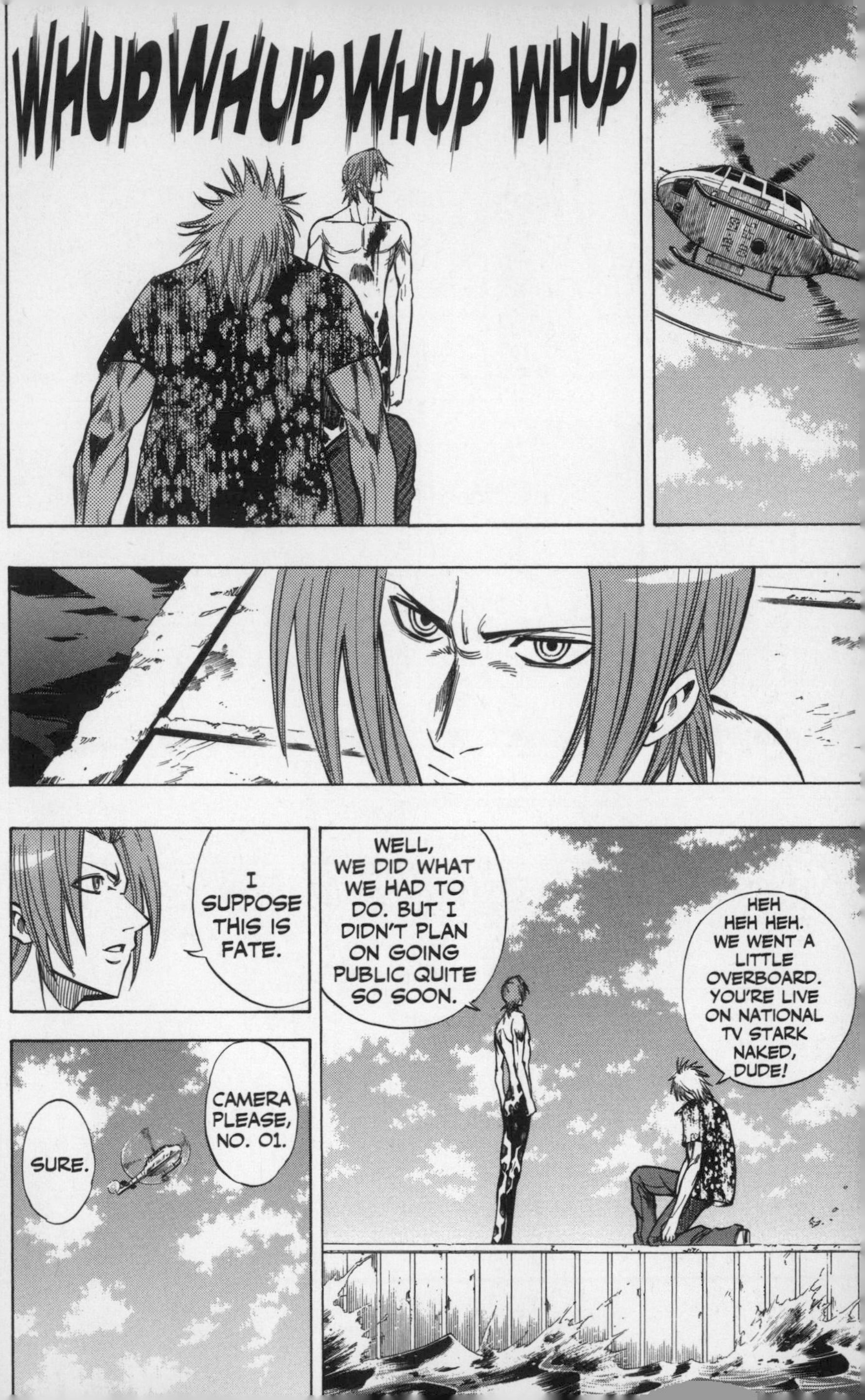
WHUP WHUP WHUP WHUP
HEH HEH HEH. WE WENT A LITTLE OVERBOARD. YOU'RE LIVE ON NATIONAL TV STARK NAKED, DUDE!
WELL, WE DID WHAT WE HAD TO DO. BUT I DIDN'T PLAN ON GOING PUBLIC QUITE SO SOON.
I SUPPOSE THIS IS FATE.
CAMERA PLEASE, NO. 01.
SURE.

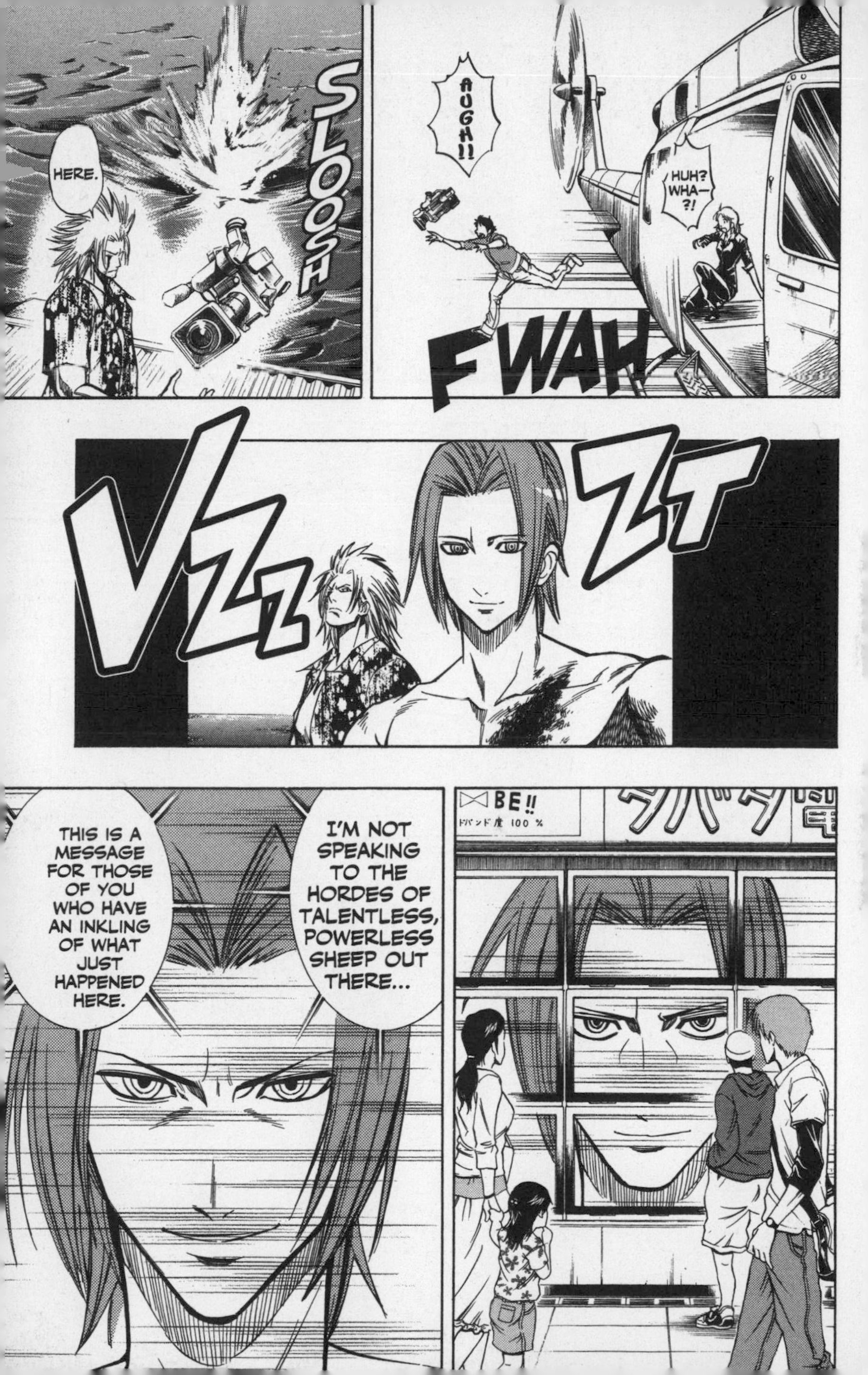
AUGH!!
HUH? WHA— ?!
FWAH
HERE.
SLOOSH
VZZZT
BE!!
I'M NOT SPEAKING TO THE HORDES OF TALENTLESS, POWERLESS SHEEP OUT THERE...
THIS IS A MESSAGE FOR THOSE OF YOU WHO HAVE AN INKLING OF WHAT JUST HAPPENED HERE.

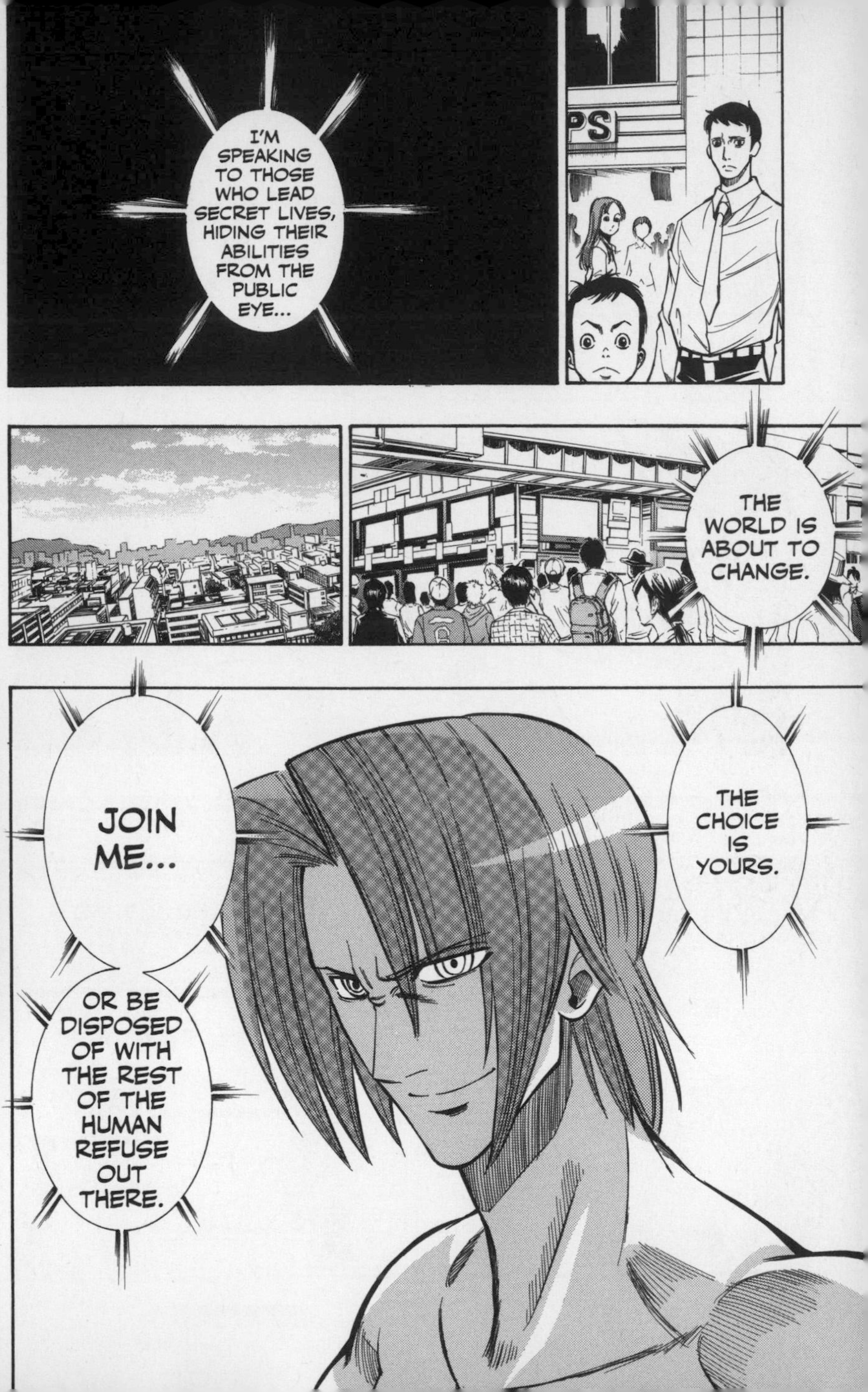
I'M SPEAKING TO THOSE WHO LEAD SECRET LIVES, HIDING THEIR ABILITIES FROM THE PUBLIC EYE...
THE WORLD IS ABOUT TO CHANGE.
JOIN ME...
OR BE DISPOSED OF WITH THE REST OF THE HUMAN REFUSE OUT THERE.
THE CHOICE IS YOURS.

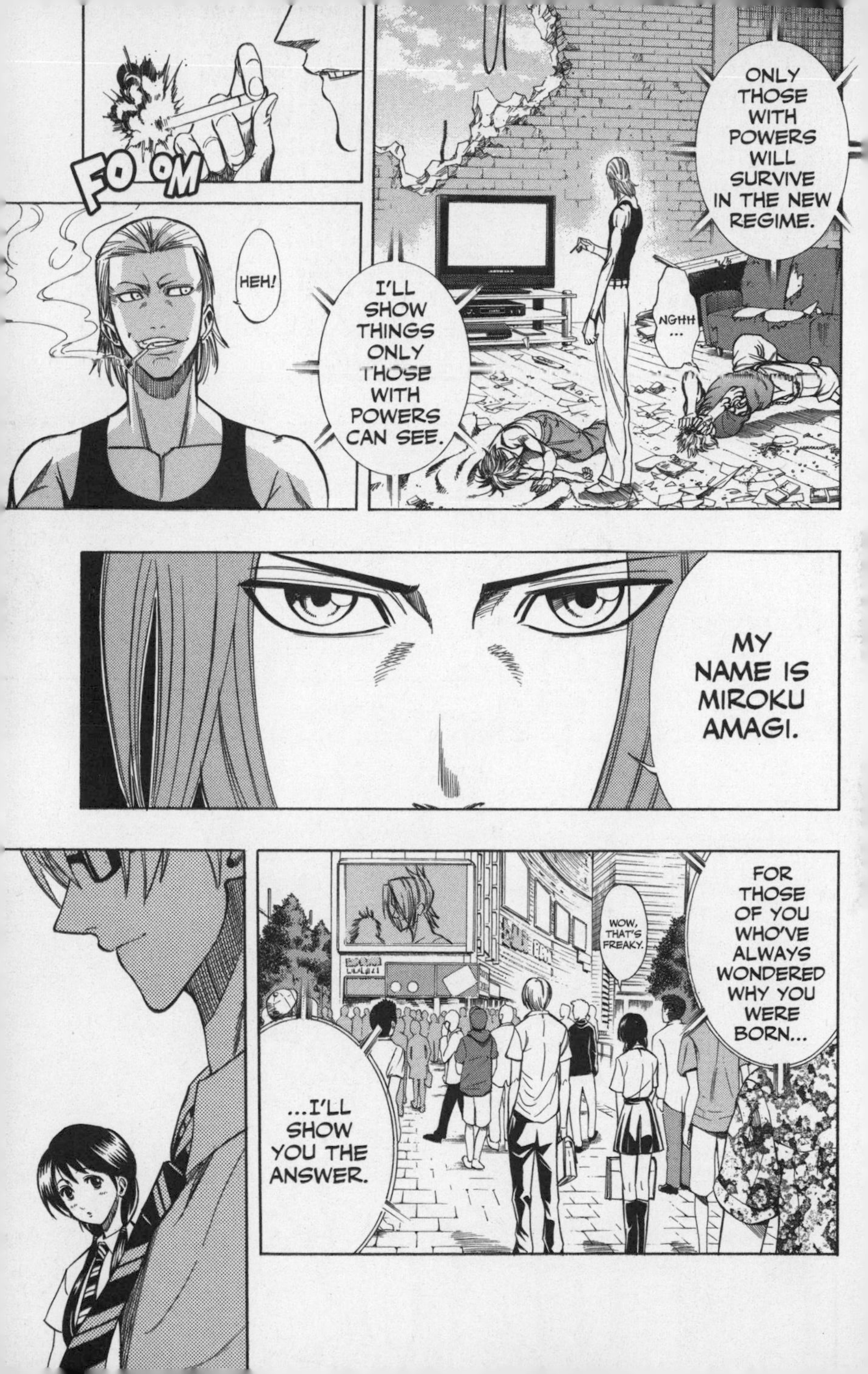
ONLY THOSE WITH POWERS WILL SURVIVE IN THE NEW REGIME.
NGHH...
I'LL SHOW THINGS ONLY THOSE WITH POWERS CAN SEE.
FOOM
HEH!
MY NAME IS MIROKU AMAGI.
FOR THOSE OF YOU WHO'VE ALWAYS WONDERED WHY YOU WERE BORN...
WOW, THAT'S FREAKY.
...I'LL SHOW YOU THE ANSWER.

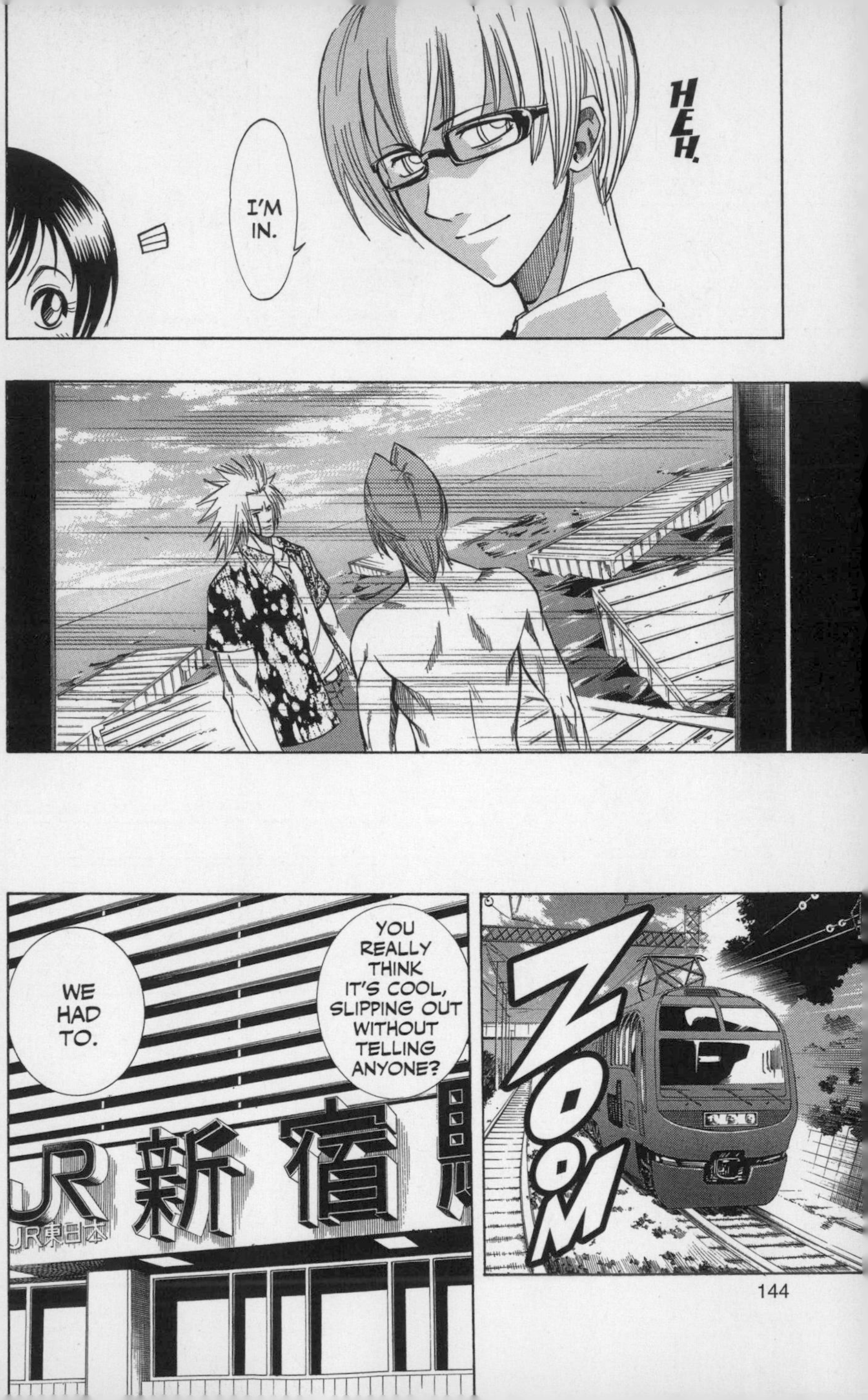
HEH.
I'M IN.
ZOOM
YOU REALLY THINK IT'S COOL, SLIPPING OUT WITHOUT TELLING ANYONE?
WE HAD TO.
新宿
JR東日本

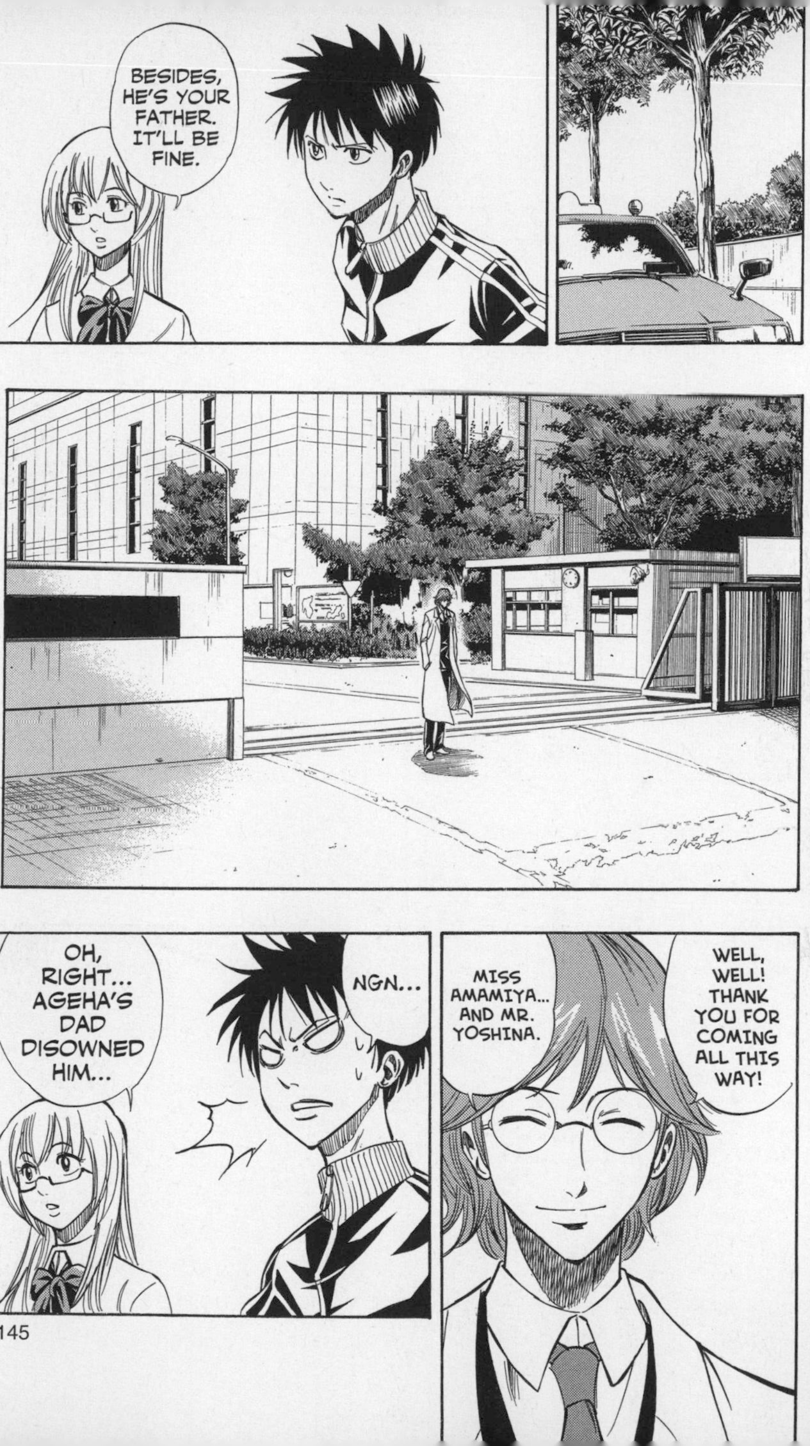
BESIDES, HE'S YOUR FATHER. IT'LL BE FINE.
WELL, WELL! THANK YOU FOR COMING ALL THIS WAY!
MISS AMAMIYA... AND MR. YOSHINA.
NGN...
OH, RIGHT... AGEHA'S DAD DISOWNED HIM...

Mutters and mumblings...

DRAWING PACE
I'VE NOTICED THAT EVEN THOUGH I'VE
GOTTEN FASTER AT DRAWING, IT STILL
BASICALLY TAKES ME JUST AS LONG
TO FINISH MY WORK.
WHAT'S UP WITH THAT?

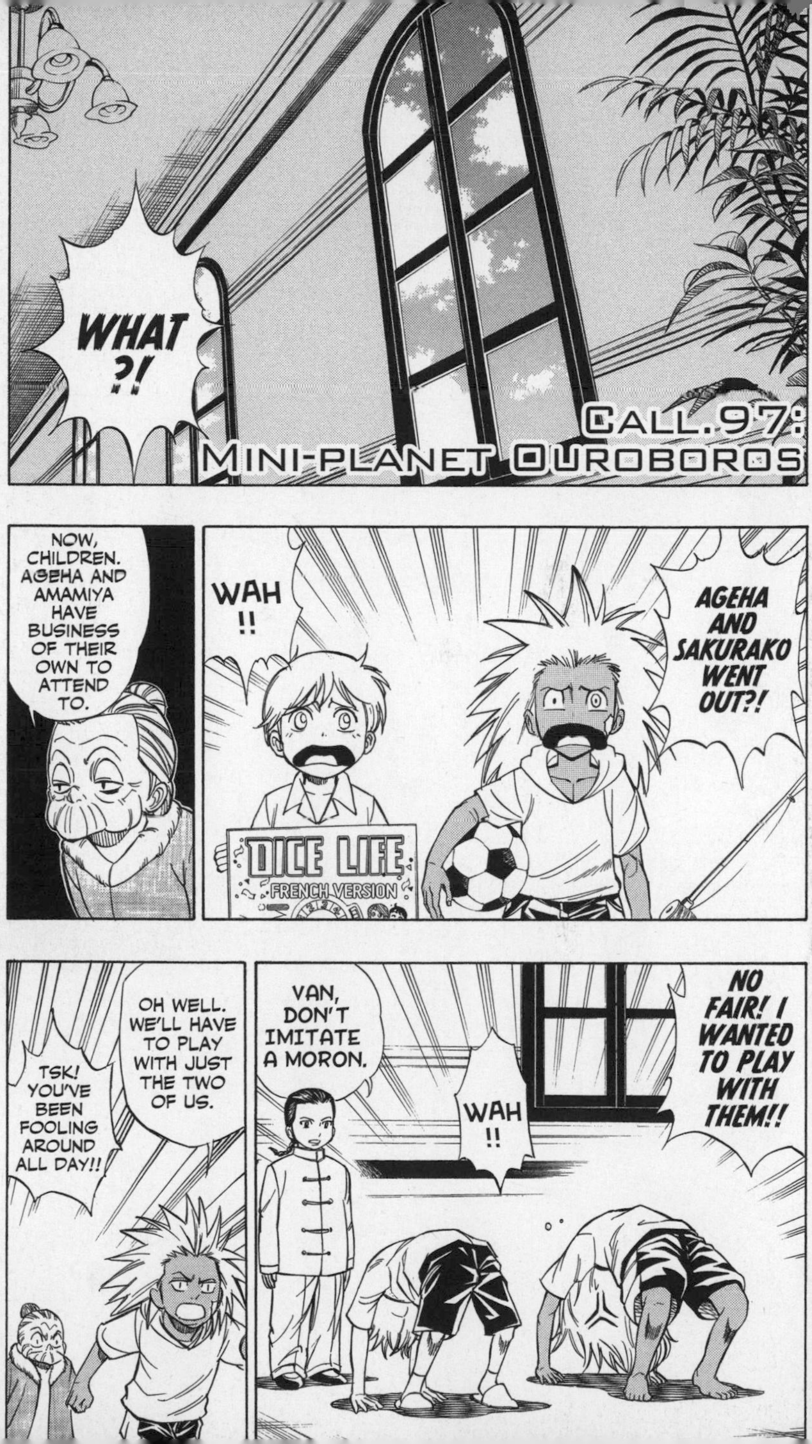
WHAT ?!
CALL.97: MINI-PLANET OUROBOROS
AGEHA AND SAKURAKO WENT OUT?!
WAH !!
DICE LIFE FRENCH VERSION
NOW, CHILDREN. AGEHA AND AMAMIYA HAVE BUSINESS OF THEIR OWN TO ATTEND TO.
NO FAIR! I WANTED TO PLAY WITH THEM!!
WAH !!
VAN, DON'T IMITATE A MORON.
OH WELL. WE'LL HAVE TO PLAY WITH JUST THE TWO OF US.
TSK! YOU'VE BEEN FOOLING AROUND ALL DAY!!

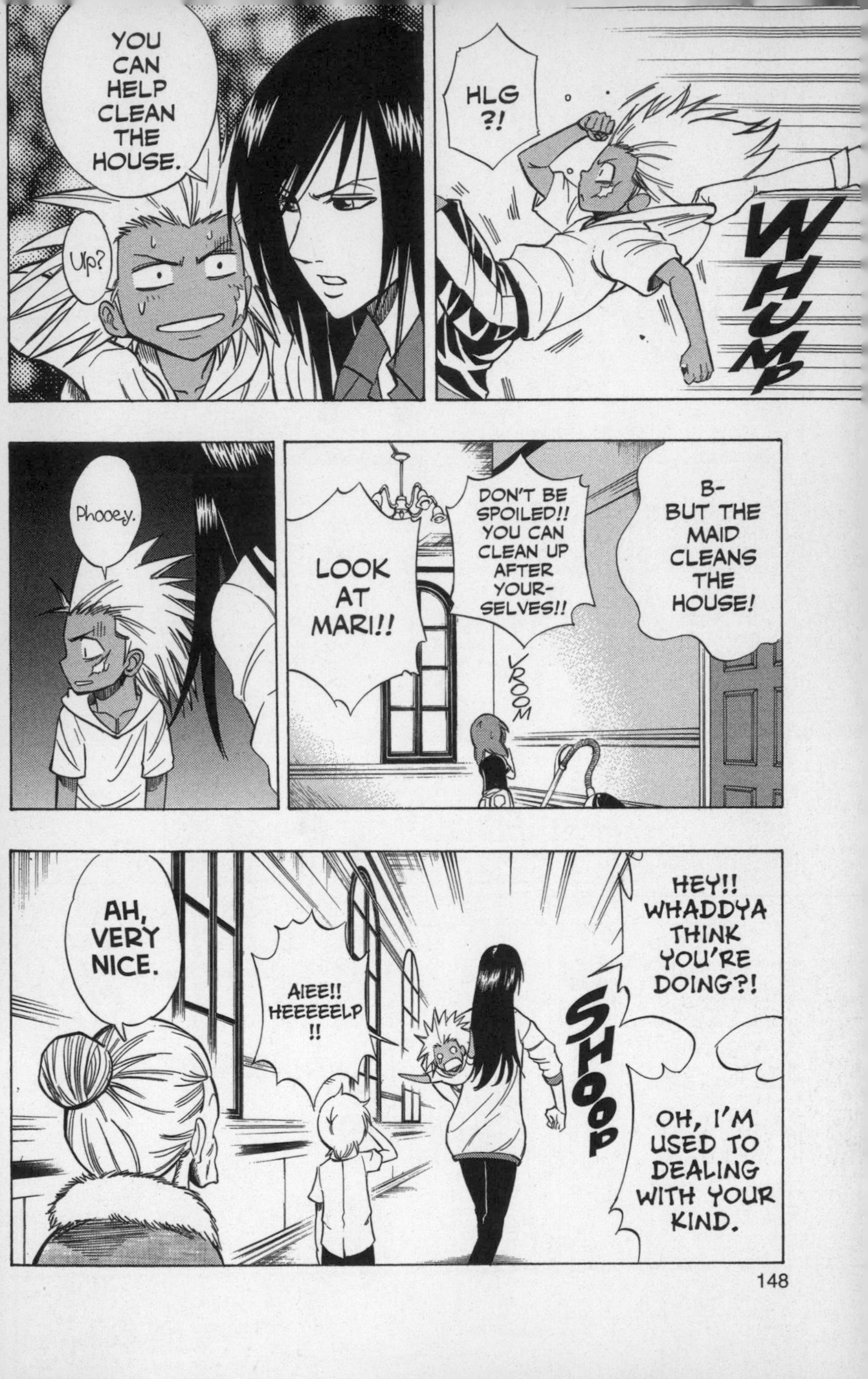
HLG ?!
WHUMP
YOU CAN HELP CLEAN THE HOUSE.
Urp?
B-BUT THE MAID CLEANS THE HOUSE!
DON'T BE SPOILED!! YOU CAN CLEAN UP AFTER YOURSELVES!!
LOOK AT MARI!!
VROOM
Phooey.
HEY!! WHADDYA THINK YOU'RE DOING?!
SHOOP
OH, I'M USED TO DEALING WITH YOUR KIND.
AIEE!! HEEEEELP !!
AH, VERY NICE.

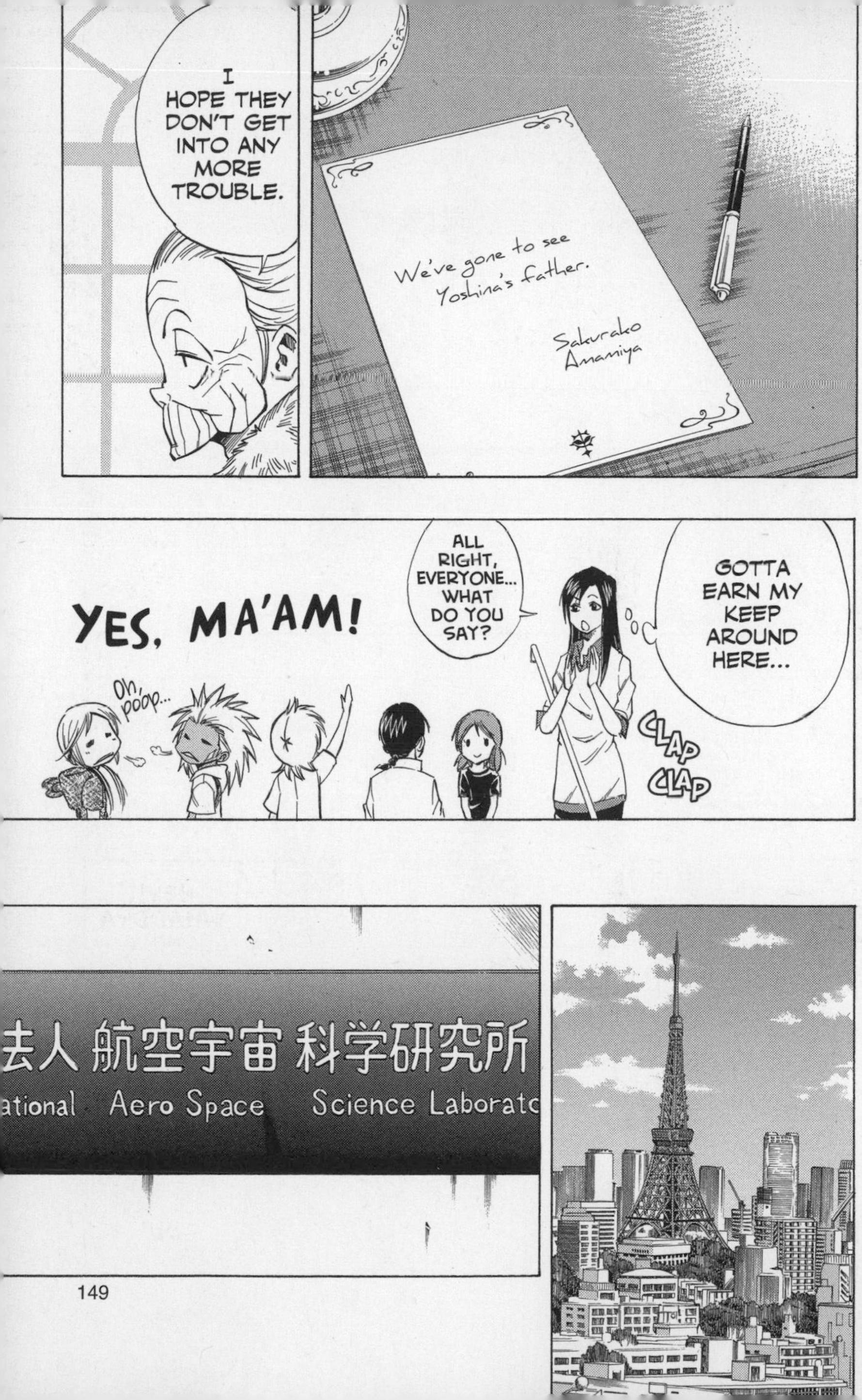
We've gone to see Yoshina's father.
Sakurako Amamiya
I HOPE THEY DON'T GET INTO ANY MORE TROUBLE.
GOTTA EARN MY KEEP AROUND HERE...
CLAP CLAP
ALL RIGHT, EVERYONE... WHAT DO YOU SAY?
YES, MA'AM!
Oh, poop...
法人 航空宇宙 科学研究所
ational Aero Space Science Laborato

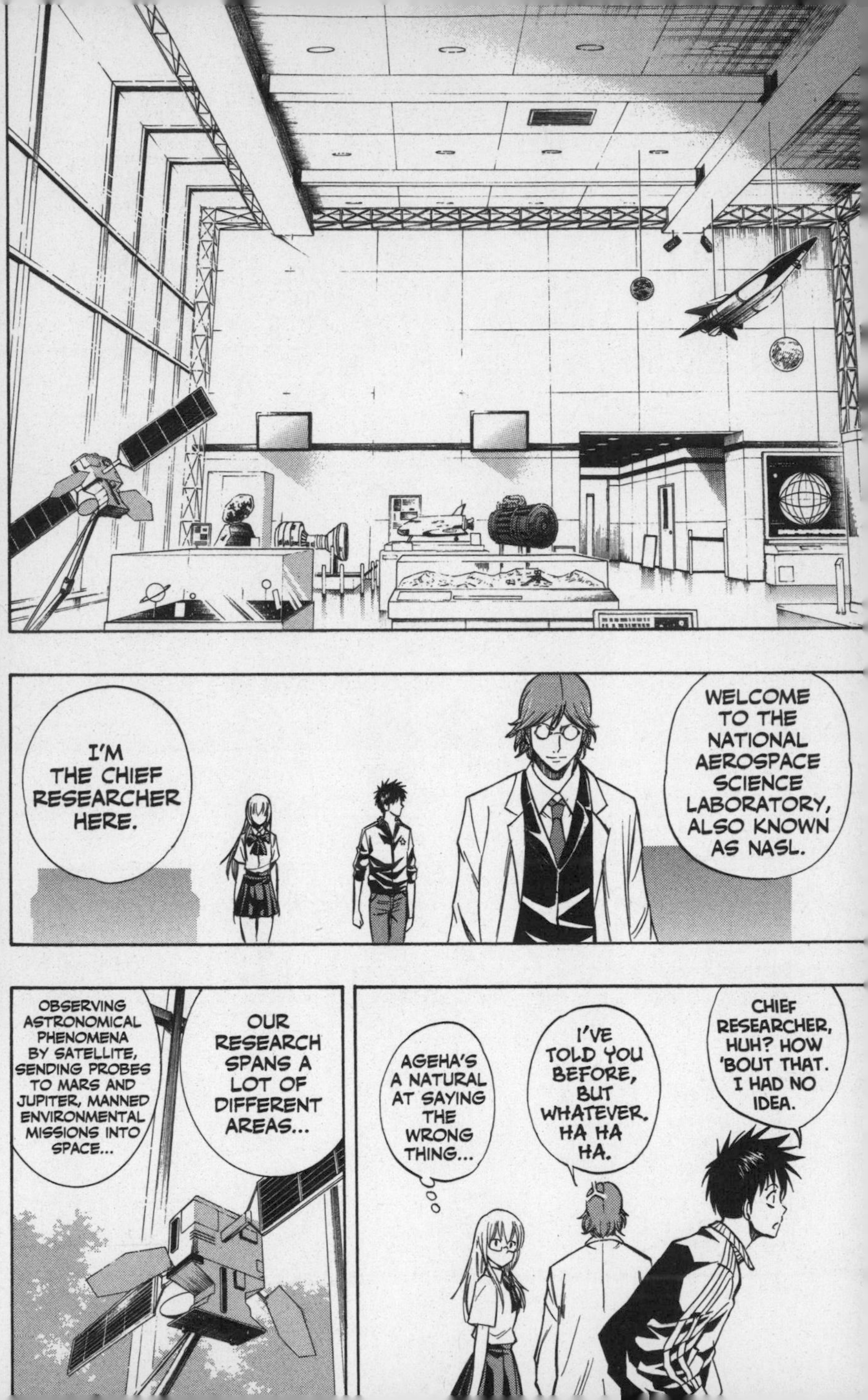
WELCOME TO THE NATIONAL AEROSPACE SCIENCE LABORATORY, ALSO KNOWN AS NASL.
I'M THE CHIEF RESEARCHER HERE.
CHIEF RESEARCHER, HUH? HOW 'BOUT THAT. I HAD NO IDEA.
I'VE TOLD YOU BEFORE, BUT WHATEVER. HA HA HA.
AGEHA'S A NATURAL AT SAYING THE WRONG THING...
OUR RESEARCH SPANS A LOT OF DIFFERENT AREAS...
OBSERVING ASTRONOMICAL PHENOMENA BY SATELLITE, SENDING PROBES TO MARS AND JUPITER, MANNED ENVIRONMENTAL MISSIONS INTO SPACE...

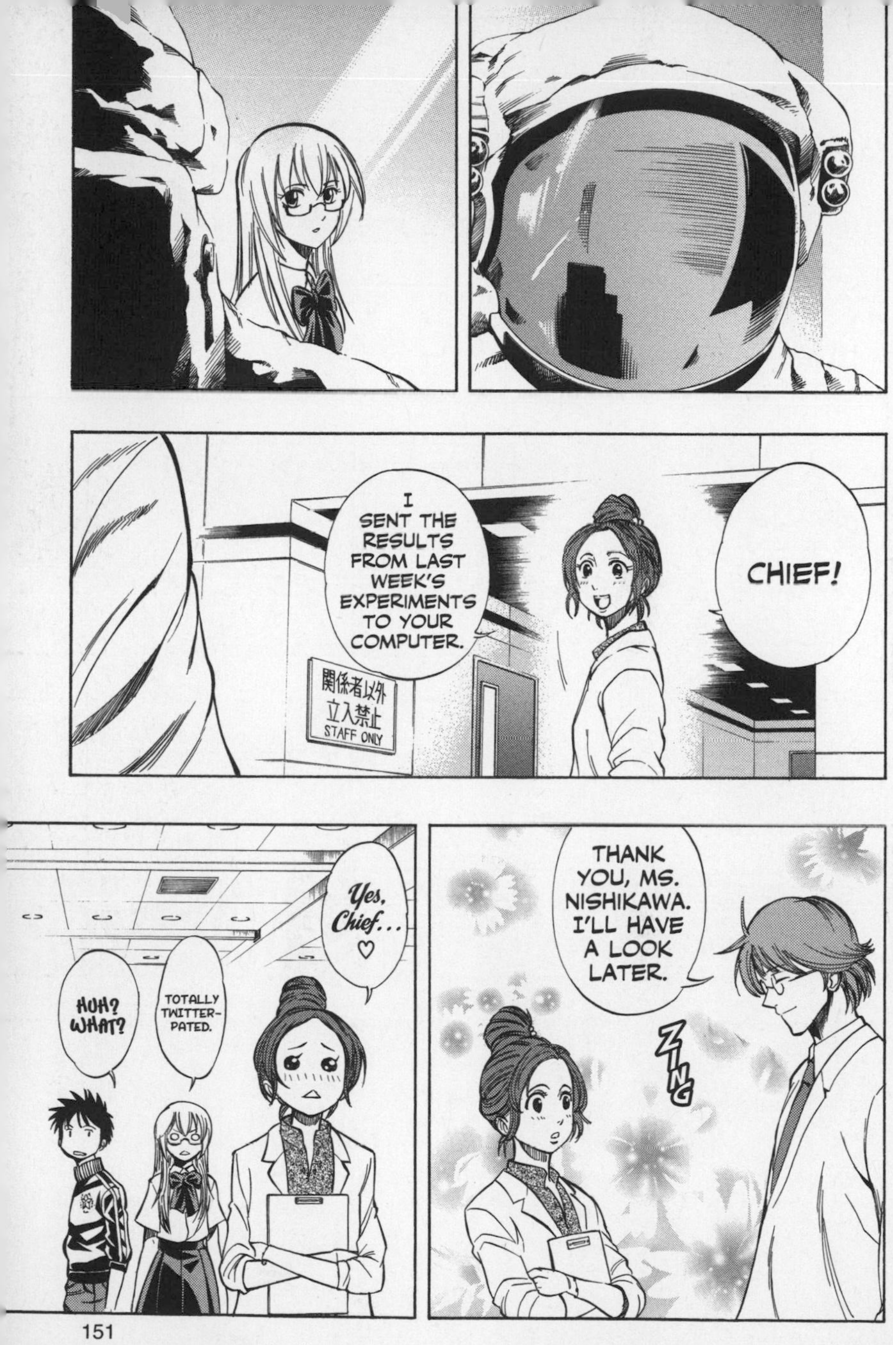
CHIEF!
I SENT THE RESULTS FROM LAST WEEK'S EXPERIMENTS TO YOUR COMPUTER.
関係者以外 立入禁止 STAFF ONLY
THANK YOU, MS. NISHIKAWA. I'LL HAVE A LOOK LATER.
ZING
Yes, Chief... ♡
TOTALLY TWITTER-PATED.
HUH? WHAT?

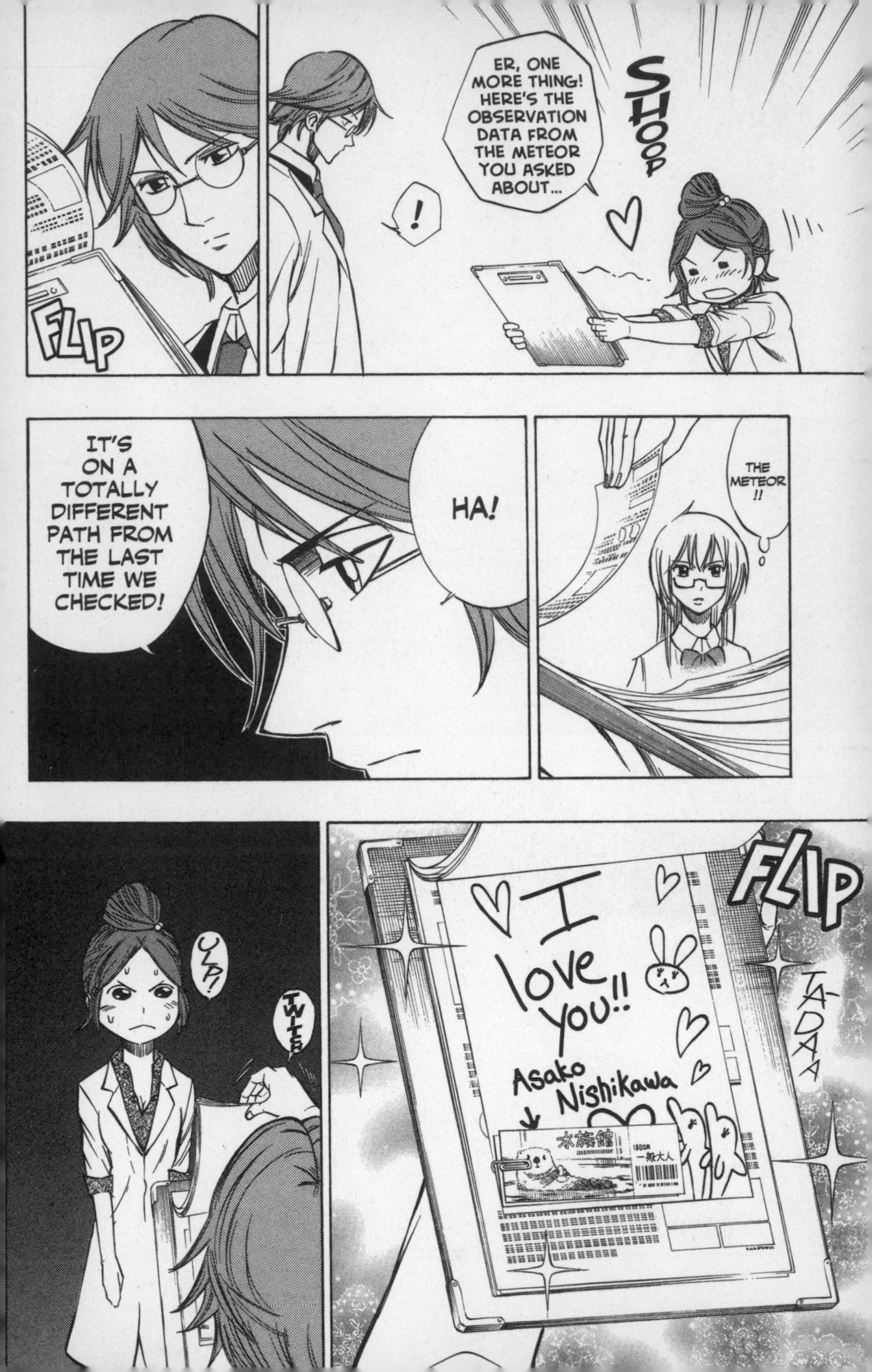
ER, ONE MORE THING! HERE'S THE OBSERVATION DATA FROM THE METEOR YOU ASKED ABOUT...
SHOOP
!
FLIP
THE METEOR !!
HA!
IT'S ON A TOTALLY DIFFERENT PATH FROM THE LAST TIME WE CHECKED!
FLIP
TA-DAA
I love you!!
Asako Nishikawa
水族館
1800円
一般大人
ULP!
TWITCH

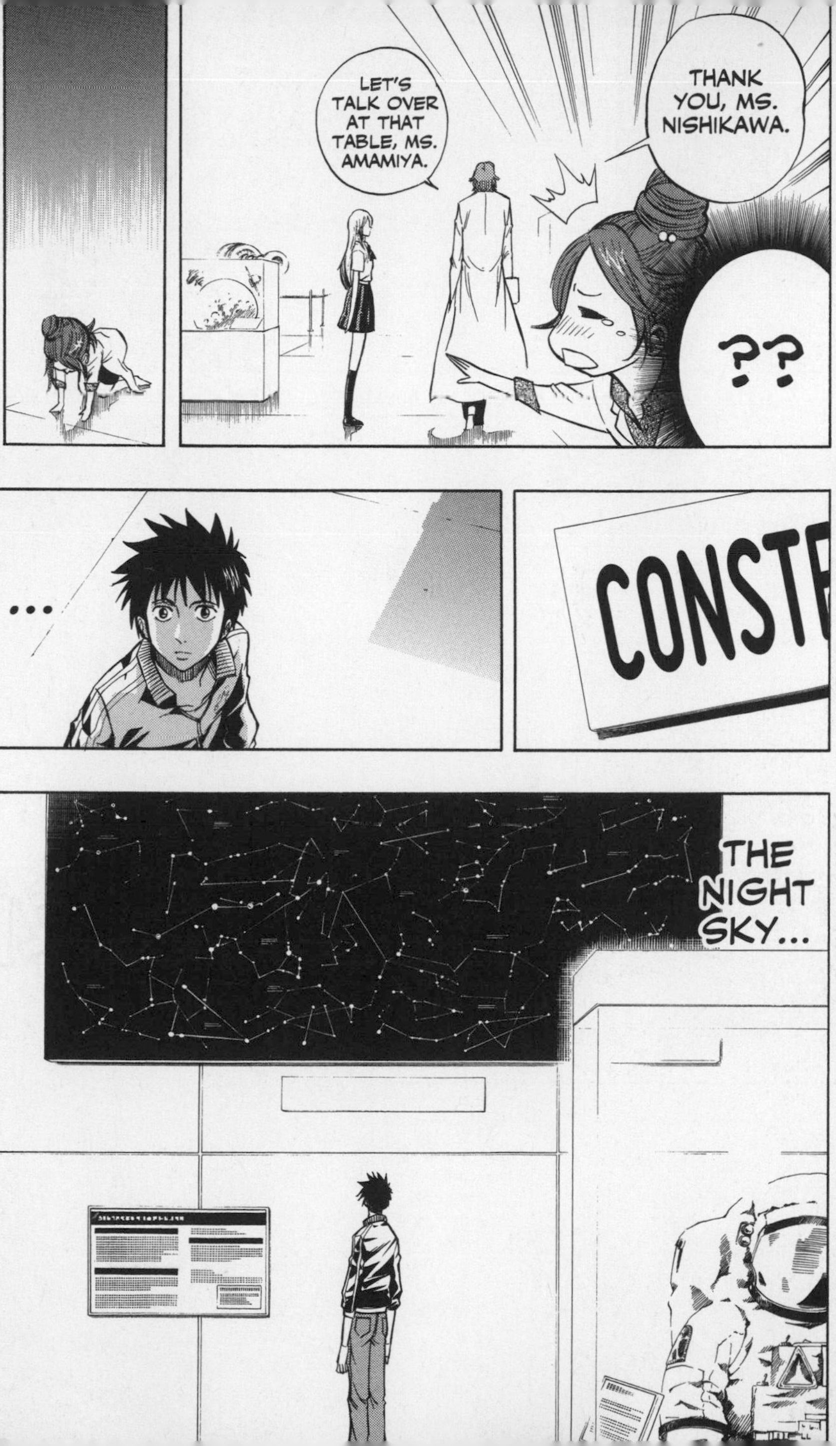
THANK YOU, MS. NISHIKAWA.
LET'S TALK OVER AT THAT TABLE, MS. AMAMIYA.
??
CONSTE
...
THE NIGHT SKY...

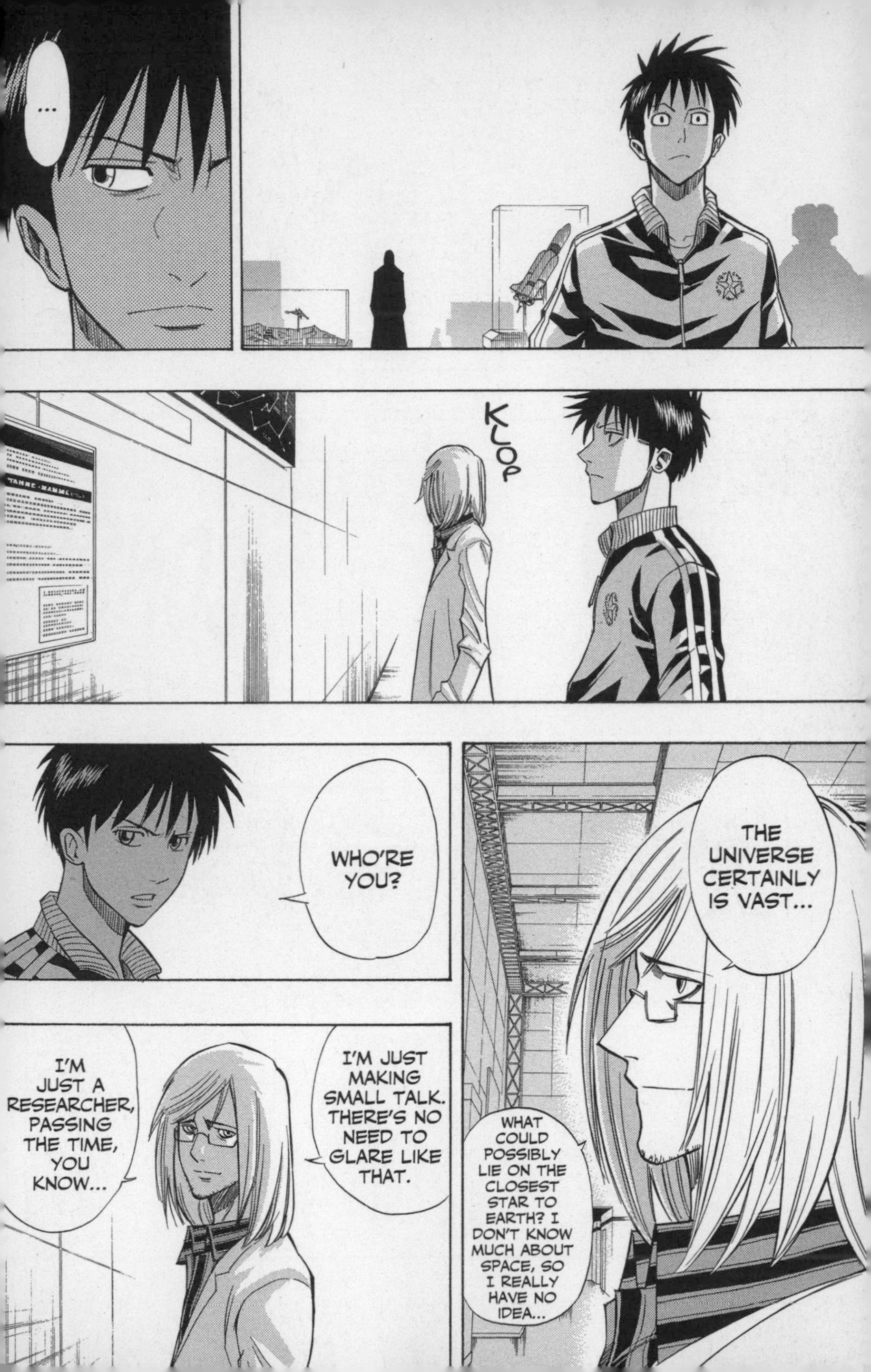
...
KLOP
THE UNIVERSE CERTAINLY IS VAST...
WHAT COULD POSSIBLY LIE ON THE CLOSEST STAR TO EARTH? I DON'T KNOW MUCH ABOUT SPACE, SO I REALLY HAVE NO IDEA...
WHO'RE YOU?
I'M JUST MAKING SMALL TALK. THERE'S NO NEED TO GLARE LIKE THAT.
I'M JUST A RESEARCHER, PASSING THE TIME, YOU KNOW...

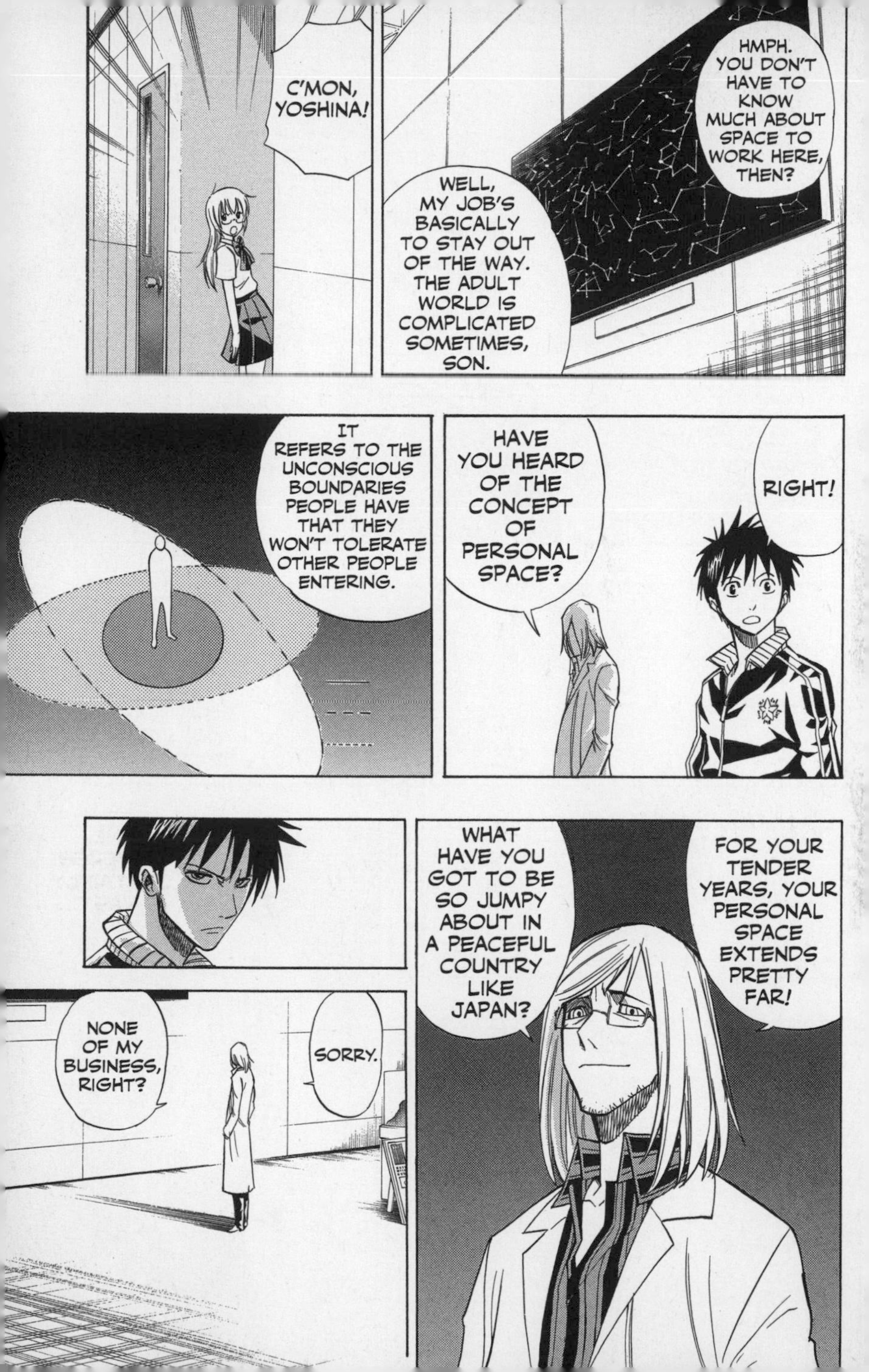
HMPH. YOU DON'T HAVE TO KNOW MUCH ABOUT SPACE TO WORK HERE, THEN?
WELL, MY JOB'S BASICALLY TO STAY OUT OF THE WAY. THE ADULT WORLD IS COMPLICATED SOMETIMES, SON.
C'MON, YOSHINA!
RIGHT!
HAVE YOU HEARD OF THE CONCEPT OF PERSONAL SPACE?
IT REFERS TO THE UNCONSCIOUS BOUNDARIES PEOPLE HAVE THAT THEY WON'T TOLERATE OTHER PEOPLE ENTERING.
FOR YOUR TENDER YEARS, YOUR PERSONAL SPACE EXTENDS PRETTY FAR!
WHAT HAVE YOU GOT TO BE SO JUMPY ABOUT IN A PEACEFUL COUNTRY LIKE JAPAN?
SORRY.
NONE OF MY BUSINESS, RIGHT?

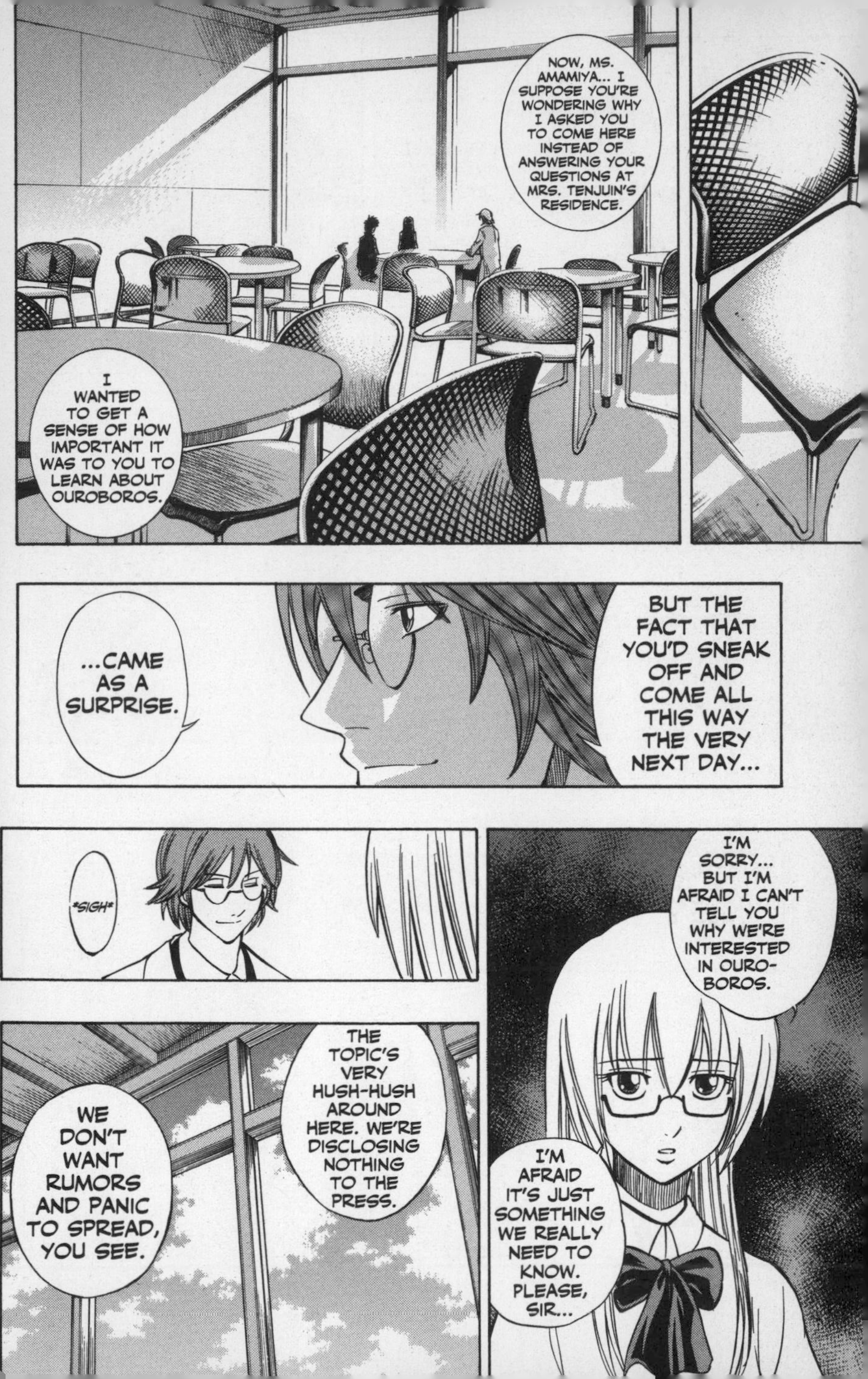
NOW, MS. AMAMIYA... I SUPPOSE YOU'RE WONDERING WHY I ASKED YOU TO COME HERE INSTEAD OF ANSWERING YOUR QUESTIONS AT MRS. TENJUIN'S RESIDENCE.
I WANTED TO GET A SENSE OF HOW IMPORTANT IT WAS TO YOU TO LEARN ABOUT OUROBOROS.
BUT THE FACT THAT YOU'D SNEAK OFF AND COME ALL THIS WAY THE VERY NEXT DAY...
...CAME AS A SURPRISE.
I'M SORRY... BUT I'M AFRAID I CAN'T TELL YOU WHY WE'RE INTERESTED IN OURO-BOROS.
I'M AFRAID IT'S JUST SOMETHING WE REALLY NEED TO KNOW. PLEASE, SIR...
SIGH
THE TOPIC'S VERY HUSH-HUSH AROUND HERE. WE'RE DISCLOSING NOTHING TO THE PRESS.
WE DON'T WANT RUMORS AND PANIC TO SPREAD, YOU SEE.

READ THIS WAY

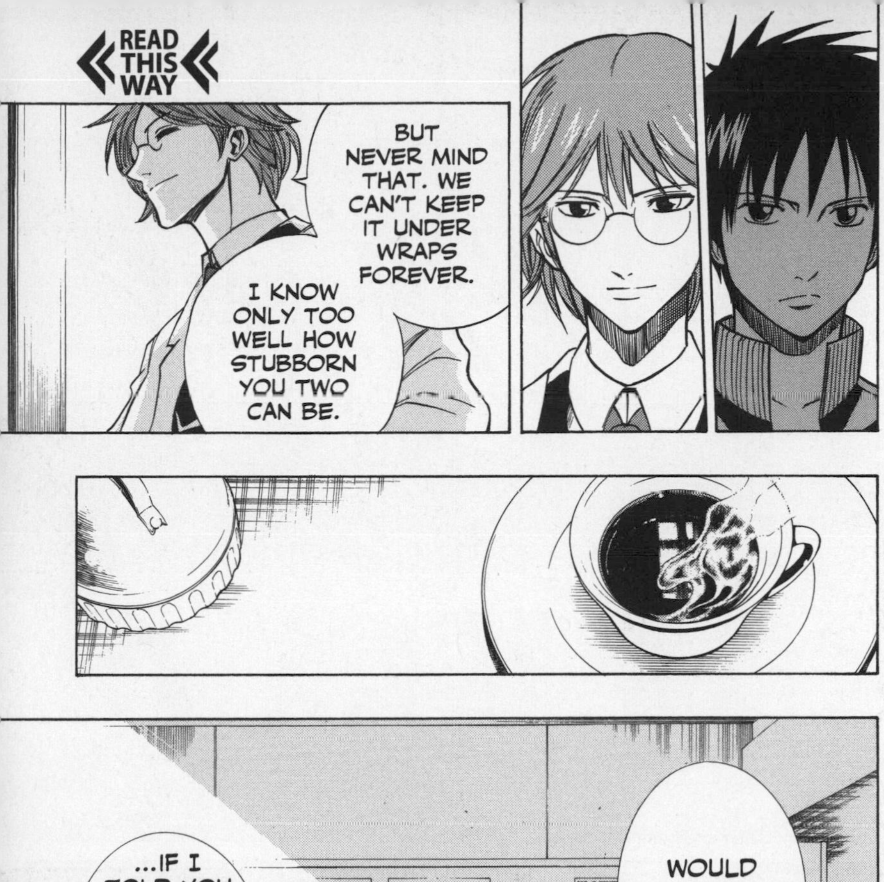

BUT NEVER MIND THAT. WE CAN'T KEEP IT UNDER WRAPS FOREVER.
I KNOW ONLY TOO WELL HOW STUBBORN YOU TWO CAN BE.
WOULD YOU BELIEVE ME...
...IF I TOLD YOU THIS METEOR HAS A WILL OF ITS OWN?

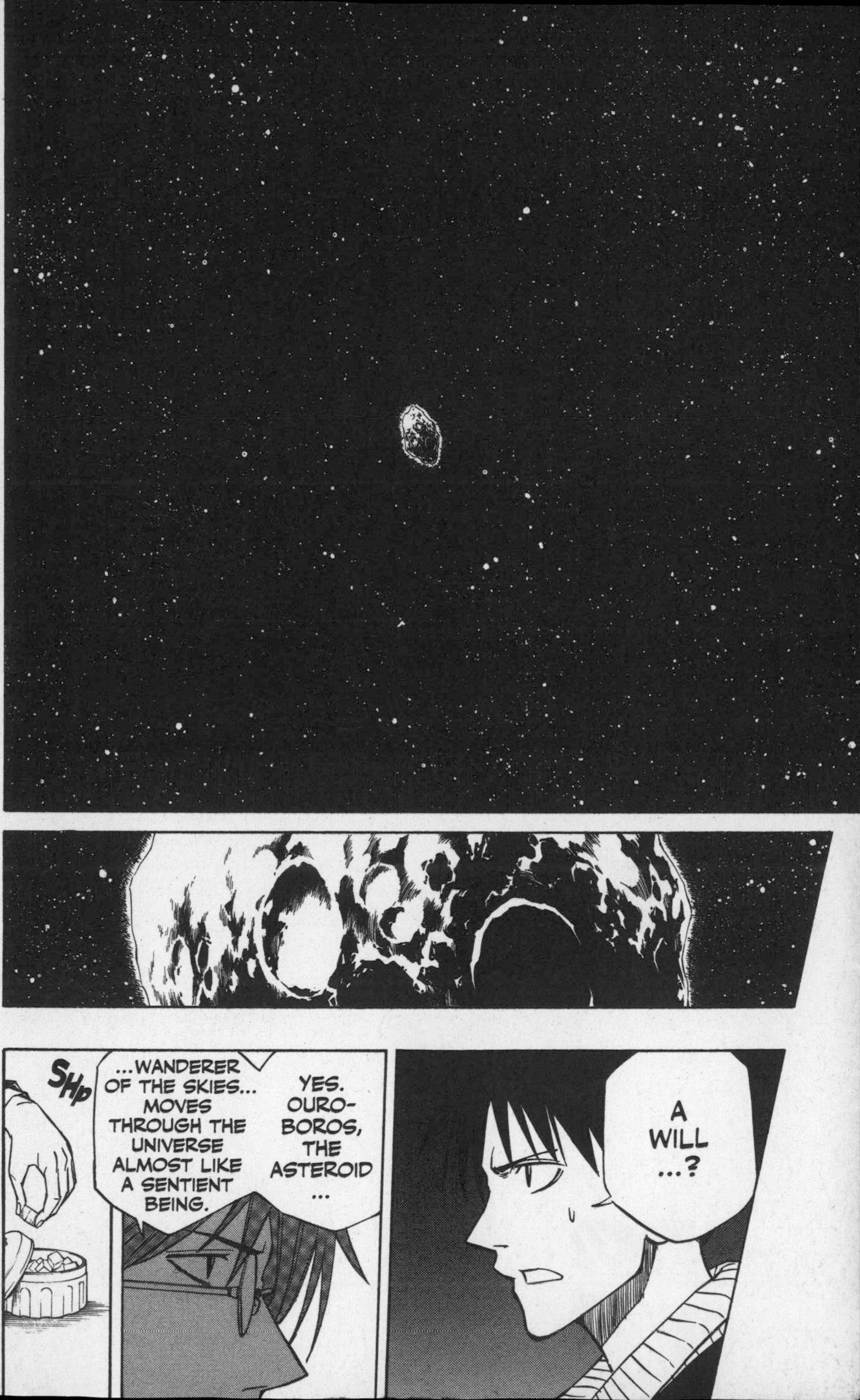
A WILL ...?
YES. OURO-BOROS, THE ASTEROID ...
...WANDERER OF THE SKIES... MOVES THROUGH THE UNIVERSE ALMOST LIKE A SENTIENT BEING.
SHp

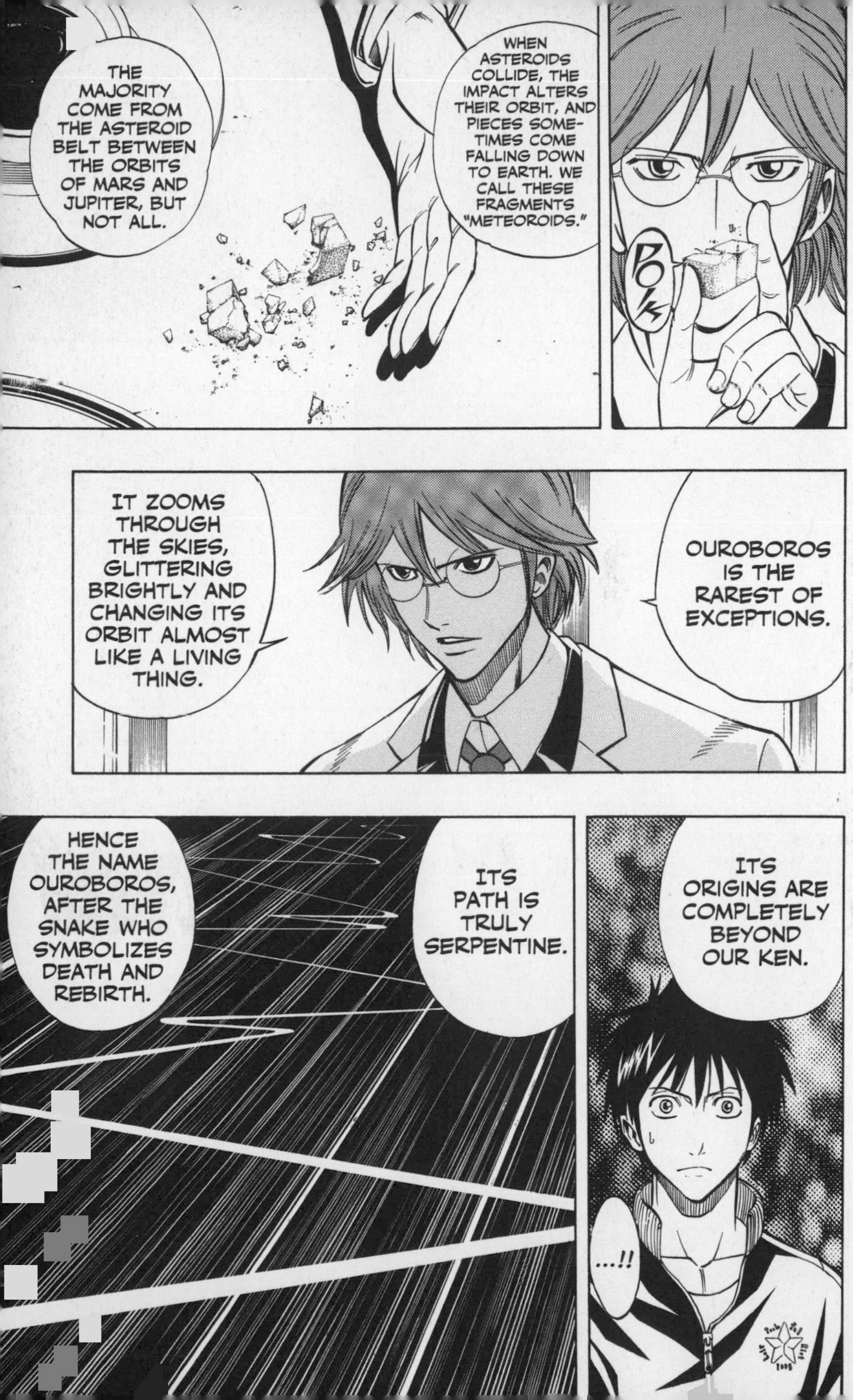
POK
WHEN ASTEROIDS COLLIDE, THE IMPACT ALTERS THEIR ORBIT, AND PIECES SOME-TIMES COME FALLING DOWN TO EARTH. WE CALL THESE FRAGMENTS "METEOROIDS."
THE MAJORITY COME FROM THE ASTEROID BELT BETWEEN THE ORBITS OF MARS AND JUPITER, BUT NOT ALL.
OUROBOROS IS THE RAREST OF EXCEPTIONS.
IT ZOOMS THROUGH THE SKIES, GLITTERING BRIGHTLY AND CHANGING ITS ORBIT ALMOST LIKE A LIVING THING.
ITS ORIGINS ARE COMPLETELY BEYOND OUR KEN.
...!!
ITS PATH IS TRULY SERPENTINE.
HENCE THE NAME OUROBOROS, AFTER THE SNAKE WHO SYMBOLIZES DEATH AND REBIRTH.

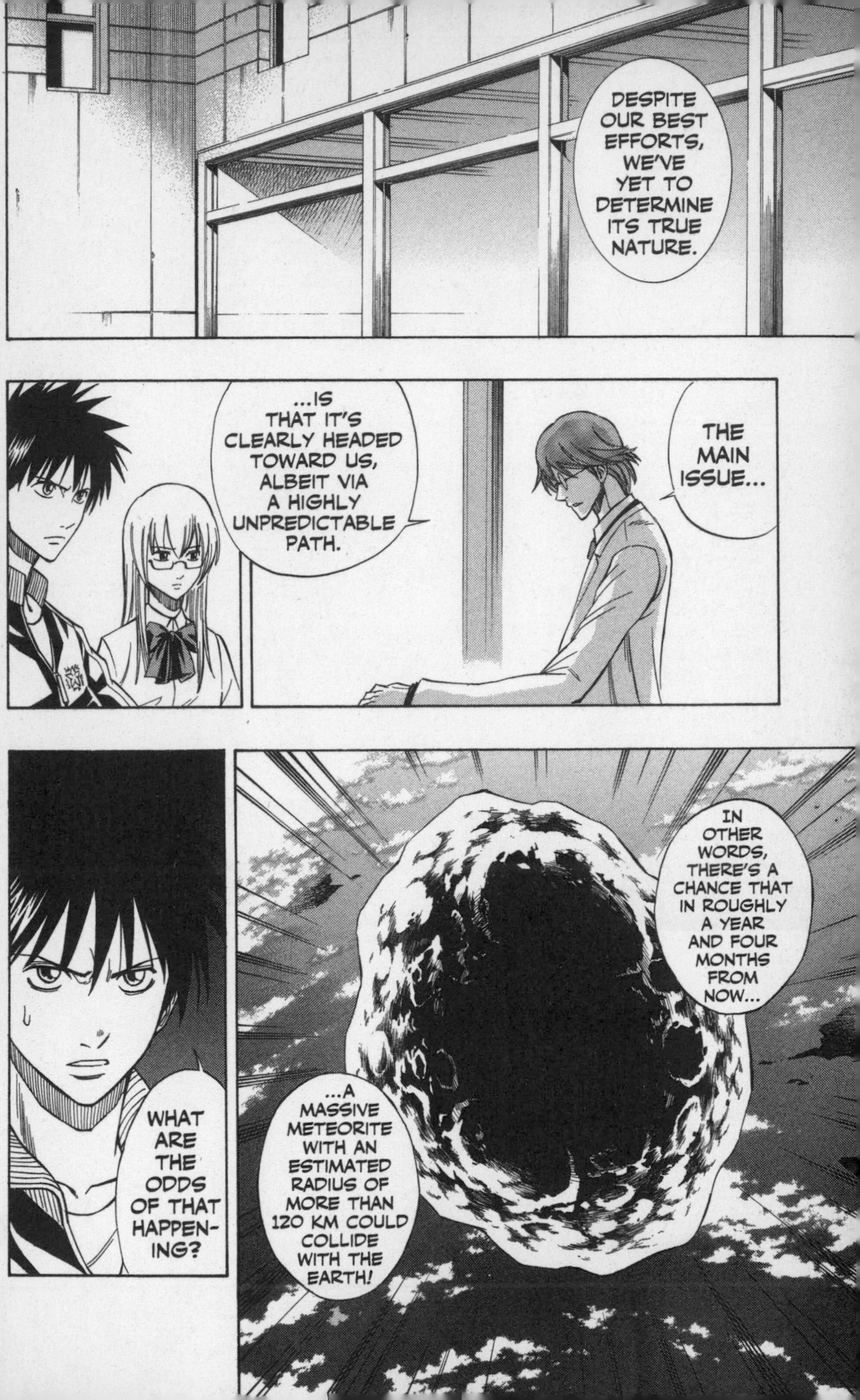
DESPITE OUR BEST EFFORTS, WE'VE YET TO DETERMINE ITS TRUE NATURE.
THE MAIN ISSUE...
...IS THAT IT'S CLEARLY HEADED TOWARD US, ALBEIT VIA A HIGHLY UNPREDICTABLE PATH.
IN OTHER WORDS, THERE'S A CHANCE THAT IN ROUGHLY A YEAR AND FOUR MONTHS FROM NOW...
...A MASSIVE METEORITE WITH AN ESTIMATED RADIUS OF MORE THAN 120 KM COULD COLLIDE WITH THE EARTH!
WHAT ARE THE ODDS OF THAT HAPPEN-ING?

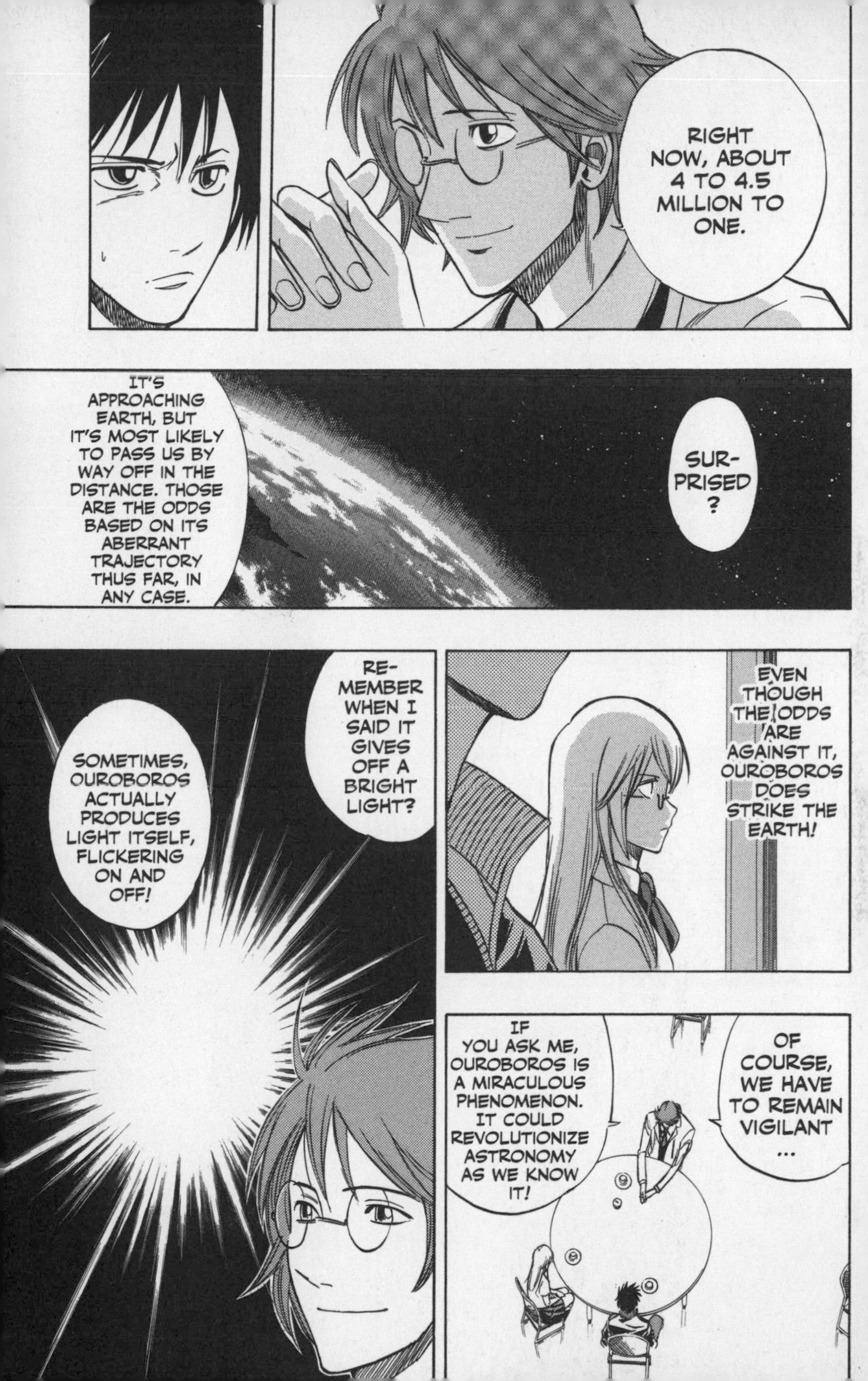
RIGHT NOW, ABOUT 4 TO 4.5 MILLION TO ONE.
SUR-PRISED?
IT'S APPROACHING EARTH, BUT IT'S MOST LIKELY TO PASS US BY WAY OFF IN THE DISTANCE. THOSE ARE THE ODDS BASED ON ITS ABERRANT TRAJECTORY THUS FAR, IN ANY CASE.
EVEN THOUGH THE ODDS ARE AGAINST IT, OUROBOROS DOES STRIKE THE EARTH!
OF COURSE, WE HAVE TO REMAIN VIGILANT ...
IF YOU ASK ME, OUROBOROS IS A MIRACULOUS PHENOMENON. IT COULD REVOLUTIONIZE ASTRONOMY AS WE KNOW IT!
RE-MEMBER WHEN I SAID IT GIVES OFF A BRIGHT LIGHT?
SOMETIMES, OUROBOROS ACTUALLY PRODUCES LIGHT ITSELF, FLICKERING ON AND OFF!

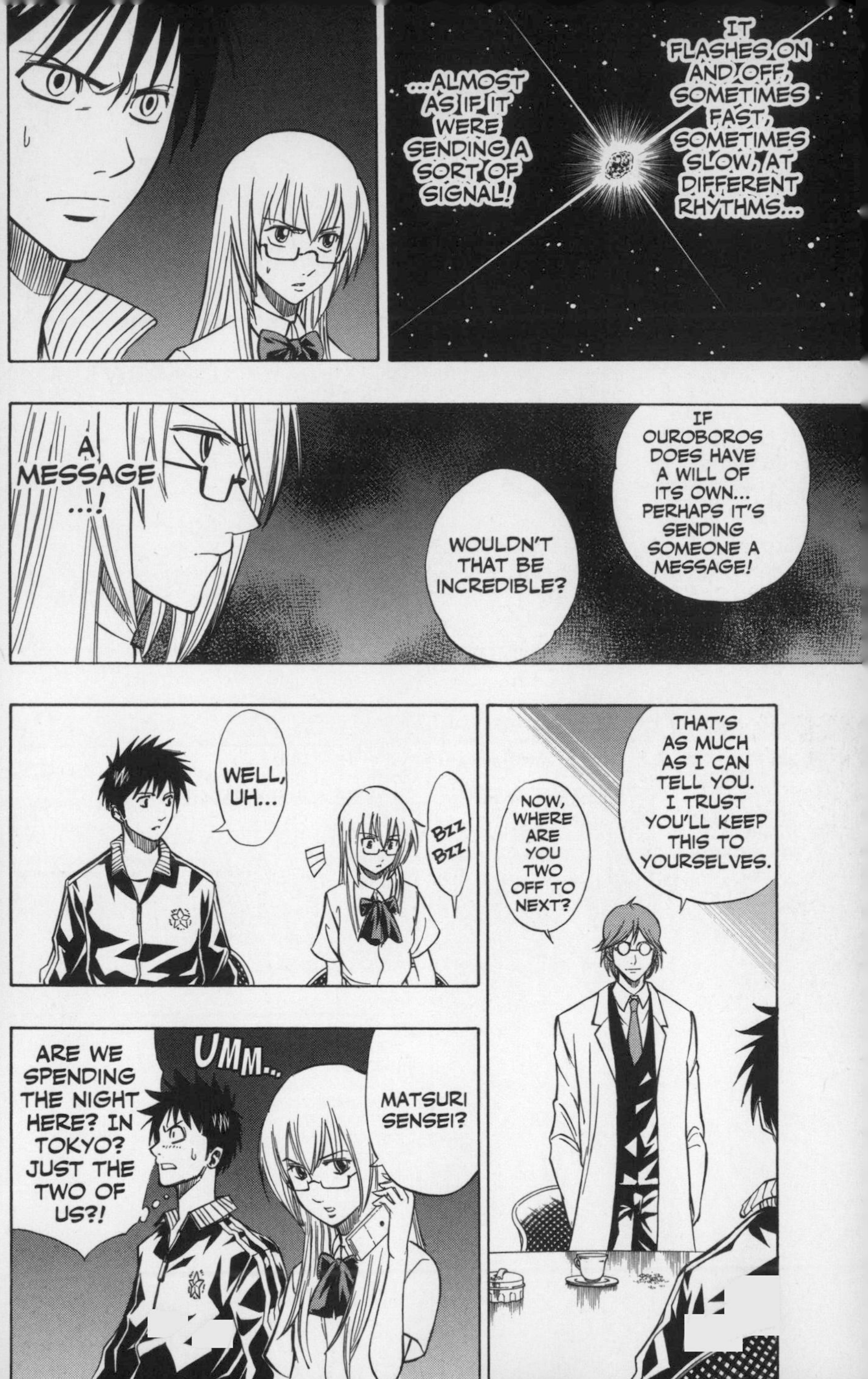
IT FLASHES ON AND OFF, SOMETIMES FAST, SOMETIMES SLOW, AT DIFFERENT RHYTHMS...
...ALMOST AS IF IT WERE SENDING A SORT OF SIGNAL!
IF OUROBOROS DOES HAVE A WILL OF ITS OWN... PERHAPS IT'S SENDING SOMEONE A MESSAGE!
WOULDN'T THAT BE INCREDIBLE?
A MESSAGE ...!
THAT'S AS MUCH AS I CAN TELL YOU. I TRUST YOU'LL KEEP THIS TO YOURSELVES.
NOW, WHERE ARE YOU TWO OFF TO NEXT?
WELL, UH...
BZZ BZZ
MATSURI SENSEI?
UMM...
ARE WE SPENDING THE NIGHT HERE? IN TOKYO? JUST THE TWO OF US?!

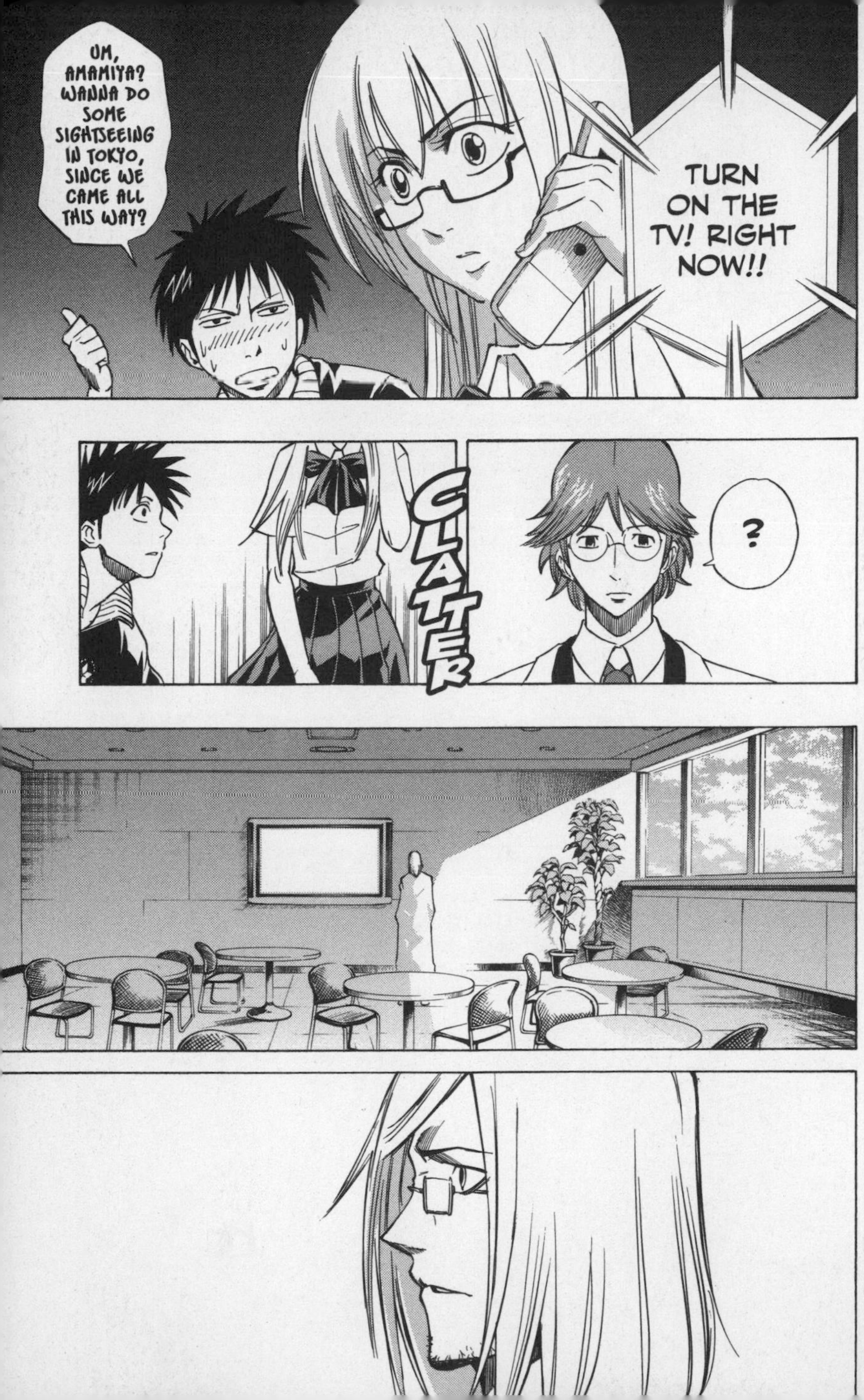
TURN ON THE TV! RIGHT NOW!!
UM, AMAMIYA? WANNA DO SOME SIGHTSEEING IN TOKYO, SINCE WE CAME ALL THIS WAY?
?
CLATTER

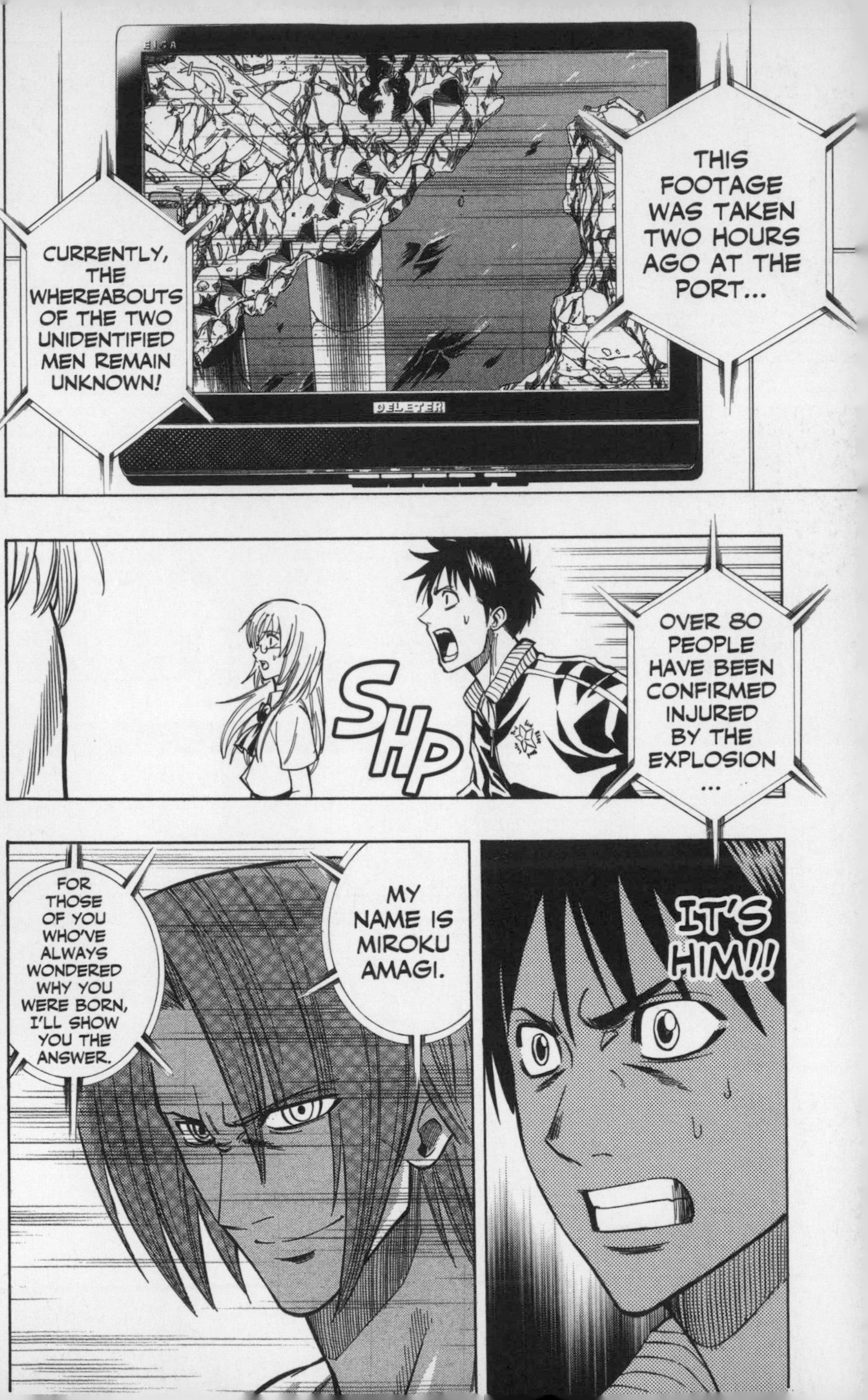
THIS FOOTAGE WAS TAKEN TWO HOURS AGO AT THE PORT...
CURRENTLY, THE WHEREABOUTS OF THE TWO UNIDENTIFIED MEN REMAIN UNKNOWN!
DELETER
OVER 80 PEOPLE HAVE BEEN CONFIRMED INJURED BY THE EXPLOSION ...
SHP
IT'S HIM!!
MY NAME IS MIROKU AMAGI.
FOR THOSE OF YOU WHO'VE ALWAYS WONDERED WHY YOU WERE BORN, I'LL SHOW YOU THE ANSWER.

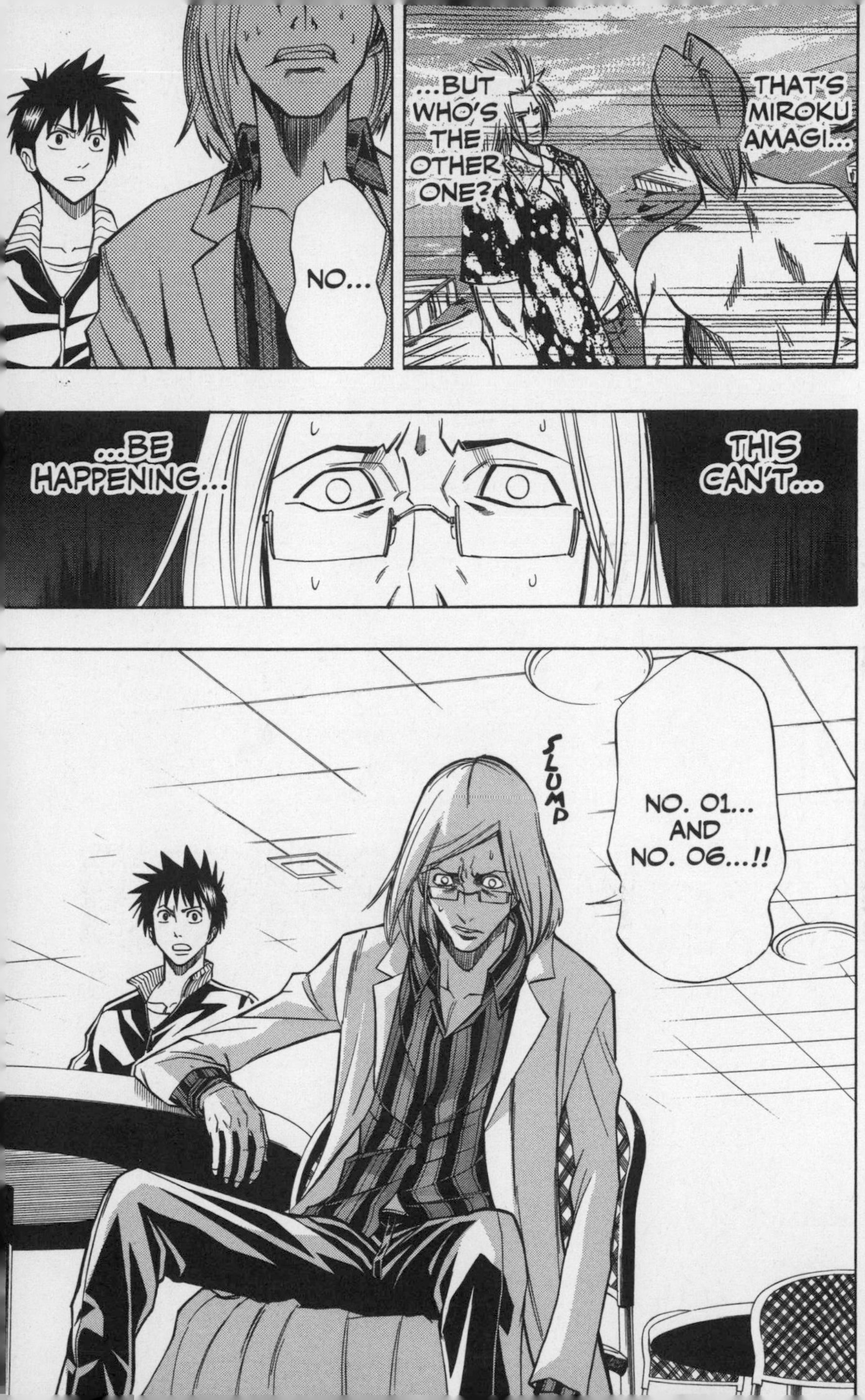
THAT'S MIROKU AMAGI...
...BUT WHO'S THE OTHER ONE?
NO...
THIS CAN'T...
...BE HAPPENING...
NO. 01... AND NO. 06...!!
SLUMP

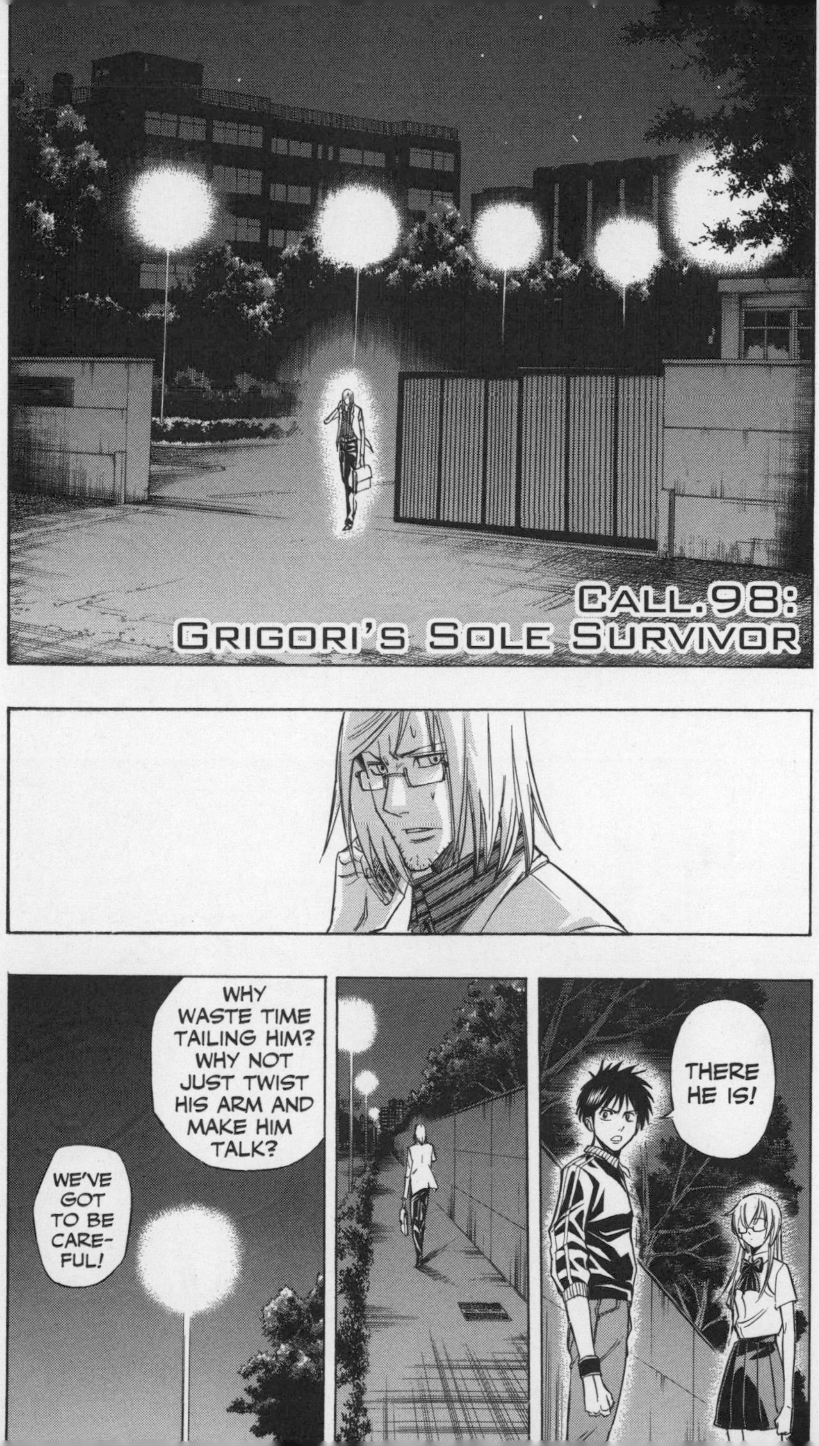
CALL.98:
GRIGORI'S SOLE SURVIVOR
THERE HE IS!
WHY WASTE TIME TAILING HIM? WHY NOT JUST TWIST HIS ARM AND MAKE HIM TALK?
WE'VE GOT TO BE CARE-FUL!

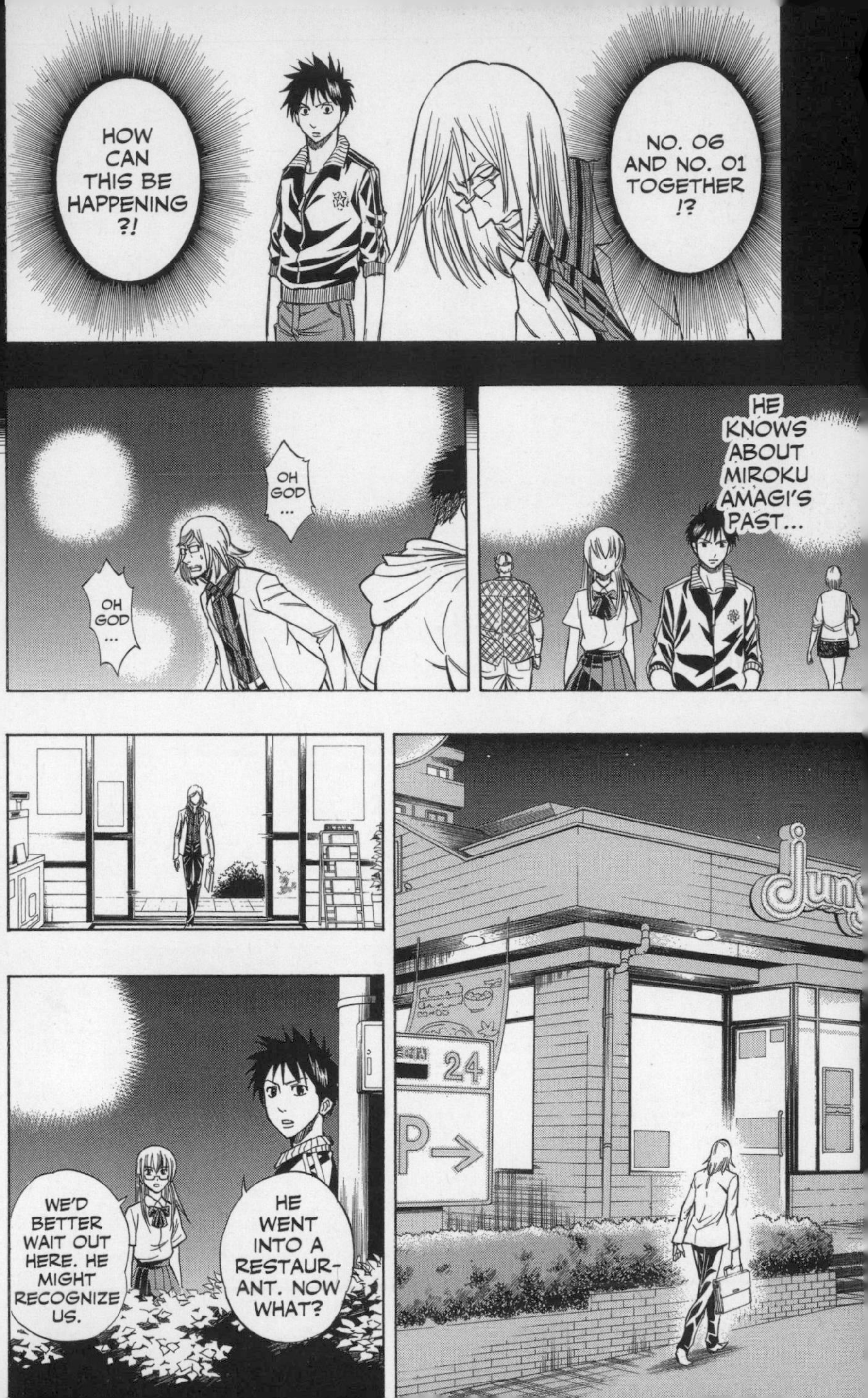
NO. 06 AND NO. 01 TOGETHER !?
HOW CAN THIS BE HAPPENING ?!
HE KNOWS ABOUT MIROKU AMAGI'S PAST...
OH GOD ...
OH GOD ...
24
P
HE WENT INTO A RESTAUR-ANT. NOW WHAT?
WE'D BETTER WAIT OUT HERE. HE MIGHT RECOGNIZE US.

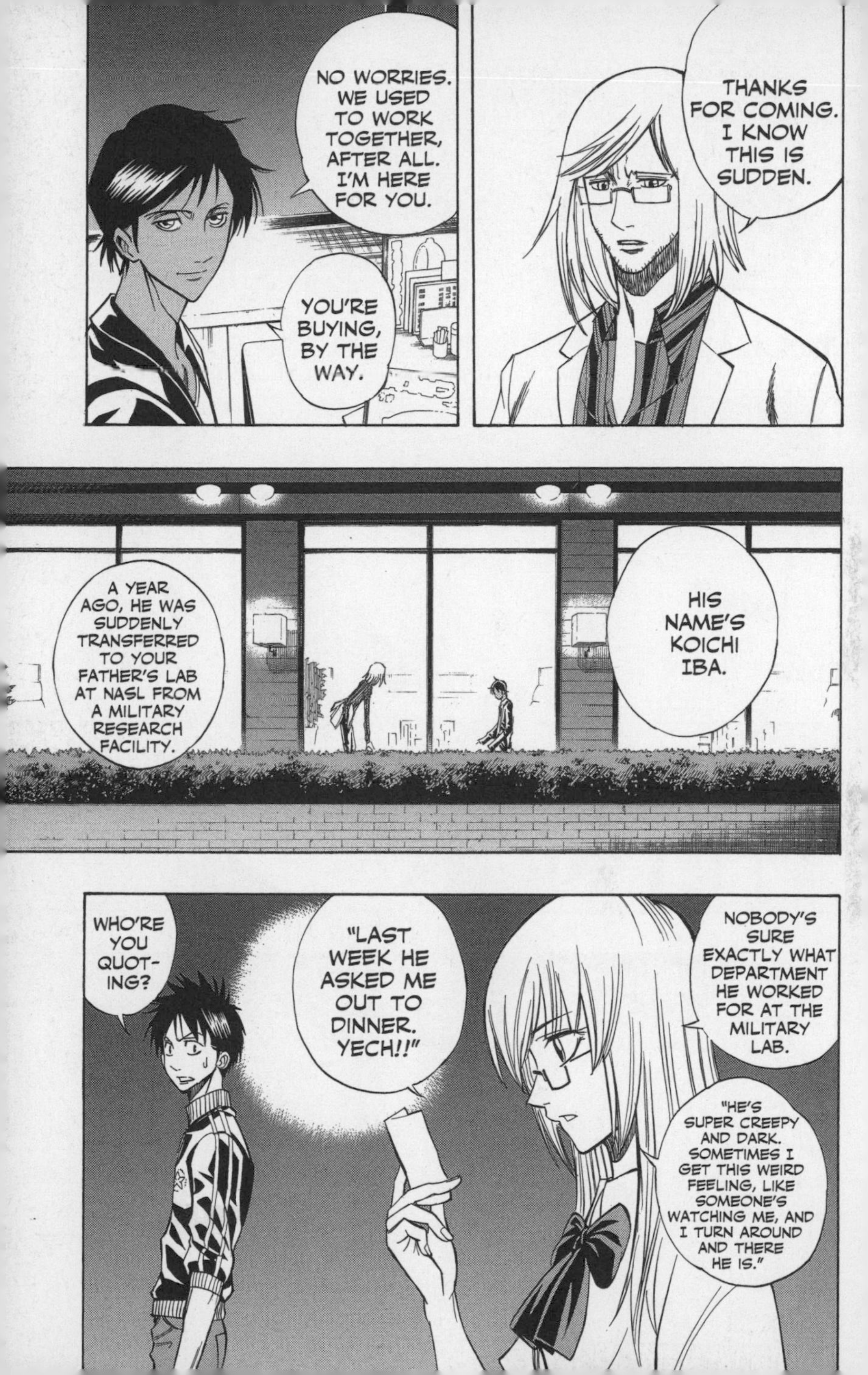
THANKS FOR COMING. I KNOW THIS IS SUDDEN.
NO WORRIES. WE USED TO WORK TOGETHER, AFTER ALL. I'M HERE FOR YOU.
YOU'RE BUYING, BY THE WAY.
HIS NAME'S KOICHI IBA.
A YEAR AGO, HE WAS SUDDENLY TRANSFERRED TO YOUR FATHER'S LAB AT NASL FROM A MILITARY RESEARCH FACILITY.
NOBODY'S SURE EXACTLY WHAT DEPARTMENT HE WORKED FOR AT THE MILITARY LAB.
"HE'S SUPER CREEPY AND DARK. SOMETIMES I GET THIS WEIRD FEELING, LIKE SOMEONE'S WATCHING ME, AND I TURN AROUND AND THERE HE IS."
"LAST WEEK HE ASKED ME OUT TO DINNER. YECH!!"
WHO'RE YOU QUOT-ING?

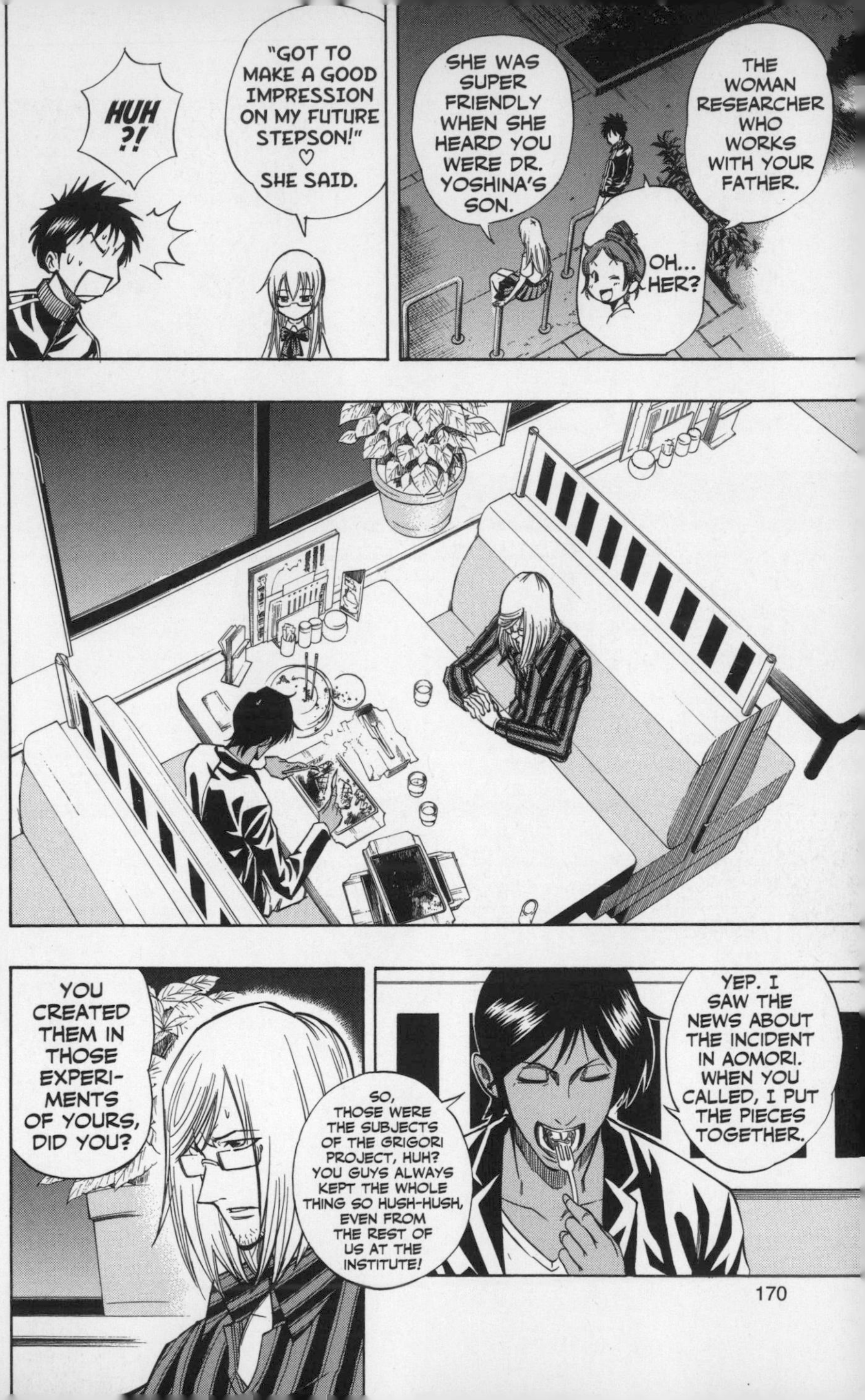
THE WOMAN RESEARCHER WHO WORKS WITH YOUR FATHER.
OH... HER?
SHE WAS SUPER FRIENDLY WHEN SHE HEARD YOU WERE DR. YOSHINA'S SON.
"GOT TO MAKE A GOOD IMPRESSION ON MY FUTURE STEPSON!" ♡ SHE SAID.
HUH?!
YEP. I SAW THE NEWS ABOUT THE INCIDENT IN AOMORI. WHEN YOU CALLED, I PUT THE PIECES TOGETHER.
SO, THOSE WERE THE SUBJECTS OF THE GRIGORI PROJECT, HUH? YOU GUYS ALWAYS KEPT THE WHOLE THING SO HUSH-HUSH, EVEN FROM THE REST OF US AT THE INSTITUTE!
YOU CREATED THEM IN THOSE EXPERIMENTS OF YOURS, DID YOU?

READ THIS WAY

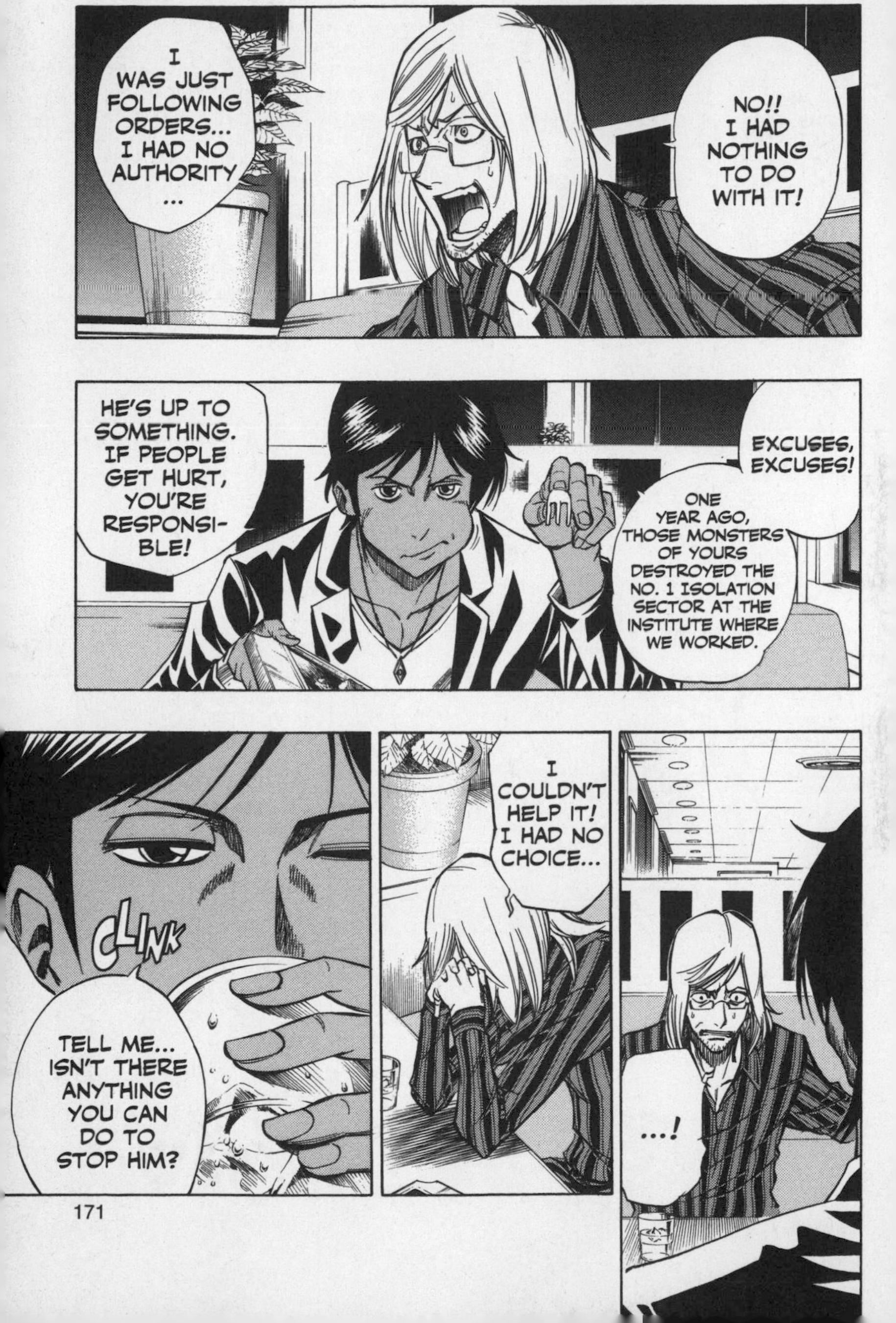
NO!! I HAD NOTHING TO DO WITH IT!
I WAS JUST FOLLOWING ORDERS... I HAD NO AUTHORITY...
EXCUSES, EXCUSES!
ONE YEAR AGO, THOSE MONSTERS OF YOURS DESTROYED THE NO. 1 ISOLATION SECTOR AT THE INSTITUTE WHERE WE WORKED.
HE'S UP TO SOMETHING. IF PEOPLE GET HURT, YOU'RE RESPONSI-BLE!
...!
I COULDN'T HELP IT! I HAD NO CHOICE...
CLINK
TELL ME... ISN'T THERE ANYTHING YOU CAN DO TO STOP HIM?

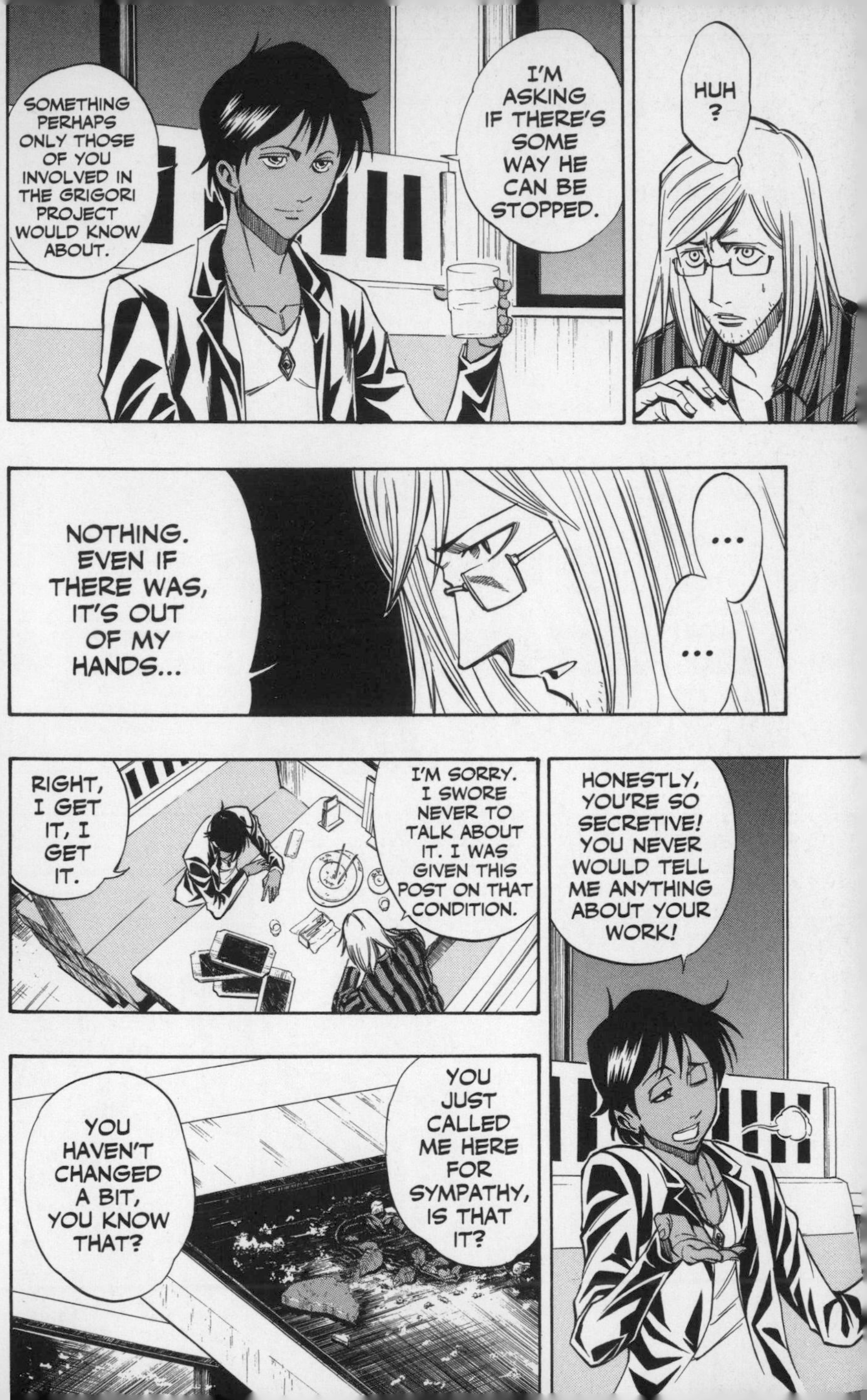
HUH?
I'M ASKING IF THERE'S SOME WAY HE CAN BE STOPPED.
SOMETHING PERHAPS ONLY THOSE OF YOU INVOLVED IN THE GRIGORI PROJECT WOULD KNOW ABOUT.
...
...
NOTHING. EVEN IF THERE WAS, IT'S OUT OF MY HANDS...
HONESTLY, YOU'RE SO SECRETIVE! YOU NEVER WOULD TELL ME ANYTHING ABOUT YOUR WORK!
I'M SORRY. I SWORE NEVER TO TALK ABOUT IT. I WAS GIVEN THIS POST ON THAT CONDITION.
RIGHT, I GET IT, I GET IT.
YOU JUST CALLED ME HERE FOR SYMPATHY, IS THAT IT?
YOU HAVEN'T CHANGED A BIT, YOU KNOW THAT?

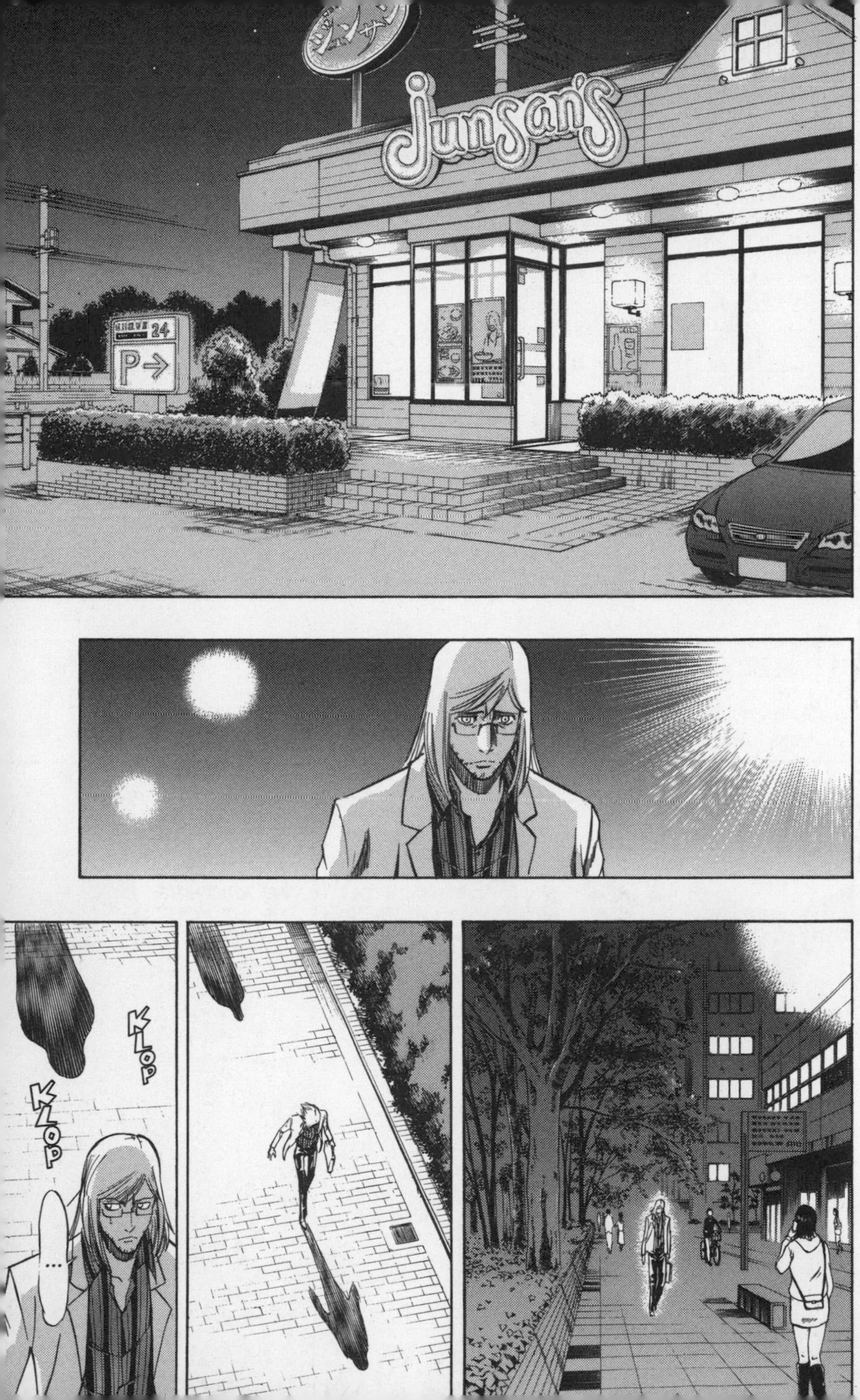
Junsan's
24
P
KLOP
KLOP
...

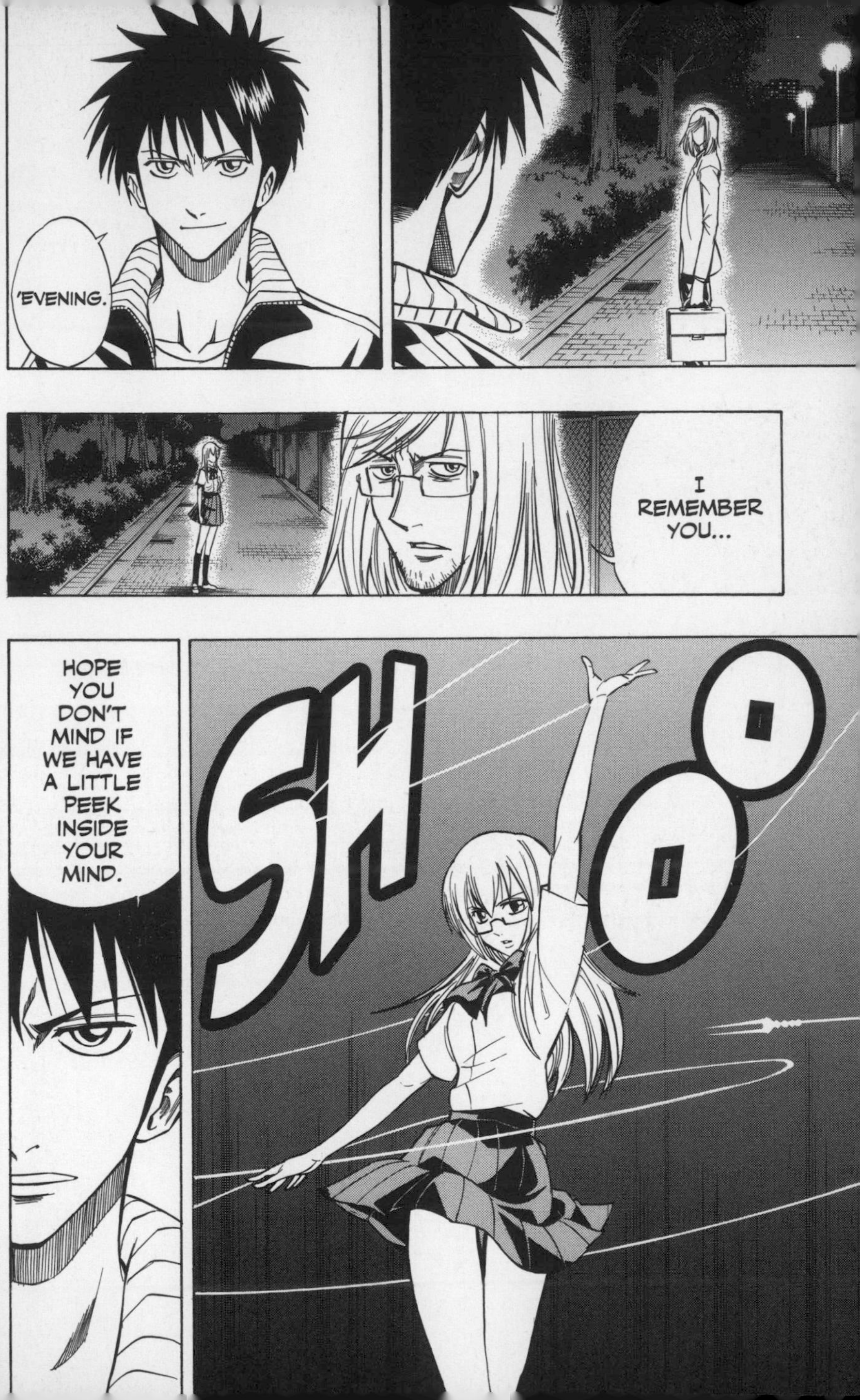
'EVENING.
I REMEMBER YOU...
SHOO
HOPE YOU DON'T MIND IF WE HAVE A LITTLE PEEK INSIDE YOUR MIND.

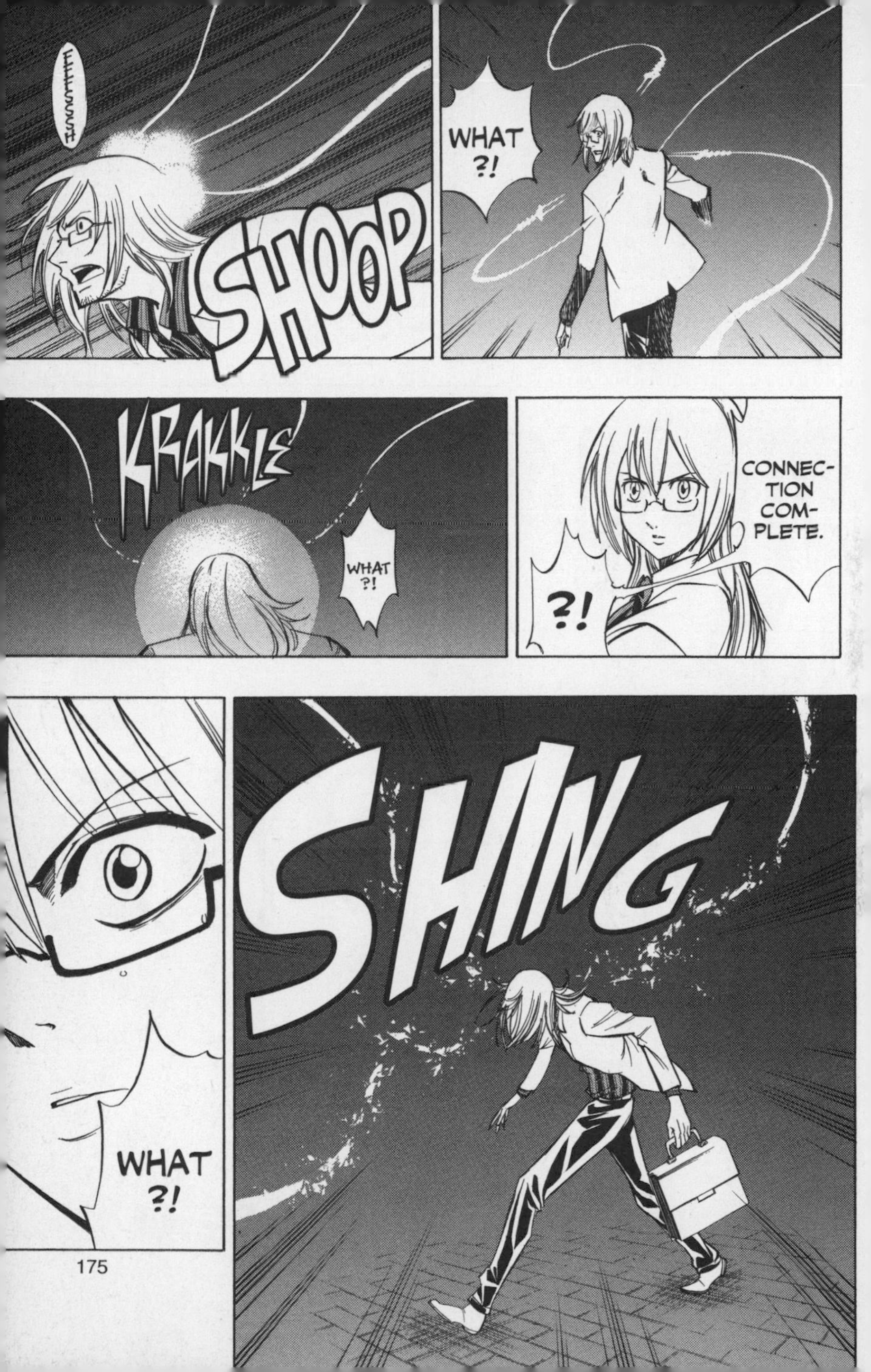
WHAT ?!
SHOOP
CONNEC- TION COM- PLETE.
?!
KRAKKLE
WHAT ?!
SHING
WHAT ?!

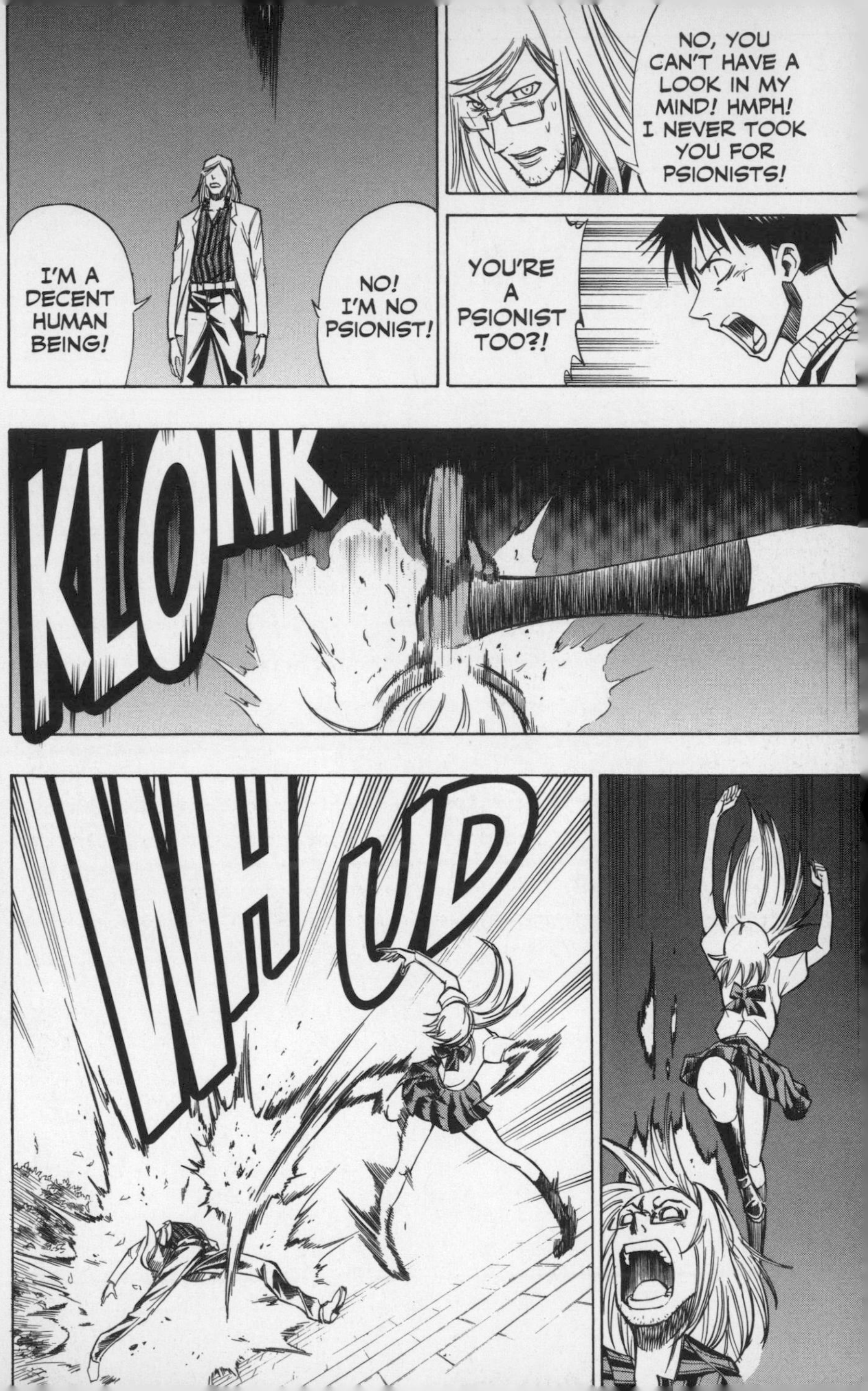
NO, YOU CAN'T HAVE A LOOK IN MY MIND! HMPH! I NEVER TOOK YOU FOR PSIONISTS!
YOU'RE A PSIONIST TOO?!
NO! I'M NO PSIONIST!
I'M A DECENT HUMAN BEING!
KLONK
WHUD

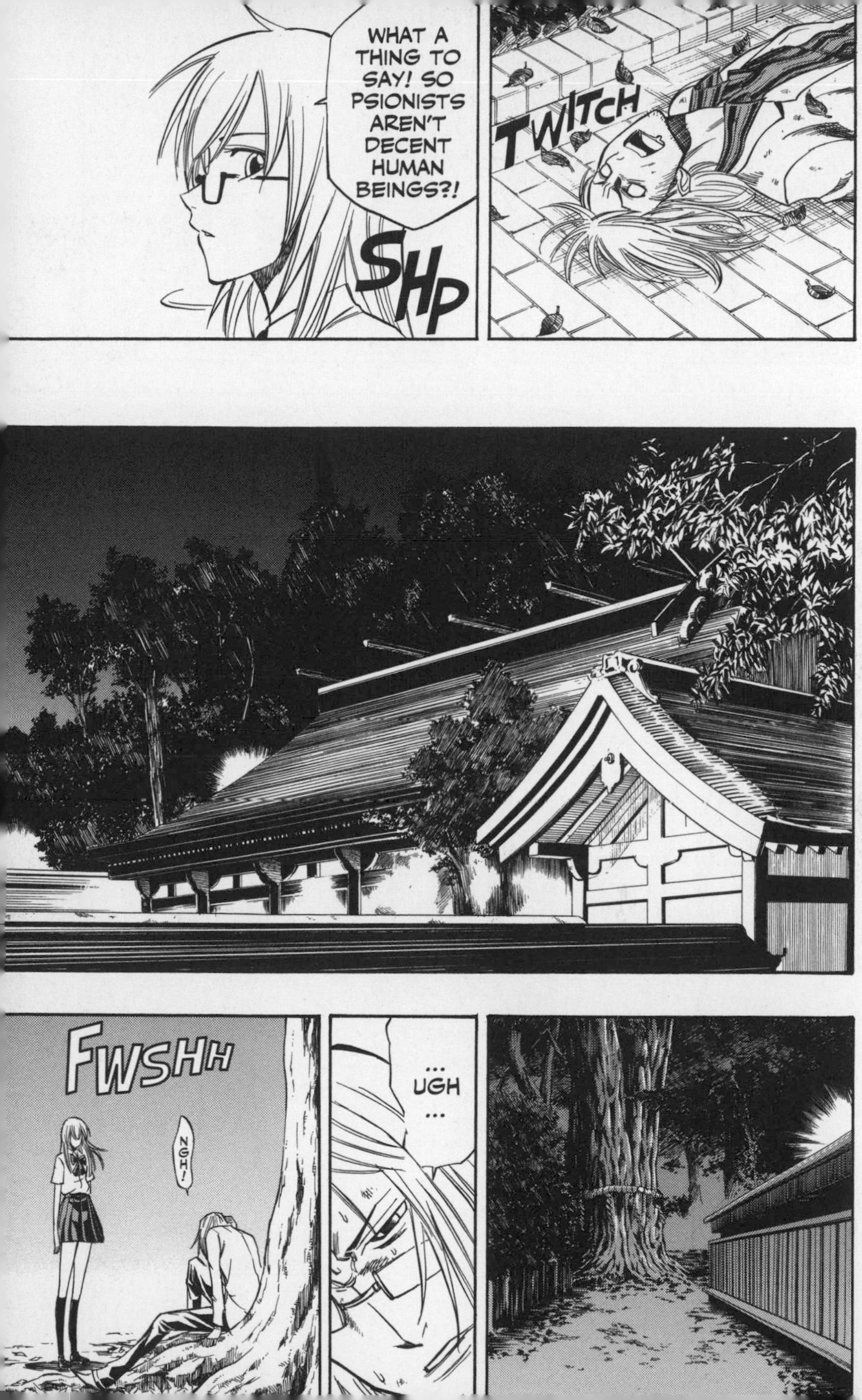
TWITCH
WHAT A THING TO SAY! SO PSIONISTS AREN'T DECENT HUMAN BEINGS?!
SHP
... UGH ...
FWSHH
NGH!

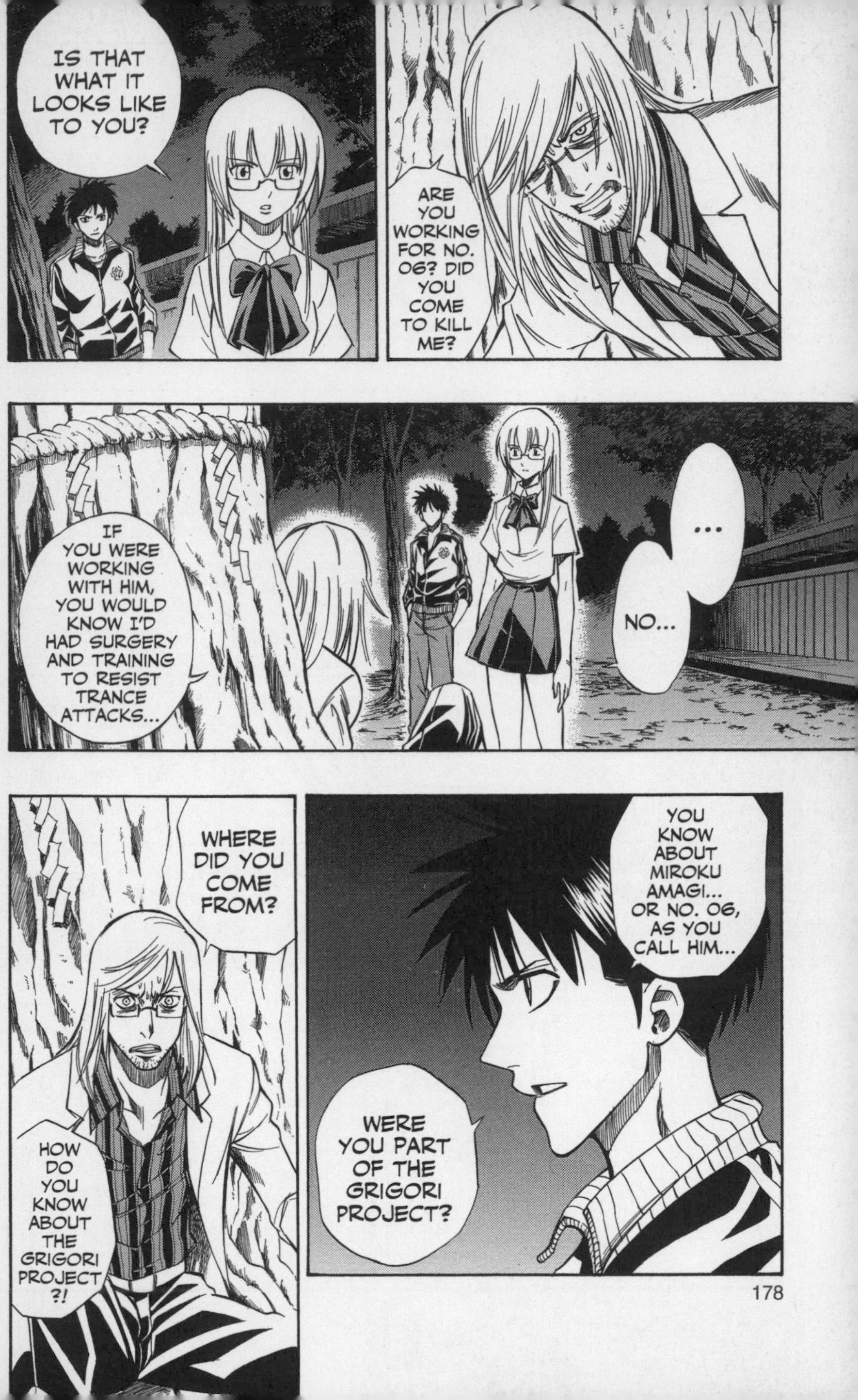
ARE YOU WORKING FOR NO. 06? DID YOU COME TO KILL ME?
IS THAT WHAT IT LOOKS LIKE TO YOU?
...
NO...
IF YOU WERE WORKING WITH HIM, YOU WOULD KNOW I'D HAD SURGERY AND TRAINING TO RESIST TRANCE ATTACKS...
YOU KNOW ABOUT MIROKU AMAGI... OR NO. 06, AS YOU CALL HIM...
WERE YOU PART OF THE GRIGORI PROJECT?
WHERE DID YOU COME FROM?
HOW DO YOU KNOW ABOUT THE GRIGORI PROJECT ?!

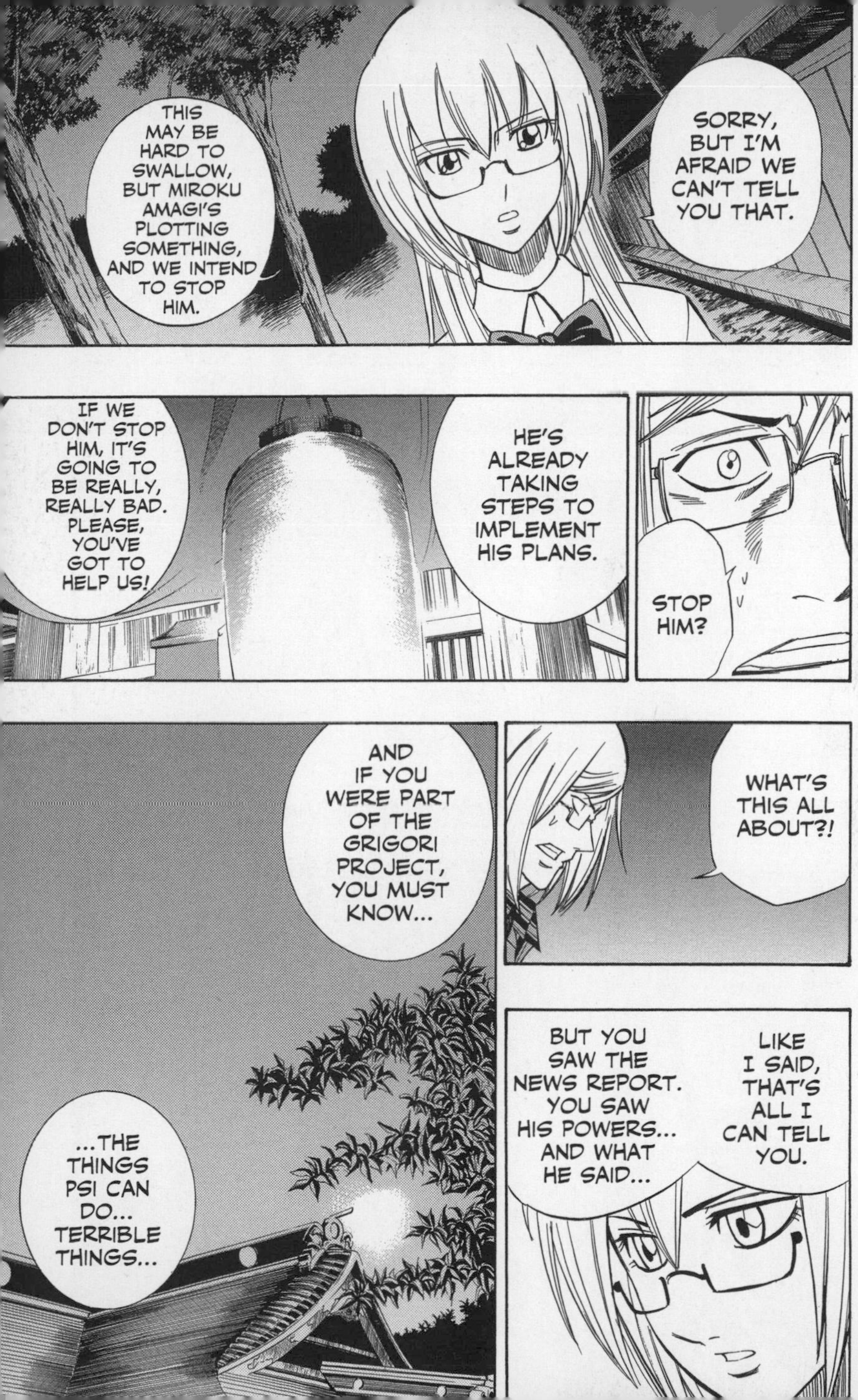
SORRY, BUT I'M AFRAID WE CAN'T TELL YOU THAT.
THIS MAY BE HARD TO SWALLOW, BUT MIROKU AMAGI'S PLOTTING SOMETHING, AND WE INTEND TO STOP HIM.
STOP HIM?
HE'S ALREADY TAKING STEPS TO IMPLEMENT HIS PLANS.
IF WE DON'T STOP HIM, IT'S GOING TO BE REALLY, REALLY BAD. PLEASE, YOU'VE GOT TO HELP US!
WHAT'S THIS ALL ABOUT?!
LIKE I SAID, THAT'S ALL I CAN TELL YOU.
BUT YOU SAW THE NEWS REPORT. YOU SAW HIS POWERS... AND WHAT HE SAID...
AND IF YOU WERE PART OF THE GRIGORI PROJECT, YOU MUST KNOW...
...THE THINGS PSI CAN DO... TERRIBLE THINGS...

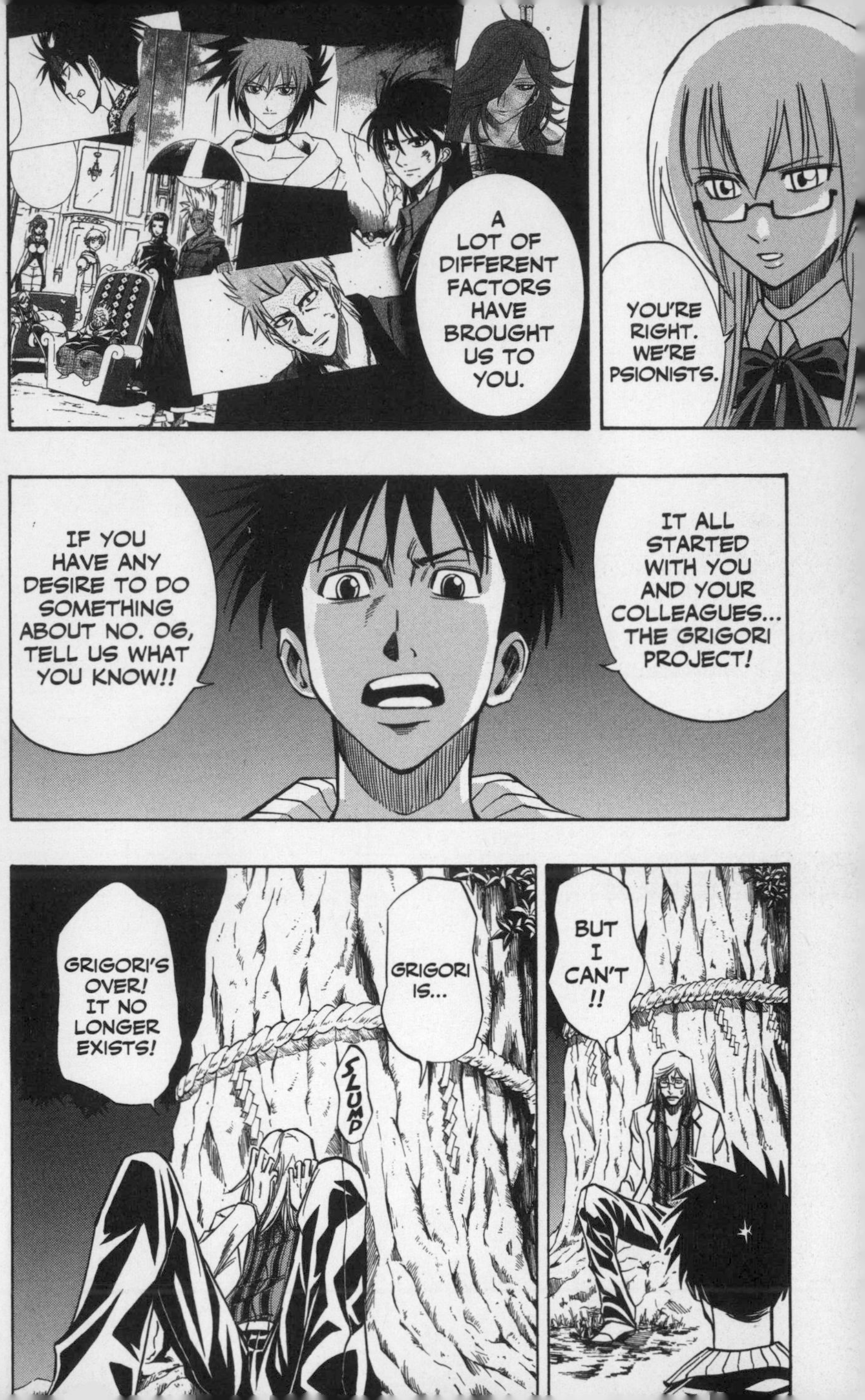
YOU'RE RIGHT. WE'RE PSIONISTS.
A LOT OF DIFFERENT FACTORS HAVE BROUGHT US TO YOU.
IT ALL STARTED WITH YOU AND YOUR COLLEAGUES... THE GRIGORI PROJECT!
IF YOU HAVE ANY DESIRE TO DO SOMETHING ABOUT NO. 06, TELL US WHAT YOU KNOW!!
BUT I CAN'T!!
GRIGORI IS...
SLUMP
GRIGORI'S OVER! IT NO LONGER EXISTS!

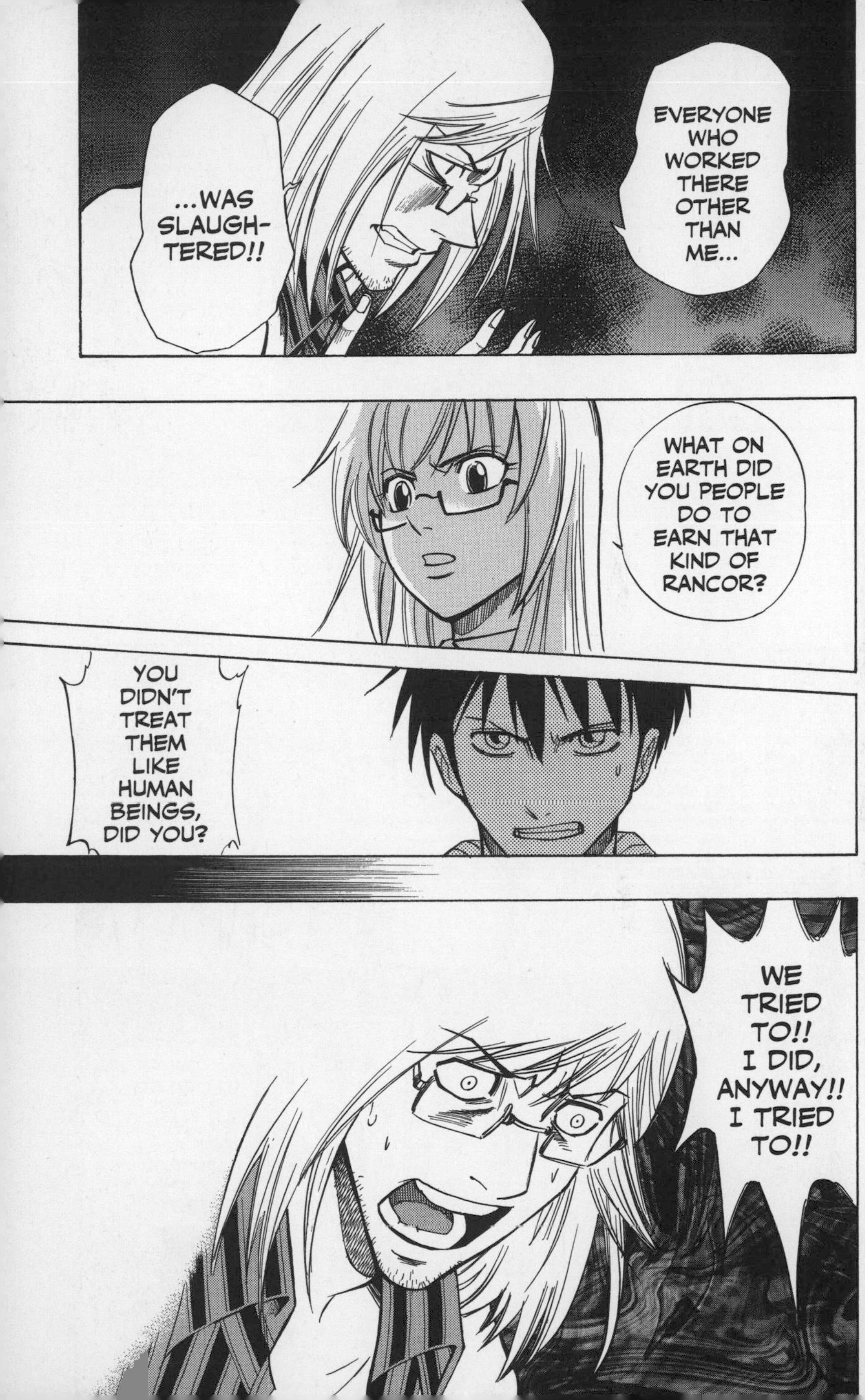
EVERYONE WHO WORKED THERE OTHER THAN ME...
...WAS SLAUGHTERED!!
WHAT ON EARTH DID YOU PEOPLE DO TO EARN THAT KIND OF RANCOR?
YOU DIDN'T TREAT THEM LIKE HUMAN BEINGS, DID YOU?
WE TRIED TO!! I DID, ANYWAY!! I TRIED TO!!

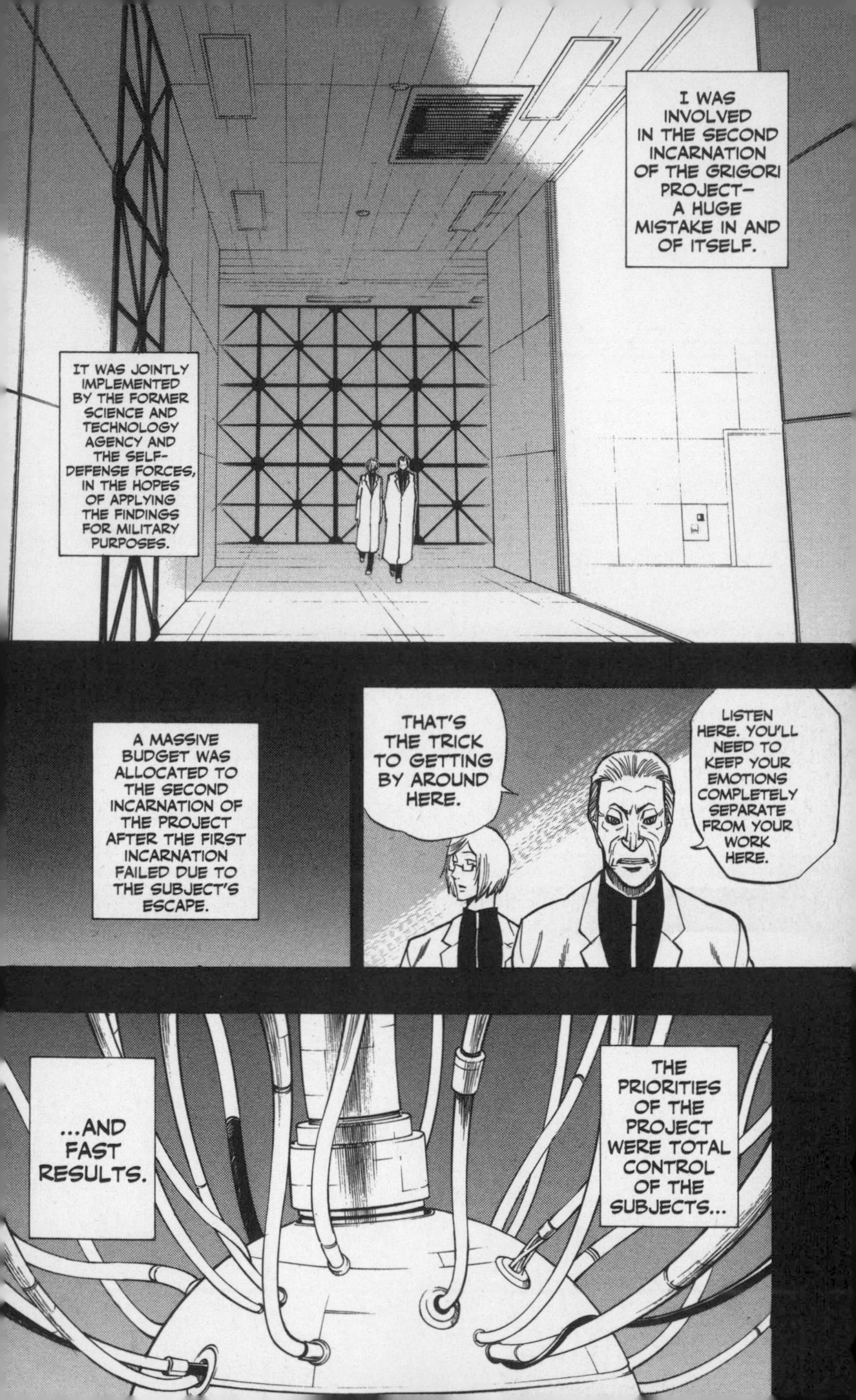
I WAS INVOLVED IN THE SECOND INCARNATION OF THE GRIGORI PROJECT— A HUGE MISTAKE IN AND OF ITSELF.
IT WAS JOINTLY IMPLEMENTED BY THE FORMER SCIENCE AND TECHNOLOGY AGENCY AND THE SELF-DEFENSE FORCES, IN THE HOPES OF APPLYING THE FINDINGS FOR MILITARY PURPOSES.
LISTEN HERE. YOU'LL NEED TO KEEP YOUR EMOTIONS COMPLETELY SEPARATE FROM YOUR WORK HERE.
THAT'S THE TRICK TO GETTING BY AROUND HERE.
A MASSIVE BUDGET WAS ALLOCATED TO THE SECOND INCARNATION OF THE PROJECT AFTER THE FIRST INCARNATION FAILED DUE TO THE SUBJECT'S ESCAPE.
THE PRIORITIES OF THE PROJECT WERE TOTAL CONTROL OF THE SUBJECTS...
...AND FAST RESULTS.

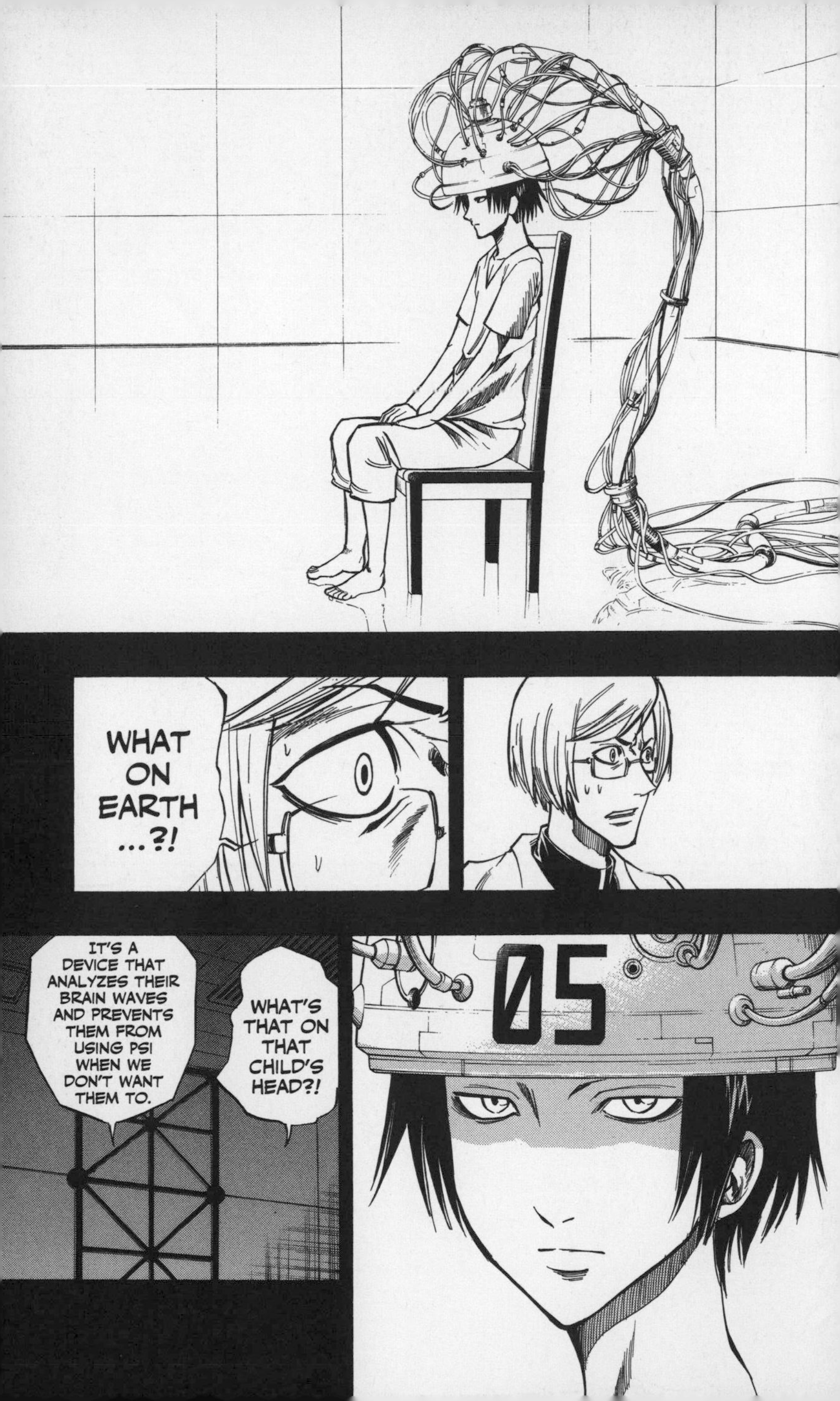
WHAT ON EARTH ...?!
WHAT'S THAT ON THAT CHILD'S HEAD?!
IT'S A DEVICE THAT ANALYZES THEIR BRAIN WAVES AND PREVENTS THEM FROM USING PSI WHEN WE DON'T WANT THEM TO.
05

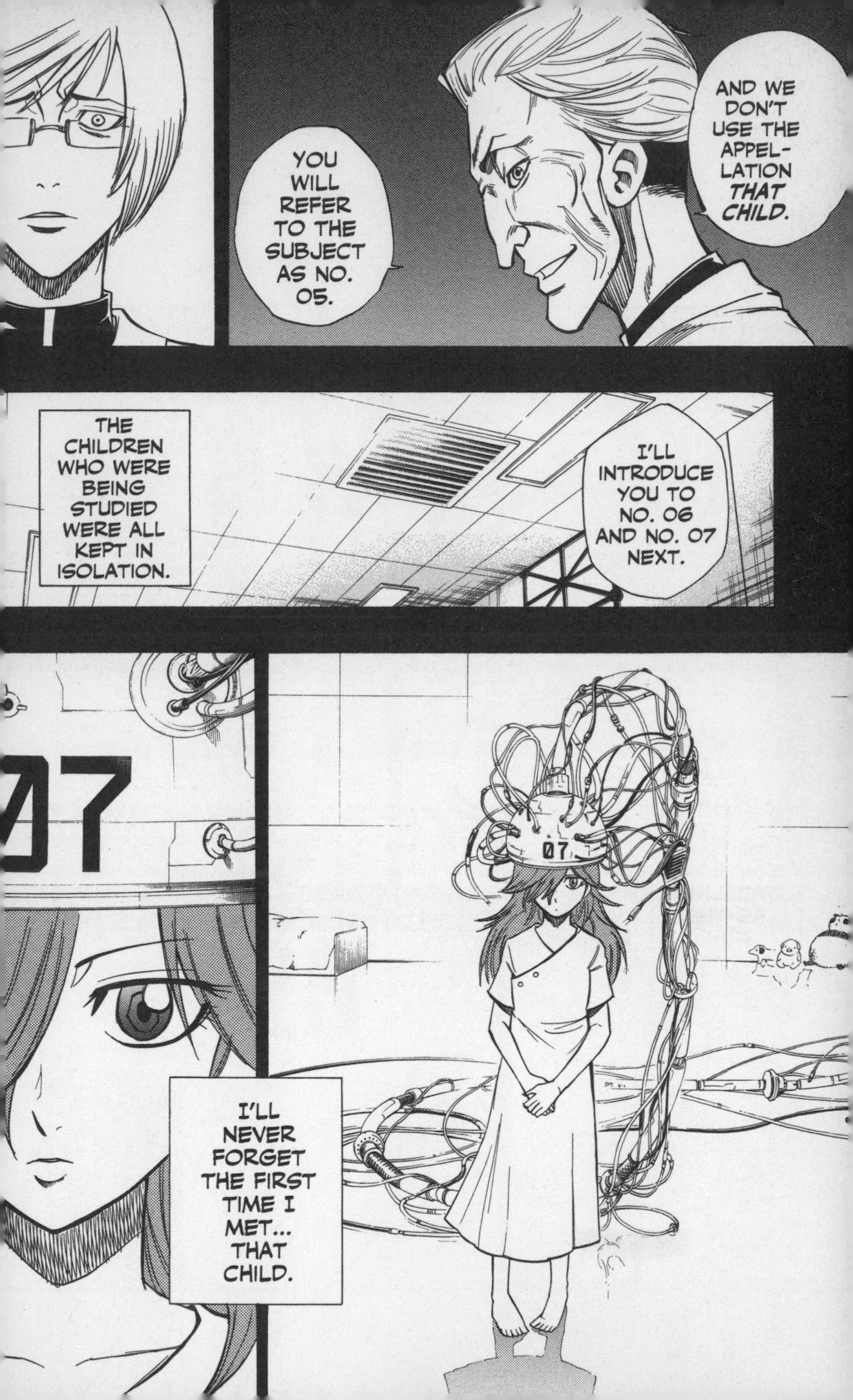
YOU WILL REFER TO THE SUBJECT AS NO. 05.
AND WE DON'T USE THE APPEL-LATION *THAT CHILD*.
I'LL INTRODUCE YOU TO NO. 06 AND NO. 07 NEXT.
THE CHILDREN WHO WERE BEING STUDIED WERE ALL KEPT IN ISOLATION.
07
07
I'LL NEVER FORGET THE FIRST TIME I MET... THAT CHILD.

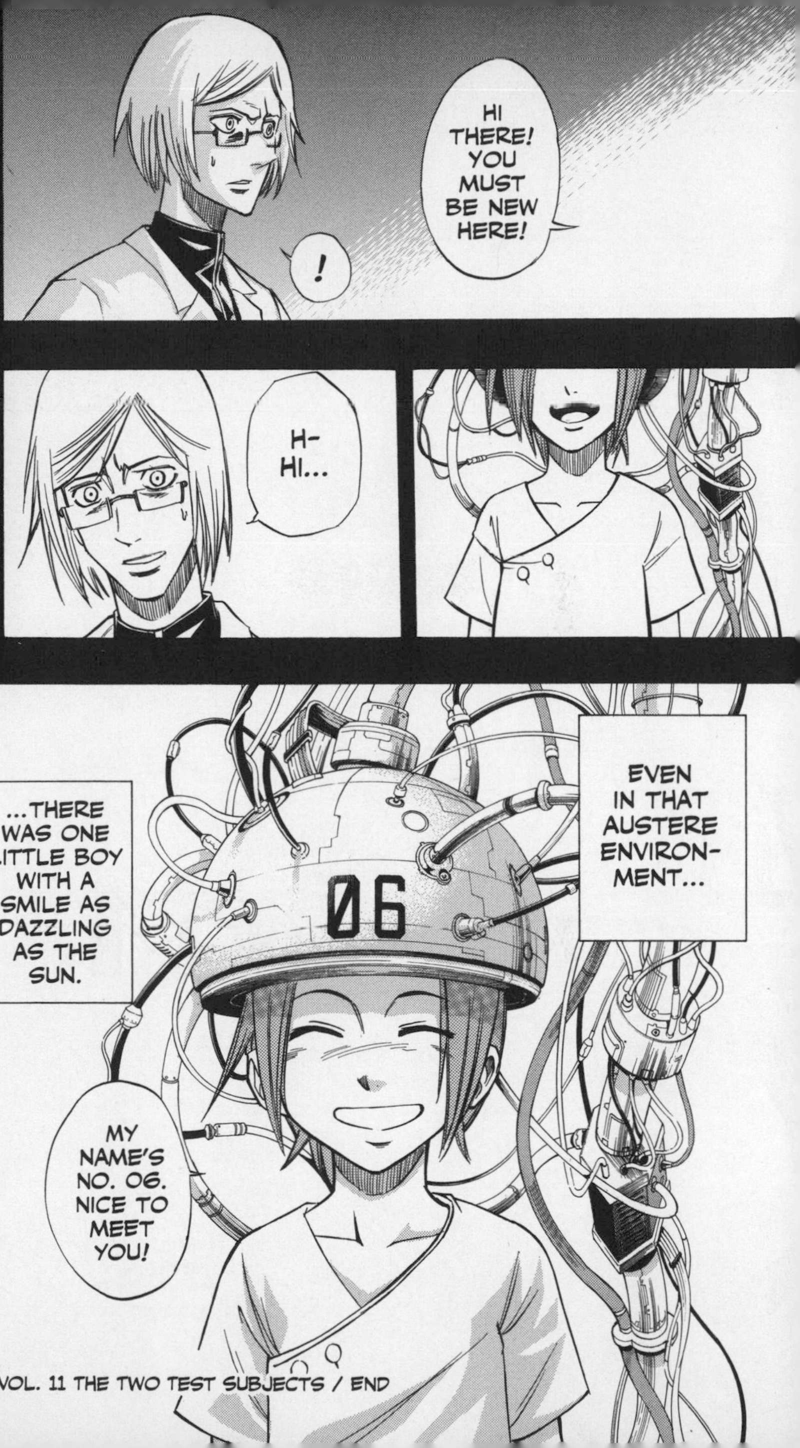
HI THERE! YOU MUST BE NEW HERE!
!
H- HI...
EVEN IN THAT AUSTERE ENVIRON- MENT...
...THERE WAS ONE LITTLE BOY WITH A SMILE AS DAZZLING AS THE SUN.
06
MY NAME'S NO. 06. NICE TO MEET YOU!

VOL. 11 THE TWO TEST SUBJECTS / END

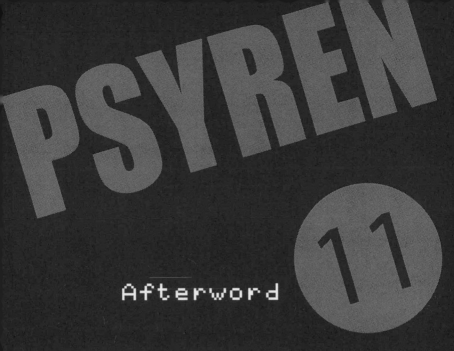

PSYREN

11

Afterword

THANK YOU FOR BUYING VOLUME 11.

THE ARC THAT BEGINS IN THIS VOLUME COULD BE CALLED "AMAGI MIROKU'S FORMATION OF W.I.S.E."

DURING MARCH, WHILE WORKING ON THIS TANKOBON VOLUME, VARIOUS TASKS KEPT COMING UP LIKE COLOR PAGE WORK AND JUMP NEXT! STUFF. IT WAS IMPOSSIBLE TO TAKE TIME OFF, AND I WAS TOTALLY EXHAUSTED BY THE END. BUT SOMEHOW I MANAGED TO MAKE IT THROUGH...THANKS TO MY STAFF. THANKS AGAIN, EVERYONE.

WELL, I'LL CONTINUE TO HANG IN THERE AND DO MY BEST! SEE YOU NEXT TIME!

TOSHIAKI IWASHIRO, MARCH, 2010

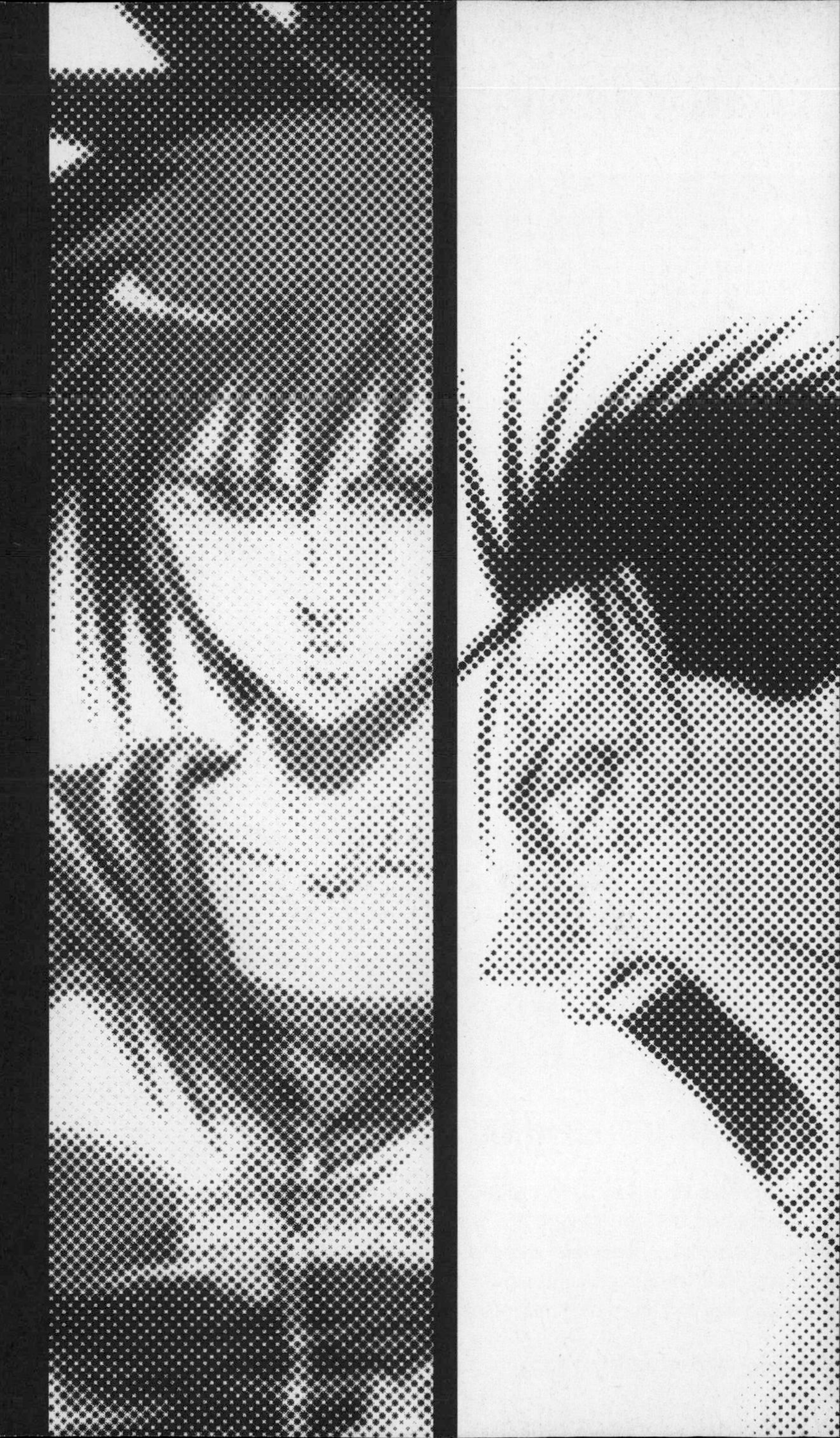

IN THE NEXT VOLUME...

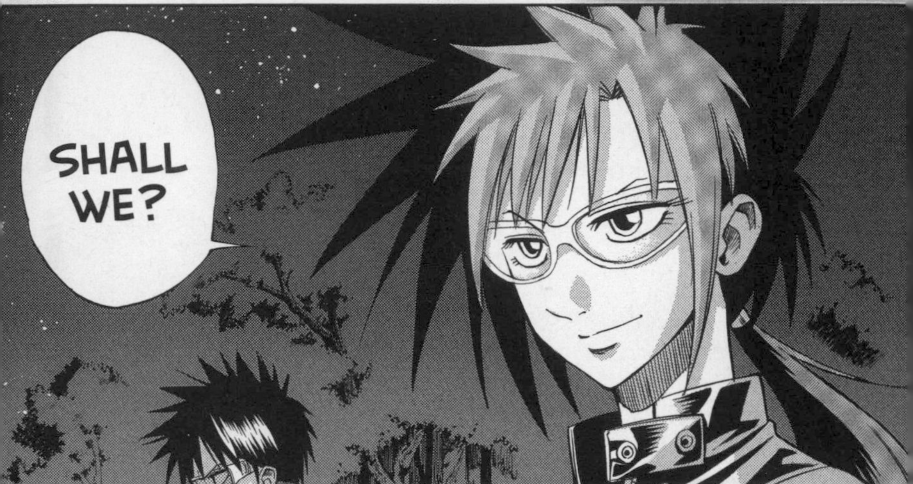

SHALL WE?
YES.

BLOOD AND DETERMINATION

Having survived their fourth trip to Psyren, Ageha and his friends set out to learn more about Miroku Amagi. A researcher from Miroku's past reveals a way to stop the madman, contained deep within a high-security research lab. Ageha and Matsuri infiltrate the lab, narrowly escaping a twisted trap, but in the process the key to stopping Miroku is lost forever.

Available SEPTEMBER 2013!

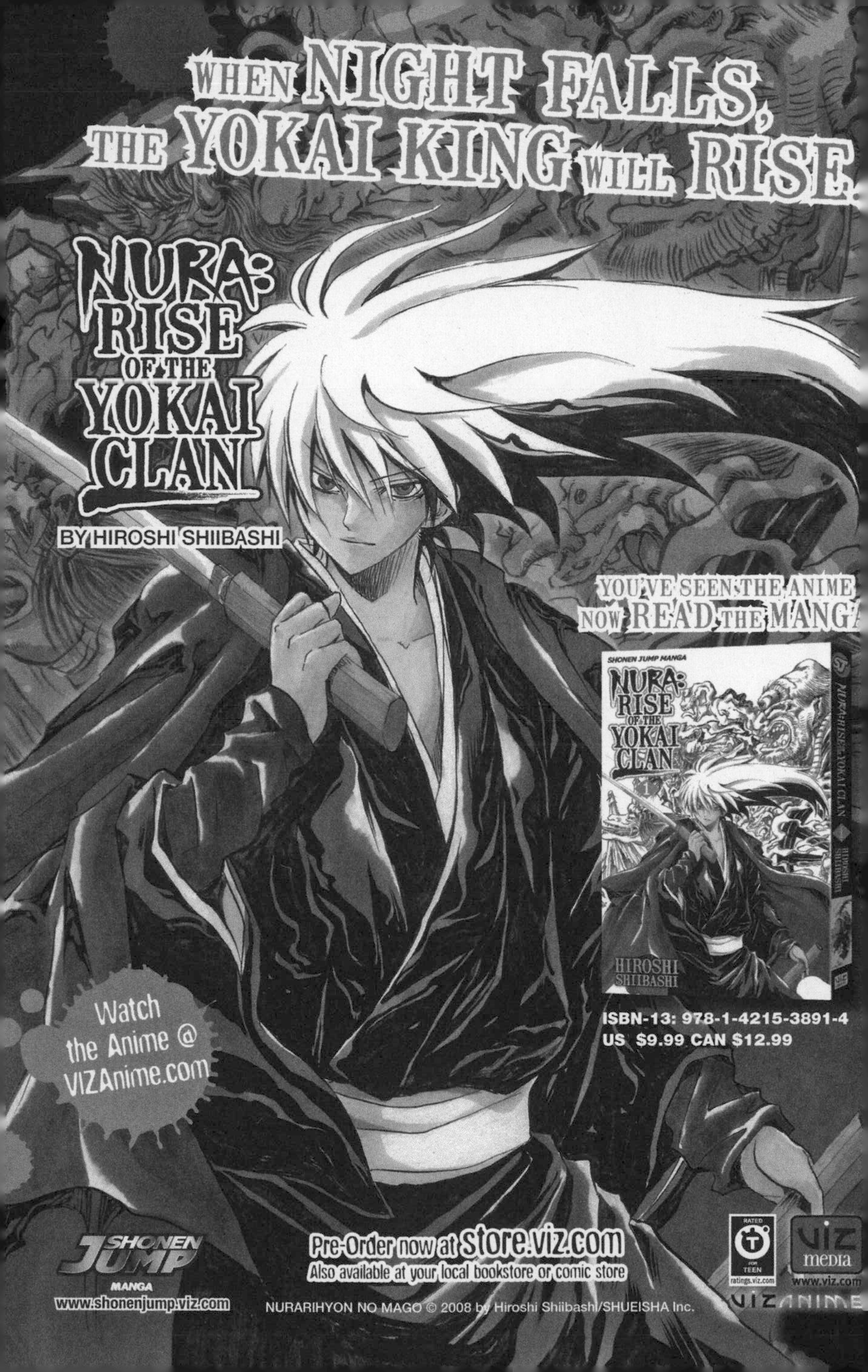
WHEN NIGHT FALLS, THE YOKAI KING WILL RISE.
NURA: RISE OF THE YOKAI CLAN
BY HIROSHI SHIIBASHI
YOU'VE SEEN THE ANIME NOW READ THE MANGA
SHONEN JUMP MANGA
NURA: RISE OF THE YOKAI CLAN
HIROSHI SHIIBASHI
ISBN-13: 978-1-4215-3891-4
US $9.99 CAN $12.99
Watch the Anime @ VIZAnime.com
SHONEN JUMP MANGA
www.shonenjump.viz.com
Pre-Order now at store.viz.com
Also available at your local bookstore or comic store
RATED T FOR TEEN
ratings.viz.com
viz media
www.viz.com
VIZANIME
NURARIHYON NO MAGO © 2008 by Hiroshi Shiibashi/SHUEISHA Inc.

DISCOVER ANIME
IN A WHOLE NEW WAY!

www.neonalley.com

What it is...

- Streaming anime delivered 24/7 straight to your TV via your connected video game console
- All English dubbed content
- Anime, martial arts movies, and more

Go to **neonalley.com** for news, updates and to see if Neon Alley is available in your area.

You're Reading in the Wrong Direction!!

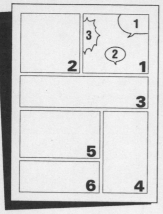

Whoops! Guess what? You're starting at the wrong end of the comic!

...It's true! In keeping with the original Japanese format, **Psyren** is meant to be read from right to left, starting in the upper-right corner.

Unlike English, which is read from left to right, Japanese is read from right to left, meaning that action, sound effects and word-balloon order are completely reversed—something which can make readers unfamiliar with Japanese feel pretty backwards themselves. For this reason, manga or Japanese comics published in the U.S. in English have sometimes been published "flopped"—that is, printed in exact reverse order, as though seen from the other side of a mirror.

By flopping pages, U.S. publishers can avoid confusing readers, but the compromise is not without its downside. For one thing, a character in a flopped manga series who once wore in the original Japanese version a T-shirt emblazoned with "M A Y" (as in "the merry month of") now wears one which reads "Y A M"! Additionally, many manga creators in Japan are themselves unhappy with the process, as some feel the mirror-imaging of their art changes their original intentions.

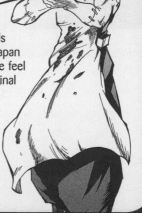

We are proud to bring you Toshiaki Iwashiro's **Psyren** in the original unflopped format. For now, though, turn to the other side of the book and let the fun begin...!

—Editor

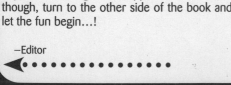